INTERWOVEN HISTORIES Contemporary Art, Migratory Narratives and Textiles

Christel Vesters

# INTERWOVEN HISTORIES
## Contemporary Art, Migratory Narratives and Textiles

nai010 publishers

# INTERWOVEN HISTORIES
## Contemporary Art, Migratory Narratives and Textiles

*Interwoven Histories: Contemporary Art, Migratory Narratives and Textiles* revolves around five contemporary works of art, each lending its own perspective to the theme of migration while drawing on the rich material, metaphorical and historical qualities of the language of textiles. It builds on a decade of research and many inspiring exchanges with artists, designers, curators and thinkers about the power of textiles in contemporary art. Parts of this body of work have found its way into essays I have written for publications at home and abroad, some of which have been adapted for this book—as well as into the activities I developed for my curatorial platform 'Touch/Trace: Researching Histories through Textiles', including the international group exhibition *Interwoven Histories: Researching Histories through Textiles* (Amsterdam, 2021).

The book in front of you is organized in five clusters, each starting with a close reading of one artwork. Juxtaposing image and text, we wander across the work's tactile surface, zoom in on its texture, explore its visual composition and listen attentively to the stories it whispers through its weaves and stitches. The second part unravels the content of the artwork. In conversation, each artist shares what inspired the work and their intent in making it, alongside the research which underpins its themes and concepts. One of the questions that arises is what drew them to textiles and how does this medium amplify the meaning of their work.

Pulling threads from the previous two sections, a third layer connects the work to a wider, diversified field of knowledge, pointing towards an ever-expanding fabric of possible associations that extends beyond the pages of this publication. Gathering some of the insights and ideas that have surfaced through its pages, each cluster wraps up with some tentative conclusions that deepen the reflection on the book's three themes—contemporary art, migratory narratives and textiles. The clusters are enriched by essays in which authors from different backgrounds and disciplines focus on a particular area of knowledge—one that either complements, juxtaposes or challenges the content of the cluster.

Textile in art remains an endlessly fascinating subject; many more artists could have been included here. Ultimately, I settled on these five artists, who have different cultural backgrounds yet are all connected to the Netherlands. Some were born and raised here, others came to study and chose to stay. Together they embody the multilayered cultural–historical fabric of Dutch society today.

Just like the artworks discussed within its pages, the book mirrors in its layout and design some characteristic aspects of the language of textiles: zooming in and out between the detail and the surface, folding and unfolding different concepts and contexts, pulling into view reverse sides, watching different connective threads emerge from the seams. It does not aim to provide a singular and conclusive interpretation, but rather it offers a patchwork of pluriform ideas, knowledge and perspectives. Ultimately, the publication seeks to address two questions: how do histories of migration shape our societies today and what makes textiles—especially in the hands of artists—such a powerful and evocative medium to offer new perspectives on these complex subjects? My hope is that readers will intuitively sense the depth, rich complexity and expressive power of textiles—not merely as beautiful objects, but as living materials and reservoirs of meaning that inspire new ways of thinking about our histories.

## INTERWOVEN HISTORIES
### Every Binding Holds a Story

Textiles tell stories about the time and place in which they were made. Stories about the arrival of new materials, visual styles and motifs. About technological innovations that changed our production systems and gradually replaced the craftsperson's hand with machinery. About the movement and displacement of people, about changes in political regime or religious beliefs, about resistance and emancipation, about the boom and bust of commercial markets. Sometimes they even tell the tale of the person who made them.

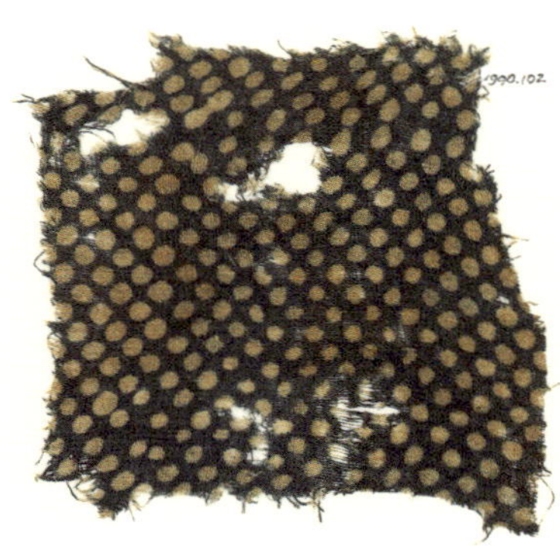

This archaeological textile fragment, bearing traces of tear and wear, was most likely made in Gujarat, West India, and discovered in Fustat, Egypt, before entering the Ashmolean Museum, Oxford University's research collection in 1941. It reappears in 2018 in Vincent Vulsma's textile work Fragment with Dots (Fustat).

Textile fragment with dots, c. 10–15th century. Cotton, resist-dye indigo blue, 18.5 × 17.5 cm.

*Interwoven Histories* is centred around the idea that textiles are inseparable from the fabric of history. Whether it is a simple calico or a precious silk, historical events have left their imprint on their surface. Take, for instance, the introduction of the jacquard loom in 1804, which made it possible to weave increasingly elaborate and intricate patterned brocades and is often seen to have revolutionized the textile industry and spur industrialization.[1] Or consider the 'discovery' of indigo blue by elite consumers in Western Europe. Its popularity ignited a global industry which soon overtook the market for locally grown woad.

The first essay in this publication is dedicated to the textile research of curator, author and collector Seth Siegelaub (1941–2013). Siegelaub placed textiles at the centre of history, regarding them as the subject of significant economic, technological and cultural developments—including the history of intercontinental trade. As he wrote, 'Rugged, resilient and portable, textiles have a unique place in the interwoven history of ornament and trade.[1] Yet these interwoven histories rarely follow a linear logic, nor do they unfold as clean-cut interactions; rather, they emerge as messy entanglements of overlapping interests and developments. Moreover, many of these interactions are propelled by broader historical currents that are not always immediately apparent.

Metaphorically, history itself can be read as a piece of textile: to understand the ways in which its narratives are fabricated, we can look, for instance, at the seams or bindings to see how individual threads interact. Like textiles, history too has a reverse side; a backstory whose image is not as flawless as its front and is preferably kept out of sight. The global indigo market, for instance, cannot be separated from the colonial exploitation of people and land, just as the industrialization of textile manufacturing cannot be disentangled from the deplorable factory working conditions of women and children in nineteenth century Europe — circumstances that, regrettably, have been carried over into the sweatshops of low-wage countries in Asia and Latin America today.

If textiles carry the imprint of history, then their traces of wear and tear bear witness to the stories of everyday life concealed behind grand historical narratives. These traces are the place where past lives become tangible. The tension between these personal stories and the overarching narrative — the thread and the fabric, the personal and the collective — is one of the recurring themes of this book.

## MIGRATORY NARRATIVES
### Threading Notions of Movement and Belonging

Textiles are inextricably linked with stories of movement and migration. When people move, textiles travel with them — as garments, tents, interior decorations, ritual cloths and, of course, as commodities of trade. Carried across transcontinental and colonial trade networks, travelling from one cultural context to the next, textiles have long played an active role in the circulation of patterns, materials and techniques. Often, these migrations of form generate new designs or hybrid aesthetics.

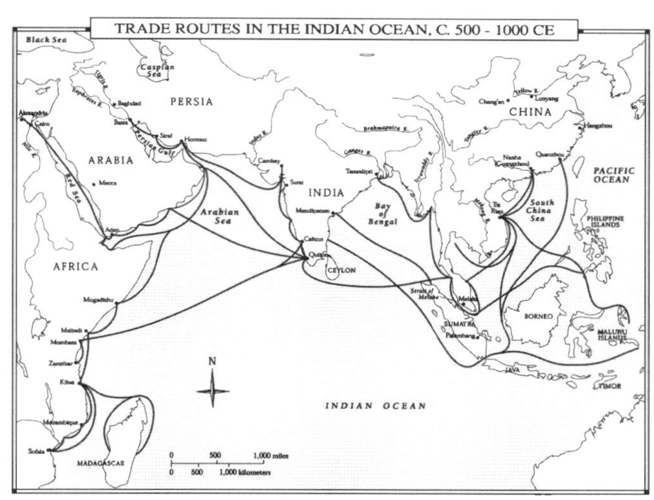


Trade Routes in the Indian Ocean, c. 500–1000 CE.

In her contribution to this book, cultural historian Ananya Jahanara Kabir describes the pattern of Vilsco's famous Angelina wax print as a 'repository of aesthetics, taste and the history of cultural exchange'. In this case the exchanges among Indian Ocean cultures and between Indian Ocean and Atlantic cultures. Taking a similar approach to Kabir, we might view textiles not merely as decorative surfaces but as indexes of migration and diasporic memory that invite us to consider the forces that propelled these migrations.

Each of the five works in this publication tells a different story of migration: *Technik*, for instance, traces the movements of a Navajo/Diné weaving pattern across different cultural contexts and spheres of production, grappling with the complex theme of cultural appropriation.[2] *Sperveri*, on the other hand, recovers the stories of women and men who had to flee their homes to escape violence and oppression, offering them refuge within a beautifully embroidered bed-tent. And *The Rise of the Prophet* engages with the contemporary realities of diasporic existence brought about by the transatlantic displacements of millions, in its exploration of the colonial histories of indigo blue.

Together the works map a broad spectrum of migratory experiences that reflects our contemporary human condition — on a personal and collective level both — one that at the moment of writing this introduction is dominated by war, displacement and growing trauma on all sides. In the words of the British writer and cultural theorist Marina Warner:

*Today, in times of dislocation and war and ever more serious threats of civil violence, confusion and violent hatred, people are on the move, and with them stories. Their own personal stories and their cultures' legacies. And in the plural encounters of these new diasporas, new narratives are constantly being formed.*[3]

A recurring theme in this publication is the interplay between these old and new histories of displacement with politics and power, colonialism, mercantilism and trade. As such, through these five works, the book engages with contemporary discussions on a wide range of subjects including postcolonialism and decolonialism, environmental crises and sustainability, and with questions of identity, ancestral traditions and cultural heritage.

One important insight gained during the research for this book is that while migration is often understood in terms of borders or nation states, textiles defy such abstract boundaries. They do not adhere to the lines drawn on world maps, nor to politically defined entities that determine the identities we carry in our passports — mainly because many textile traditions predate those political boundaries. Politics can change, ideologies can shift, but weaving patterns evolve far more slowly. For this reason, textiles offer a distinctive blueprint for the movements and transformations that have taken place with time to shape the hybrid cultures and identities of the present.

## TEXTILE IN ART
### Affective Entanglements Evoking Connections

Artists seem to intuitively grasp the complex entanglements of histories of migration. They weave, stitch, quilt and embroider to engage with the often forgotten undersides of these narratives, picking up different, sometimes contradictory, threads and inserting them into the fabric of the present. Their works make material what the British anthropologist Tim Ingold terms 'that peculiarly human ability to weave stories from the past into the texture of present lives,'[4] when he reflects on the storied nature of knowledge and the ways in which past and present converge in lived experience.

As a medium, textile allows artists to communicate concepts and ideals that are not easily put into words. 'Textiles express connectedness', observes patricia kaersenhout in our interview when discussing *Vrouwen van VOS*, her series of banners that celebrates international and intergenerational networks of female solidarity. She adds: 'I'm interested in creating a communal body, and textile is the perfect medium to achieve this. It brings people together, but it's also a spiritual way of connecting with the world, and what was here before us.'

This sense of kinship and connection — temporal, communal, ancestral and ecological — recurs in all five artworks. Whether apparent in the juxtaposition of four textile objects made at different periods yet connected by a shared indigenous motif (*Technik*); in the stitching together of disparate textile fragments into a variegated whole (*The Rise of the Prophet*); or in the collective creation of embroideries while remembering the women who came before (*Sperveri*), textiles embody an intrinsic quality of connectedness.

In many works of art that involve textiles, this relation is linked with themes of healing and repair — a healing, for instance, of colonial wounds that tore communities apart and severed ties to land and indigenous knowledge. Some artists featured in this publication seek to suture these wounds by reconnecting certain textile objects or materials with their ancestral origins, for example indigo dye. Others, working in a more personal and intimate register, move toward healing by applying intricately embroidered stitches that evoke beauty and joy.

Although textile crafts have long been associated with eye-pleasing needlework and fine weaving, artists today employ textiles to support their political and activist messages too. Neatly finished surfaces, craftsmanship and skill are not their main objective, as is apparent in the countless loose hanging threads, crooked stitching and fringes on view amongst these pages. Rather, it is the subversive, DIY aesthetic of their art that drives home the message they seek to communicate.

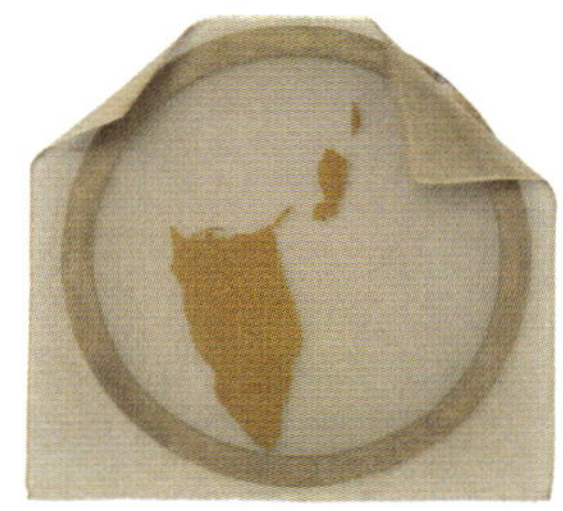

Territori occupati (Occupied Territories), Alighiero Boetti, 1969.
Wool embroidery on jute cloth, circular wooden frame, 120 × 127 cm.

Textile communicates on a different, more affective register than, say, old or new media. One work of art which illustrates this point (although it is not featured in this book) is Alighiero Boetti's embroidered *Terri Occupati* (*Occupied Territories*, 1969). It shows the contours of the Palestinian territories on the last day of the Six-Day War between Israel and the neighbouring states of Egypt, Jordan and Syria. Boetti (1940–1969) asked his wife Annemarie Sauzeau (1938–2014), to embroider the outline of an inset map that had appeared along a newspaper article.[5] With their clean, straight lines, these newspaper graphs reduce geopolitical crises to mere data—names, places, dates—stripping away the bloodshed, terror and trauma, and thereby dehumanizing the impact of conflict on both sides of the border.

However, worked in plain cross-stitch technique, using ochre-coloured woollen threads on a piece of jute, the abstract contours are transformed into a solid patch of land. Stitch by stitch, Sauzeau's hands granted the abstract shape attention, time and a human touch that seems able to bridge the distance between here and there, now and then. *Territori Occupati* shows the conceptual power of textile as an artistic medium; it shows how a simple cross-stitch becomes political.

Textiles are part of everyday life. We wear them close to our skin. This may be one reason why they speak to us on such a personal and intimate level, stimulating a different mode of knowing—one that is intuitive and emotional, rather than factual and objective. These evocative qualities, coupled with the poetic language of textile give this medium the unique capacity to make abstract ideas tangible. A small number of stitches can hold entire histories while preserving their complexity. Our time calls for new perspectives—new ways of imagining the world we live in, honouring its complexity and diversity, while striving for deeper connections. And as a medium textile communicates just that.

1. These developments did not happen without opposition. In France, the Saboteurs resisted industrialization by damaging machinery, and in the United Kingdom the Luddites took to the streets to protest wage cuts and poor working conditions, inspiring the rise of labour unions to negotiate worker's rights and protect jobs. See, for instance, my essays 'Activist Threads' (2021); 'Jacquard's Machine' (London, 2019) and 'Some Notes on Women, Labour and Textile Crafts' (Amsterdam, 2018).
2. The terms Navajo and Diné both refer to the same Indigenous people of the Southwestern United States. Diné means 'the people' in their own language, while Navajo is widely used in public discourse. Throughout this book I use the term Navajo for consistency and accessibility, while acknowledging and respecting the preference of the community for the name Diné in appropriate contexts.
3. Marina Warner, 'Stepping beyond Words: Narratives on the Move in Cultural Conflicts', lecture presented at the Warburg Institute, London (2019). Apropos Warburg, his thinking on the migration of form, or rather the wandering of visual motifs was extrapolated from a somewhat anecdotal fact about Flemish tapestries. In the 14th and 15th centuries, Flemish aristocrats would have their tapestries transported with them from their Belgian castles to their Florentine winter palaces for comfort purposes in the cold months. Thus, they introduced patterns and 'Bildermotive' specific to the Flemish tradition of wall tapestries to the 15th Florentine Renaissance milieu. Warburg demonstrated his theory in his famous *Bilder Atlas Mnemosyne*, which in turn inspired the encyclopaedia-like tableaux that intersect the pages of this book. See also my essay 'Travelling Carpets' (2020/2021).
4. Tim Ingold, *Being Alive: Essays on Movement, Knowledge and Description* (2011), p.201.
5. The caption beneath the inset map reads '10 June 1967 (Gaza, Jerusalem, Sinai and Golan)'.

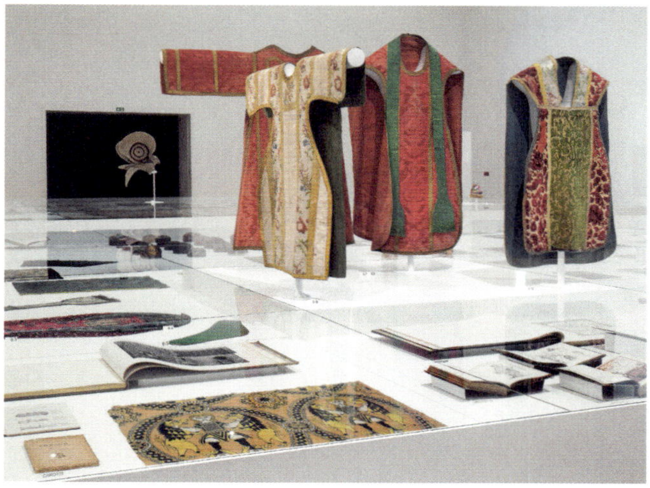

Seth Siegelaub: Beyond Conceptual Art, exhibition view Stedelijk Museum Amsterdam, 2015–2016.

Seth Siegelaub is probably best known for collaborating with emerging conceptual artists in 1960s and 1970s New York. His revolutionary approach to exhibiting their work resulted in a radical departure from the conventional white cube space in *The Xerox Book* (1968) and *January 5-31, 1969*, and in experiments with the 'catalogue-as-exhibition'. But Siegelaub was much more than a legendary curator. He published political pamphlets, engaged in political activism, ran a one-man press and news network, drafted the first artist contract, was a self-taught researcher, archivist and bibliographer. And he collected old textiles and books on all things related to textile.

*I am unpacking my library. Yes, I am. The books are not yet on the shelves, not yet touched by the mild boredom of order. (...) Instead, I must ask you to join me in the disorder of the crates that have been wrenched open (...) to join me among piles of volumes that are seeing daylight again after two years of darkness, so that you may be ready to share with me a bit of the mood—it is certainly not an elegiac mood, but rather one of anticipation—which these books arouse in a genuine collector.*[1]

# A TAPESTRY OF THOUGHTS
## Seth Siegelaub's Center for Social Research on Old Textiles

The invitation is Walter Benjamin's, asking the reader to share in his excitement at rediscovering his books after being separated from them for years. His 1931 essay 'Unpacking my Library' is not so much about the accumulated knowledge contained in his library as it is about the exhilarated state of mind of the book collector. Benjamin, a genuine collector, observed that the passion of every collector borders on the chaotic, and that the library, in essence a chaos of books, finds its counterpoint in the order of its catalogue: 'There is in the life of the collector a dialectical tension between the poles of order and disorder.'[2]

I had to think of Benjamin's remarks when I found myself sitting amid a clutter of books, dozens of half-unpacked cardboard boxes and some amateurishly wrapped textiles. They belonged to Seth Siegelaub, and their contents needed to be catalogued after his unexpected death in 2013. Administrative drudgery, you would think, but no: every box I opened revealed an inspiring and exhilarating 'chaos' of books. A box could hold a year's issues of 1930s magazines on embroidery, including patterns of a variety of motifs, antique manuscripts with dye recipes, and various titles on textile crafts from around the world, such as the richly illustrated *Guatemalan Textiles Today: The Art and Technique of Weaving, Dyeing,*

1. Walter Benjamin, 'Unpacking my Library: A Talk about Collecting', July 1931, in *Selected Writings: Volume 4, 1938-1940* ([1991] 2006), pp. 486-493.
2. Ibid. p. 487.

*Spinning, Crocheting, Looping*, and *Netting in Guatemala* (1978), or *The Art of Bobbin Lace: A Practical Text Book of Workmanship* (1908). That same box might also contain titles on the social history of specific crafts, or the economic development of the textile industry and trade, such as *The Pre-Industrial Economy in Wingland 1500–1750* (1971) or *La Technique et l'Organisation de la Draperie à Bruges, à Gand, et à Malines au milieu de XVIe Siècle* (1920).

As I worked my way through the boxes with a growing curiosity of what I might find next, the intellectual and poetic potential of Siegelaub's accumulated books and textiles started to dawn on me. I could sense that it had something to do with the myriad ways in which textiles are interconnected with social, political, economic and technological change down the ages. Little did I know at the time, sitting in a cold garage hauling boxes, noting down titles and cryptic numeral codes, that I would spend the next fifteen years exploring that idea, spurred on by the work of various contemporary artists who, like me, are captivated by both the beauty and history of textiles. But the random juxtaposition of books and textiles triggered another question: If historical knowledge helps us to understand textiles, can textiles help us understand history? What emerged from those boxes of colourful and delicate fabrics, and knowledge related to textiles, was the idea that the entire history of humanity might be understood as a tapestry made of connecting and sometimes conflicting threads.

The books scattered on the floor were part of the Center for Social Research of Old Textiles (CSROT), a one-man research institute dedicated to investigating the social history of handmade textiles, founded by Seth Siegelaub in 1986.[3] His ambition was to build an exhaustive library on the history of handwoven textiles that would enable people to produce research on a critical history of their social, economic, commercial and political aspects.

In an interview, Siegelaub once compared his passion for collecting with 'a very extensive love'.[4] When he passed away in 2013, his collection of books contained over 7,300 titles. His textile collection, which he simply named 'Seth Siegelaub Textiles: 750 items'. His affection for textiles started in the 1960s, when he owned a gallery in Manhattan and displayed oriental rugs alongside contemporary art. But, as he explained, 'Much of that interest moved from actual rugs to books about rugs (...) to understand the history; how they looked or were used since antiquity. Methodologically that appealed to me more.'[5]

Twenty years later, Siegelaub would start working tirelessly to compile a detailed and systematic reference bibliography in which he organized, categorized and annotated the wealth of information he had accumulated. In 1997, he published his magnus opus, the *Bibliographica Textilia Historiae: Towards a General Bibliography on the History of Textiles*, which he described as 'the first general bibliography attempting to outline and document all facets of the literature of the world history of textiles'. The hefty volume contains over 5,000 references — printed books and pamphlets,

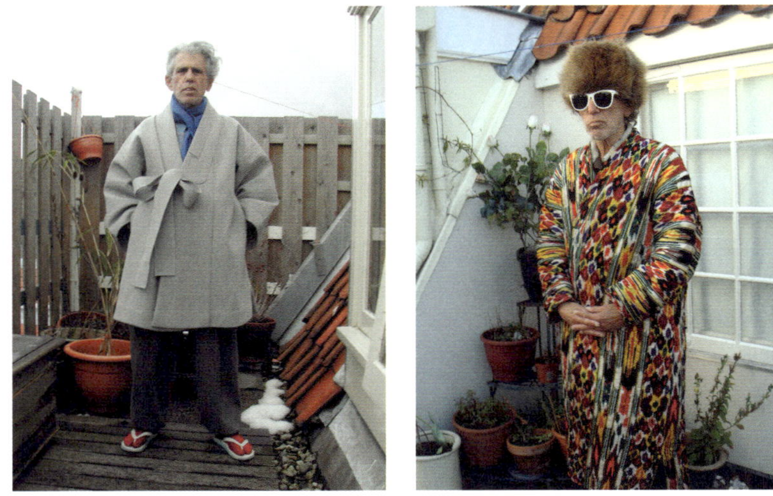

Seth Siegelaub wearing a Korean priest's robe (left) and an ikat woven caftan (right) from his SST collection.

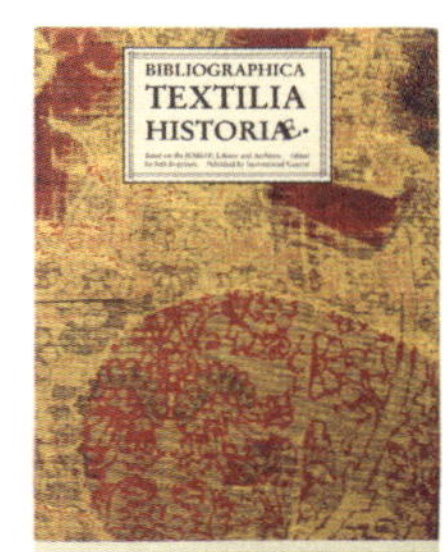


Cover of Bibliographica Textilia Historiae: Towards a General Bibliography on the History of Textiles Based on the Library and Archives of the Center for Social Research on Old Textiles, Center for Social Research on Old Textiles and Seth Siegelaub (New York: International General, 1997).

The Bibliographica Textilia Historiae offers an annotated index of the CSROT's research library and archive. Its content can also be accessed through the website of the Egress Foundation, the umbrella organization set up by Siegelaub in the final years of his life, which brought together all his projects and collections.

3. The collection is held at the Antonio Ratti Foundation in Como, Italy.
4. 'Seth Siegelaub in Conversation with Rike Frank and Grant Watson' (2012), p. 226.
5. 'Nothing Personal ... An Interview with Seth Siegelaub', in cat. ex. *The Stuff That Matters* (2012).
6. Seth Siegelaub, 'Introduction: Notes Towards a Critical History of the Literature of Textiles' (1997), p. 17.
7. Ibid. p. 10.
8. Ibid.
9. *The Stuff That Matters: Textiles Collected by Seth Siegelaub for the CSROT*, Raven Row, London, 1 March–5 May, 2012. Four years later, large parts of his CSROT and textile collection were included in the survey exhibition *Seth Siegelaub – Beyond Conceptual Art*, curated by Leontine Coelewij and Sara Marinetti for the Stedelijk Museum Amsterdam, 12 December 2015–16 April 2016.
10. Siegelaub, *Bibliographica Textilia* p. 10.

serials, articles and offprints, dissertations, royal decrees and laws — published in all languages since the late fifteenth century to the present. Its systematic order feels somewhat at odds with the inspiring chaos of the clutter of books I'd encountered before. The entries are arranged alphabetically by author and title, not indexed by subject, to allow the reader 'to chance upon works that would otherwise be lost in any type of detailed subject index.'[6] Siegelaub's research project seems be driven by this never-ending dance between those 'two poles of order and disorder'.

What set Siegelaub's CSROT apart from other research projects at the time was not only its scope and openness to textile cultures worldwide, but the fact that his interest in textiles moved far beyond their conventional study, which stuck to beyond the surface, so to speak, the aesthetic appearance, provenance and dates, and did not pay attention to social, cultural and economic aspects. Instead, Siegelaub placed textiles right at the centre of society.

'Textiles', he writes in the introduction to his *Bibliographica Textilia Historiae*, 'have played a very special role in the history of humanity because of their unique and contradictory dual character: they are at the same time very delicate and vulnerable to the natural elements and human use on the one hand, while on the other hand, they are very rugged, resilient and portable...' It is this characteristic, he says, 'that has given textiles a unique place in the interwoven history of ornament and the history of trade (...) and with this trade, an essential means of communication for motifs, designs, cultural values, and ideas, as well as the power behind them'.[7]

By way of demonstration, Siegelaub points to the fundamental role textiles played in the rise of the capitalist system, referring to wool production as the first large-scale capitalist industry and to the industrial revolution, their role in architecture, and their place in colloquial language. To Siegelaub, all these things were connected, just as 'it was only logical that the development of the jacquard loom in France at the beginning of the 19th century would be an inspiration for the work of Charles Babbage in England, which directly led to the invention of the computer in the 20th century'.[8]

In keeping with the nature of his interest in textiles, which concerned not merely their aesthetic beauty, but the histories they convey, Siegelaub acquired handmade fabrics only, most of them bearing traces of wear and tear. The holes, fringes and loose hanging threads testify to another dimension of 'textile's intimate relationship with society'. The fact that most of the items are fragments and not complete pieces can also be seen as marks of lived history and the biography of things. Precious textiles were often cut up by merchants and collectors who were only interested in the decorated parts of the cloth. Regardless of their condition, Siegelaub's collection contains some exquisite pieces: beautiful eighteenth century embroidered silks, ancient indigo-died weavings from Peru, lush velvets, vividly coloured brocades, Tapa fragments from Fiji. All simply too hard to resist to not touch.

In 2012, Raven Row in London staged the exhibition *The Stuff That Matters: Textiles Collected by Seth Siegelaub* for the CSROT. It was the first time Seth Siegelaub and Marja Bloem, his partner in life and work, showed some of his textile and book collections to a larger public.[9] Curated by Sara Marinetti, Alice Motard and Alex Sainsbury, the exhibition featured an eclectic mix of textile fragments, some combined with books and historical documents from the CSROT collection. It was also the first time that the two collections were laid over each other, both literally and figuratively. Intuitive correspondences connections between knowledge and 'stuff' formed in the blink of an eye, turning textiles from eye-catchingly beautiful objects into what Siegelaub understood them to be: 'essential means of communication for motifs, designs, cultural values, and ideas, as well as the power behind them', with just as much agency and advocacy as the book lying next to it.[10]

Books and textiles, textiles and books. I have often thought about that first encounter with those piles of boxes, one holding a *mer à boire* of historical and practical knowledge, the other a sensuous explosion of colour, textures and details, and how that juxtaposition of intellectual and sensuous knowledge undid years of academic studies that had trained me to separate high art and low art, knowledge and sensuous information, and all my preconceived ideas about the value of textiles.

In many ways, Siegelaub's social research into old textiles remains an important reference to my own thinking on textiles. He taught me to mine various forms of knowing and pay attention to objects and ideas that may fall outside the mainstream. Some speak to the mind, some to the eyes. Others reveal a knowledge that cannot be expressed in words. History, be it the history of art, economics, technological innovation or textiles, should not be understood as strictly separate fields or categories, but as a tapestry, emerging from interwoven threads and knotted networks.

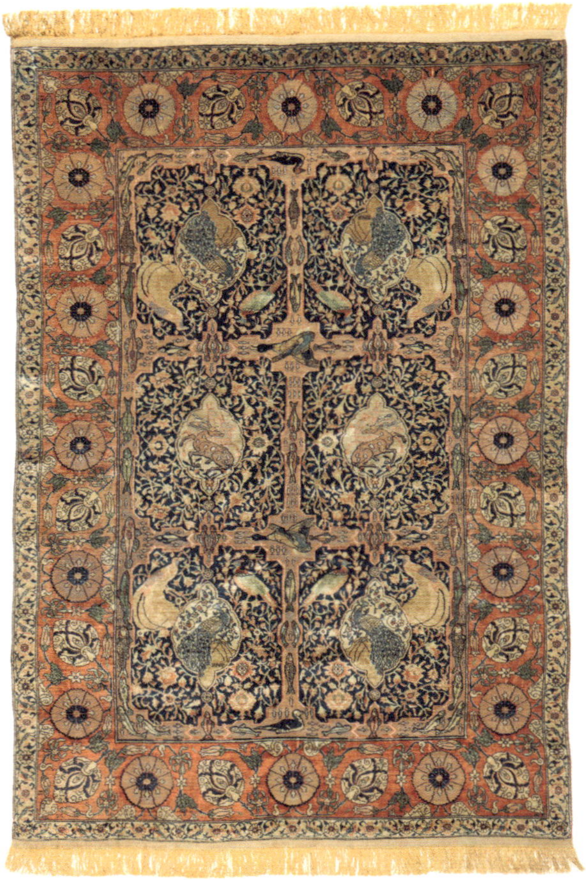

Kumkapi rug, Hagop Kapoudjian, c. 1900. Silk and silver thread, knotted, 216 × 136.5 cm. Collection Calouste Gulbenkian Foundation, Lisbon.

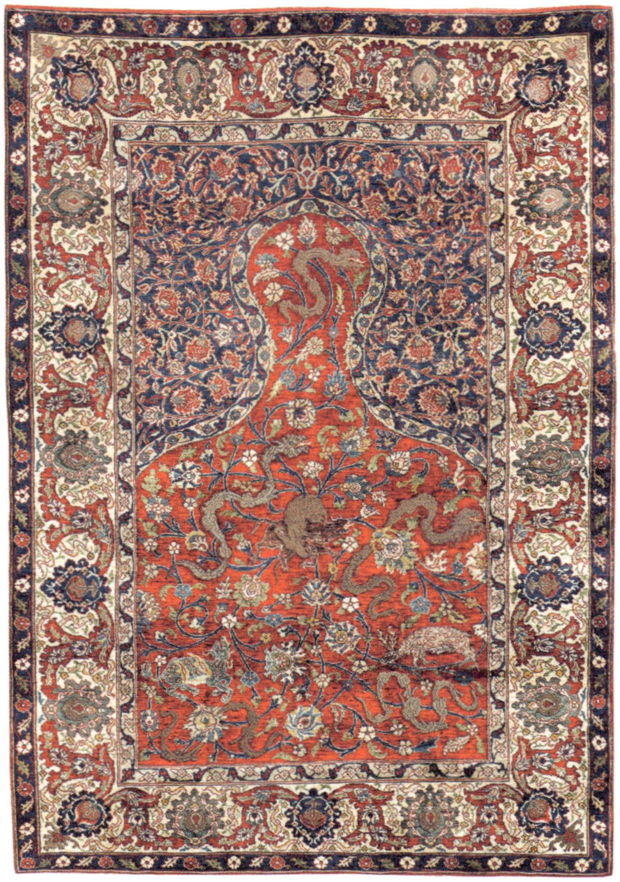

Kumkapi rug, Hagop Kapoudjian for Tosunyan, late-19th century. Silk and silver thread, knotted, 181 × 125 cm. Collection Arkas Holding, Istanbul.

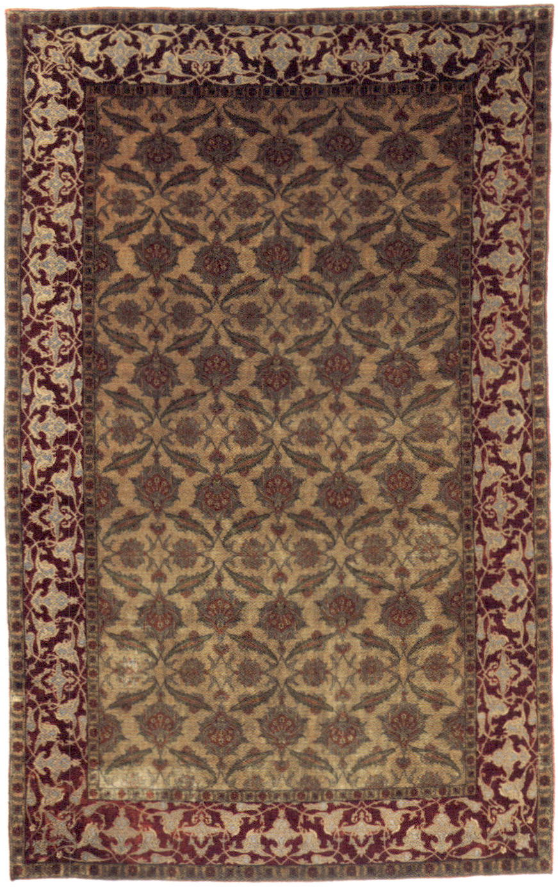

Kumkapi rug, Hagop Kapoudjian, c. 1900. Silk and silver thread, knotted, 181 × 125 cm. Collection Calouste Gulbenkian Foundation, Lisbon.

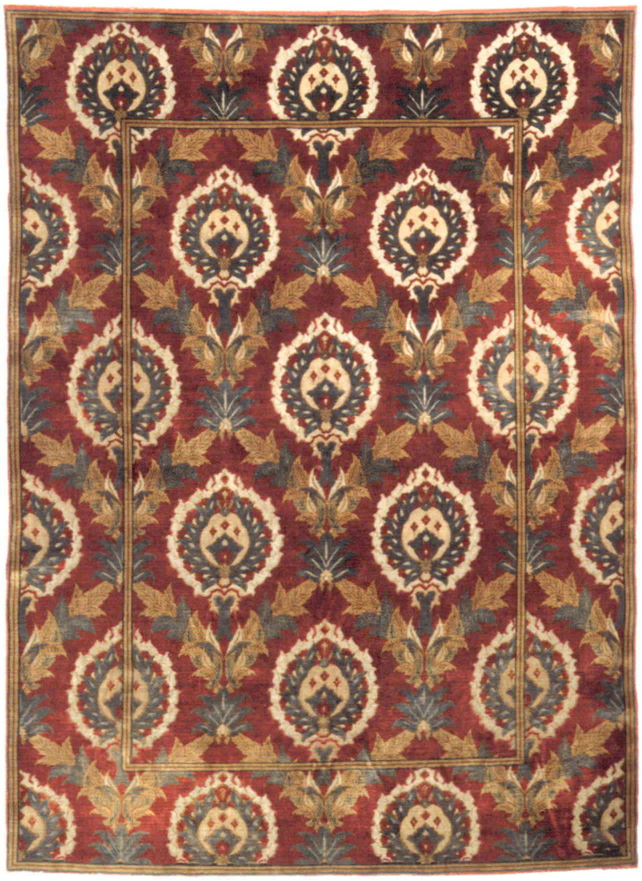

Kumkapi rug, Hagop Kapoudjian, c. 1900. Silk and silver thread, knotted, 181 × 125 cm. Collection Calouste Gulbenkian Foundation, Lisbon.

This essay explores a unique type of rug that emerged in late nineteenth century Istanbul and disappeared abruptly after 1915. Known as Kumkapi rugs, these fine silk carpets blend the technical mastery of Armenian weavers with vibrant sixteenth century Persian designs and luxurious materials like Bursa silk and French gold thread. Woven into their intricate surfaces are material traces of history's upheavals — echoes of persecution and ethnic cleansing. That history is recounted here through the life and work of Kumkapi master weaver Hagop Kapoudjian (Kayseri, 1870–Paris, 1946).

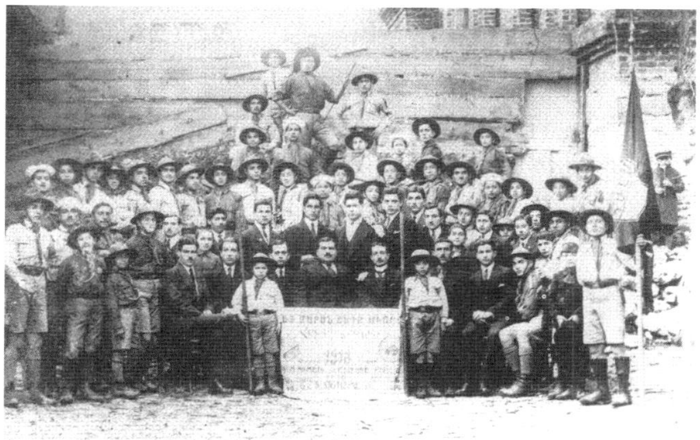

Group portrait taken at the inauguration of the KumKapi Boy Scouts' Troop in Istanbul, 1918, with Hagop Kapoudjian standing in the middle of the front row. This is the only existing photograph of the master weaver.

# KUMKAPI
# Travelling Carpets

There are no official records documenting Hagop Kapoudjian's arrival in Istanbul, nor do we know much about his life or training prior to that time. The information available comes from secondhand sources: personal communications — written or verbal — between carpet dealers and collectors. These eventually made their way into auction and exhibition catalogues.[1] Some sources mention that Hagop moved to Istanbul with his family as a boy, while others claim he arrived in the capital as a young man around 1890.

What we do know is that Kapoudjian was born in 1870 in Kayseri, a thriving town along key trade routes with a strong economy based on carpet weaving, textiles and commerce. It was also home to a diverse population of Turks, Armenians and Greeks.[2] He likely received his training in the local tradition of knotted-pile rug weaving, distinguished by a high wool pile and solid knotting using the so-called double Ghiordes or Turkish knot. These rugs featured bold primary colours — yellow, red, blue and dark brown — and strongly stylized, geometric animal and floral motifs.

## ANATOLIAN WEAVINGS

As with many regional weaving traditions, the same rug types were likely woven for generations. Locally available materials such as leaves, roots or fruits were used to colour the woollen threads. Rugs were woven at home or in local workshops and reflected a distinct and enduring regional aesthetic and visual rendering of patterns and motifs.[3]

Only a few early examples of rugs woven by Armenian hands from Central Anatolia still exist. However, we can get a good impression of their colours and style by examining paintings from the fifteenth century Venetian Renaissance or the seventeenth century Dutch School, where 'rugs from the East hang down as holiday decorations from windows and balconies; carpets serve as floor coverings in private homes and public palaces, and lie as spreads upon the table'.[4]

1. There is very little written documentation on the weavers of the Kumkapi School. The biographical information on Hagop Kapoudjian — also known as Kapuciyan and 'Rotund (Fat) Hagop' — presented in this essay is drawn from the publication *Hagop Kapoudjian: The First and Greatest Master of the Kum Kapi School* (1993), by George F. Farrow et al. Farrow's monograph offers detailed descriptions of silk rugs from his collection, including works by Kapoudjian and fellow Kumkapi weavers such as Zareh Penyamine.
2. Kurtuluş Cengiz, 'The Tale of Industrialization in a Small Town in Turkey: Hacilar-Kayseri' (2019), p. 59.
3. As artist and textile scholar Belkis Balpinar notes in her study on the origins of Anatolian Kilims: 'Kilim weavers are not composers; they are very good performers,' explaining that a specific type of kilim was unique to one tribal group and distinct from all others, serving as both a statement and a symbol of unity. See Belkis Balpinar, 'A Discussion on Central Asian Türkmen Influence on Anatolian Kilims' (2001), pp. 7-16.
4. Willem Bode et al, *Antique Rugs from the Near East*, ([1902] 1958), p. 15. Willem Bode's *Antique Rugs* was the first comprehensive European study on antique knotted rugs from the 'Near East'. It was written in response to the rising popularity and booming market for 'Oriental rugs' in northern Europe in the late 19th century, spurred on by public exhibitions such as the Vienna Carpet Exhibition in 1891. The book focuses on determining the age and provenance of ancient carpets, while also acknowledging the limitations of such efforts and the risk of erroneous conclusions based on false assumptions.

From the fifteenth century onwards, so-called Turkey rugs became prized possessions among the European nobility and wealthy elite—first in the courts and clergy of Venice, then in Spain, and later north of the Alps. 'The Anatolian rug captivated Europe by its often enigmatic and mysterious designs, which were thought to embody an ancient symbolic system.'[5] For example, seventeenth century portraits of Dutch regents and burghers—known as governor pieces—often feature Turkish rugs used as table covers or floor pieces, signalling the wealth and worldliness of those portrayed. The popularity of 'Oriental rugs' continued well into the twentieth century, spurred by public exhibitions such as the Vienna Carpet Exhibition of 1891. This growing demand significantly boosted the weaving economies of Central Anatolian towns like Kayseri, Sivas and Tokat.

Workshops in Kayseri would have employed both Armenian and Turkish weavers. Christian Armenians and Islamic Turks had coexisted as weavers in relative peace since the region was secured by the Ottomans in the fifteenth and sixteenth centuries.[6] However, by the time Hagop Kapoudjian was born, peace between the two communities had begun to erode, giving way to growing anti-Armenian sentiment and violence. This spurred many Armenians to leave the region and seek refuge in the western parts of the Ottoman Empire.

By the late nineteenth century, a group of Armenian weavers had settled in the Kumkapi district of Constantinople, present-day Istanbul. Located on the northern shore of the Sea of Marmara, Kumkapi (meaning Sand Gate in Turkish) was a poor immigrant neighbourhood with a large Armenian population. Its narrow, dirty streets and small, dimly lit workshops stood in stark contrast to the splendour of the nearby Topkapi district, home to the Blue Mosque, Hagia Sophia and Topkapi Palace—where many of the Sultan's treasures, including remarkable examples of sixteenth century Safavid rugs, were on display. Two women, Reara Agha Kayseri and Apraham Agha, established looms in Armenian churches and orphanages, where young but skilled Armenian girls wove rugs in exchange for food. Their efforts laid the foundation for what would become known as the Kumkapi School.

## PERSIAN DESIGNS

Armenian weavers, including Kapoudjian, likely chose Istanbul as their destination due to its proximity to the town of Hereke—an important centre of textile production that offered migrant weavers stable work and income. Hereke was renowned for its finely hand-knotted silk carpets. In 1843, Ottoman Emperor Sultan Abdülmecid I established the Hereke Imperial Factory, which was tasked exclusively with producing carpets, curtains and upholstery for the Ottoman Court—particularly for the newly constructed Dolmabahçe Palace in Istanbul. The Imperial workshops employed only the finest weavers and designers from across the country, including Armenian weavers from Kayseri.

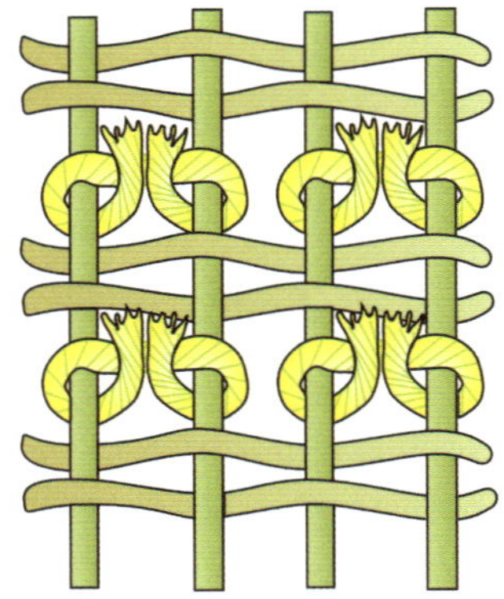

A.

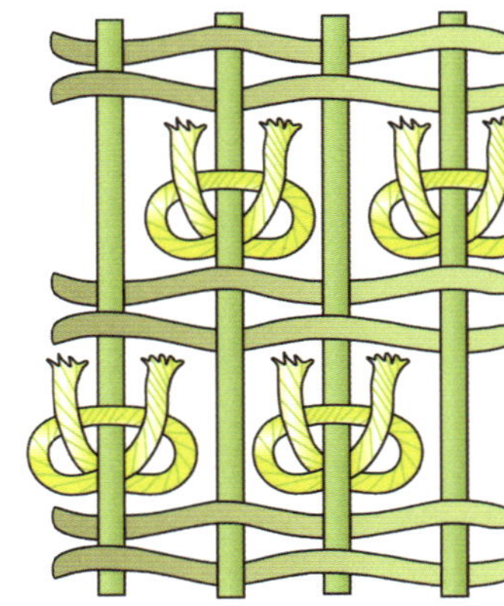

B.

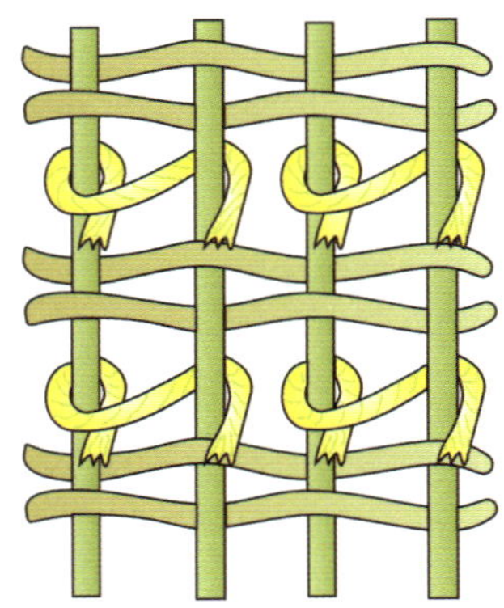

C.

KNOTS
Of the traditional rug weaving techniques, knotted pile rugs have received the most attention. Their basic structure consists of warp, weft and pile. The pile is created by knotting yarn around the warp using either continuous or cut yarn. Different knotting techniques produce distinct visual effects. Warp and weft are generally made of cotton, while the pile may consist of various materials, including wool and silk.

A. Turkish knot (Ghiordes knot): A symmetrical knot in which both ends of the yarn are pulled up between two warp threads – either upwards, downwards or in reverse; commonly used in long-pile carpets due to its durability and secure hold. The knot is thought to have originated in the northern regions of Iraq.

B. Spanish knot: Either symmetrical or asymmetrical, this knot is formed by looping the pile around pairs of warp threads instead of single warps. A variation uses a single warp and is quick to produce.

C. Persian knot (Sehna knot): An asymmetrical knot where one end of the yarn is tightly looped around a warp while the other end is left loose; allows for a higher knot density and more intricate patterning than the Turkish knot. A Persian knot can be open to either the left or the right, depending on the desired design.

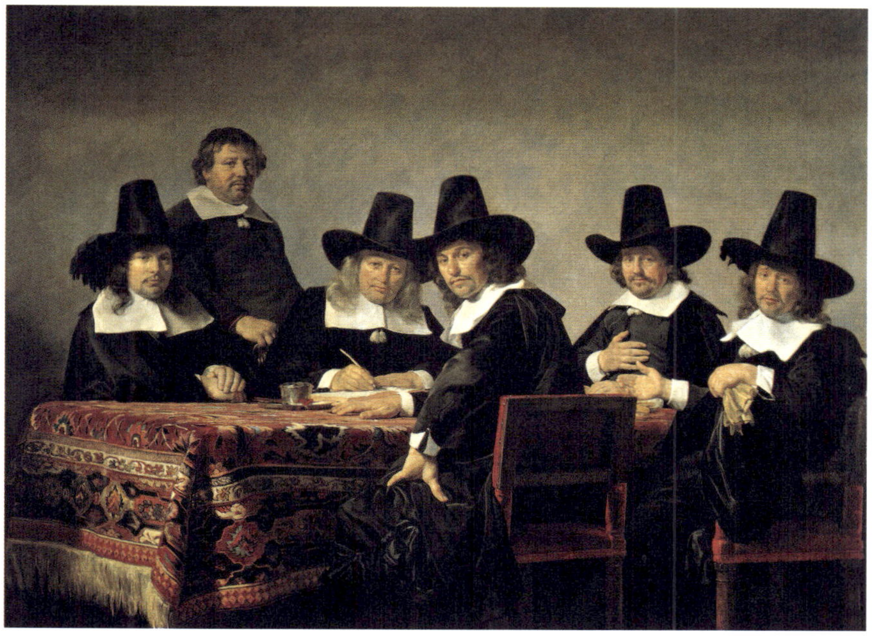

The Regents of the Children's Almshouse in Haarlem, Jan S. de Bray, 1663. Oil on canvas, 186 × 250 cm.

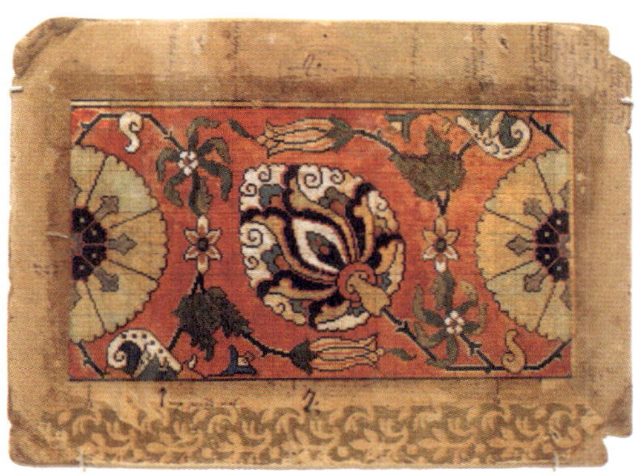

Weaving cartoon from Hagop Kapoudjian's workshop, c. 1890–1920.

It is unclear whether Kapoudjian was ever formally employed by the Imperial workshops, but it is evident that he was heavily influenced by the style and techniques of the Ottoman Court weavings. He went on to master several of these, including brocade weaving with silk and gold- or silver-wrapped threads. Court-style carpets were themselves partly inspired by the Safavid carpets of sixteenth century Persia. Kapoudjian must have studied these Persian designs — characterized by symmetrical layouts, central medallions, floral arabesques and delicate curvilinear patterns — during visits to Topkapi or Dolmabahçe Palace. Over time, his own carpets began to incorporate increasingly refined details that echoed the visual language of Persian rug-making.

By the turn of the century, Kapoudjian was a celebrated master weaver, the owner of one of the Kumkapi weaving workshops, and a respected member of the Armenian community. His rugs stood out for their technical excellence, exceptionally high knot density, use of precious materials and unrivalled designs. While rooted in Turkish carpet traditions, they also drew inspiration from the intricately patterned silk Safavid carpets of sixteenth century Persia.

In the early twentieth century, Kumkapi rugs had become internationally renowned and highly sought-after by both the Ottoman elite and European collectors. However, in April 1915, the production of the Kumkapi carpets came to an abrupt end. Although Ottoman authorities had already begun targeting Armenian minorities, the situation escalated on the night of 23 April with a coordinated raid in Istanbul — known as Red Sunday — during which 250 Armenian intellectuals and community leaders were imprisoned. Most Armenian weavers either fled the city that year or became victims of ethnic cleansing. Kapoudjian escaped to Paris, where he died in 1946.

## AFTERLIFE

Sometimes, the biography of a thing echoes the biography of its maker. It bears witness to the hands that created it — to the skill, artistic vision and hours of dedicated labour someone invested in mindfully (perhaps even lovingly) shaping its texture, form and design. In this sense, textile objects become tactile documents of lives lived, and, when viewed more broadly, of the historical circumstances that shaped those lives. Kumkapi carpets reveal how the twists of history are — sometimes quite literally — inscribed in its threads. They are an example of cross-pollination, brought about by the forced migration of Armenian weavers to Istanbul, the encounter between Armenian weaving tradition characterized by its primary colours and geometric motifs, and the intricate and lush designs of sixteenth century Persian tapestries, resulting in a group of extraordinarily precious silk carpets.

As Arjun Appadurai explains in the introduction to *The Social Life of Things* (1986),[7] the biography of a thing may extend long after it left the workshop of its maker — as is the case with the Kumkapi rugs. Their status as extraordinary carpets continues into the present.[8] But in the aftermath of the

5. Bode, *Oriental Rugs*, p. 156. In 2014, the Metropolitan Museum in New York organized the exhibition *Carpets from the East in Paintings from the West*. The exhibition showed three mid-17th Dutch paintings alongside three actual rugs from the East dating to the same period.
6. Armenians are one of the four indigenous populations of modern nation-state Turkey. Since ancient times, Christian Armenians have inhabited the mountainous plateau of Eastern Anatolia, living side by side with Muslim Kurds and other ethnic groups. In the 11th century, Turkic nomadic groups migrated to the region from East Asia. During the fifteenth and sixteenth centuries, the area was secured by the Ottoman Turks and integrated into the vast Ottoman Empire. While most Armenians were poor peasants, some found success as merchants and artisans, participating in international trade from the sixteenth to the eighteenth centuries and earning a reputation in Istanbul, India and Europe.
7. Arjun Appadurai, ed, *The Social Life of Things: Commodities in Cultural Perspectives* (1986).

Armenian genocide, Kumkapi rugs came to represent more than mere commodities — they became symbols of the cultural heritage of a people whose history has been marked by conflict and exile. As treasured heirlooms carrying memories of a lost homeland, these rugs found their way into both public and private collections. Often initiated and supported by affluent members of the Armenian diaspora, such institutions are dedicated to preserving cultural memory, raising awareness and fostering a sense of a shared cultural identity.

The urgency of these initiatives becomes apparent when we open a standard handbook on Turkish weaving traditions, only to find that the Armenian origins of Kumkapi rugs are rarely mentioned.[9] Instead, they are categorized as Turkish. As the eminent Armenian-American historian Dickran Kouymjian points out: 'The history of Armenian carpet weaving is still a fragmented discourse (...) Many of its basic facts are or have been challenged, or simply rejected, by determined nationalistic policies of neighboring political authorities, foremost among them the Republic of Azerbaijan and more subtly, but for a longer time, Turkey.'[10] These mechanisms of cultural erasure and denial, 'aided and abetted by the idea that whatever was produced historically in the boundaries of a modern nation-state or, in an earlier time, an empire, must be subsumed under the name of the dominant political constituency of the country' are common to many nation-states. But as Turkey's denial of the Armenian genocide persists, and Armenian civil rights continue to be undermined, any appraisal of the history and origins of Kumkapi rugs becomes, inevitably, a political act.

8. To illustrate the economic value of Kumkapi rugs, in 2019, a Kumkapi rug sold at Christie's Auction House in London for GBP 20,000. A smaller rug from the same lot sold for GBP 11,250. Both were listed as being in 'good condition'. In 2011, Bonhams Auction House sold a Kumkapi rug in excellent condition for GBP 24,000.
9. Dickran Kouymijan, 'The Berlin Dragon-Phoenix Carpet and Its Probable Armenian Origin' (2014), pp. 5-8. As an example, Kouymijan refers to his 1978 copy of the two-volume. Early Caucasian Carpets in Turkey with its censored map blacking out the word 'Armenia'. I encountered the same 'omission' in the catalogue published in 2017 to accompany the exhibition *Kum Kapi Rugs from the Arkas Collection* at TIEM, Istanbul organized as part of the second annual Istanbul Carpet Week organized by the Istanbul Carpet Exporters' Association (IHIB).
10. Ibid., p. 5.

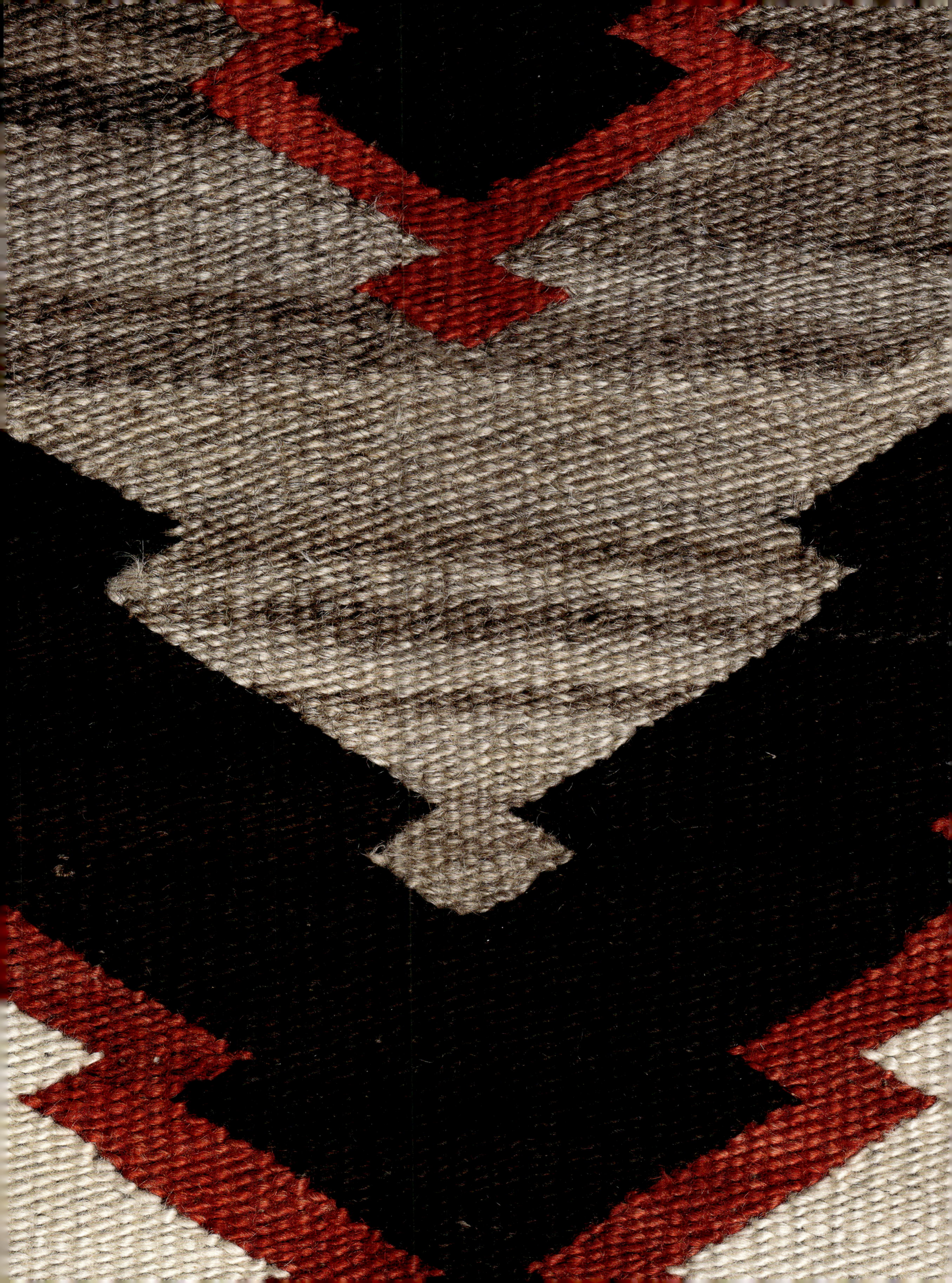

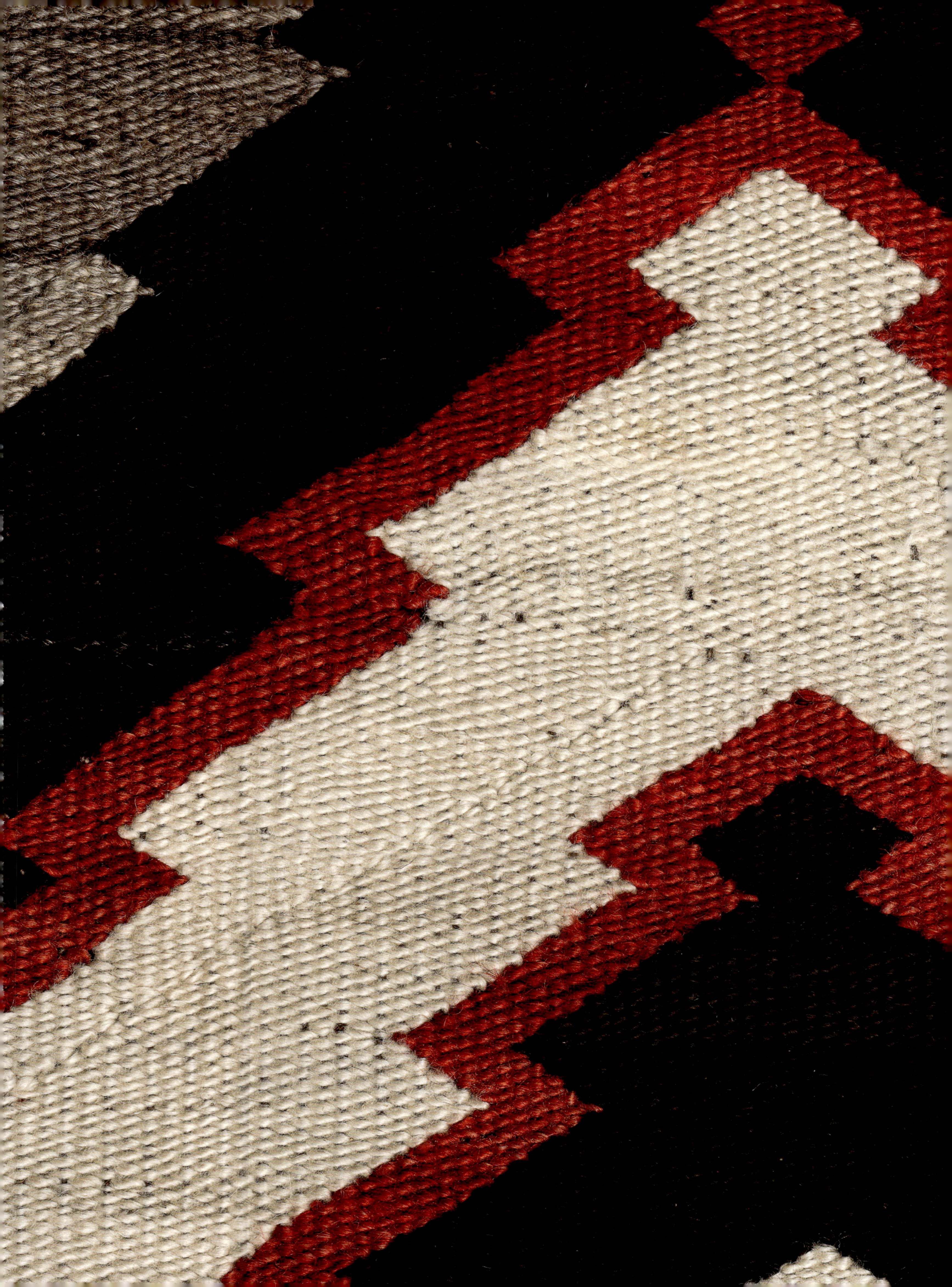

*Technik*

Elisa van Joolen & Vincent Vulsma

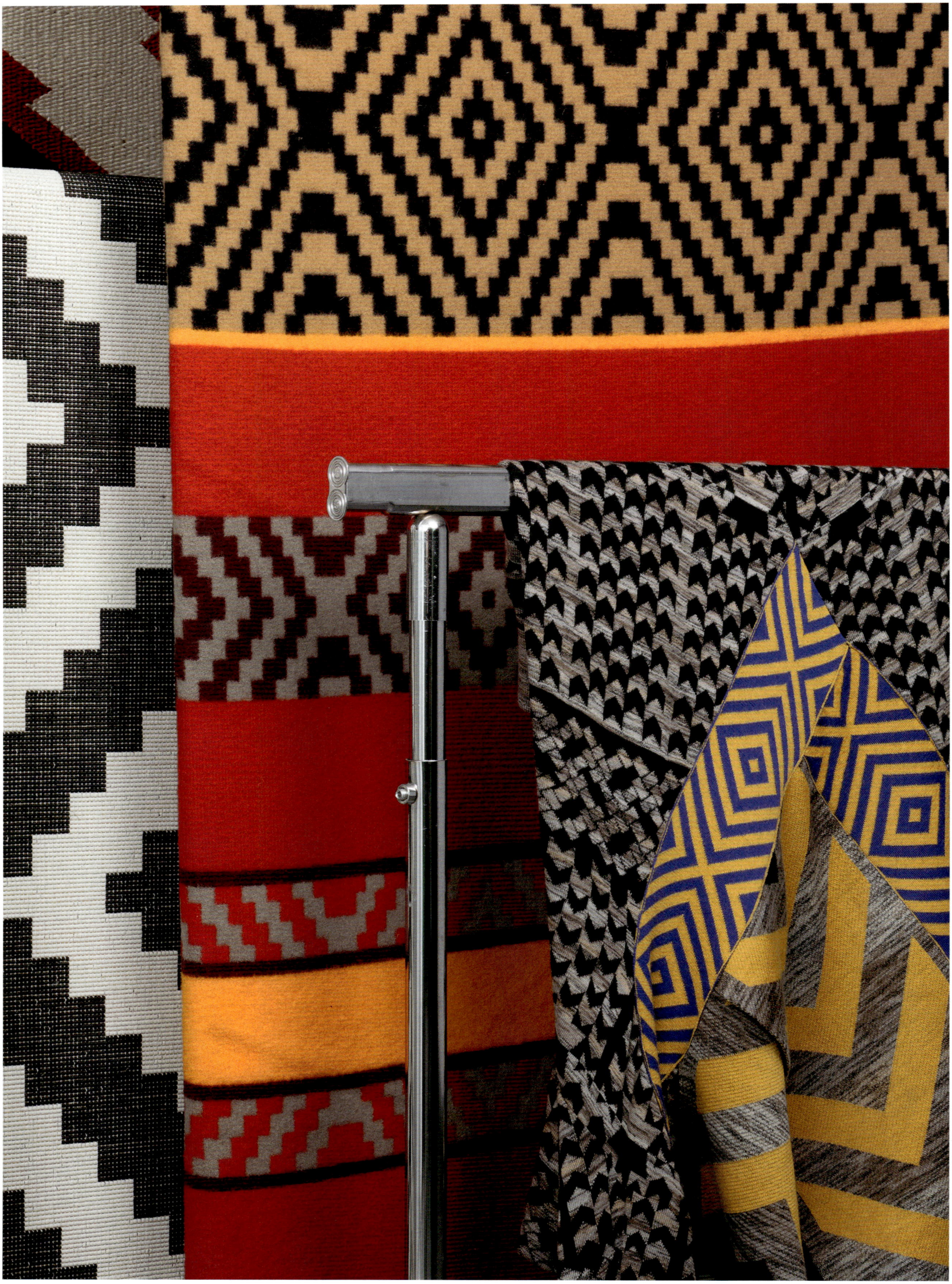

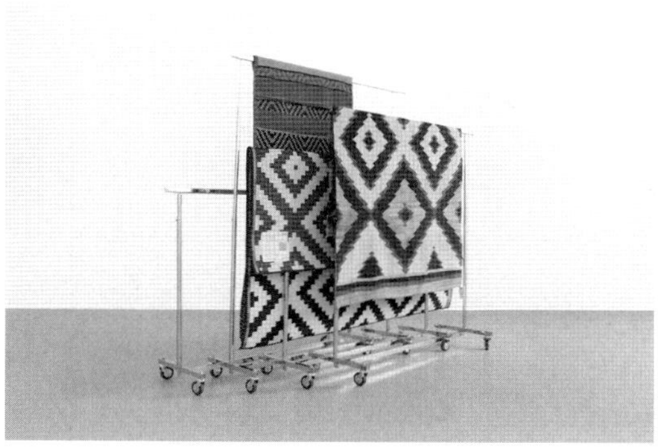

Technik, Elisa van Joolen & Vincent Vulsma, 2012–2013.

Navajo Indian weaving, Transitional Period, c. 1890s, handwoven, natural wool, 139.7 × 213.4 cm; Pendleton Indian Trade Blanket, J. Capps & Sons Tribute #2, 2010, based on an original design c. 1910, felt binding, pure virgin wool and cotton, made in the USA, 162.6 × 182.9 cm; Lappljung Ruta, design by Anna Evferlund for IKEA, machine woven, polypropylene, made in Egypt, 200 × 200 cm; Bernhard Willhelm, Chevron Print Sweater, size S, AW collection 2012/2013, knitted, cotton and mohair, made in Belgium; metal clothing racks, dimensions variable.

*Technik* comprises four pieces of textile, each draped over a chrome-metal clothing rack. The racks are adjusted to different heights and placed back to back, their wheels locked into a grid of metal beams. Together, the racks and textiles create a dynamic tableau of overlapping surfaces that partly obscure one another. From back to front we see a handmade flat-woven Navajo rug in natural wool, dated around the 1890s; a machine-woven rug made of polypropylene designed by Anna Evferlund for IKEA; a Pendleton Indian Trade Blanket made of wool and cotton, produced by Pendleton Mills; and a knitted, cotton and mohair sweater designed by Bernhard Willhelm for his AW collection 2012/2013.

Moving around the installation, we get a sense of the materiality and weight of the textiles. We can also examine the back of each piece. The artists have left the labels attached, providing us with snippets of information about origin, material composition, mode of production and, in some cases, the name of its maker.

What these textiles share is their use of the same geometric pattern and colour scheme, which has become known by its colloquial name, Navajo pattern. In its most rudimentary form, this pattern is based on a repetition of a triangular or diamond-shaped motif, often using basic earth tones like red, brown, grey, golden yellow, white and black. The pattern appears in different variations and designs, even though the Navajo rug and black-and-white IKEA rug were produced a century apart. In the Bernhard Willhelm sweater, the motif appears at various scales synthesized into one design.

The repetition of the pattern in various shapes and sizes connects the four products across time and place. In terms of texture and materiality, however, these textiles are worlds apart. Even without touching them, we can sense that the sweater is soft and smooth, whereas the IKEA rug looks coarse and stiff. Similarly, the 1890s Navajo weaving, made of wool, looks prickly and less comfortable than the Pendleton Indian Trade blanket, which is made of pure wool and cotton. Zooming in on surface textures, we detect significant differences in the woven structures. In the IKEA rug the interlocking of warp and weft is a clearly visible and an integral part of the design, creating a firm and even look. In the Navajo textile, on the other hand, the threads are uneven and the rhythm of warp and weft irregular, making the handwoven rug appear more animated and alive, more authentic and unique. The type of yarn used in each of the four pieces — wool, cotton, synthetic — also determines material expression and the vividness of the colours. The various choices and combinations of weaving technique, quality of yarn and type of binding lend each textile in *Technik* its individual material and tactile identity.

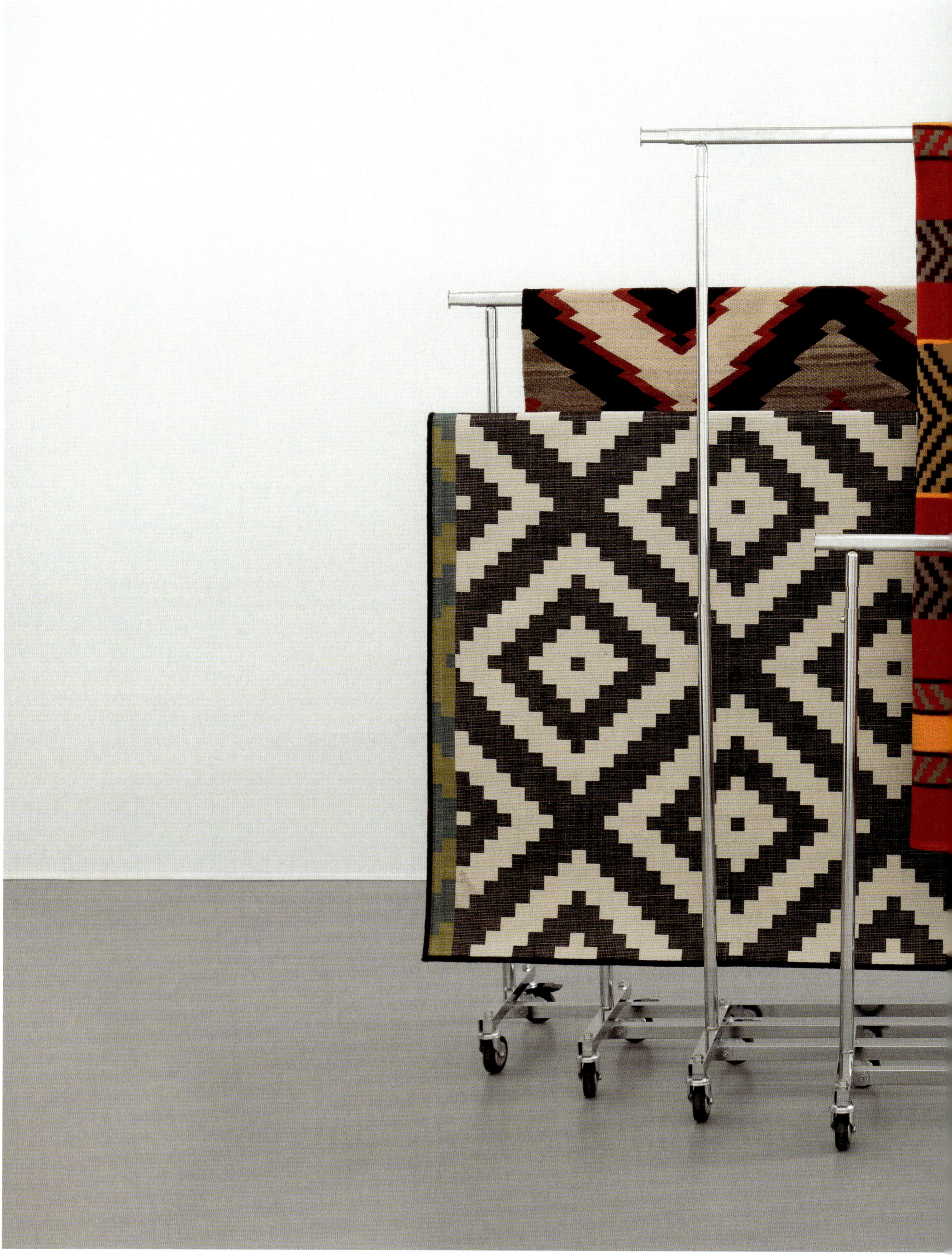

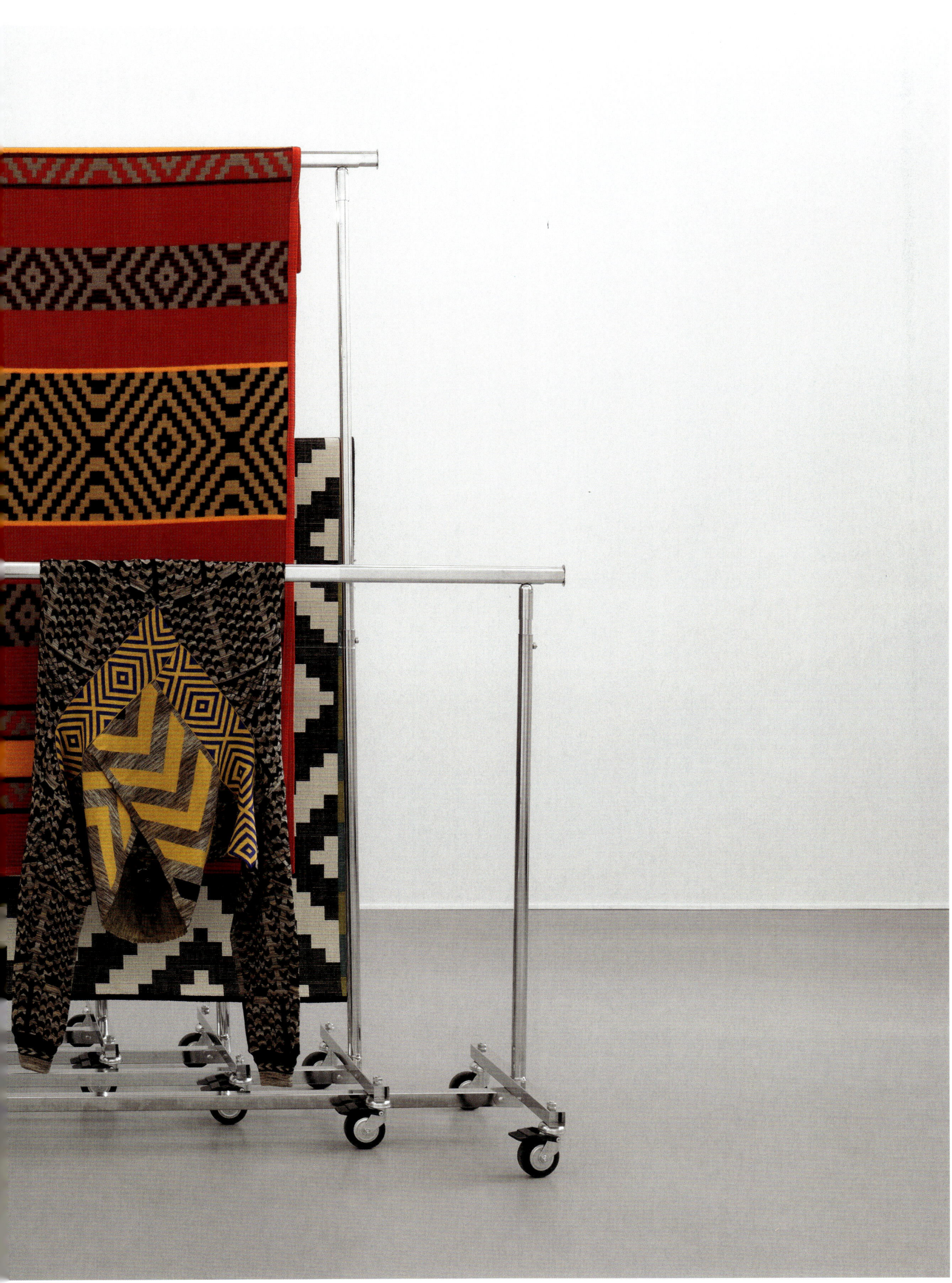

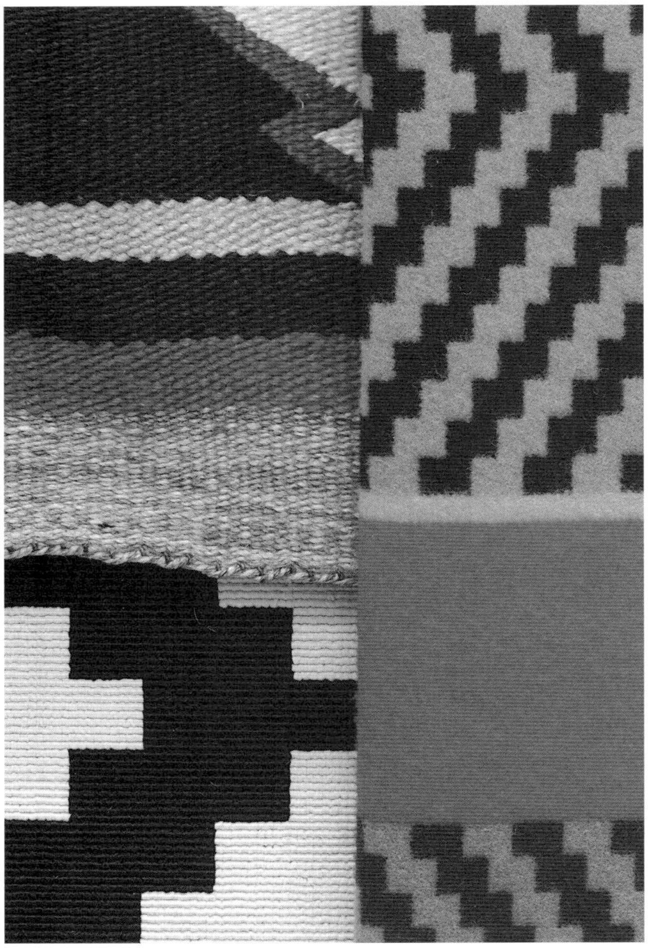

Detail Technik, overlapping Navajo weaving, Pendleton Indian Trade Blanket and IKEA rug.

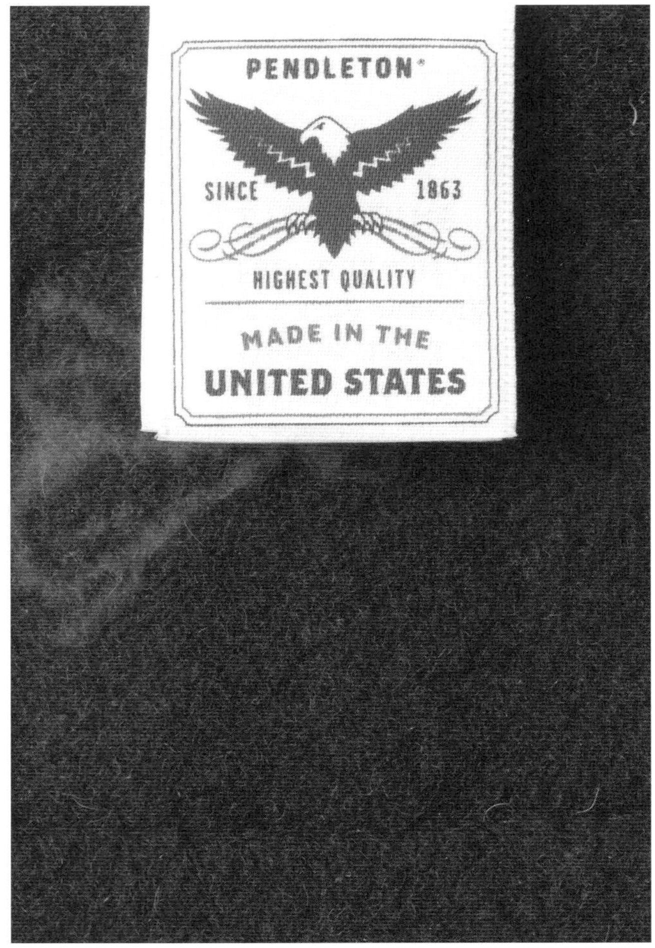


Detail Technik, label Pendleton Indian Trade Blanket.

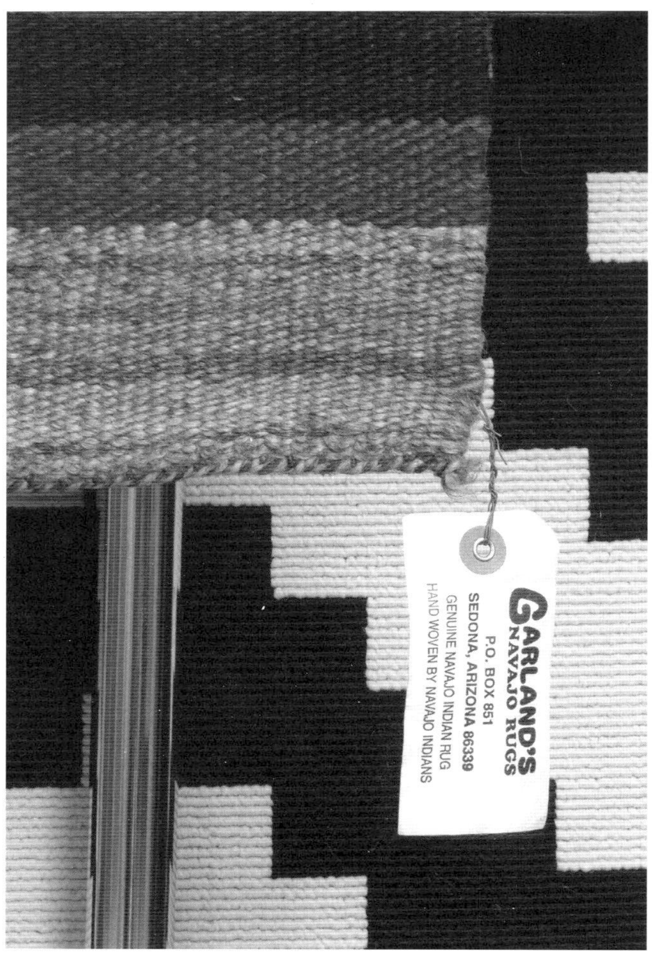


Detail Technik, label Garland's Navajo Rugs, Arizona.

# UNRAVELLING TECHNIK
## In Conversation with Elisa van Joolen & Vincent Vulsma

The collaborative artwork *Technik* (2012–2013), by Vincent Vulsma and Elisa van Joolen, brings together various textile representations of a Navajo design, known as the diamond motif. It tells the story of how one pattern migrated over time from one context to another, and about the events that propelled these shifts in the history of Navajo weaving. Between the works, *Technik* critically speaks of appropriation that is inextricably linked with imperialism and colonization, with consequences extending far beyond the formal and aesthetic.

CHRISTEL VESTERS — What prompted you to make this artwork?

ELISA VAN JOOLEN & VINCENT VULSMA — The installation is one of the few works we've made together. It's the result of our shared interest in the mechanism of cultural appropriation. In the summer of 2012, when we were in New York together, we noticed how many items in popular design stores such as Urban Outfitters and Opening Ceremony featured representations of the geometric, diamond-shaped Navajo pattern. We decided to take this specific pattern as the focus of our research.

When we investigated the origins of the pattern, we came across the story of the original 'trade blankets', and the ambiguous role Pendleton and other American companies have played in the circulation of Navajo designs since the late nineteenth century. The company opened its first woollen mill in Oregon in 1895 and soon started producing so-called Indian Trade Blankets which they traded with Indigenous Americans living across the Colombia Plateau. Their patterns and colours were based on the blankets and robes woven by local Indigenous Americans, and after a few years Pendleton Woolen Mills started to collaborate with indigenous weavers on the design of their blanket collections, and later on a clothing collection. In 2009, to celebrate its centenary, Pendleton launched its Tribute Series, reissuing some of the historical Indian Trade Blanket designs. The appropriation of Navajo designs and other cultural motifs is not uncommon in fashion and design.

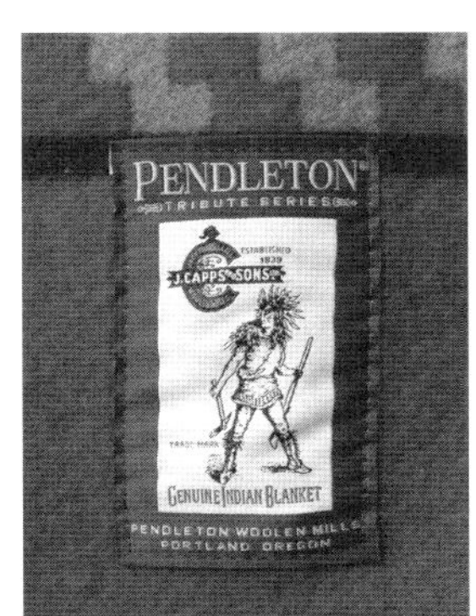


Detail Technik, label Pendleton Mill Tribute Series: J. Capps and Sons, 2017.

In a way, Pendleton contributed to a greater familiarity with and popularity of the Navajo textile tradition, but there is also a lesser-known and perhaps less honourable side to this story. Pendleton

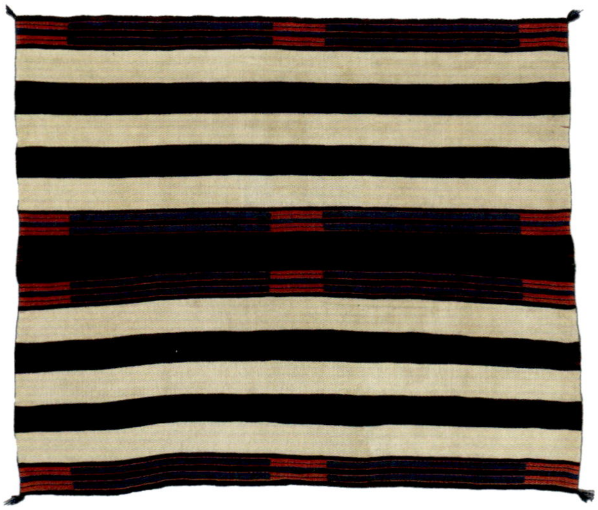

05

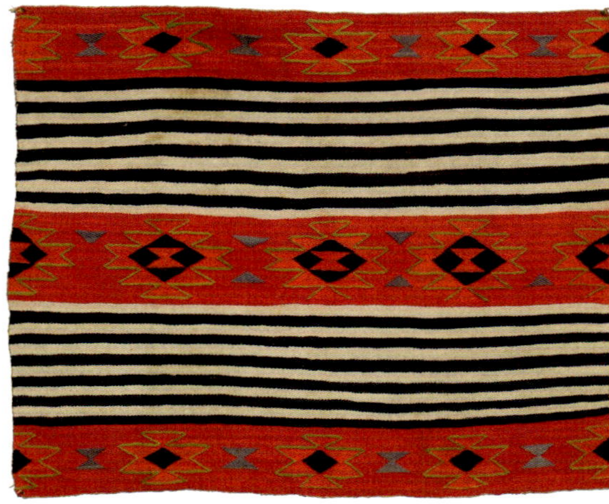

06

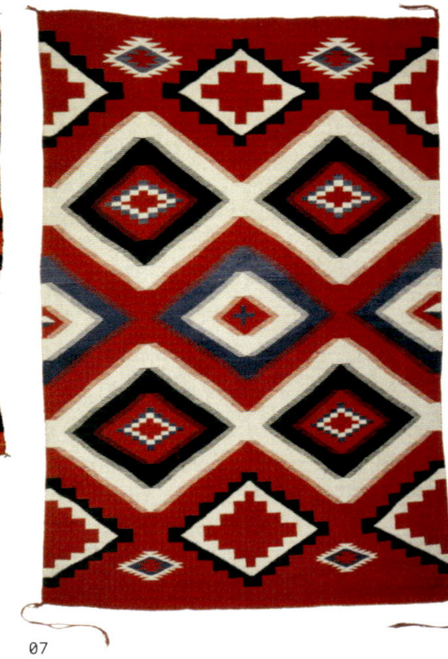

07

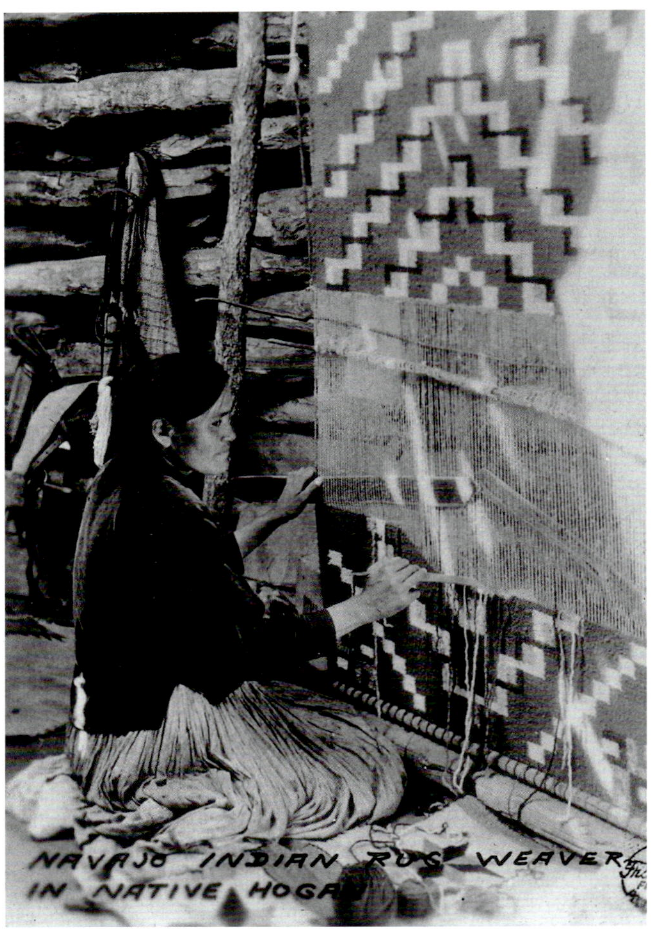


01

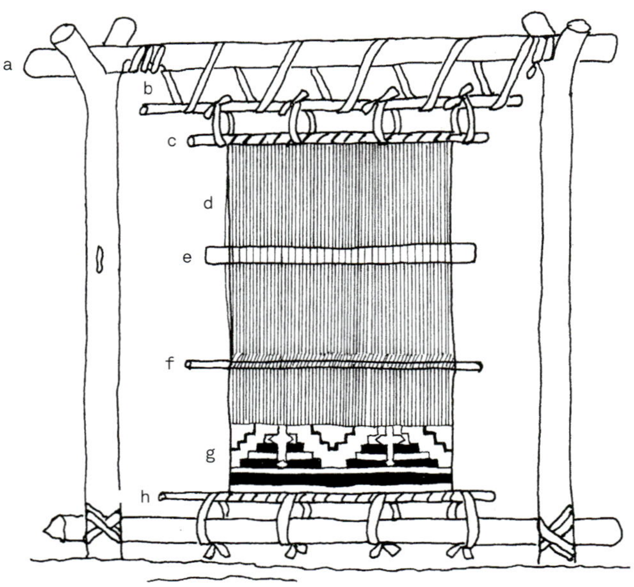


02

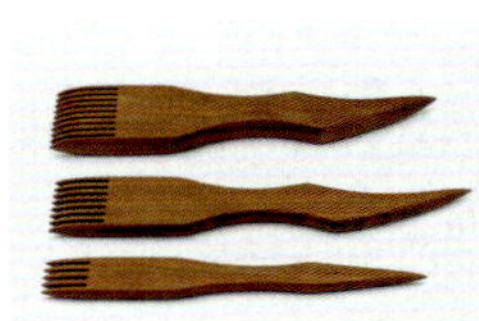

03

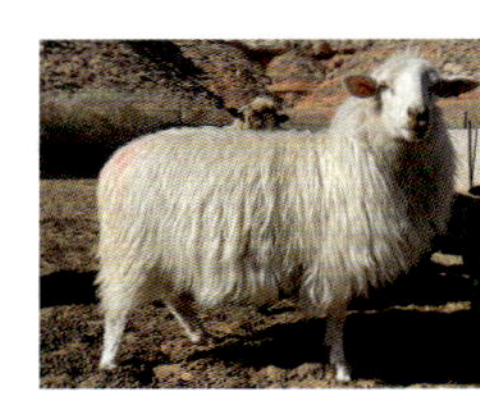

04

NAVAJO WEAVING
Weaving plays a prominent role in Navajo culture. Renowned for its geometric patterns and natural colours, their woollen blankets were used as cloaks, saddle blankets, night covers or 'doors'. The exact origins are uncertain, but Navajo weaving probably dates back to the 17th century when women learned the technique from neighbouring Pueblo tribes. Churro sheep introduced by the Spanish provided the wool. A few examples of 18th century Navajo weaving survive; most show plain stripes, some feature terrace and diamond motives, characteristic of later Navajo weaving.
The Navajo used blankets as barter long before European settlers and traders entered the south-west. Its commerce accelerated with the trading post system in the late 19th and early 20th century. This period saw the introduction of new design elements, dyes and yarns, such as Germantown yarns and vibrant aniline dyes, often encouraged by traders to cater to a non-native clientele.

01. Navajo weaver in hogan, 1933.
02. Vertical loom, Pueblo/Navajo type.
(a) vertical supports; (b) rope tension adjustment; (c) upper warp beam; (d) warp threads; (e) batten or weaving sword; (f) harness stick with string heddles; (g) rug in progress; (h) lower warp beam or cloth beam
03. Weaving tools.
04. Navajo-Churro sheep (Dibé dits'ozí), with its renowned dual coat consisting of long fleece outercoat and soft downy undercoat, Navajo-Churro sheep are strong and adaptable to harsh desert environment.
05. Chief Blanket (First Phase), c. 1855–1860.
Hand-spun wool, natural white, natural dye black, indigo blue, bayeta (ravelled) yarn, tapestry weave, horizontally woven, 157.5 × 186.7 cm.
Woven before 1860, First Phase Chief Blankets were characterized by their simple, bold stripes in natural colours, using natural dyes and repurposed yarns. These blankets were traded widely among Indigenous American tribes and Euro-American settlers.
06. Woman's Chief Blanket, c. 1890s.
Hand-spun wool, natural white, natural dye black, aniline-dye red, tapestry weave, horizontally woven, 139.7 cm × 172.72 cm.
Typically, Woman's Chief-style blankets combine striped panels with rows of stylized medallions with centred diamond motives. The hourglass motive, woven in grey yarn, symbolizes Spider Woman.
07. Transitional Blanket, c. 1897–1912.
Hand-spun and commercial wool, undyed white, natural black and synthetic red dye, tapestry weave, interlocked and diagonal joins, 231.5 × 156.5 cm.
08. Eyedazzler Germantown Blanket, c. 1890–1910.
Wool, aniline-dyed commercial yarns, tapestry weave, dovetailed and diagonal joins, 144 × 95.5 cm.
While interned at Bosque Redondo, Navajo were issued new aniline-dyed yarns which they combined with wool from their

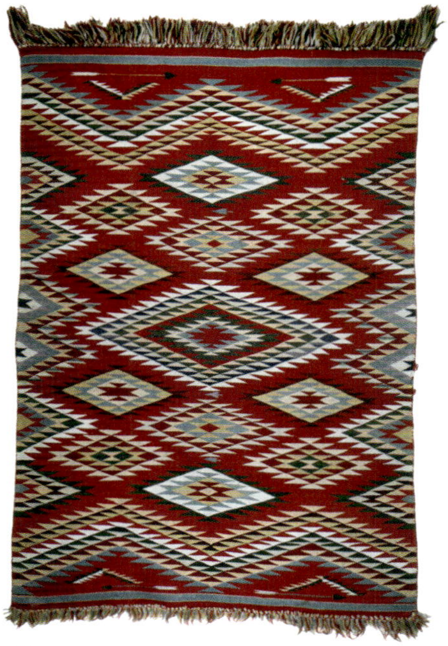

08

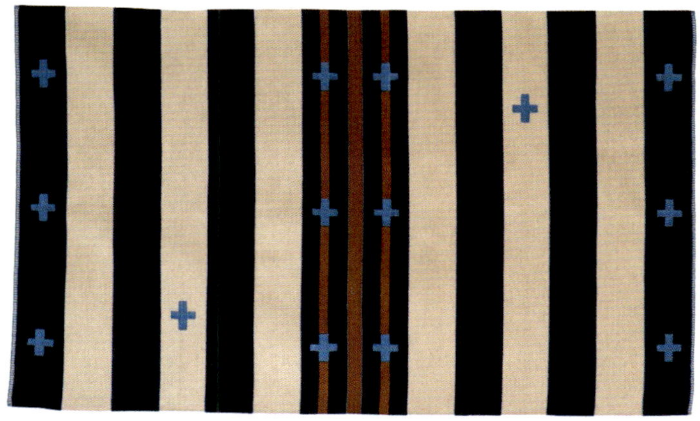

09

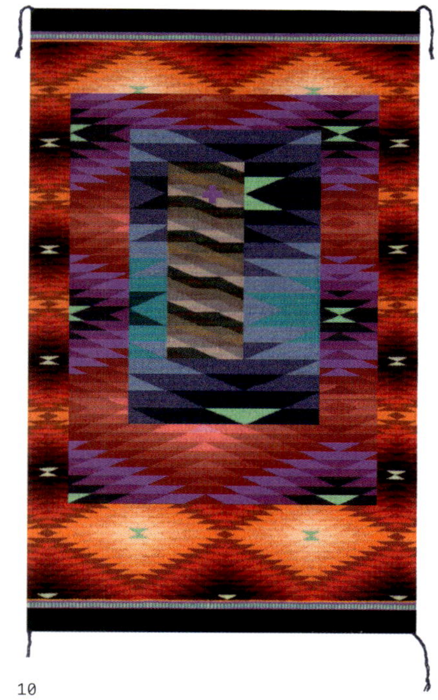

10

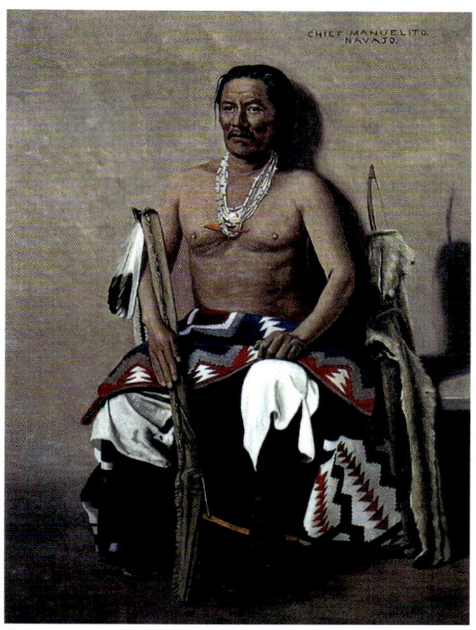


11

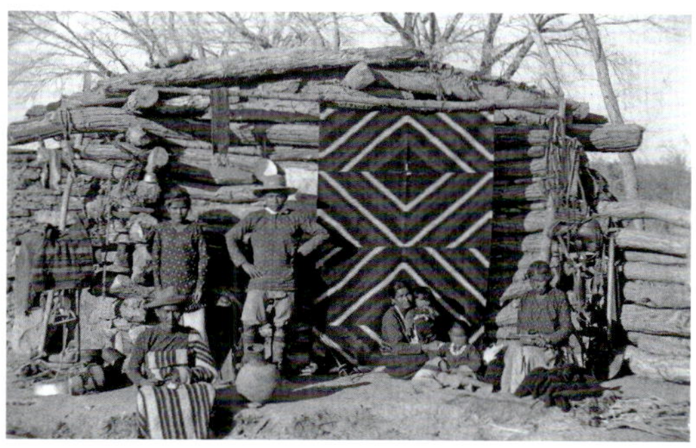

12

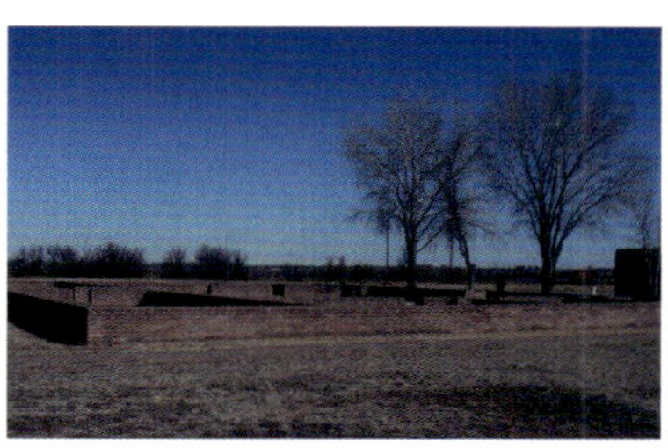

13

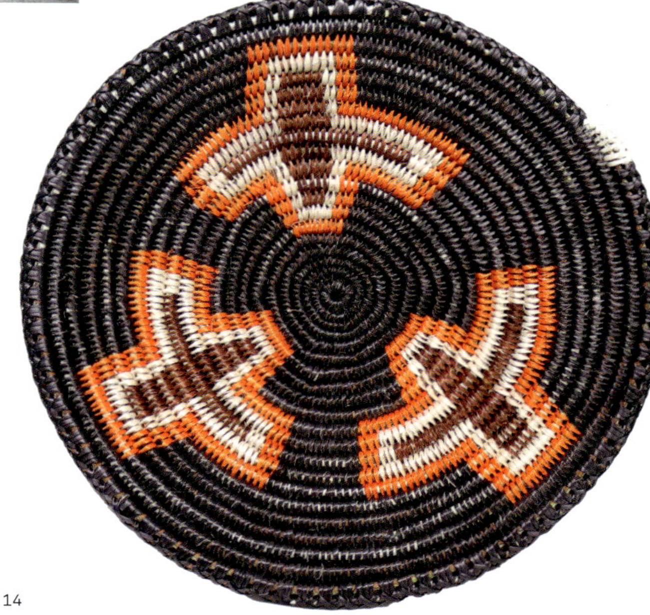

14

last few sheep. Close to Mexico, Navajo adopted and adapted the elaborate serrated diamond style from the Saltillo sarape textile, turning it into eye-dazzling geometric designs.

09. Turquoise Crosses Rug, Pendleton Home Collection.
Hand-spun, hand-dyed wool, hand-woven in a flatweave. Available in various sizes.
Based on traditional Navajo Chief Blankets, this rug is woven by Zapotec artisans in Oaxaca, New Mexico.

10. Woven in the Stones, Melissa Cody, 2018.
Wool warp, weft, selvedge cords, aniline dyes, handwoven in a flatweave, 93.3 × 64.1 cm.
A fourth generation Navajo weaver, Melissa Cody (b. 1981) is renowned for her vibrant colours and geometric patterns. Revitalizing historic Navajo 'Germantown' weaving, Cody creates modern art pieces that honour and innovate her heritage. In Woven in the Stones she uses the traditional Navajo hourglass motive, symbolizing Spider Woman.

BOSQUE REDONDO AND AFTER

While Navajo weaving thrived throughout the 19th century, the Navajo people entered a dark period. Set on expanding their territory in the south-west after the Mexican-American war (1846–1848), the United States government stepped up its campaign against Indigenous tribes. What followed was a systematic destruction of their crops and livestock, including the Navajo-Churro sheep. In 1864, the Navajo were forced from their land and incarcerated at Bosque Redondo. After four years, they signed a treaty that allowed them to return home. To replace their Churro, each family was given one sheep of a different breed, providing lesser quality wool.

11. Studio portrait of Chief Manuelito, c. 1887–1891.
With text written on rear: 'Manuelito, the once fierce chief of the Navajo.'
Chief Manuelito or Hastiin Ch'il Haajiní (c. 1818–1893) was one of the principal headmen of the Navajo before, during and after the Bosque Redondo period.

12. Photograph of a Navajo family in front of a timber and earthen hogan near Bluff City, Utah, c. 1880–1910.
A rug, cloth belt and horse tack hang from the house.

13. Ruins of military Fort Sumner, New Mexico, which oversaw the internment of the Navajo people in the adjacent Bosque Redondo reservation.

14. Spider Woman Crosses Basket, 1994.
In the Navajo Creation Story, Spider Woman, or Na'ashjéii Asdzáá (Diné name), emerged from nothingness and created the world. She wove together threads of light to form everything we see today, including mountains, rivers and even the sun itself. She taught the first humans spinning and weaving, and passed on patterns and techniques that have been used by generations of Navajo women weavers. She is symbolized by the so-called Spider Woman Cross which can be found in weavings and other Navajo craft objects.

was one of those nineteenth century American companies that greatly benefitted from the controversial restrictions imposed on indigenous communities across the United States. For centuries, indigenous communities, including the Navajo, had produced *and* traded hand-woven woollen blankets. They herded their sheep, harvested the wool, spun it and dyed it to create their uniquely designed blankets. But as colonization spread, more and more Indigenous Americans were forced to leave their land, losing their herds and their income. Ironically, the Pendleton Indian Trade Blankets owe their name to the fact that they were traded with those communities whose own production was undercut.

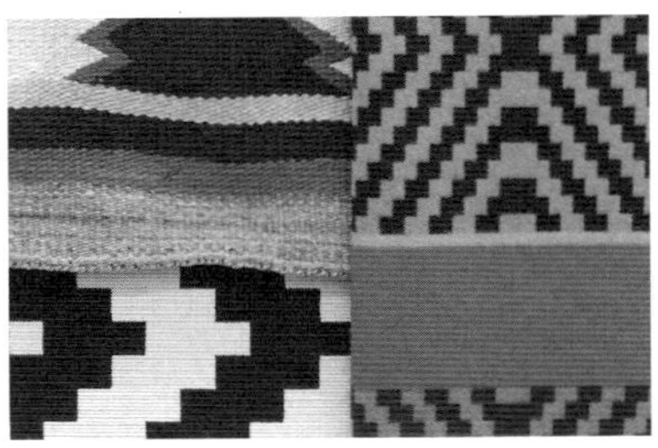

Detail Technik, Pendleton Indian Trade Blanket (front), Navajo Blanket (middle) and IKEA rug (back).

CHRISTEL — In *Technik* you placed an original 1890s handwoven Navajo blanket next to a machine-woven blanket from the Pendleton Tribute Series with a design based on a that of a 1910 blanket manufactured by another commercial mill, J. Capps & Sons from Jacksonville, Illinois. The original Navajo weaving, as well as the Pendleton remake, are a testimony to a history in which cultural appropriation and the migration of form resulted in new designs. They also illustrate a kind of cultural appropriation that is inextricably linked with imperialism and colonization, with consequences extending far beyond the formal and aesthetic. In that sense, *Technik* can be read as a post-colonial critique.

ELISA & VINCENT — This was one of the things we discovered when we searched for more background information on the Pendleton Trade Blanket. And yes, it is one of the ingredients in the work, but for us it is more than a post-colonial critique per se. *Technik* points to a number of consecutive shifts, or moments of translation if you like, in the history of the Navajo pattern. The pairing of the authentic white and sand-coloured Navajo blanket with the Pendleton remake shows the transition of the pattern from a handwoven craft to an industrial product, a development that not only unfolded along technical and industrial lines, but also brought about significant socio-economic changes.

CHRISTEL — Are you referring to the appropriation of labour? That moment in the nineteenth century when the weaver's hand was replaced by machines and artisanal knowledge of manual weaving lost its value and significance.

ELISA & VINCENT — Yes, the impact of this historical development reached far beyond an improvement in material quality or larger production quantity. It introduced goods into the indigenous communities that were often cheaper and offered more choice than the Navajo themselves could make by hand.

Similarly, the IKEA rug, which was designed in Sweden, mass-produced in Egypt, and sold in stores worldwide, represents the pattern's circulation within the contemporary context of global production. It represents a global economy where a product can be designed in one place and mass-produced in low-income countries like India, Bangladesh, or in this case Egypt — places that have very rich textile traditions of their own. The Bernhard Willhelm sweater represents the high end of the spectrum, where handmade items are perceived as exclusive, and the pattern acquires a different cultural and economic value.

There are many examples of indigenous textile designs that have undergone revivals in Western fashion and design. The revival of the geometric Navajo pattern is no exception. We wanted to show the abstraction that happened in the process as this pattern migrated into various contexts and consumer markets. You could argue that there is no such thing as *the* Navajo pattern. Even that category is fluid. Like the pillows at Urban Outfitters, the IKEA rug is an example of this abstraction and standardization. Aesthetically speaking, the pattern is a simplification. But in terms of cultural origin it has become a commodity, part of a universal vocabulary that is omnipresent and accessible to all. Thanks to stores like IKEA, anyone anywhere can own a Navajo-inspired carpet.

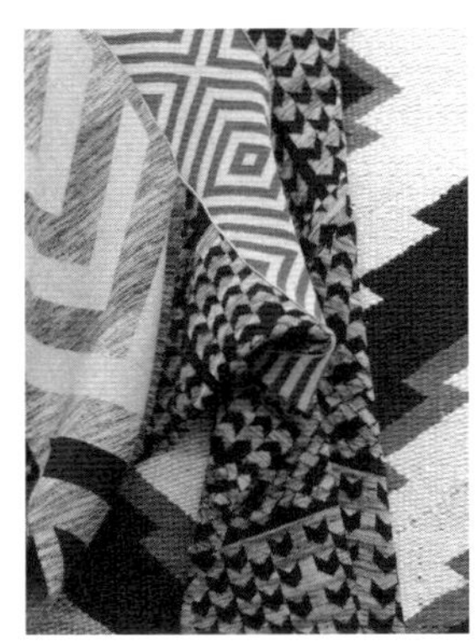

Detail Technik, Bernhard Willhelm sweater (front) and Navajo Blanket (back).

Neither IKEA nor the German fashion designer Bernhard Willhelm mention the Navajo weaving tradition as a source of inspiration for their designs. The choice to include the knitted sweater from his 2012/2013 collection in *Technik* was based on some speculation on our part. Although his fashion designs have always been highly eclectic, we don't know if he consciously selected a Navajo pattern to work with for his design. At the time we made *Technik*, his collections represented this trend of 'everything goes' where people appropriated patterns, motifs and models from all over without scruples. You took what you liked, you mixed and matched, you used anything that fit your narrative. Of course, this is problematic.

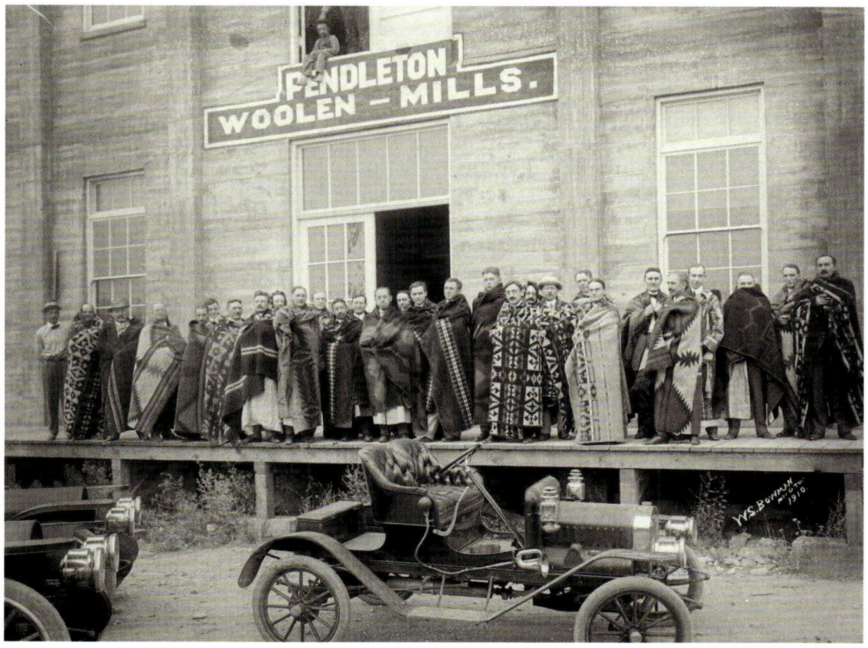


15

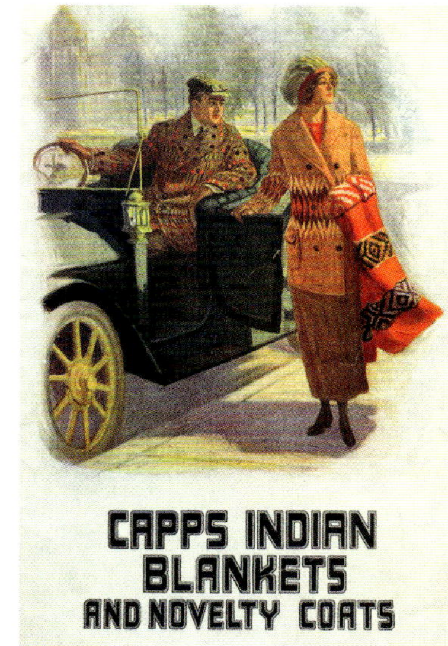


17

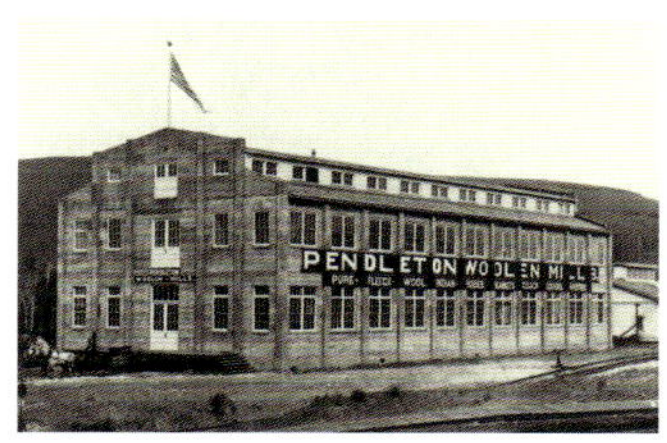

16

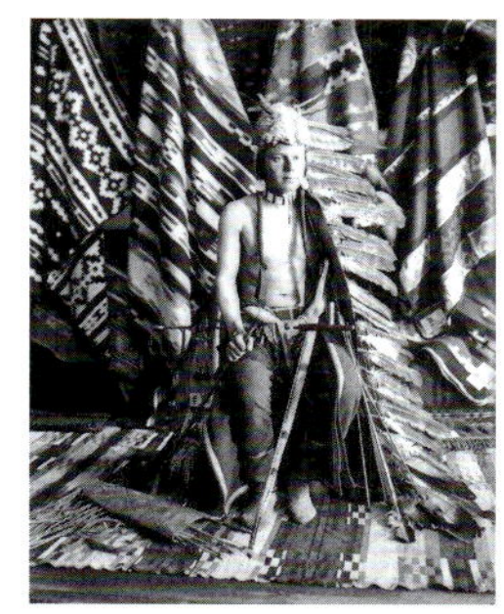

19

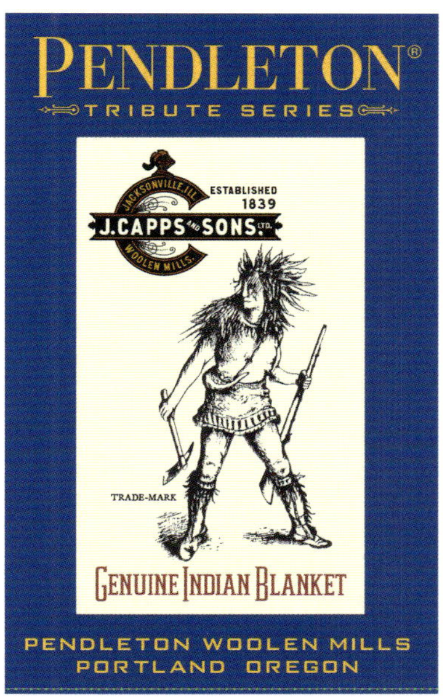


18

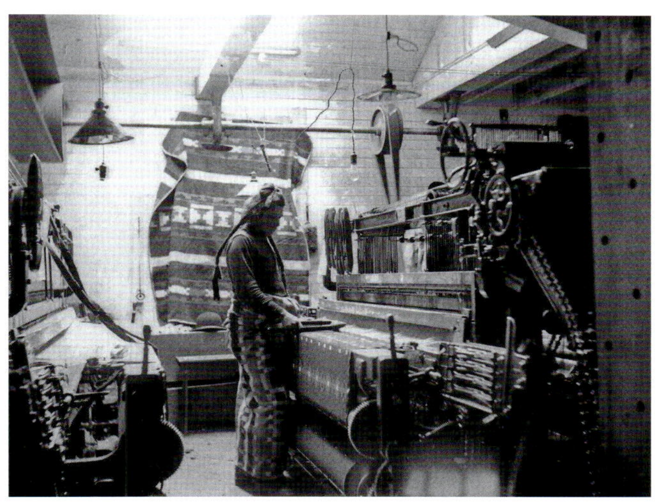

20

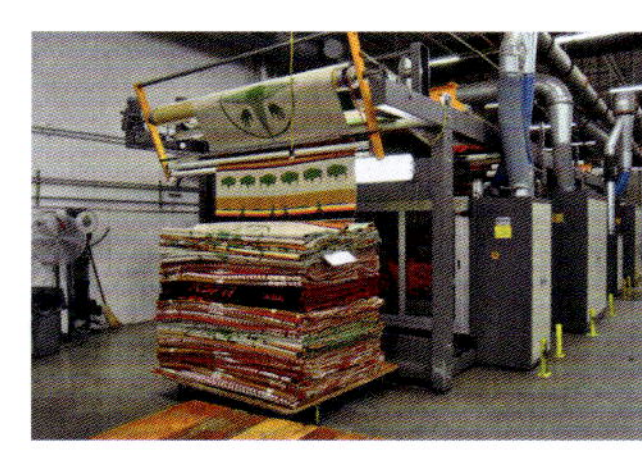

21

PENDLETON
Pendleton's version of its all-American heritage brand starts in 1853 when the young English weaver Thomas Kay (1838–1900) headed to America's newest state, Oregon. Kay, born in the heartland of England's textile industry, started working in mills at a young age and became an expert weaver and 'loom boss'. The immigrant's expertise ensured his employment in several mills, until he was able to open his own mill in 1889. As the Pendleton company states: 'From these humble beginnings rose a dyed-in-the-wool American success story.' In 1909, Kay's sons, known as the Bishop brothers, bought a woollen mill in Pendleton, a European-American settlement and trading post in Umatilla County, Oregon. They installed state-of-the-art mechanical looms and produced vividly coloured wool blankets based on the designs of the trade blankets woven by Indigenous tribes living in the region.

15. Pendleton Woolen Mills in Pendleton, Oregon, 1910. Local businessmen, draped in blankets, pose on the loading dock during a tour of the Pendleton Mill.
16. Pendleton Woolen Mills in Pendleton, Oregon, 1910. Photograph from the Pendleton archives.
17. Advertisement of Capps & Sons Woolen Mill promoting their collection of Indian Blankets. J. Capps referred to the design of the red blanket hanging over the lady's arm as 'Cheyenne Basket pattern, a Riot of Color.' Capps & Sons was the first to manufacture blankets for the trade with Indigenous Americans. Their designs were mostly created by Portuguese weavers.
18. Label from the Pendleton Tribute Series, J. Capps & Sons, #2, 2009. Celebrating its centenary, Pendleton issued a series of blankets based on historical designs as a homage to four 'American Mills that thrived during the Golden Age of Native American Trade', including Racine Woolen Mills, Oregon City Mills, and J. Capps & Sons.

NAVAJO TRADE BLANKET
Adapting to new circumstances after returning to their homeland in 1868, Navajo women continued to weave, but had to compete with commercial woollen mills like Pendleton and J. Capps & Sons. Paradoxically, Indigenous people became the most important clientele for industrially manufactured trade blankets, whereas Navajo women mainly wove blankets for non-native clientele. To promote blankets among Indigenous Americans, Pendleton used Navajo, Pueblo or Walla Walla people as models in its promotional materials.

19. Tribal man in regalia with weapons, seated among display of Pendleton Woolen Mills blankets (original title), photographed by Major Lee Moorhouse, c. 1900–1910. Glass plate negative, 15.2 × 20.3 cm.
20. Looms in Pendleton Woolen Mills, Indian 'working' loom (original title), photographed by Major Lee Moorhouse, c. 1900–1910. Glass plate negative, 15.2 × 20.3 cm.
21. Pendleton's industrial loom today, 2023.

CHRISTEL — When you were making decisions about how to present this research, how important were the physical textiles to you? I mean, did your research focus on the transitions and migrations of the image motif, or did its material manifestations also play a role?

ELISA & VINCENT — Both are equally important. Apart from the pattern's visual existence, which was very easy to research on the internet, we wanted to know what material the various objects were made of, how they felt, how big or small they were, how heavy. That's why we started to acquire the actual textiles. We were interested in the 'real' material information.

The repetition of the pattern is an obvious element in *Technik*. In that sense, the installation refers to the copying of images that has become standard practice in visual culture today. But we also wanted to foreground the material translations of the pattern. Showing the real things invites people to look closely and engage with them, rather than perceiving them only as images. When you look closer you can see that the Pendleton design is quite different from the original Navajo patterns. It is inspired by the original rather than a copy of it. However, Pendleton's Navajo-inspired patterns have become the point of reference for what is now generally referred to as the 'Navajo Indian' pattern.

CHRISTEL — Can you say something about the spatial and visual composition of *Technik*, and why you hang the textiles back to back, presenting them as vertical surfaces, rather than as functional objects?

ELISA & VINCENT — We want to evoke the image of multiple search windows on a computer screen, each window holding a world onto its own, referring again to notions of flattening and flatness. On a computer screen, everything gets the same technical treatment; every image is translated into pixels, zeros and ones. In a way, they are all placed on the same visual plane, regardless of their time and place of origin, or make. Material information gets lost if you use online sources or printed images only. It's another example of abstraction. We were interested in real material information. On the other hand, the reference to computer screens also suggests the ease with which we can access any pattern or design from across world. So, in that sense, the technical flattening of an image on a computer screen becomes synonymous with the cultural flattening of an object by isolating it from its context. All the histories it holds get lost in translation.

Hanging them on commercial clothing racks, stacked one behind the other, as if they were rolled in from storage, also points to their status as commodities in the design and fashion industry, with all the negative connotations of overproduction and mass consumption this entails. But more importantly, we wanted to draw attention to the repositioning of these textile objects from a context of trade and daily use to the precious space of art, where different value systems and different modes of perception dictate how we interact with objects. Presenting them as vertical surfaces and evoking that vertical gaze that is typical of looking at art also directly questions the way museums display non-art objects (for want of a better term). They pull the object out of its social context and then reconstruct the context with texts describing the object's biography.

CHRISTEL — *Technik* can be read along various lines, various threads that intertwine the history of an indigenous weaving tradition with histories of colonization, cultural appropriation and capitalism. But the work also echoes some of the invisible yet powerful lines that the Western art canon has drawn to demarcate what is art and what is not. I am thinking of the marginalized position of textiles and folk art, and the discussion around copies and originals, the original being authentic and therefore having more value than the copy. Am I right in saying that *Technik* evokes a loss of authenticity through the process of cultural appropriation and technical and material translation, as well as maybe the loss of culture heritage?

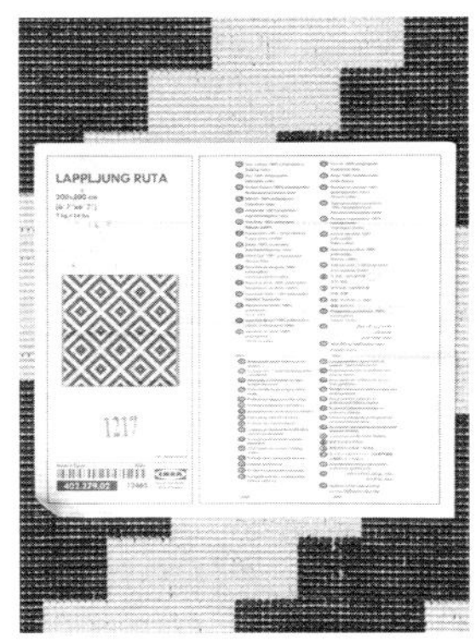


Detail Technik, label Lappljung Ruta Rug, IKEA, design by Anna Efverlund.

ELISA & VINCENT — We didn't want to establish a hierarchy between the four textiles, or state that the traditional Navajo blanket is the only true original pattern. We are more interested in how the same pattern is used by various people and how it emerges in various contexts. And how, conversely, this multitude of contexts gets absorbed in each item. This is why we decided not to include an explanatory text with the work but only to show the labels instead, which disclose all the essential facts about the date and place of production, materials and techniques used and so on. If you look closely, you will find the dealer's tag on the Navajo rug, which states that the rug is a 'Genuine Navajo Indian Rug — Hand woven by Navajo Indians', or the label on the Ikea rug including information about the materials and where it was produced. The labels gently nudge viewers to reflect on the various origins and contexts of the items, the way they are produced, branded and marketed.

We approached the work as an assemblage in which separate pieces, each with its own story, when put together, create a new narrative about the appropriation, decontextualizing and recontextualizing of cultural objects, in this case a pattern. Showing them in art spaces opens up a perspective that is rooted in a long tradition of looking at objects vertically, and as abstractions, as if they were modern abstract paintings.

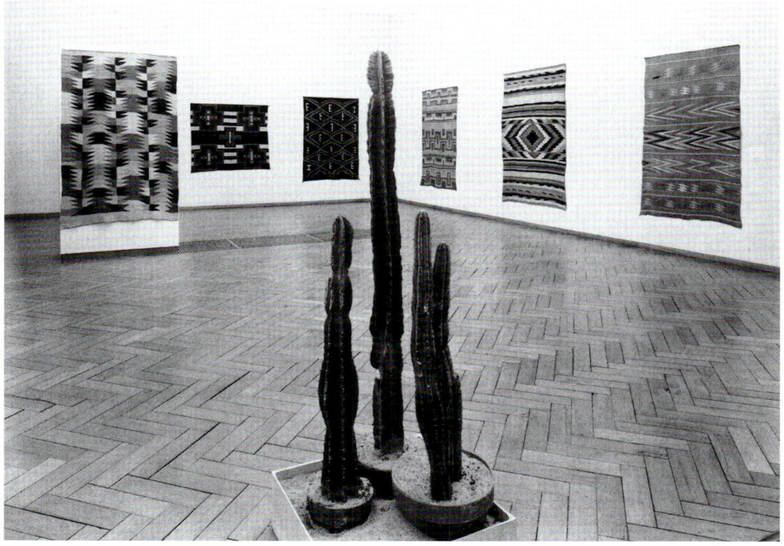

22

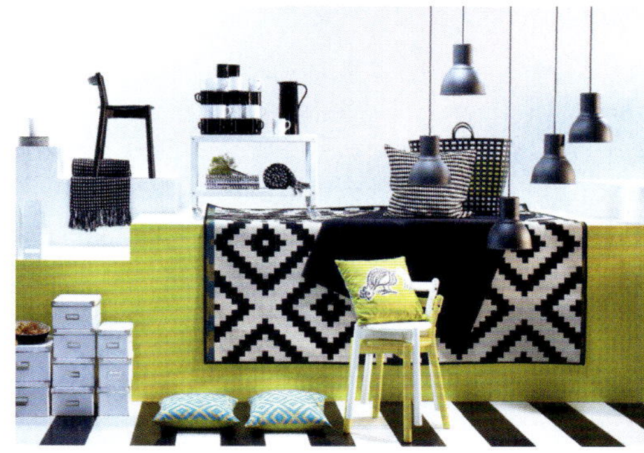

23

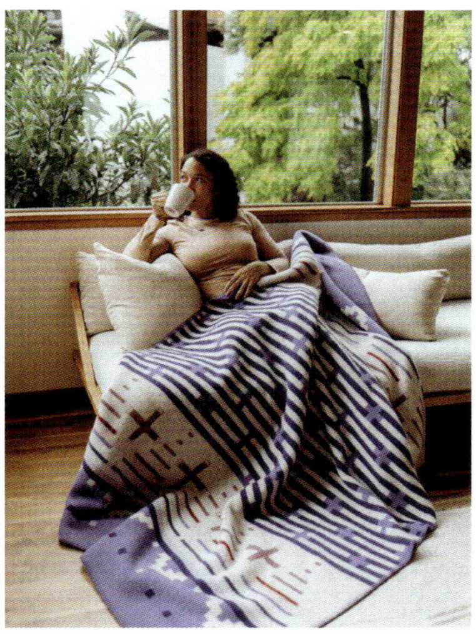

26

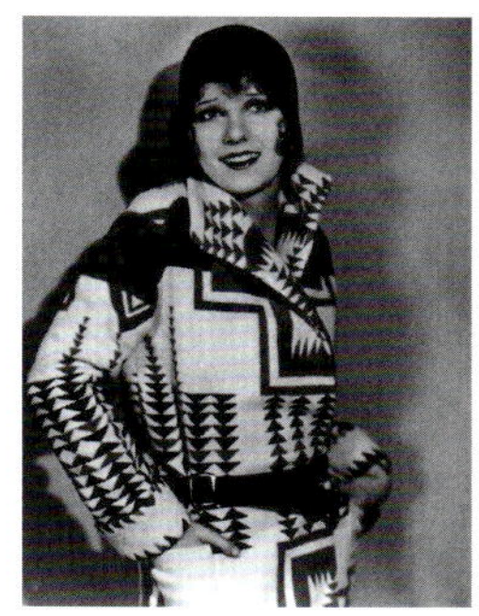

24

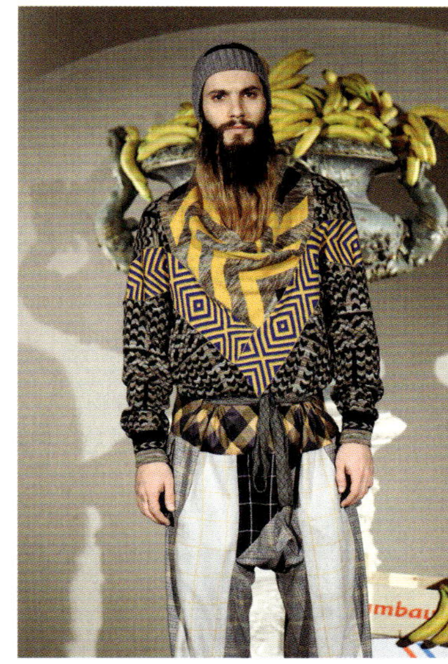

25

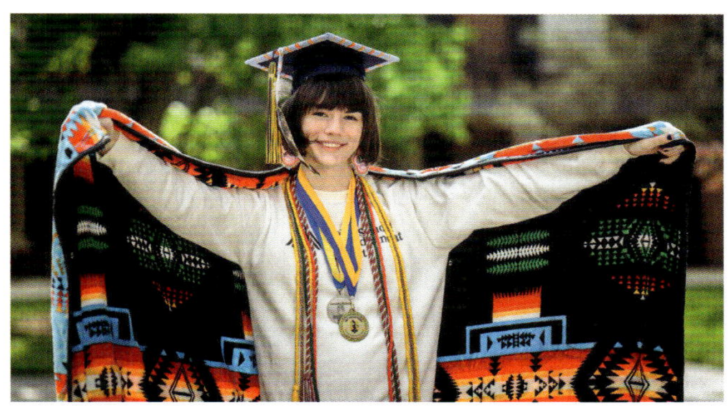

28

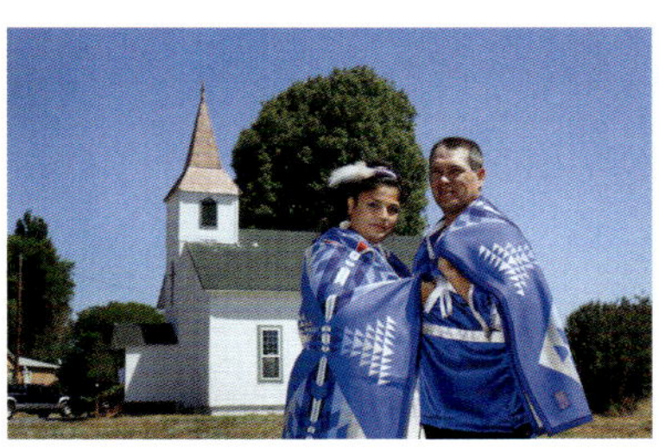

27

CULTURAL APPROPRIATION
In recent decades, Navajo patterns have appeared in mainstream culture: from high-end designer clothing to streetwear and mass-produced home decoration. For centuries, blankets have been a gift of honour among Indigenous communities. They are given at graduations, birth celebrations and funeral ceremonies. At the same time, criticism of the appropriation of this cultural heritage has intensified, leading to greater awareness and new initiatives for social and economic justice and cultural ownership.

22. The Navajo Blanket, an exhibition at the Stedelijk Museum Amsterdam, 8 March–20 April 1975.
A subtle form of cultural appropriation happens when non-Western ethnographic objects are displayed on the white walls of Western art museums. In the 1960s, Navajo blankets were 're-discovered' by modernist painters like Frank Stella and Donald Judd, who took inspiration from them. Recognizing the flaws in the modernist framing, Stedelijk Museum curator Marja Bloem chose to emphasize the history of the Navajo people and their experiences of social and political repression to reconnect the blankets with their cultural origins.
23. IKEA Catalogue Winter 2011, showing the Lappljung Ruta Rug designed by Ann Evferlund. This bestselling rug has made its way into living rooms across the globe. Designed in Sweden, produced in Egypt, and bought everywhere.
24. Actor Anita Page wearing a Pendleton coat, date unknown. Copy of a black & white negative, 4 × 5 inch.
25. Model wearing Chevron Print Sweater from Bernhard Willhelm Autumn/Winter Collection 2012/2013. Knitted, cotton and mohair, made in Belgium.
26. Spider Woman Wool Blanket, 2024, designed by Lynda Teller Pete for Eighth Generation. 2-sided, Norwegian wool, machine woven, made in Norway, 200 × 135 cm.
Eighth Generation is the first Native-owned company to produce woollen blankets. Designed by Native artists under the tagline 'Inspired Natives TM, not Native-inspired', the blankets are sustainably crafted. Fifth generation Diné/Navajo artist Lynda Teller Pete has dedicated her career to keeping the culture of Navajo weaving alive. Her Spider Woman blanket pays tribute to the teachings of the first weaver and the legacy of the women who followed her.

BLANKET CEREMONY
Blanketing is a deeply meaningful tradition among Indigenous communities: a way to mark a special event, show respect, say thanks or give blessing. The type of blanket, colours and patterns hold symbolic meaning. At weddings, the bride and groom are wrapped individually in a blue blanket, representing their past lives. After the blessing, these are removed and the couple is wrapped in a single white blanket, symbolizing their union.

27. Native American Wedding Ceremony at the Williamson River Indian Mission church, Chiloquin, Oregon.
28. Graduate Sky Kihuwa-Mani with Pendleton blanket, 2022.
Sky Kihuwa-Mani (Onondaga and Tuscarora) photographed at her graduation blanket ceremony of the Native American Students Association at UNC Greensboro.

CHRISTEL — After *Technik* you both continued your careers in your respective fields, critical fashion and visual art. Vincent, you explored the history and economy of trade through textiles and made some superb works in which you pushed these subjects to such a level of abstraction that they almost disappeared behind their appearance (simulation) as a work of modern art. I am thinking of *Fragment with dots* (*Fustat*) from 2018, which you based on a black-and-white catalogue image of an archaeological textile fragment found at an Egyptian burial site. How does abstraction operate here?

VINCENT — Abstraction is often the result of different moments of translation. In terms of materiality, *Fragment with dots* (*Fustat*) is based on the 1997 black-and-white catalogue photo of the original textile, which is a resist-dye indigo fabric with a pattern of white dots. In the analogue photograph the textile is mechanically translated into a grid of black halftone dots, losing some of the nuances in colour and texture. To produce a new weaving using a computerized Jacquard loom, I translated the half-tone image into digital data using a dithering algorithm, and finally I replaced the white paper background of the photograph with undyed cotton and the black ink dots with white paper yarn, translating the photograph back into a white-on-white cloth over ten times the size of the original fragment.

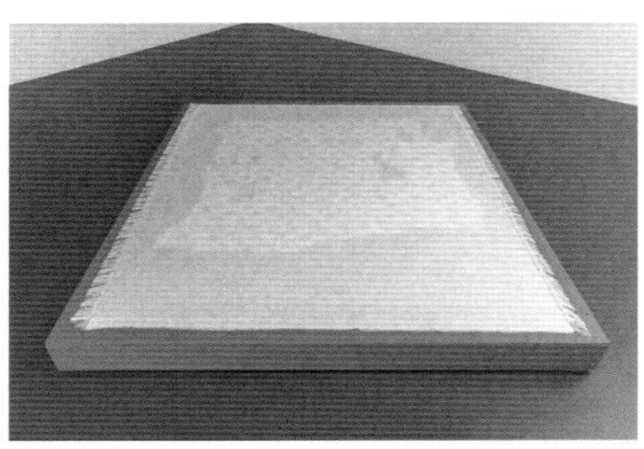

Fragment with Dots (Fustat),
Vincent Vulsma, 2018.
Cotton and paper yarn, jacquard woven, 202 × 180 cm.

CHRISTEL — But these translations in terms of technique and material also have a conceptual, maybe even an ideological, meaning, don't they? When I saw the piece lying flat on its low platform lifted centimetres off the floor in the exhibition, I was intrigued by the changing effect of the fabric, and the way the image appears and disappears depending on the angle of view, and how the light entered the gallery.

VINCENT — I've always been fascinated by the conceptual overlaps between the production of textiles and the production of history. What I try to do is bring to light the workings of history, not only the way we construct these narratives but also, more concretely, the workings of invisible forces of colonial imperialism and capitalism. In *Fragment with dots* (*Fustat*) I wanted to address the fact that long before Europeans dominated global trade on the Indian and Atlantic Ocean, long before colonial powers appropriated designs and textile techniques and turned them into a profitable commodity, there existed a thriving trade in textiles between city states on the Asian coast, and the African coast. The archaeological fabric I used as a starting point for this work is an example. It was created in Gujarat some time between the tenth and fifteenth centuries, and found in Egypt, before it was bought (or maybe looted) by the British Egyptologist P. E. Newberry in the early 1930s and became part of the collection of the Ashmolean Museum in Oxford. It was in the early sixteenth century that the Portuguese forcefully took ownership of this intra-Asian trade network and extended it to Europe, that these existing routes were capitalized on and became a vital infrastructure in the trading of goods, and later of people. And part of that history is that from a western perspective the existing textile crafts and textile trade between India and the Arab world were blotted out, forgotten.

CHRISTEL — So, like *Technik*, the work is not only about the geographical movement of textiles or the migration of patterns, but also about bringing to light the hidden and marginalized histories that set these movements in motion.

*Technik* tells the history of a weaving pattern as it moves through different cultural contexts and spheres of production: from its origins as a domestic craft deeply embedded in Navajo/Diné culture, to its transformation into a mass-produced commodity circulating the global market. Each textile object in the installation—rug, blanket, sweater—marks a point along this trajectory, representing some of the twists and turns in the larger fabric of Navajo weaving history. The artwork also shows how these transitions modified the materiality and form of the diamond-shaped pattern and how it was adapted to prevailing trends and tastes along the way.

However, while the migration of the pattern functions as a leitmotif, *Technik* is equally concerned with what lies beneath its material surface: the often-unseen techniques of cultural appropriation. Between the 1890s Navajo Trade Blanket and the 2010 Pendleton Tribute remake (the original and the copy-of-a-copy, so to speak) *Technik* opens up a discursive space in which critical questions are raised about the asymmetrical power relations that underpin cultural appropriation, whether economic, colonial, political, social or racial in nature. In the case of Navajo weaving, the commercial success of the Trade Blankets—based on Navajo designs and produced by companies such as Pendleton Mills and Caps & Sons—cannot be separated from the colonial aggression, disownment and displacement the Navajo people endured: internment in Camp Bosque Redondo by the US government and the loss of their Churro sheep, which drastically reduced their wool supply. Other factors, such as the fact that commercial mills had access to state-of-the-art looms or the wool tariffs imposed by state governments, further contributed to the disenfranchisement of Navajo weavers.

A more subtle form of cultural appropriation occurred in the late 1960s and early 1970s, when Navajo blankets were 're-discovered' by modernist painters such as Frank Stella, Donald Judd and Mark Rothko, who drew inspiration from them and curated exhibitions with the weavings. Hung on white museum walls, the rugs were viewed as paintings, subjected to a modernist aesthetic gaze. As anthropologist Kathy M'Closkey finely unfolds in her contribution to this book, this transition from the domestic sphere into the white cube greatly impacted the economic circumstances of the Navajo weaver.

Weaving is a deeply spiritual practice in Navajo culture. It embodies the principles of *hozho*—harmony, balance, beauty and well-being—which guide relationships with family, community and the natural world. Each pattern reflects the sacred relationship between the weaver, their ancestors and the land that sustains them. The appropriation of Navajo weaving into other contexts severs these connections and erases the spiritual knowledge embedded in the textiles, ultimately contributing to a loss of cultural heritage. We could therefore read *Technik* as a story of loss: a loss of authenticity, of material quality and of cultural agency. Yet the story continues to weave forward. In recent years, companies such as Pendleton have become aware of their part in this history and are changing their practices, while Native-run enterprises are reclaiming their heritage and taking the production of Navajo blankets back into their own hands, thus honouring its true essence.

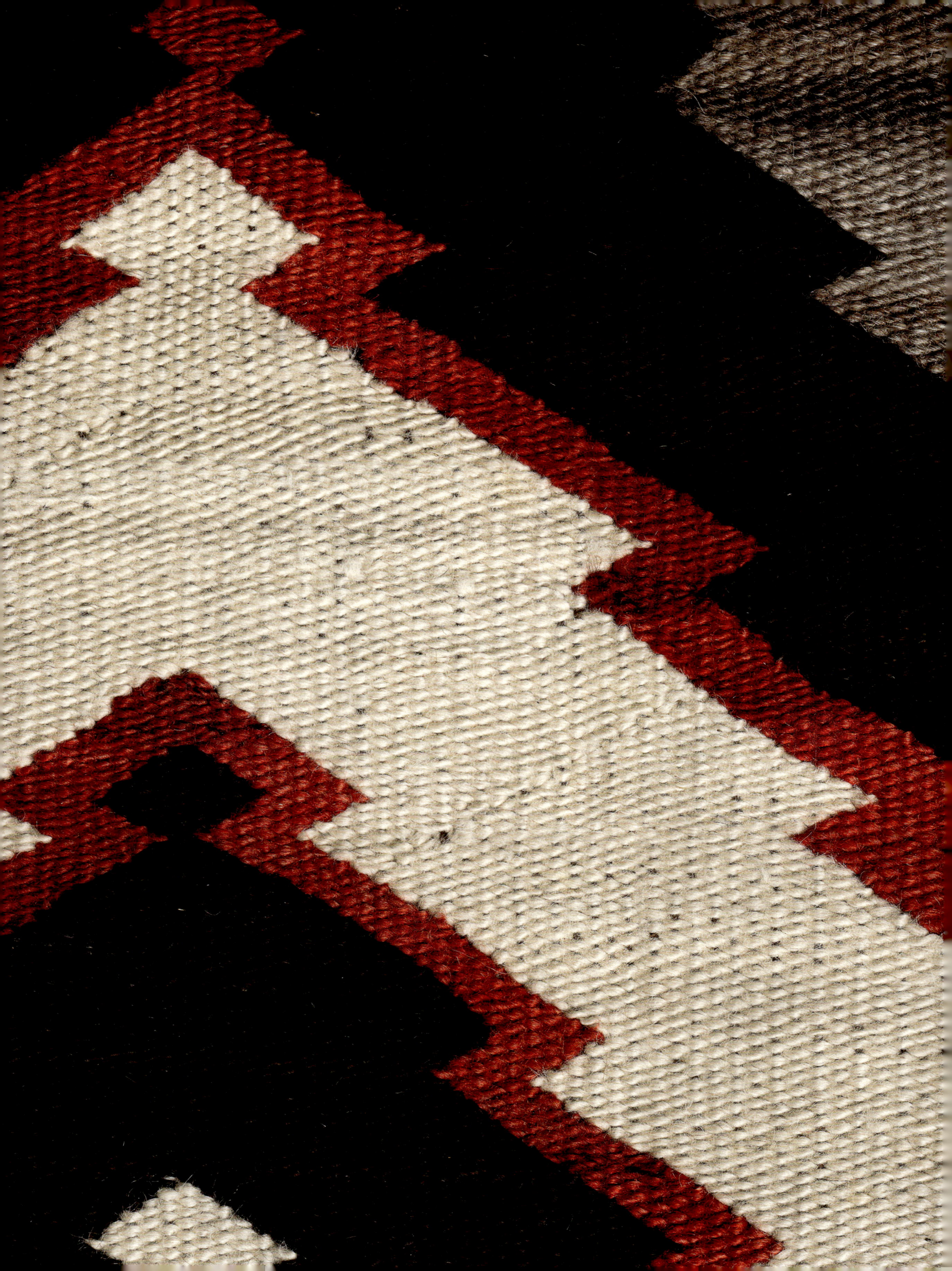

Anthropologist Kathy M'Closkey has devoted much of her academic career to supporting the struggle for social justice among Navajo people. Her extensive research has led her into hitherto overlooked archives, unearthing business records and economic data that reveal the appalling truth: the disenfranchisement and impoverishment of the Navajo people, especially women, was sustained by an imposed economic system that ensured that the more they wove, the poorer they became. In the following essay, M'Closkey writes those women and their labour into the historical record.

# THE POLITICS OF DISCLOSURE
## How the Culture of Connoisseurship Disenfranchises Navajo (Diné) Weavers

Kathy M'Closkey

In their ground-breaking book *Plunder: When the Rule of Law is Illegal*, professor of law Ugo Mattei and legal anthropologist Laura Nader argue that plunder is the single most significant factor producing and sustaining poverty in the world. They query 'how have anthropologists, unwittingly perhaps, contributed to a legitimization of plunder...?' In this essay I will highlight how the conditions of plunder have been normalized through the construction of Navajo textile history by generations of scholars who chose to view weaving through the lens of art history.[1] My second argument stresses how women weavers have categorically been erased from the dominant historical narrative.

For generations anthropologists were the primary authorities publishing on south-western Native American art and material culture.[2] More than six thousand articles and books were published about the Navajo between 1970 and 1990. In his 1999 book *Diné Bibliography to the 1990s*, sociologist Howard M. Bahr indexes four entries under 'economics', and more than 55 under 'catalogues, collections, and exhibitions', thereby demonstrating the emphasis on Navajo weaving as 'art'.[3] In 1987, anthropologist Gary Witherspoon conservatively estimated that 100,000 women wove 1,000,000 textiles over the previous two centuries.[4] The available literature claims that by 1890, increasing tourism and the Arts and Crafts Movement ostensibly drove the demand for Navajo textiles. Yet weavers' productivity remains unhistoricized, because scholars' publications severed it from the global wool market.

### HISTORICAL CONTEXT

Of the 400,000 Navajo, or Diné, living within the United States, 70 per cent of the population occupy a 70,000 square kilometre reservation, straddling

1. Multispecies feminist theorist Donna Haraway critiques the dominant history of Navajo weaving narrated in romantic pastoral ways, thereby marginalizing women's labor shaped by the context of production. She offers an alternative holistic interpretation of human and non-human beings-in-relation with Churro sheep as companion species. This symbiosis, or collective creation sustains *k'e*, (kinship), and other relational ontologies crucial to survivance. See Donna Haraway, *Staying with the Troubles: Making Kin in the Chthulucene* (2016), pp. 89-97.
2. Nancy J Parezo, 'The Challenge of Native American Art and Material Culture' (1990), p. 13. By 1990, anthropologists had authored 75 per cent of the literature on Native American arts, crafts and material culture.
3. Howard M. Bahr, *Diné Bibliography to the 1990s* (1999).
4. Gary Witherspoon, 'Navajo Weaving: Art in its Cultural Context' (1987).

Arizona, New Mexico and Utah.[5] Thirty per cent of the population lacks running water, electricity, or both. Per capita income is 30 per cent of the national average. Historically they managed a broad subsistence base that included farming, herding, raiding and trading, but they gained a major portion of their income from weaving and livestock production.[6]

Anthropologists Van Valkenburg and McPhee claim that the Navajo wearing blanket was the mother from which all external trade developed. During 1863, to 'civilize' the Navajo, and open their homeland for settlement, the federal government forced 10,000 to relocate to eastern New Mexico. Attempts to farm the alkaline soil failed, and with few sheep, insufficient rations and rampant diseases, an estimated 20 per cent of the population died. Weavers supplemented the hardy, coarse-wool from the few remaining Churro sheep, which they had herded since the sixteenth century, with unravelled and respun red bayeta cloth and commercial yarns of lesser quality supplied with their annuities.

On June 1, 1868, a treaty was signed between Navajos and the federal government, allowing them to return to their homeland, which by then had been reduced by 80 per cent. Upon leaving Bosque Redondo, each Navajo was issued two Churro sheep to re-establish self-sufficiency. Although weaving became their primary source of income, women lost control of marketing since the government licensed settler Anglo traders to buy and sell Navajo products, thus determining their value. Furthermore, textile production rapidly increased due to the detrimental consequences of integration into the national markets, formidable competition from commercial trade blanket manufacturers appropriating Navajo designs, and the rise in the cost of living. The weak demand for Navajo wool prompted traders to pressure weavers to turn wool into rugs. Navajo self-sufficiency was undermined due to dependence on external markets.

Although one of the most studied peoples on earth, an enormous amount of evidence reveals how the inimical effects of free trade over a century ago triggered Navajo impoverishment and remains absent from Navajo weaving history.[7] Over the last 20 years my fact-finding has focussed on in-depth research in relevant archives, unearthing information missing from the extant literature. My inquiry reveals that the more Navajos wove, the poorer they became. In my previous and forthcoming books, my intention is to write the women *and their labour* into the historical record.

## WOOL — THE 'MISSING LINK'

Recently published (but uncited) information extracted from archives (1880s–post WWII), reveals how Navajo history was intertwined with the history of the global carpet wool market and the US domestic wool tariff.[8] By 1890, the Navajo were the only woolgrowers raising Churro, carpet wool sheep designated Class III. My research reveals that after 1893, free trade in carpet wool under the Wilson-Gorman tariff drove textile production, accelerating the transformation from wearing blanket to rug. This tariff (1893–1897) placed all classes of wool on the duty-free list, bankrupting one-third of domestic

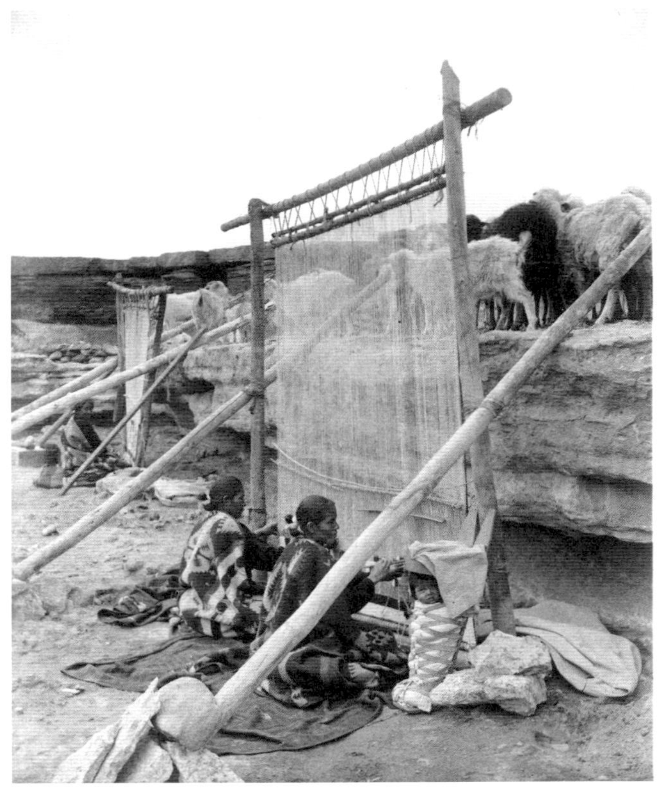

Navajo women weaving on vertical looms, with flock of Churro sheep on ledge above, photographic print, c. 1914.

5. The Navajo people call themselves Diné, or The People. Early Spanish invaders referred to them as Navajo, an altered form of a Tewa Pueblo word for farmed fields in the valley. First Nations are reclaiming their ancestral names, discarding those imposed by invaders. However, I will use the term Navajo because it coheres with the historical context in which my usage is situated.
6. Spanish explorers introduced a hardy, coarse-wooled sheep called Churro, into the region during the 16th century.
7. Because of this wide-angled perspective, 80 per cent of the information utilized in my forthcoming book is drawn from archives untapped by Navajo studies scholars (*Why the Navajo Blanket Became a Rug: Excavating the Legacy of Modernization and Development*). Information was drawn from Bigelow-Sanford Carpet Company Records, and Edmund P. Graves Papers, Baker Business Library, Harvard; The Hubbell Trading Post Papers, University of Arizona Library, Special Collections, Tucson; Bulletins of the National Association of Wool Manufacturers, Newberry Library, Chicago, IL and U. S. Government, Superintendents' Annual Narrative and Statistical Reports, Navajo Agencies 1910-1935. BIA, RG75, National Archives, Washington, DC.
8. See for instance Kathy M'Closkey 'Unravelling the Narratives of Nostalgia: Navajo Weavers and Globalization' (2010); 'Up for Grabs: Assessing the Consequences of Sustained Appropriations of Navajo Weavers' Patterns' (2012a).
9. Superintendents' Reports to CIA, cited in M'Closkey, 'Novica, Navajo Knock-offs and the 'Net: A Critique of Fair Trade Marketing Practices' (2012b).
10. David M. Brugge, *Hubbell Trading Post, National Historic Site* (1993).
11. Kathy M'Closkey, *Swept Under the Rug: A Hidden History of Navajo Weaving* ([2002] 2008), p. 76 and *Why the Navajo Blanket Became a Rug: Excavating the Legacy of Modernization and Development* (forthcoming).

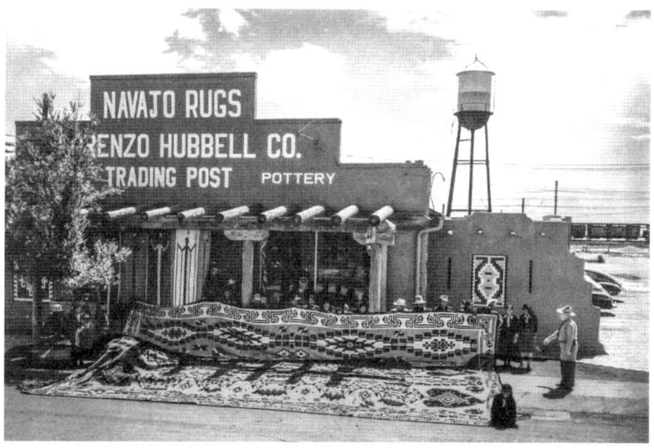


Hubbel Trading Post in Winslow, Arizona, with the Hubbel Joe Rug, photographic print, 1932.

The Hubbell Trading Post was established in 1878 in Ganado, Arizona, by John Lorenzo Hubbell. The Hubbell family operated several trading posts in the early 20th century, including this one in Winslow. During the Great Depression, Hubbell needed an attraction to draw tourists into his Trading Post, and commissioned Julia Joe, a well-known weaver from Greasewood, Arizona, to weave the 'World's Largest Navajo Rug'.

woolgrowers, and prompting traders to continue wholesaling weaving by weight as a more lucrative means to market 30 per cent of Navajos' coarse carpet wool clip. Bureaucrats also embedded weaving in the wool and livestock statistics, since they viewed textile production as an extension of the livestock industry.[9] The rest of the clip acquired by traders amounted to only *one week's* supply for domestic carpet manufacturers, whose looms consumed half a million pounds per day. The rest of the demand was met by carpet wools imported from over thirty countries. Powerful captains of industry demanded permanent removal of tariff protection for Class III carpet wools, when the Dingley tariff passed in 1897, with high tariffs placed on clothing wools, Classes I and II, while Class III carpet wools remained on the duty-free list. Given that Navajos were the sole producers of Class III wool in the country, they were the only growers negatively impacted by the new tariff. For eighty years, hand-spun and woven saddle blankets and rugs were wholesaled like other livestock products, graded, bundled and shipped to regional wholesalers to pay down traders' debts.

Lorenzo Hubbell of Ganado, Arizona, is by many considered the czar of Navajo trade, and the 'father' of the Navajo rug.[10] Hubbell, his sons and extended family members shipped over 275 *tons* of weaving between 1893 and 1913. Rug and saddle blanket values were pegged to duty-free carpet wool values and marketed *by weight* until the late 1960s.[11] Analysis of the family's business records reveals that weavers averaged less than two cents an hour in book credit for decades, expending 40 to 60 hours of labour for every pound of weaving produced. Thus, the evidence in traders' business records ruptures the master narrative—that traders like Hubbell 'saved' Navajo weaving by developing off-reservation markets.[12] Huge shipments reveal the magnitude of gendered injustice, as weavers and their families became increasingly impoverished.

## STOCK REDUCTION

For sixty years (from the 1870s to the early 1930s), the federal government had restricted traders from purchasing breeding stock to ensure self-support. This proscription coupled with a lack of price supports for purchase of non-breeding stock to relieve overcrowding resulted in an overgrazed range. Thus, conflicting government policies culminated in stock reduction (1934–1940) during the Great Depression. The carpet-woolled Churros that provided the best wool for thousands of weavers, were destroyed. This horrific event still resonates and is often referred to as cultural genocide.

Although weavers' output was valued at $1 million by 1930, providing one-third of reservation residents' income, the market collapsed as the Depression deepened. The wool was too unstandardized for manufacturers, and because it lacked tariff protection, only wholesale slaughter of Churros 'solved the problem'. For decades, the hardy Churro had out-reproduced the breeds introduced by traders and bureaucrats to 'upgrade' flocks. If Churro genes persisted, they argued, the fleece from Navajo flocks would fail to meet national standards required by woollen manufacturers, standards that they implemented themselves to ensure high-quality clothing wools suitable for commercial needs.[13]

Weaving served as a means of economic diversification for traders coping with fluctuations in the global market due to duty-free imports of 70 to 140 million pounds of carpet-grade wool annually, much of it shipped from China. This 'alternative means to market wool' sustained the trading post system. Between 1900 and World War II, both the Navajo population (22,000/48,000+) and the number of reservation trading posts doubled, (from 79 to 170), while the value of textiles shipped from the reservation rose twenty-fold.[14] Today, these old 'pound blankets' are continuously recycled in the antiquities' markets, depressing the demand for contemporary rugs woven by an estimated 20,000 weavers.

My book *Swept Under the Rug* (2002) incorporates eleven tables and eight figures that illustrate the cost of goods at the Hubbell trading posts, and the annual wholesale averages of Navajo livestock products, including textiles, acquired between 1881 and 1943. Chapter 3 'Traders, Weavers and Trade Blankets', details the destruction of the market for Navajo wearing blankets driven by the escalation of commercially manufactured trade blankets bearing 'Indian' designs. Because authors neglect to access primary data from pertinent archives, most literature emphasizes the influence of traders on weavers' designs. Such assumptions are overdetermined due to the magnitude of production. Navajo women wove at home, not in factory-like conditions, in which supervisors provided inputs, controlled designs and quality of outputs.

Hundreds of invoices located in the two tons of Lorenzo Hubbell Trading Post Papers (1865–1965), housed at the University of Arizona Special Collections Library, Tucson, affirm the importance of women's textile production in subsidizing the trading family's business empire. Available since 1977, their business records also reveal that commercial trade blankets cost from three to six times more per pound than the value of hand spun, handwoven saddle blankets or rugs, because trade blankets were woven from domestic and imported clothing wools *protected by high tariffs*.[15] The income generated by hundreds of weavers often bridged the gap between starvation and survival of Navajo families.[16] A century ago, regional warehouses were stuffed with authentic rugs. Today they are crammed with knockoffs.[17] Meanwhile, dealers and trading posts located in reservation border towns hold large inventories of historic and contemporary textiles, and unredeemed pawn.[18]

## HOW PAST PRODUCTIVITY HARMS CONTEMPORARY WEAVERS

Many of the 'pound' blankets and rugs wholesaled by weight currently fetch very high prices in the collectors' markets. Sales increased exponentially after the first exhibit of historic weaving was borrowed from the collections of twenty prominent artists including Kenneth Noland, Frank Stella and Andy Warhol, and toured internationally from 1972 to 1976.[19] From $70 to $100 million worth of historic

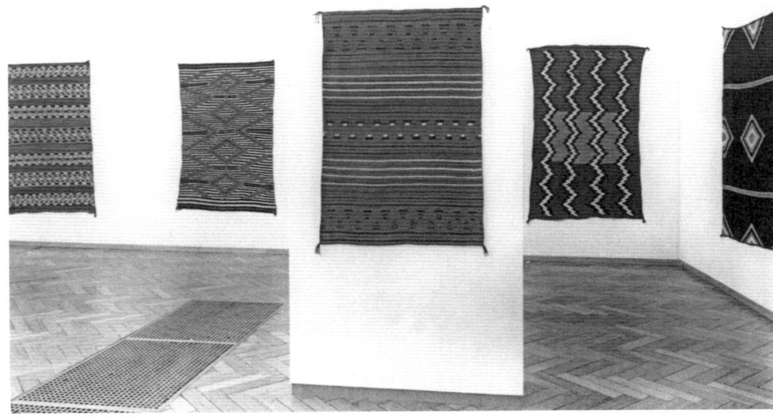

Installation view of the exhibition The Navajo Blanket at the Stedelijk Museum Amsterdam, March 8–April 20, 1975.

The exhibition in the Stedelijk Museum was based on the travelling exhibition curated by Anthony Berlant and Mary Kahlenberg and included 59 fine 19th century Navajo blankets from private and public collections in the United States and Europe, as well as various ethnographic objects from the Museum voor Volkenkunde in Leiden.

13. Kathy M'Closkey, *Navajo Blanket* (forthcoming).
14. Lawrence D. Weiss, 'The Development of Capitalism in the Navajo Nation' (1984), p. 151.
15. Trade blankets, however, were never sold by weight.
16. Colleen O'Neill, *Working the Navajo Way: Labor and Culture in the Twentieth Century* (2005), pp. 55-80.
17. Kathy M'Closkey, 'Navajo Knock-offs' (2010b); 'Up for Grabs' (2012a).
18. Fieldnotes (2006-ongoing).
19. Anthony T Berlant et al, *Walk in Beauty* (1977), Joe B Wheat, *Blanket Weaving in the Southwest* (1974). There are images of this exhibition when it travelled to Amsterdam in other parts of the chapter.
20. Extrapolated from Karl E Meyer, *The Plundered Past* (1973), p. 81.
21. See for instance Marian E Rodee, *Old Navajo Rugs: Their Development from 1900 to 1940* (1981); Anne L Hedlund, *Navajo Weavings from the Andy Williams Collection* (1997) and Kathleen Whitaker, *Southwest Textiles: Weavings of the Pueblo and Navajo* (2002).
22. Hubbell Trading Post Papers; U. S. Government Annual Narrative and Statistical Reports.
23. Brad Goldfarb, 'In His Element' (2013).
24. Hedlund, *Navajo Weavings*; Wikicollecting, downloaded 30 August, 2013.
25. Hubbell Trading Post Papers (1902), Curio Catalogue, Box 545 (13).
26. M'Closkey, *Swept Under the Rug* (2002), Chapter 6 and 'Diasporas of and by Design' (2019).
27. *Weaving Worlds* documentary.
28. Kenneth Hudson quipped: 'Ethnographical museums may collect widely, but they do not dig deeply. The political consequences of doing so would be too serious, or so it is felt.' See 'How Misleading Does an Ethnographical Museum Have to Be?' (1991), p. 489.
29. 'Is It All Loot? Tackling the Antiquities Problem', *The New York Times*, March 29, 2006.
30. Roshii Montano et al, 'Blanketing the Plains: *Hanoolchaadi* in Indian Country' (2017), p. 25.
31. Ann Stevenson personal communication, 19 December 2005.
32. 'Fake Navajo Rug Alert', ATADA (2005).
33. M'Closkey, 'Up for Grabs'.
34. Jennifer N Denetdale, *Reclaiming Diné History: The Legacies of Navajo Chief Manuelito and Juanita* (2007a), pp. 22-23, 32-33 and 'Navajo Saddle Blankets' (2003).
35. Kate P Kent, 'Pueblo and Navajo Weaving Traditions and the Western World' (1976), p. 101.

weaving has changed hands since that time.[20] Emphasis on historic weaving focuses upon individual textiles, their provenance and pedigree, while ignoring the chronic economic problems. Museologists continue to 'order, dissect and classify' by determining the kinds of dyes, yarns, number of warps and wefts, and types of fleeces incorporated in historic textiles located in museum collections.[21] Crucial information located in government and business archives providing evidence of the conditions endured by weavers to provision their households, receives scant attention.[22] The 'narratives of nostalgia' spun by southwest scholars aid and consolidate the conditions for plunder, by turning hard won, exploited labour into 'collectibles'.

## RECENT COLLECTOR ACTIVITY

The following information highlights two vignettes from recent collector activity. One issue of *Architectural Digest* features designer Ralph Lauren's huge Colorado ranch.[23] The buildings are adorned with dozens of Navajo 'pound' blankets and rugs. Lauren's brand defines a lifestyle, and for decades he has mined Navajo designs to create his 'Beacon Print' clothing line. Singer Andy Williams passed away in 2012. His collection, valued at over $1 million was auctioned by Sotheby's in 2013.[24] A single 'chief's' blanket sold for $221,000. Sotheby's evaluated a double saddle blanket at $2,000. It sold for $13,000. Hubbell had jobbed similar textiles for $4.00 each.[25]

These examples illustrate how old textiles sell avidly, and internet sales have escalated exponentially.[26] Currently thousands of weavers within the vast Navajo Nation lack an infrastructure to market their rugs because of the trading post system's collapse. Few weavers make an adequate living, and unemployment hovers around 50 per cent. Further, there are no reservation-wide co-ops, micro-finance programmes or fair-trade organizations to assist weavers. Weavers with decades of experience auction their textiles monthly at a local school gymnasium in Crownpoint, New Mexico, nearly sixty miles from the closest motel, with sales averaging $225 per rug.[27]

With few exceptions, off-reservation private enterprise continues to control marketing, a consequence of pressure exerted by the United Indian Traders' Association formed in 1931, to thwart the development of cooperatives as promoted by Commissioner of Indian Affairs John Collier. The number of dealers who retail contemporary rugs exclusively has plummeted. Thus, thousands of weavers are pushed to the periphery as their ancestors' creations are endlessly replicated or sold at auction. Scholars who ignore the context of production unwittingly engage in historical amnesia through their refusal to acknowledge 'the elephant in the room', the escalation in poverty that occurred in tandem with increased production.[28]

During 2006, the *New York Times* featured a series of articles on the entangled relationships between major museums and the international antiquities trade.[29] The New School in New York City sponsored a panel titled 'Who Owns Art?' Discussion highlighted the controversy surrounding antiquities and their provenance. SUNY Stoney Brook archaeologist Elizabeth Stone spoke out in criticism of scholarly involvement in authentication: '...when you publish, as a scholar, you're authenticating the object. And when you authenticate it, its value goes up. You're participating in the trade.' The following section critiques how southwestern museologists do just that.

In 1989 Sotheby's auctioned a rare First Phase chief's blanket owned by real estate mogul Edwin Janss for over $500,000. Harmer Johnson, Sotheby's appraiser, had estimated its value between $100,000–150,000. The auction house contacted retired archaeologist Dr Joe Ben Wheat (2003), acknowledged as the dean of Navajo textile studies. He wrote a one-page description, noting that Herman Schweizer of the Fred Harvey Company had sold it to CIA John Collier (1933–1945), thus adding anecdotal value to the object. Very few blankets of this type remain in private hands. One surfaced at an *Antiques Roadshow* filmed in Tucson, Arizona in 2002, and the 2012 sale of the Chantland blanket by John Moran Auctioneers, set a record at $1.8 million.[30]

Several south-west state and private museums have featured exhibits curated by antiquities dealers and/or hosted appraisal days modelled after *Antiques Roadshow*. Such events draw hundreds of participants anxious to discover the value of their treasures. However, due to the potential conflict of interest such occasions might entail, the Museum of Anthropology at the University of British Columbia in Vancouver cancelled a similar programme.[31] Textile dealer Mark Sublette and the Antique Tribal Art Dealers' Association provided some financial backing for 'Navajo Weaving at the Arizona State Museum: 19th Century Blankets, 20th Century Rugs, and 21st Century Views' in Tucson, Arizona.[32] In their newsletter, the organization warned about knockoffs on eBay advertised as historic rugs. Members were informed that the images were taken from books on historic textiles and told that 'Navajo-style weavings done by other cultural groups are not a new phenomenon... [and] are perfectly acceptable as derivative contemporary rugs'. However, 'if these forgeries enter the mainstream market under the guise of genuine antique Navajo textiles, a great deal of harm will be done to a robust and vibrant market and to the textile dealers who market the real antique pieces'. The bloated knockoff market has also precipitated a rapid decline in the value and sales of Navajo rugs.[33]

## KNOCKOFFS AS AN EXTENSION OF THE COMMERCIALIZATION OF NAVAJO DESIGNS

As a principal source of outside knowledge, scholars consistently portrayed the Navajo as great 'borrowers' — sheep from the Spanish, the loom from the Pueblos, and designs from traders.[34] Art historian Kate Peck Kent wrote: 'Navajo weaving has no deep historical roots...it's always been a commercial link with others...thriving on innovation, change and outside contacts...'[35] Anthropologist Gladys Reichard categorized functional textiles as non-sacred craft commodities because she believed commercialization had submerged any sacred associations that weaving may have previously held.[36] Thus, scholars labelling textiles as secular commodities have inadvertently enabled both the volatile collector–investment and knockoff markets. Lacking communal copyright protection, historic patterns reside in the public domain.

The on-going appropriation of patterns by entrepreneurs such as Ralph Lauren, Dusty Henson and Pendleton™ has escalated dramatically over the past five decades. The importation of textiles woven in Navajo patterns increased exponentially during the 1980s.[37] The mostominous threat began in the early 1980s, when US wholesalers and store owners began visiting the Teotitlan region of Mexico and purchasing handwoven textiles which were far cheaper than their Navajo counterparts. By 1986, there were 110 merchants actively working with more than a thousand Zapotec weavers.

Feminist political economist Lynn Stephen describes the growing popularity of *appropriated* Navajo patterns as the primary contributor to the economic success of hundreds of Zapotec households.[38] Of the four levels of textile production, the third level comprises: 'mass produced pieces, up to five by seven feet...Navajo designs currently dominate...This is the largest sector of the market in Teotitlan.' The 1980s were marked by a surge of orders for Navajo designs. Entrepreneurs who imported and retailed these finished products into the US earned profits from 200 to 1000 per cent.[39] Currently knock-offs are imported from over twenty countries including Guatemala, Peru, Egypt, Turkey, India, Hungary, Romania, Moldova and Mexico. If knockoffs are labelled 'Indian made', or 'Navajo-made', sales are illegal and violate the Indian Arts and Crafts Board Act, a truth in advertising act that protects consumers from false advertising. El Paso Saddleblanket Company™ has thousands of wholesale accounts globally, with multimillion dollars in sales and over forty years in the business.[40] Their catalogues and website reveal how textiles, jewellery, pottery, etc., capture the 'essence of the Southwest'. Initially the owners maintained a factory on the Mexico border housing one hundred looms. Many of the knockoffs they currently sell are imported from India, Pakistan and Romania. The company has advertised extensively, claiming: 'Our yarn, our looms, our factory means your savings.' By 2005, their enormous store advertised '200,000 rugs'.

Pendleton™ trade blankets also participate in this egregious appropriation, because until recently the company advertised 'Navajo-inspired' rug designs woven in Mexico, ranging from throw rugs to room-sized textiles selling for thousands of dollars. However, the company is not in violation of the Indian Arts and Crafts Act, because they disclose that the rugs are woven by Zapotec. Paradoxically, the Navajo comprise the largest population of native consumers of Pendleton products. In 2019, I met with Pendleton marketing and design executives and presented a petition signed by over eighty people who had attended the Diné Studies Conference, (Tsaile, Navajo Nation) the previous year. The multi-million-dollar company had advertised eight knockoffs under the 'home' category on

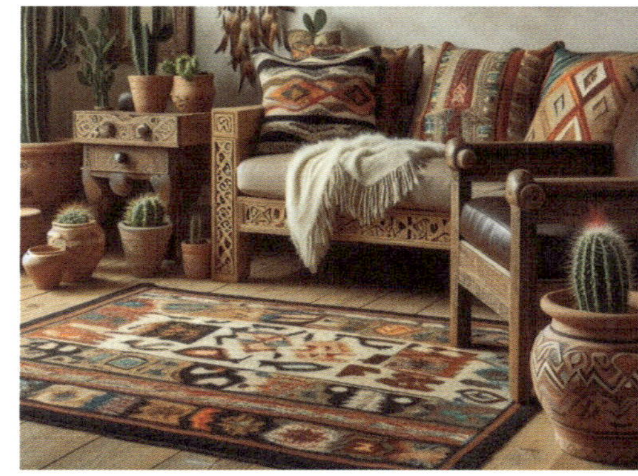

Southwestern Decor by Lord Decor Interior Design.

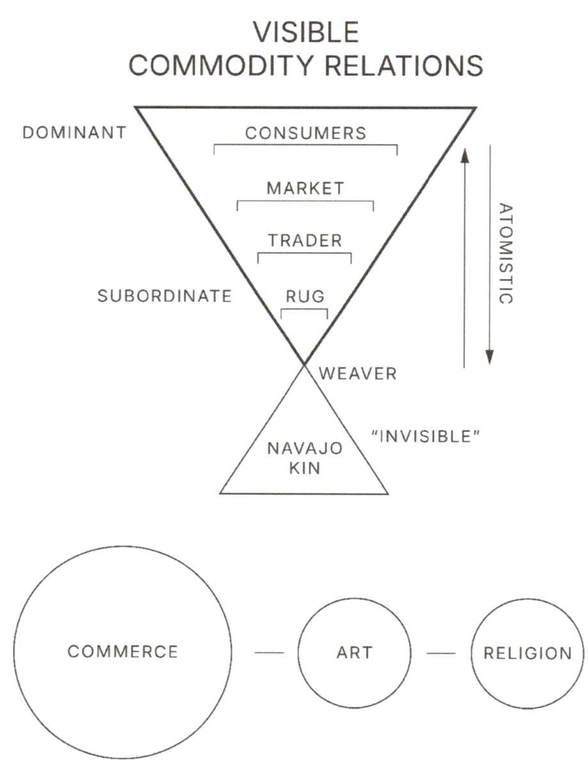


Visible commodity relations.

their website. None of the conference signatories knew that the company had been marketing knockoffs for years, because they purchase their Pendleton™ blankets from local retailers. After learning that weaving was a sacred practice rooted in Navajo cosmology, the director of international marketing indicated that the company would likely cease production of knockoffs. Although the word Navajo has disappeared from their website, several Navajo designs are currently displayed under unaffiliated names.[41]

On July 7, 2017, the Senate Indian Affairs Committee held a Hearing in Santa Fe, on 'Modernizing the Indian Arts and Crafts Act'. In her testimony, Diné weaver and museum curator Joyce Begay-Foss stated that 'we can't make a living', due to the influx of knockoffs'. She mentioned how the appropriation of designs is in violation of the Native American Religious Freedom Act. It also violates Articles 11, 20, and 31 of UNDRIP, the United Nations Declaration on the Rights of Indigenous Peoples, to 'maintain, control, protect and develop their heritage, traditional knowledge and expressions... including designs'. Pueblo fetish carver Andy Abeita acknowledged 'the world-renowned recognition of southwest arts and crafts does not reflect what goes on within impoverished makers' homes'. Because poverty among artisans is a much-neglected topic, consumers lack awareness of current circumstances.

For generations, ethnologists' publications depicted artisans as 'cultural performers' and downplayed the labour involved. According to Andy Abeita because of such massive appropriation, craft production by Native American artisans, a crucial aspect of cultural preservation, is being driven to oblivion.[42] Former SWAIA director Bruce Bernstein has stated that $0.85 of every $1 spent on contemporary Indian art now goes for knockoffs.[43, 44] The contexts of interpretation deployed in the past to describe weavers' production privileges settler history. Subsequent publications have emphasized the evolution of various styles and traders' influences on their development. Such extant interpretations have blocked a deeper understanding of the values of weaving for Diné.

In this critique I reveal the profound disconnect between the high value attached to historic textiles, and the low value attached to their context of production. Severing women's textile production from the livestock and wool markets was a major blunder, a prodigious amount of archival evidence confirms the essential importance of women's non-waged labour in subsidizing the trading post system for eighty years. Thousands of weavers and their families have paid a very high price for this neglect. Although we are accustomed to thinking of art as a significant complement of civilization, ethnographers and museum scholars concerned with cultural preservation are not accustomed to thinking of art collections as potential vehicles of cultural fragmentation.

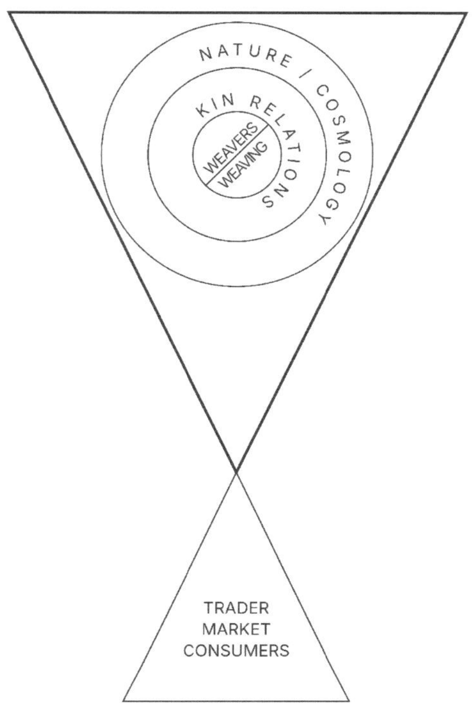


Navajo relations.

## HÓZHÓ

*Objects in museums are living entities. They embody layers of meaning, and they are deeply connected to the past, present, and*

36. Gladys Reichard, *Navajo Shepherd and Weaver* (1936).
37. Lynn Stephen, *Weaving in the Fast Lane* (1993).
38. Lynn Stephen, 'Export Markets and Their Effects on Indigenous Craft Production' (1991a), p. 384; 'Culture as a Resource' (1991b) and 'Weaving in the Fast Lane', p. 47.
39. In 2005, Santa Fe, New Mexico, reputedly the third largest art market globally, was designated a UNESCO City of Design, Crafts and Folk Art. Several knockoff dealers operate out of Santa Fe and other cities and towns in the southwest US.
40. Dusty Henson et al, *Rugs to Riches: The Amazing Story of the El Paso Saddle Blanket Company* (2001).
41. *Eighth Generation* is a First Nations' substitute for trade blankets. Located in Seattle, WA, it opened in 2008. Nooksak artist/founder Louie Gong's mantra heralds 'Support Inspired Natives instead of Native Inspired'.
42. Andy Abeita, 'Pressing Concerns for the Future of Native American Arts and Crafts' (2006).
43. Bruce Bernstein, 'Remarks' (2010).
44. The Hubbell Trading Post Papers became available for research in 1977, about the time the twin threats of the investment market for old textiles and the knockoffs emerged. In fact, the beautifully illustrated coffee-table books featuring historic textiles are frequently shipped abroad and used as templates for future production of knockoffs (fieldnotes 2011, 2015).

*future of Indigenous communities. Every engagement with objects...should begin with this core recognition. We are not just looking at interesting pieces. In the presence of objects from the past, we are privileged to stand as witnesses to living entities that remain intimately and inextricably tied to their descendant communities.*[45]

The patterns of relations that brought rugs into existence are fractured through adherence to dualisms. Cultural theft has been sanctioned in multiple ways. Such activities are midwifed by the binary between the sacred world of religion and the secular or profane world of commodity production and commercialization, as conceived by academics. Complex patterns of relations were occluded through the epistemological lens of the colonizers, including ethnographers, and perpetuated by scholars after that. Although scholars acknowledged the importance of kinship relations (*k'é*), they failed to recognize that the process and products of weaving serve as recursive enactments of the Creation Story, thereby linking cosmology, kinship solidarity, harmony *and* provisioning.

I developed this image based on feedback from two dozen Navajo, including weavers.[46] To weave a rug is to re-enact the process of creation because weaving calls the rain. While filming *Weaving Worlds*, weavers confirmed the importance of *k'e* in working with wool. As companion species, sheep are the foundation; they teach you how to live a Diné way of life. Weaving sustains ecological continuities and that recursive process links ecological aesthetics to epistemology.[47] This perspective evokes Hopi filmmaker Victor Masayesva's comment: '...there is such a thing as an Indian aesthetic, and it begins in the sacred'.[48] Weavers' eloquent comments provide deep insight into the centrality of weaving as a means of survivance.[49]

Weaver and educator Bonnie Benally Yazzie noted recently, '...the theft of our rug designs has negatively affected the market for our weaving, and destroyed much of our local economy...nearly all trading posts have closed, and traders in border towns pay very little because they are overstocked... the sacredness of the rugs is being taken away by the knockoffs...all of our designs have sacred meanings and come from our minds influenced by teachings and the Diné lifeways.'[50]

Bonnie's heartfelt testimony evokes Navajo historian Jennifer Denetdale's pithy comment: 'Important critiques...have revealed Western scholarship to be simply another kind of imperialism that reinscribes existing structures of power.'[51] The numerous designs generated by weavers were perceived as an intellectual *terra nullius,* empty of content, thus ripe for appropriation.[52] Given the extensive commercialization for more than a century, one wonders how thousands of Navajo can possibly survive as weavers in the future in an increasingly globalized, hyper-competitive world. Two centuries of plunder underscores US president Thomas Jefferson's (1801–1809) assertion: 'Money, not morality, is the principal commerce of civilized nations.'[53]

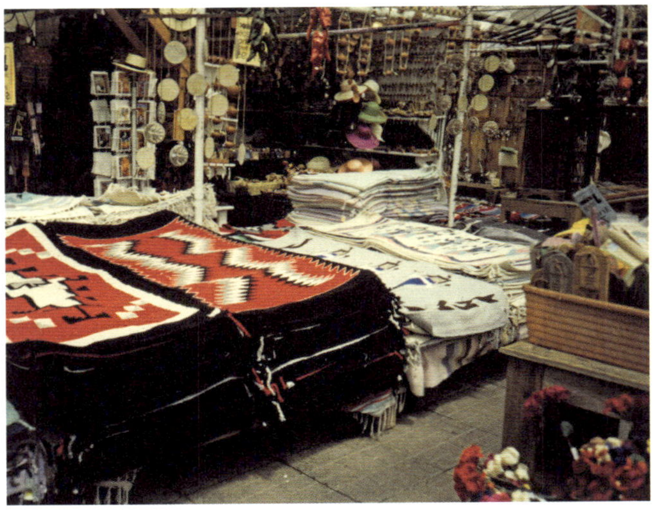

Knockoff Navajo rugs on display in Jackalope store, New Mexico, c. 2000.

45. Ho-chunk author Amy Lonetree, *Decolonizing Museums: Representing Native America in National and Tribal Museums* (2012).
46. M'Closkey, *Swept Under the Rug*, p. 18 and 'Towards an Understanding of Navajo Aesthetics' (2004a). The Diné concept of hózhó expresses beauty in a holistic way. The loom and weaving tools have a place and a purpose in the Origin stories as they were made by the Holy People, and they have life-giving names that go with the songs and prayers. After cosmic creation the Holy People retreated to the mountains, springs and canyons. The responsibility for maintaining hózhó was passed on to Diné. We cannot fully appreciate weavers' stories without considering their ecological views of their local environments and how those recursively map human/non-human relations.
47. M'Closkey, 'Towards an Understanding'.
48. Steven Leuthold, *Indigenous Aesthetics: Native Art, Media and Identity* (1998).
49. M'Closkey, *Swept Under the Rug*, Ch 7 & 8; Pete et al, *Spider Woman's Children: Navajo Weaving Today* (2018); *How to Weave a Navajo Rug, and Other Lessons from Spider Woman* (2020) and Rosemary Willink, *Weaving a World: Textiles and the Navajo Way of Seeing* (1996).
50. Bonnie B Yazzie, 'Spider Woman, Our Grandmother's Teachings Woven into Our Diné (Navajo) Lifeways', personal files (2021).
51. Denetdale, *Reclaiming Diné History*, p. 33.
52. Ugo Mattei et al, *When the Rule of Law is Illegal* (2008), p. 21.
53. goodquotes.com.

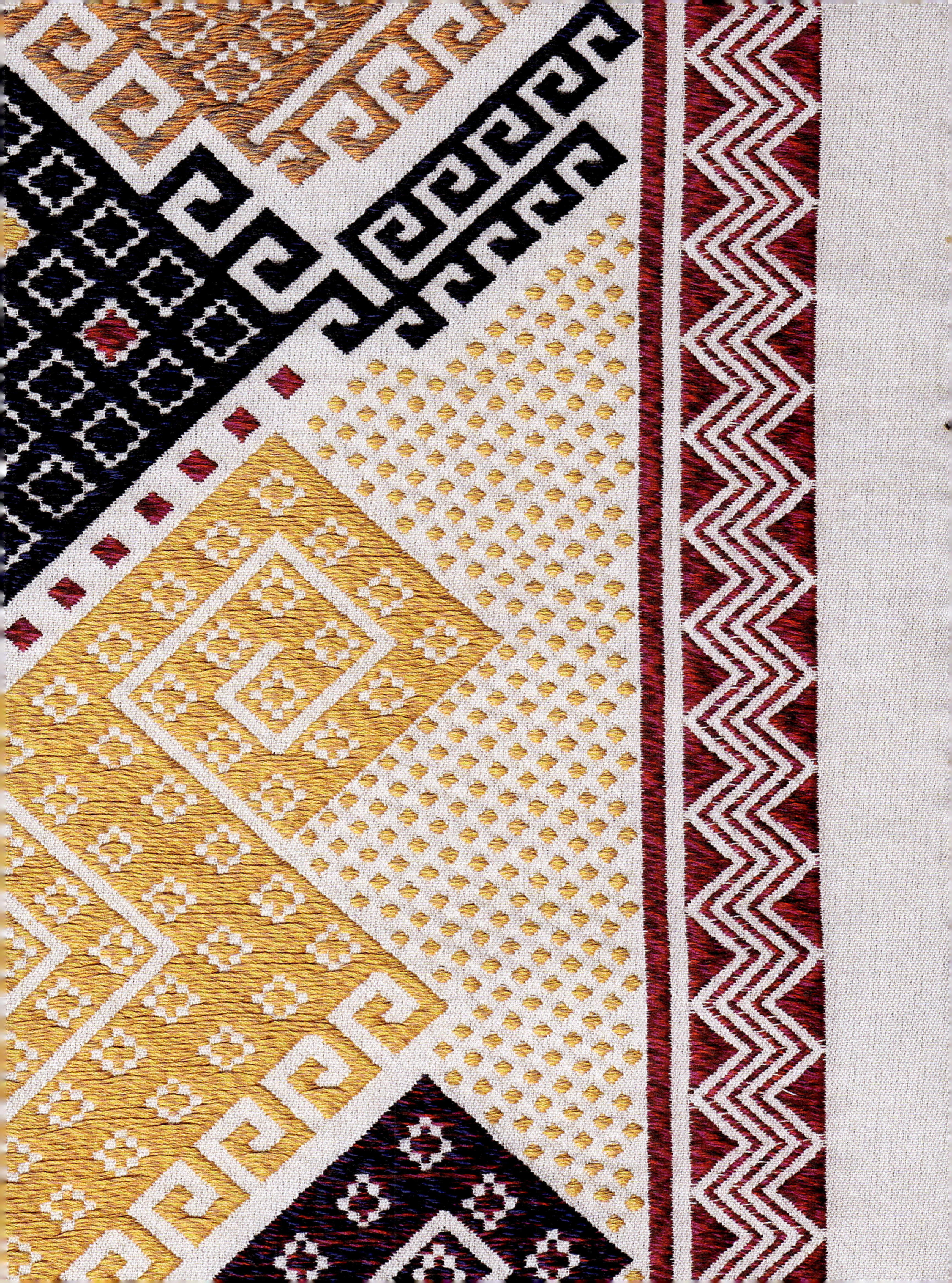

*Tampan*
Jennifer Tee

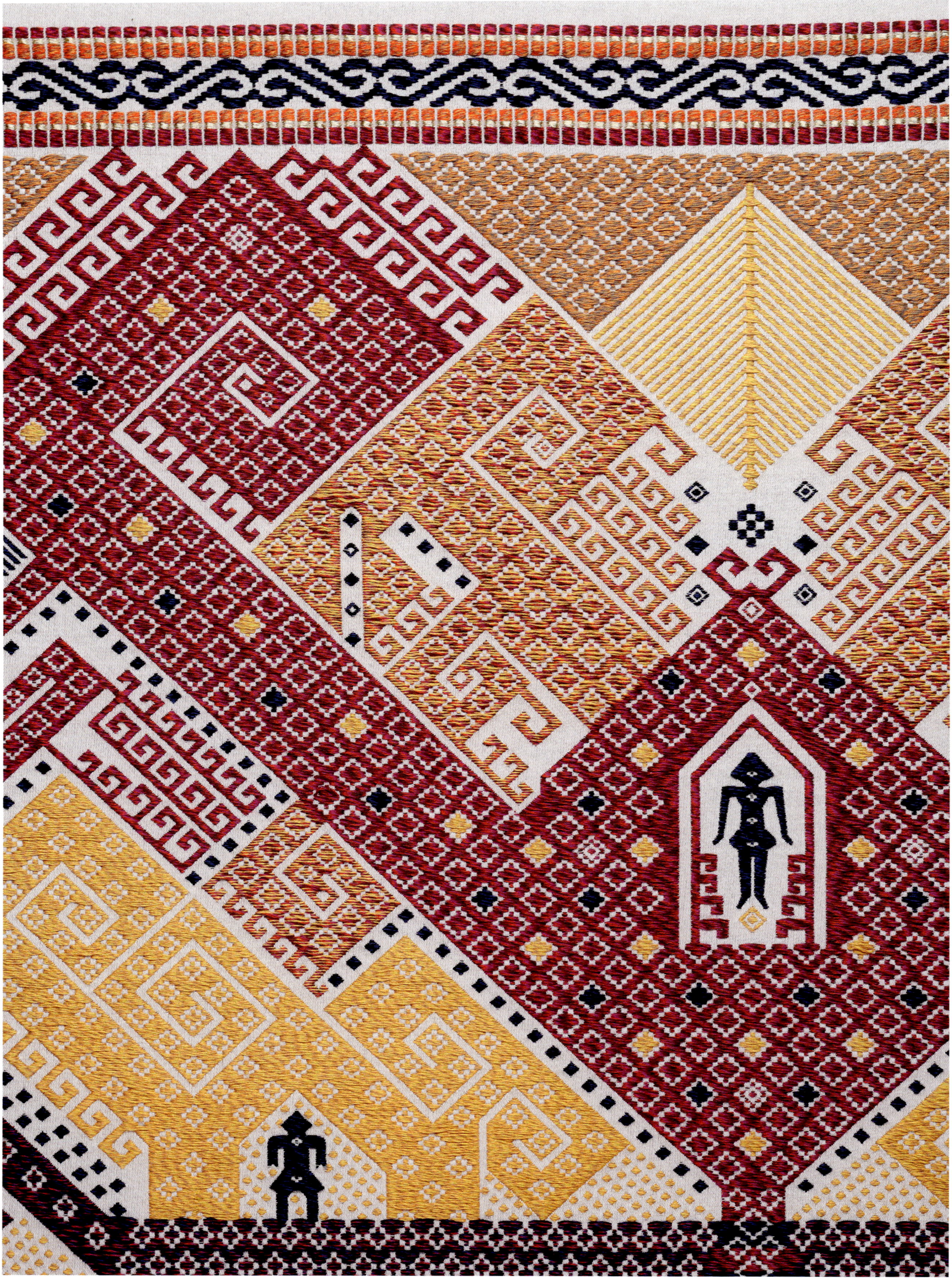

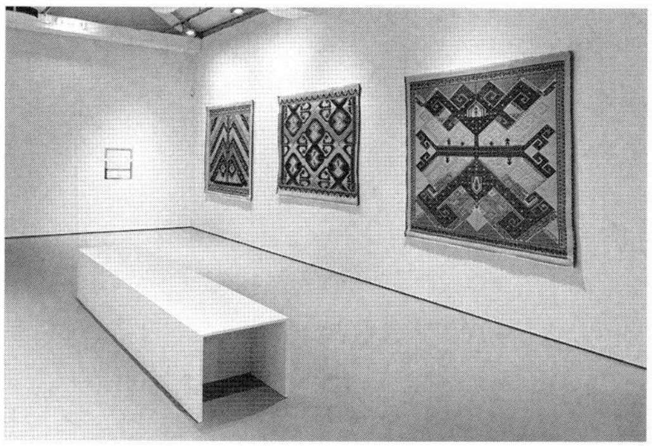

Tampan Tree of Life, Tampan Womb of Time, Tampan Mirrored Ship #3, Jennifer Tee, 2016.

Wool, cotton, linen, elirex, jacquard woven, 170 × 159 cm, 154 × 164 cm, and 180 × 164 cm.

*Tampan Tree of Life*, *Tampan Womb of Time* and *Tampan Mirrored Ship #3* are intricately woven jacquard tapestries, drawing inspiration from the traditional *tampan* and *palepai* weavings from the Lampung region in Indonesia. The three tapestries share a palette of earthy tones: deep burgundy, muted red, warm yellow, rusty orange and steel blue-black. *Tampan Tree of Life* features sharp, pointed shapes; *Tampan Womb of Time* emphasizes curved, enclosed forms; and *Tampan Mirrored Ship #3* combines these elements into a multi-layered composition.

The designs synthesize geometric patterns — triangles, squares, zigzag and meandering lines — with stylized depictions of human figures, houses, plants, animals, trees and birds. While some are immediately recognizable, others are reduced to elemental graphic forms that require closer observation to be identified. Zooming out, we see that the patterns and figures form cohesive images. In *Tampan Tree of Life*, the yellow, brown and black patterns extending diagonally from the centre, resemble branches of a tree, with meandering motifs representing curly leaves. Hanging from the trunk are diamond-shaped 'bubbles' containing stylized human figures. In *Tampan Mirrored Ship #3*, the meandering motifs on the left and right sides form the prow and stern of a ship, mirrored along its horizontal axis. On second look, we recognize the same ship archetype at the base of the tree in the first work. The prow and stern also feature in the design of the central tapestry, combined with curved shapes holding one or two human figures. However, a central organizing motif, like the tree and ship, seems to be absent here. Instead, the overall image is organized along two zigzag lines. The tapestries are bordered by decorative friezes that incorporate repeating geometric patterns that also appear in the central imagery.

Symmetry and repetition create harmony across the three tapestries. In *Tampan Tree of Life*, motifs are mirrored vertically, while in *Tampan Womb of Time* and *Tampan Mirrored Ship #3*, patterns are mirrored both vertically and horizontally. Closer inspection, however, reveals subtle disruptions in the symmetry — such as the horizontal axis being slightly off-centre in *Tampan Mirrored Ship #3* or an uneven distribution of figures in *Tampan Womb of Time* — which introduce visual tension.

Jennifer Tee's tapestries were woven on a digitized jacquard loom, a technique that ensures precision and smooth surfaces. Yet the use of thick yarns and floating threads create a sculpted texture that interacts with light. The weft comprises multicoloured plied threads — steel blue-black is made from black, anthracite and marine-blue yarns; warm yellow twists together yellow, gold and camel hues, bringing vibrancy to woven surfaces. Even the reverse sides of the *Tampan* are intriguing. They reveal floating threads typical of jacquard weaving, forming a hieroglyphic-like accumulation of lines that provide a more intuitive, haptic rendering of the design. They also show the deep storage of inactive threads that only intermittently become visible on the front.

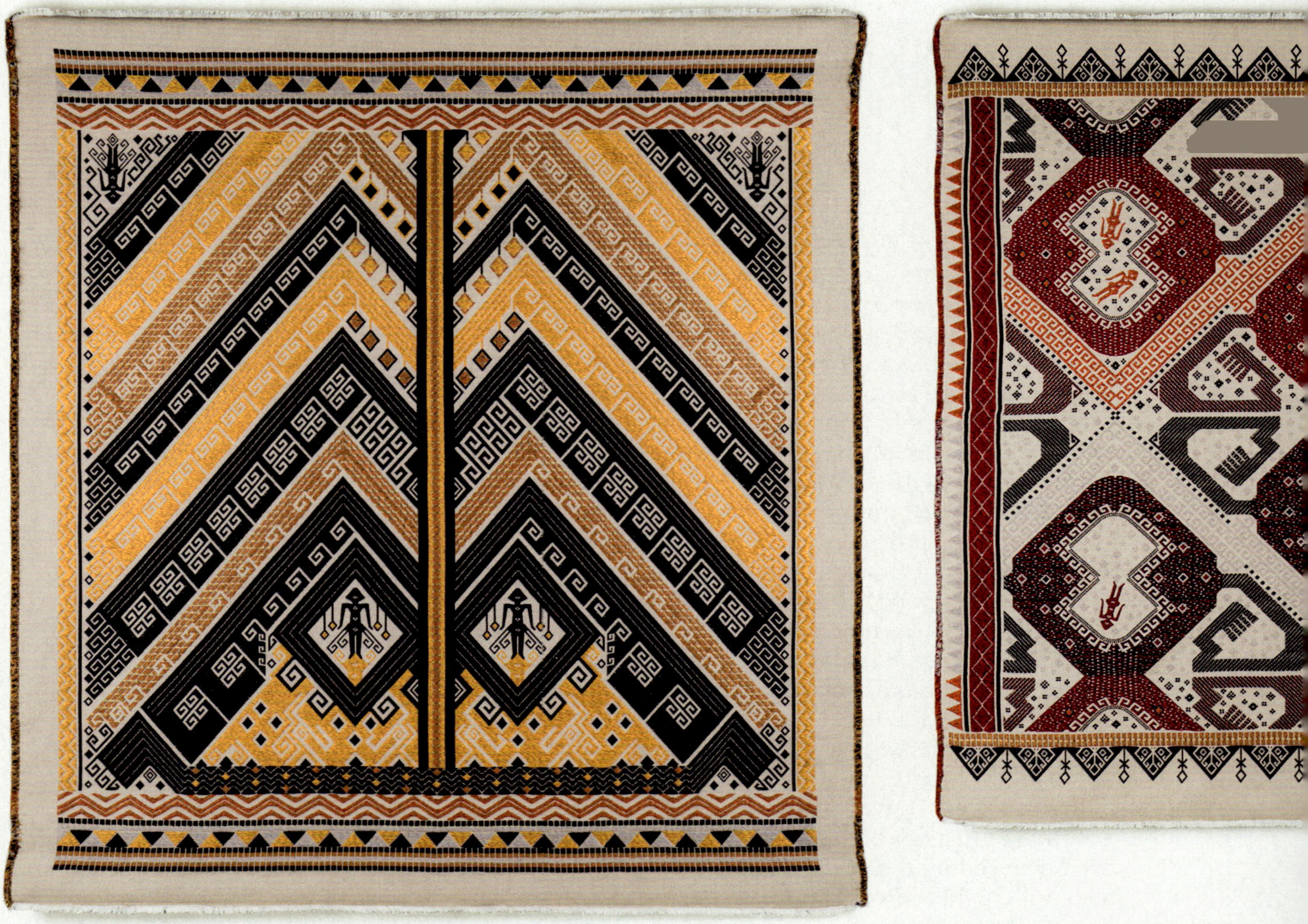

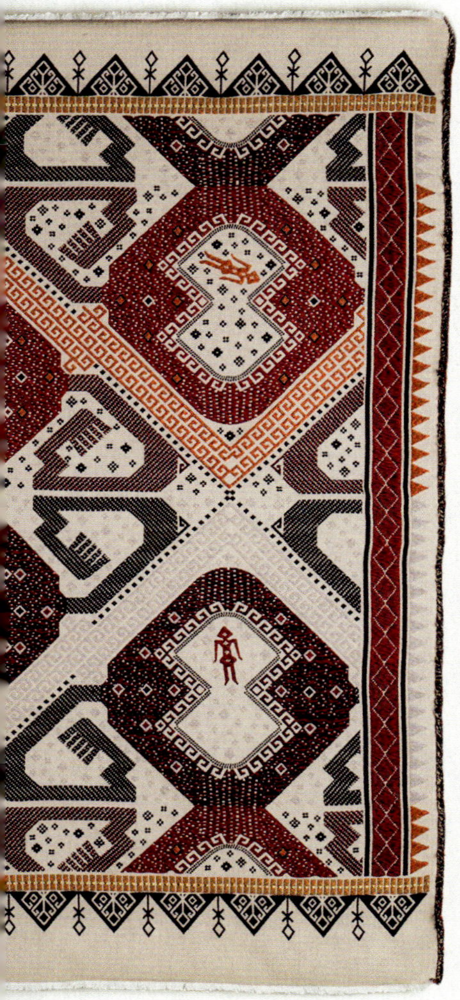

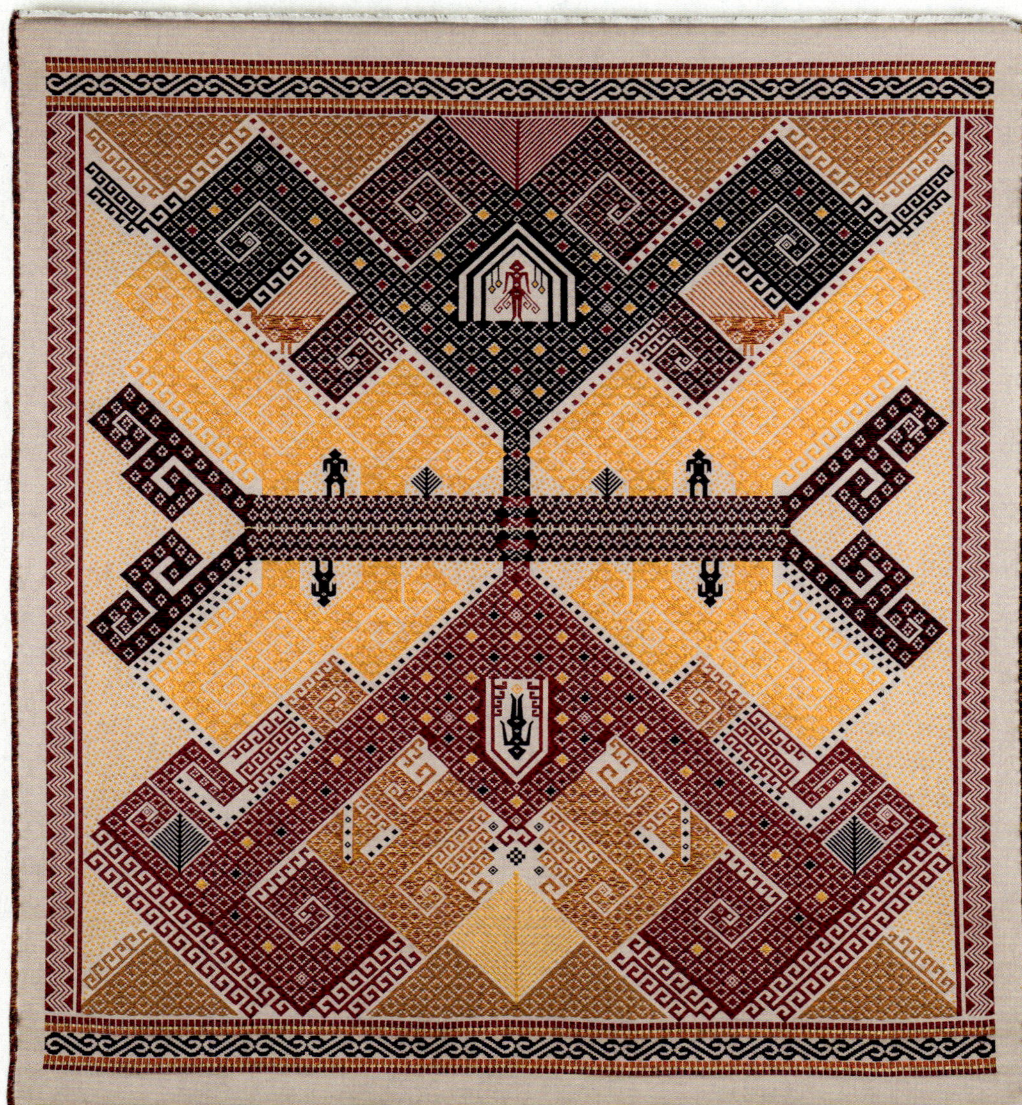

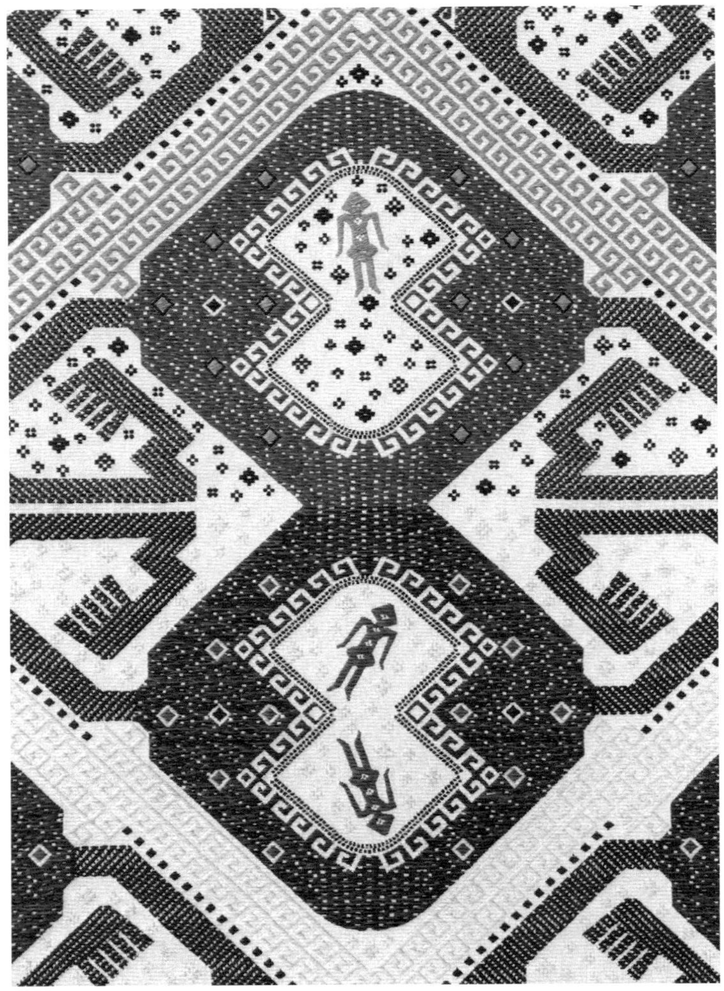

Detail Tampan Womb of Time, diamond-shaped ‘bubbles’.

Detail Tampan Tree of Life, meandering motifs.

# UNRAVELLING TAMPAN
## In Conversation with Jennifer Tee

Jennifer Tee's artistic practice spans diverse media and disciplines including ceramics, textiles, tulip petal collages and performance. Over the past decade, she has created a body of work inspired by the ceremonial *tampan* and *palepai* textiles from Indonesia, including the *Tampan* series of jacquard-woven pieces featured here. Depicting ships as their central motif, these ceremonial cloths resonate with Tee's ongoing exploration of movement, migration and the experience of being suspended in an in-between state. Through her study of their spiritual, historical and material dimensions, Tee reinterprets their symbolic language as powerful mementos for contemporary life.

CHRISTEL — The palepai and tampan textiles from the Lampung region of South Sumatra have inspired you for over a decade. What drew you to them initially?

JENNIFER — I first encountered tampan and palepai textiles in 2010 while researching a public art commission. I was studying ceremonial Indonesian textiles in the collection of the Wereldmuseum in Leiden and was struck by their iconography and symbolism. To me, they reflected ideas of migration and transition. In Europe, these ceremonial cloths are often called 'ship cloths', named after the prominent ship motif. They were used in rites of passage such as naming ceremonies, weddings and burials. The ship was seen as a vessel guiding individuals through life's transitions. They also featured in rituals marking a person's rise in social status.

CHRISTEL — You've often said that these textiles hold personal meaning for you as well?

JENNIFER — My family's history is shaped by migration and displacement. My mother is half Dutch, half British. My father's family is Chinese Indonesian. He came to the Netherlands in the 1950s by ship, along with his parents and sister. For me, the ship motif symbolizes his journey, which has become part of my story and my identity: I'm a quarter Dutch, a quarter English, and half Chinese Indonesian, a blend of cultures and histories.

Beyond these family ties, the Lampung ship cloths inspired work around ideas of movement, belonging and transformation. In many cultures, ships symbolize the journey, whether physical, like migrating from one continent to another, or spiritual, like crossing from this world to the next. These motifs intuitively captured something I couldn't quite articulate: the feeling of being a soul in limbo, always in transition, caught in an unnameable in-between. That state often involves loss: of life, of homeland, of tongue.

CHRISTEL — What about the design and materiality of the textiles?

JENNIFER — Yes, the visual quality of the tampan and palepai attracted me too: the symmetry of their composition and the tension between abstraction and figuration. Take the stylized ship motif, for instance, where the mast branches into a tree of life. Its image merges two central elements into a

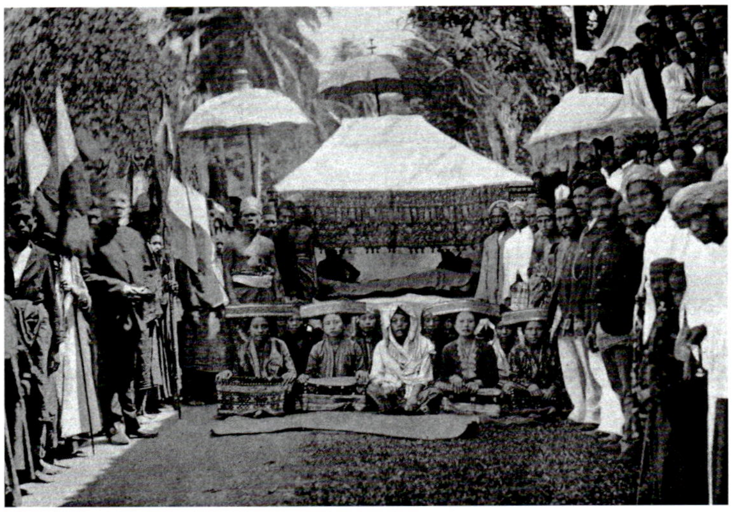

01

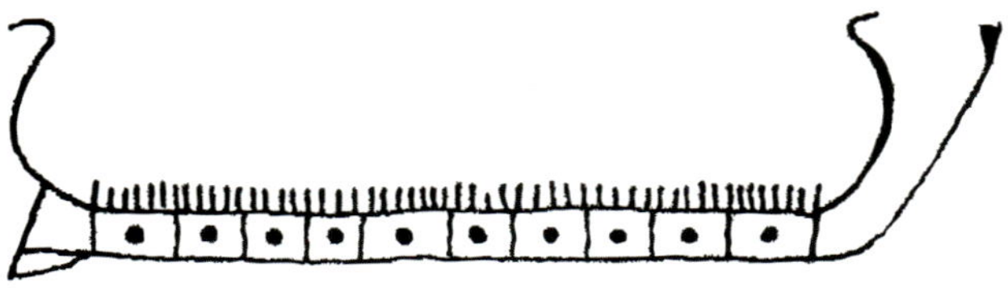

02

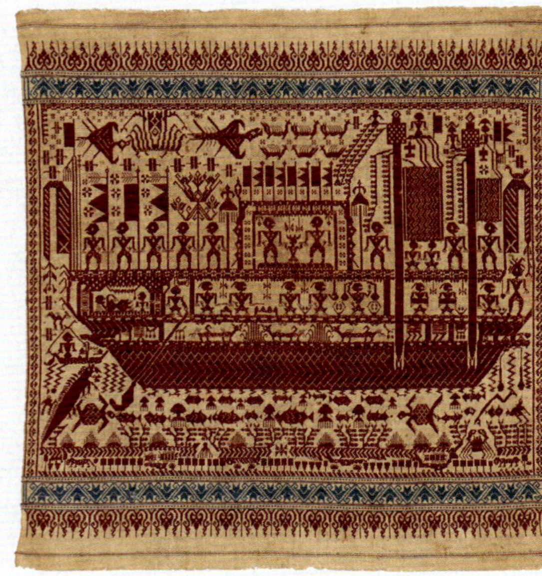

03

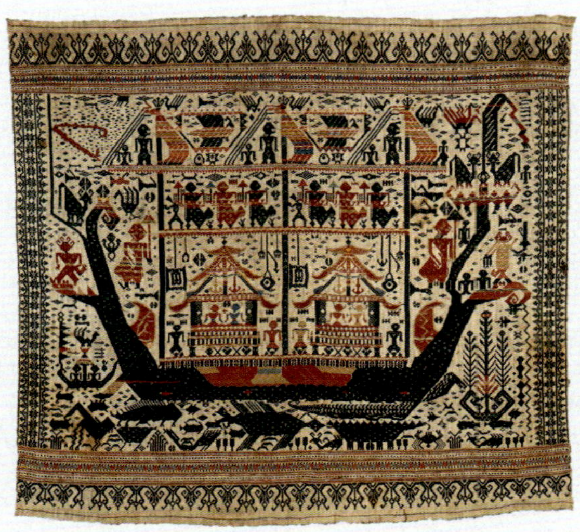

04

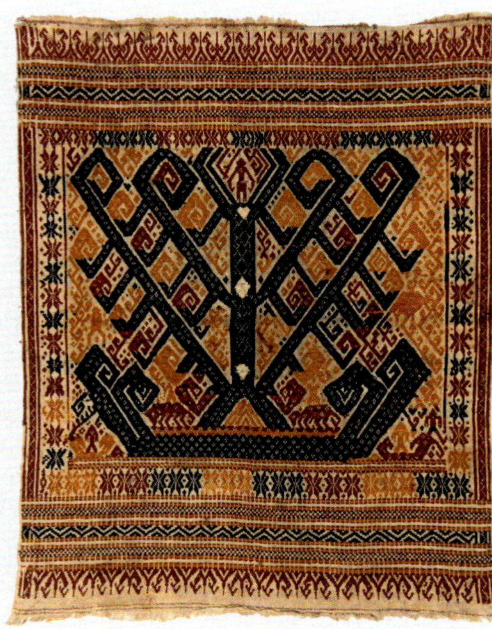

05

SHIP CLOTHS
'Tampan' and 'palepai' are ceremonial cloths woven in Lampung, South Sumatra. They were used during important rites of passage, including marriage, burials and status-raising ceremonies. Their principal motif is a ship, which led to their being referred to as 'ship cloths' in Europe. The ships were commonly understood to symbolize movement and transition – whether as a 'ship of the dead', transporting the soul of the deceased to the land of the ancestors, or as a 'spiritual lifeboat', guiding a person from one stage of life to the next.
More recent interpretations view the ship as a representation of organized society, which resonates with the literal meaning of the name Lampung: 'floating on the water'. Lampung people saw themselves as the crew aboard the world-as-ship, drifting between heaven (the upper world) and the sea (the underworld). Ship cloths were produced until the end of the 19th century.

01. Burial ceremony, Sumatra, c. 1900. Photo by G.F.M. Liebert, Eigen Haard, 1900, no. 44. Ceremony honouring a village elder. Under the canopy lies the deceased. His widow sits in the middle of the front row of female mourners.

02. Drawing of a prehistoric rockcarving of a ship found at Himmelstadlund (Sweden). Between 1910 and 1920, Swedish archeologist Arthur Nordén studied the Himmelstadlund rockcarvings. Alfred Steinmann reproduced Nordén's drawings in his 1946 trilogy 'The Ship of Dead in Textile Art', in which he noted similarities between ship motifs found in south-east Asia and northern Europe.

TAMPAN
Tampan are intricately woven, square-shaped cloths traditionally made by women. They served multiple ceremonial functions: to cover a newborn presented to grandparents, to wrap gifts and food during rituals, to be displayed or exchanged at marriages, tied to the ridgepole of a newly built house, and placed beneath the head of the deceased during burial rites. Their pictorial content varied by region. Examples from Sumatra's inland areas, 'tampan darat', feature stylized natural subjects and geometric designs, while coastal weavings, 'tampan pasisir', depict richly detailed ships surrounded by symbolic motifs.

03. Tampan pasisir, Piya, Lampung, South Sumatra, 19th century. Cotton, handwoven, 78.7 × 72.4 cm.
04. Tampan pasisir, Kalianda, Lampung, South Sumatra, c. 1650–1680 or 1764–1801. Cotton, linen, handwoven, 75 × 70 cm.
05. Tampan darat, Lampung, South Sumatra, before 1940. Cotton, handwoven, 75 × 58 cm. This Tampan combines ship and tree motifs, in which the mast branches out into a tree.

SHIP MOTIF
The ship is a favourite motif among seafaring cultures worldwide. Images of rowing boats and small sailing ships have been found in rock carvings in Scandinavia

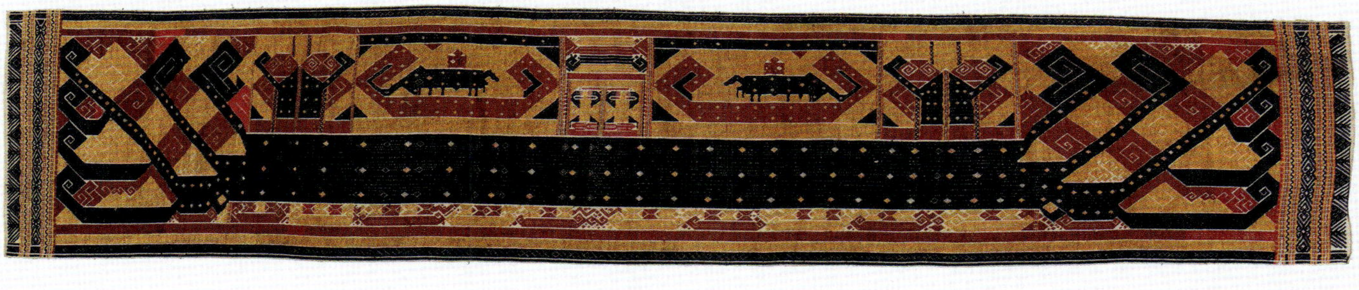

06

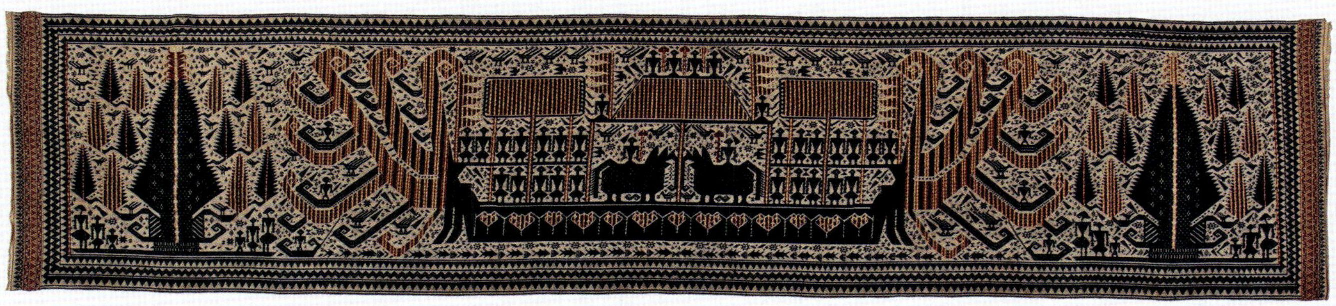

07

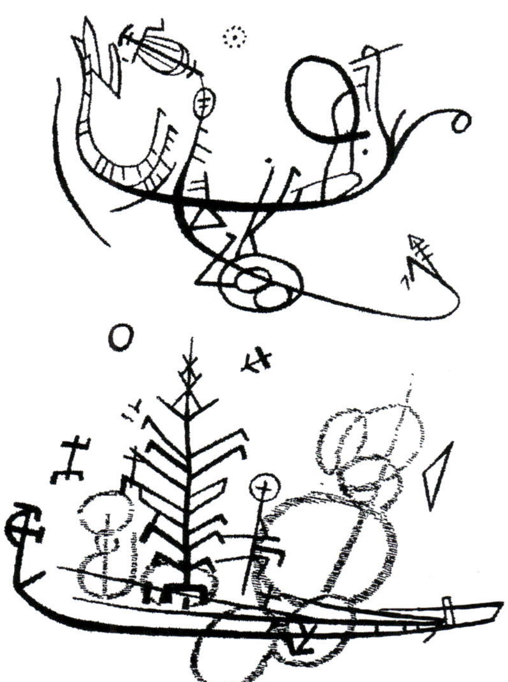

08

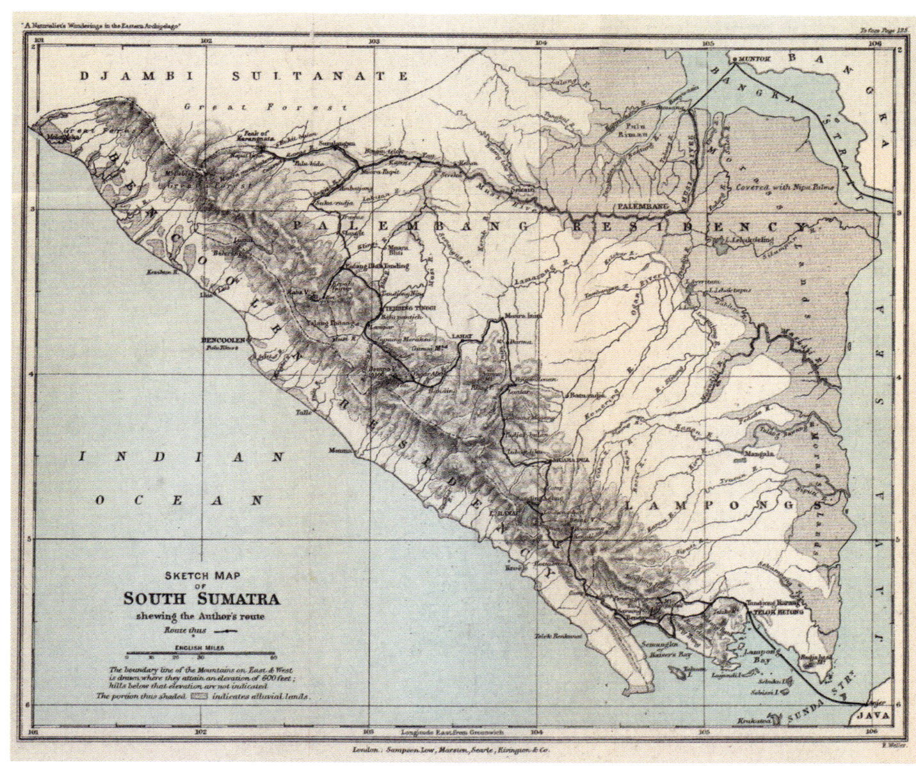


09

dating back to the Bronze Age, as well as on clay tablets from Egypt as early as 4000 BCE. In many ancient civilizations, sea-going vessels held spiritual significance and were associated not only with the journey to the afterlife, but also with fertility.

06. Palepai, ceremonial cloth, Lampung, South Sumatra, c. 1900–1925.
Cotton, handwoven, 62 × 324 cm.
07. Palepai, ceremonial cloth, Lampung, South Sumatra, c. 1900–1925.
Cotton, handwoven, 62 × 324 cm.

PALEPAI

The oblong-shaped palepai were reserved for the aristocracy, representing their wealth and status. Three metres wide, these textiles formed part of the family heirloom and were used as ceremonial backdrops during rituals celebrating a person's rise through the social ranks. Their name probably derives from the Old Javanese word lepih, meaning 'to fold' or 'to double' – possibly a reference to their symmetrical composition. Palepai feature a limited repertoire of motifs, typically including one or two vessels with a forked stern and a canopy on top. The boats are often populated with large animals, such as water buffalo or elephants, symbolizing bravery, wealth and prosperity.

08. Scratch drawings of representations of ship of death with tree, moon and sun symbols found in Papua New Guinea. After J. Röder, c. 1938–1939.
09. Map of Lampung Region, 1885. This map was published as an addendum to Henry O. Forbes' 'A naturalist's wanderings in the Eastern Archipelago: A Narrative of Travel and Exploration from 1878 to 1883', in which the Scottish explorer, ornithologist and botanist detailing his journeys through the area. It was drawn by John B. Gibbs based on the authors sketches.

LAMPUNG

The province of Lampung is located at the southern tip of the Indonesian island of Sumatra and is the ancestral homeland of the Lampung people. The first settlers on the island were Austronesians, who brought with them distinct customs and cosmological beliefs. Over time, various cultures and religions have left their mark on Lampung culture, including the prehistoric Dong Son culture, as well as Hindu-Buddhist, Chinese and, more recently, colonial influences from Asia, the Middle East and Europe.
Lampung's strategic position along the Sunda Strait made it part of the ancient maritime trade route between India and China. The region gained its wealth through pepper production. In 1690 it became an important trading post for the Dutch East India Company. In 1752, the Dutch annexed the region and introduced the so-called transmigration programme, relocating people from Java to Lampung. The 1883 eruption of the Krakatoa volcano devastated much of Lampung's coastline and wiped out its weaving tradition. Today, Provinsi Lampung is part of the Republic of Indonesia.

single geometric design, while the animals and human figures on the boat and in the surrounding sky and sea are depicted more figuratively.

CHRISTEL — The material and tactile qualities of your work are key to how it behaves in an exhibition space and how people interact with it — whether it's a tulip petal collage, a textile floor piece, ceramic objects or a choreographed performance. The three *Tampan* featured here were woven on a state-of-the-art industrial jacquard loom. Instead of using single-coloured yarns, they are woven with multi-coloured plied threads, sometimes mixing different materials such as cotton, wool and gold thread. What was your thinking behind these choices?

JENNIFER — I wanted to make works where you could sense the artist's hand — something standard jacquard production lacks in terms of tactility. The original tampan were woven by women at home on simple handlooms. That weaving tradition has largely disappeared. My wish was to create tapestries that echo the rich tones of the naturally dyed threads in the historical tampan and palepai, with their yellows, blues and browns obtained from turmeric, noni bark, indigo or iron-rich mud. Unlike the uniformity of industrially dyed yarns, these old yarns varied in tone and intensity, making the old textiles feel alive. So I began exploring alternatives to standard industrial yarns using the available techniques.

CHRISTEL — You mentioned that, to you, tampan and palepai textiles are not just flat surfaces symbolizing movement and transition, but that migration is deeply embedded in their fabric. Could you explain?

JENNIFER — In Lampung society, the ship motif isn't just about rites of passage or spiritual journeys, but also represents trade and sea voyages. Lampung has long been a crossroads of cultures, strategically positioned along the Sunda Strait between Java and Sumatra. The region prospered through the pepper trade, and Bandar Lampung was a key port. This brought the Lampung people into contact with crafts and traditions from Vietnam, China and wider South and South-East Asia, as well as the Arab world and, later, Europe. Some motifs and patterns introduced by foreign traders and artisans still appear in tampan and palepai made centuries later. These cloths carry the cultural memory of the region, embodying histories of migration and trade that shaped its identity.

CHRISTEL — In addition to the ship, another prominent motif in the ceremonial textiles is the tree of life, a symbol that, in Lampung cosmology, represents growth, life and the connection between the earthly and ancestral realms. In recent years, an important theme in textile-based conceptual art has been the duality between 'roots and routes'. The tree and ship motifs could be read as metaphors for these ideas: a sense of belonging and heritage on the one hand, and movement and migration across the earth's surface on the other. I'm curious how this symbolism has entered your artistic vocabulary?

JENNIFER — I see the entanglement of 'roots and routes' slightly differently. Yes, the ship symbolizes the modern experience of migration, of being in constant transition, and the tree of life reflects the complexity of one's origins, of family histories, and the intertwining of maternal and paternal lineages, both human and non-human, rooted in the earth. To me, tampan and palepai express the entanglement of the local and the universal. Their visual language is deeply tied to the specific cultural context in which they were created, as seen in the differences between regional styles and motifs. Yet their symbolism, the journey through life, is universal. The image of a ship appears in many ancient seafaring cultures as a metaphor for transition from life to death. Think of Charon's ferry in Greek mythology, carrying souls across the River Styx. In that sense, I believe their symbolic meaning still resonates today.

CHRISTEL — True, ship and tree are archetypical symbols, part of a universal cosmological imaginary that in your work takes on a contemporary meaning. I'm thinking of the public artwork *Tulip Palepai: Navigating the River of the World* (2017), developed for the entrance hall of Amsterdam's North-South metro line at Central Station. The diptych is a good example of how you've revitalized the iconography of this lost textile tradition. What made you choose this image for that specific space?

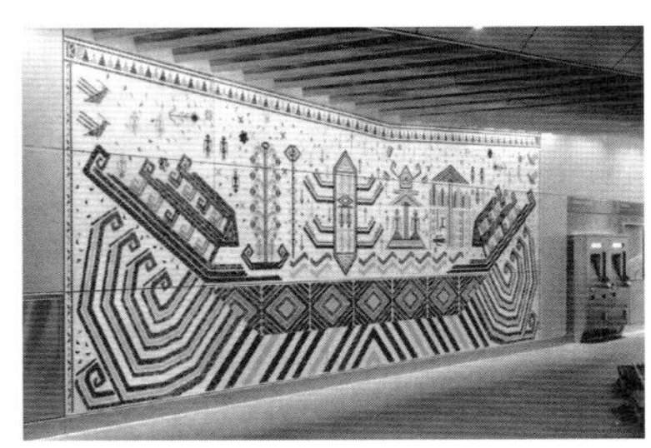

Installation Tulip Papelai: Navigating the River of the World, Amsterdam Centraal Station, Jennifer Tee, 2017.

JENNIFER — The entrance hall to the metro is one of the busiest stations in Amsterdam. Thousands of people pass through each day, rushing to work or visiting the city for the first time. I wanted to create a work that lingers in the mind, one that appeals both spiritually and physically.

CHRISTEL — Can you elaborate? What do you mean by 'spiritually and physically'?

JENNIFER — In the context of a metro station, the symbolism of the palepai can be taken quite literally: people are journeying from one place to another, most knowing where they came from and where they're going. That sense of belonging is reflected in the motifs I included, which reference the Dutch landscape, abstracted windmills and canal houses. But for some travellers, their destiny may be unknown or uncertain.

When I was sketching the work, many people were arriving in Europe and the Netherlands

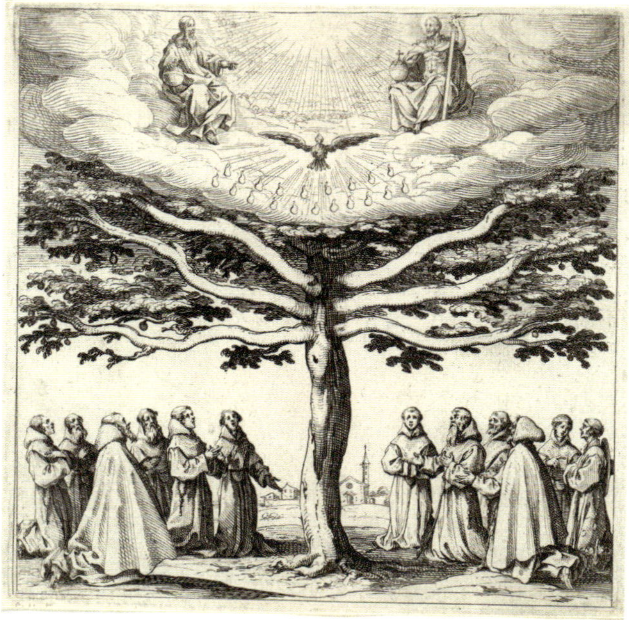

10

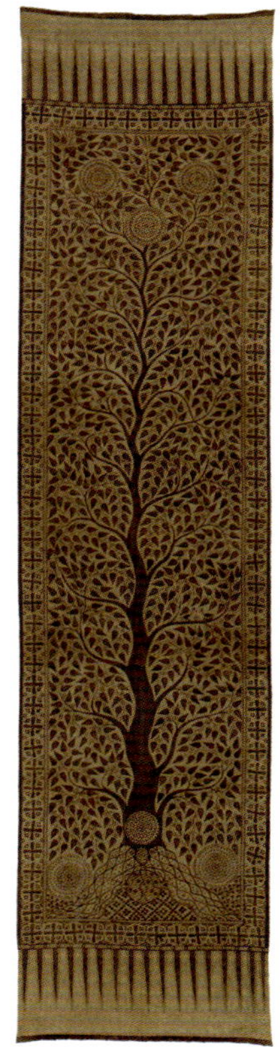

12

13

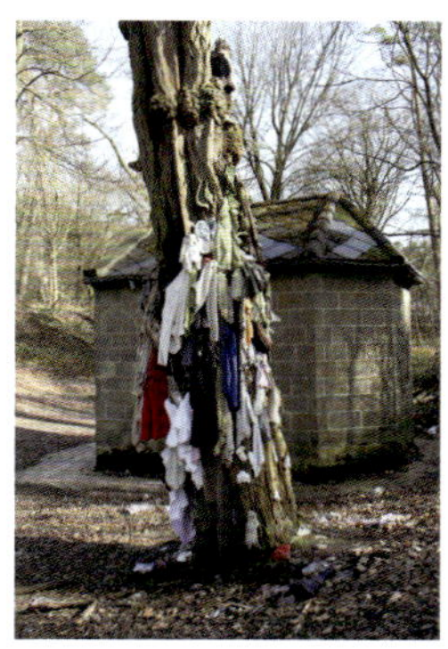

11

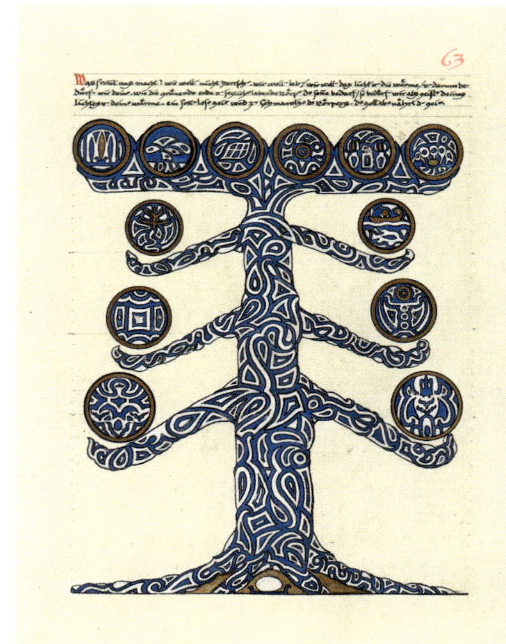

14

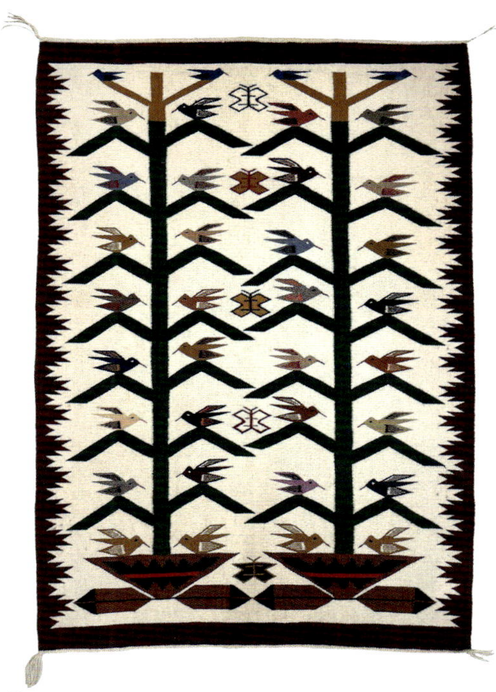

15

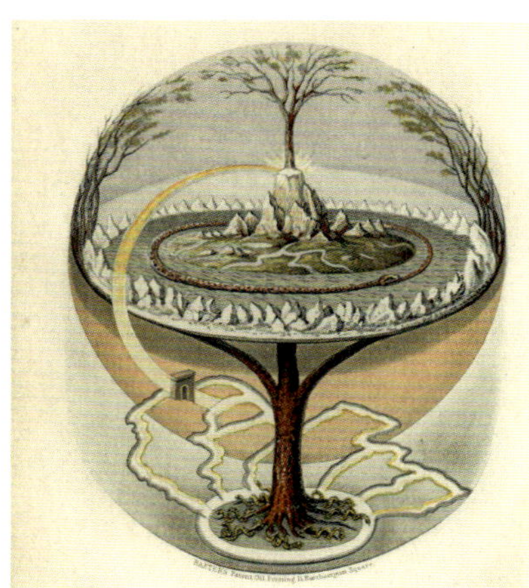

16

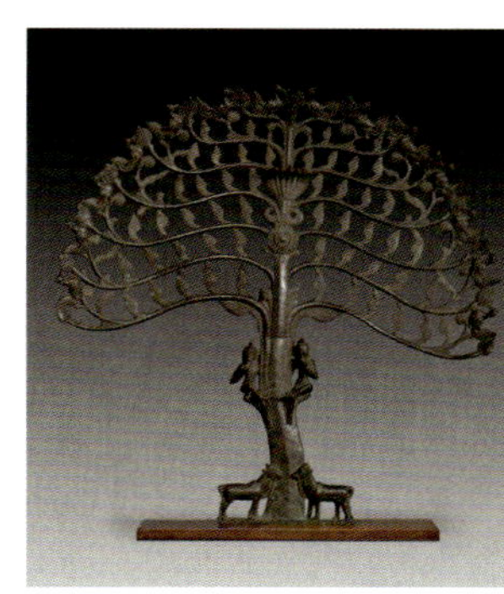

17

TREE OF LIFE
The tree of life is a common symbol in many mythologies, religions and philosophical traditions. It is closely related to the sacred tree, important in animist beliefs; the Tree of Knowledge of Good and Evil, central to the Christian creation story, and 'Yggdrasil', the World Tree, representing the axis mundi and connecting all parts of the cosmos in Norse cosmology.

10. L'Arbre de St. François (The Tree of St. Francis), Jacques Callot, Nancy, France, early 17th century.
    Etching on paper, 19.3 × 19.2 cm.
11. Koortsboom or Lapjesboom (Rag Tree), Chapelle Notre-Dame de l'Arbre-au-Puits, Stambrugge, Flanders, 2007.
    In folk belief, a fever tree could absorb a person's illness. At night, a relative would tie a strip from the patient's clothing to the tree's branches in hope of healing. If someone removed the cloth, the illness was believed to pass to them. Many fever trees were felled to eradicate the custom, yet during the COVID pandemic, the tradition quietly resurfaced.
11. Mawa or Mbesa (Sacred heirloom textile), Toraja people, Sulawesi, Indonesia, early 20th century.
    Cotton, natural dyes, painting, block printing, 374 × 89 cm.
    In many Indonesian cultures trees symbolize the link between the earth (abode of humans) and the heavens (realm of the gods). In many designs, trees sprout from a mountain. Some legends say the original ancestors emerged from mountains and volcanoes to establish the first settlements.
13. Sampler with Tree of Life, Jantje Meinderts Boorsma, Friesland, the Netherlands, 1848.
    Wool, cotton, cross- and back stitch, 42 × 34 cm.
    Appearing in various forms, the tree of life has long been a prominent motif in Dutch embroidered samplers. Often seen as biblical, it also reflects a deep, magical reverence for nature.
14. Carl G. Jung, Liber Novus (The Red Book), page 63, 1914–1930.
    In Carl Jung's archetypal language, the tree stands for life, growth and the link between conscious and unconscious. It also symbolizes the journey towards self-realization – its upward reach and resilience mirroring the strength of the human spirit.
15. Tree of Life, Wedding blanket, unknown Navajo/Diné artist, Grand Canyon, 2014. Wool, plain weave, 152 × 107 cm.
    This blanket shows two corn stalks emerging from a Navajo Wedding Basket, with birds. Corn is believed to have been given to the Navajo at creation. The tree of life weaving represents their connection to the nature and the importance of harmony and balance.
16. Yggdrasil, Oluf Olufsen Bagge, 1847.
    Painting reproduced in the English translation of the 'Prose Edda'.
17. Tree of Life, part of a devotional lamp, Kerala, India. c. 1575–1625.
    Bronze, 60.96 × 58.42 cm.

seeking refuge from war and poverty. Many made that precarious journey by boat, and some didn't survive. I don't want to make work that's too literal or too illustrative, but if you look closely, you'll see that some of the human figures are upside down, as if falling from the ship.

CHRISTEL — The public artwork *Tulip Palepai*, along with the jacquard-woven *Tampan* featured in this chapter, are early examples of your work inspired by Lampung textiles. In 2016, you also began the *Tampan Tulip* series, collages made from dried tulip petals, based on motifs from historic tampan and palepai. Looking back on this decade-long process, would you say the tampan and palepai have accompanied you on your journey too? What transitions or transformations occurred along the way?

JENNIFER — Although the tradition has died, many tampan and palepai are preserved in museum collections in Indonesia and Europe, which gave me the opportunity to study them in more detail — their materials, symbolism and visual language. And I discovered that these textiles are not one-dimensional; they are richly layered and symbolically complex.

At first, I was drawn to the central motifs, the ship and the tree of life, which aligned with themes important to me then. But over time, other elements emerged: *garuda* birds, the snake- and dragon-like forms, and sea creatures that surround the ship. Initially, I wasn't sure how they related to the central motif. Gradually, I realized they all form part of a broader cosmology, an understanding of the world and of the connections between all living things across time and space.

The more recent *Tampan Tulip* collages feature mountains, mythological creatures and animal motifs. One reason I replaced the ship and human figures on deck with elements from the natural world is that I want to create works where nature, rather than humanity, takes centre stage. This non-human imagery resonates more deeply with an ecological consciousness, something I'm engaging with in my practice today.

CHRISTEL — Could you say a bit more about that?

JENNIFER — Ancestor worship is an important aspect of the pictorial narrative of the tampan and palepai, and of traditional Indonesian culture more broadly. But this sense of ancestry goes beyond familial ties; it relates to kinship with all species, human and non-human, and how these connections evolved over Earth's time. To me, the scenes depicted on tampan and palepai bear witness to this worldview.

The coexistence of diverse species — animals, humans, seaweed, abstract plant forms — on one visual plane expresses a deep awareness of the kinship among all living beings. Humanity is not central or superior; instead, tampan and palepai show us that everything is interconnected and mutually dependent: humans and non-humans, the material and spiritual worlds, past, present and future. These textiles, along with ceremonial rituals and other objects, embody a profound understanding of our origins, of what sustains us, and how to live within ecological time.

I believe that the women who created these cloths held a deep cosmological wisdom, of the world around us and humanity's place in it. Like shamans, they sought to share this knowledge visually. Sometimes that knowledge appears in the use of symmetry, mirroring sea and sky, reflecting the balance of the cosmos and the parallels between earthly and spiritual realms.

And when you live on an island like Sumatra and see animals arriving from the north to escape winter and returning again in April, your understanding of migration is cyclical. Movement becomes part of life's rhythm and the cosmos itself. The sea is not just a space to cross, but a living realm, teeming with creatures and meaning.

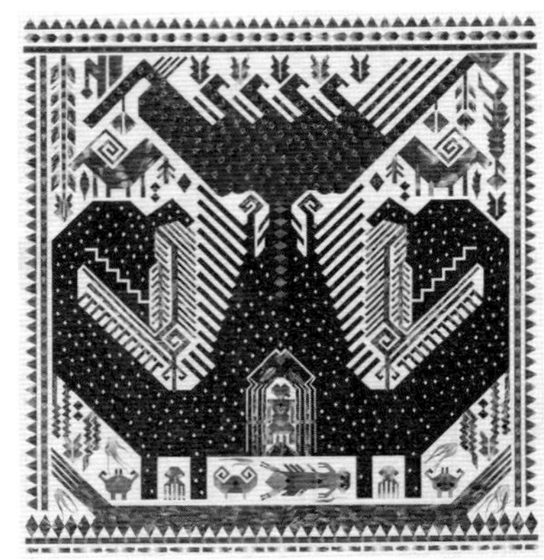

Tampan World Mountain, Ancestral Creatures, Jennifer Tee, 2022.

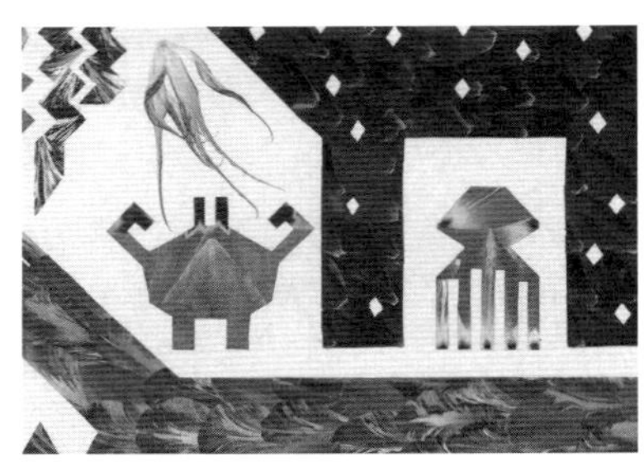

Detail, Tampan World Mountain, Ancestral Creatures, 2022.

CHRISTEL — What I hear you saying is that the tampan and palepai are not simply ethnographic artefacts locked into their own time-space continuum. Instead, they continue to convey essential wisdom about life and our world today, the most timely 'lesson' being that all things, human and non-human, are interconnected. Perhaps they still function as spiritual guides, accompanying humanity during its next rite of passage, as we transition from a human-centred to a nature-centred way of being in the world?

JENNIFER — In our so-called modern world, we tend to focus only on the short period that humans have existed on Earth, while ecological time, the time of the universe, is far broader and more encompassing. Earth's development spans 4.5 billion years. We must address the current ecological crisis and rethink how we want to live on this planet. I believe we'd benefit from weaving ourselves back into

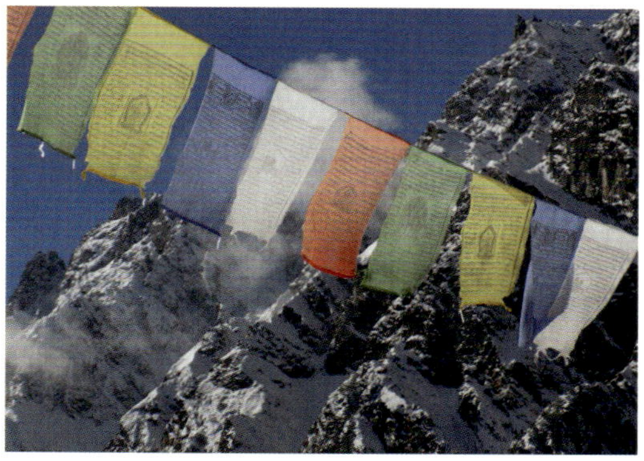

18

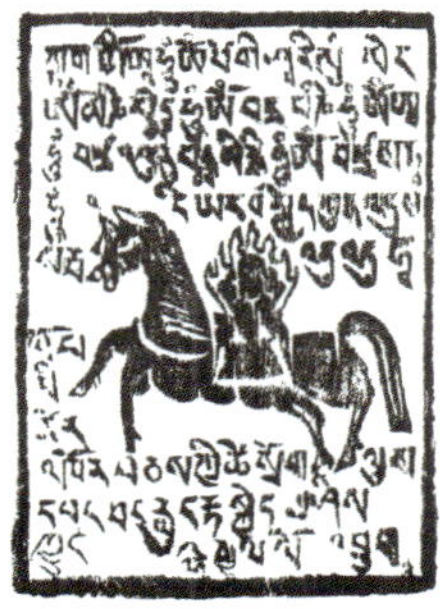

19

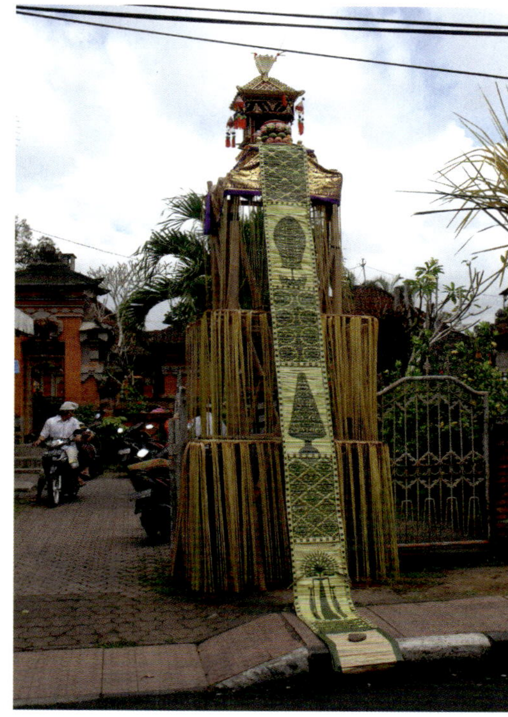

20

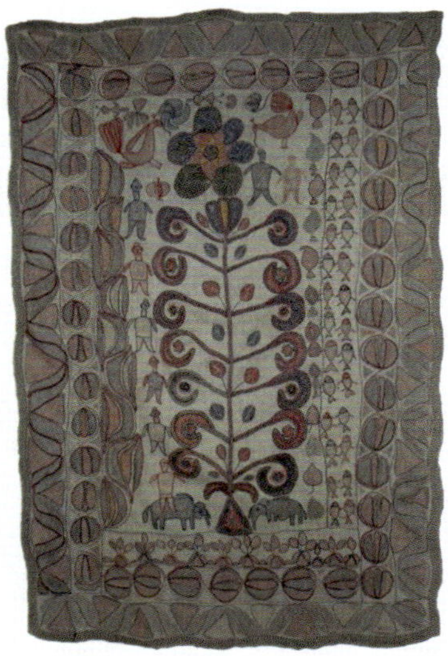

21

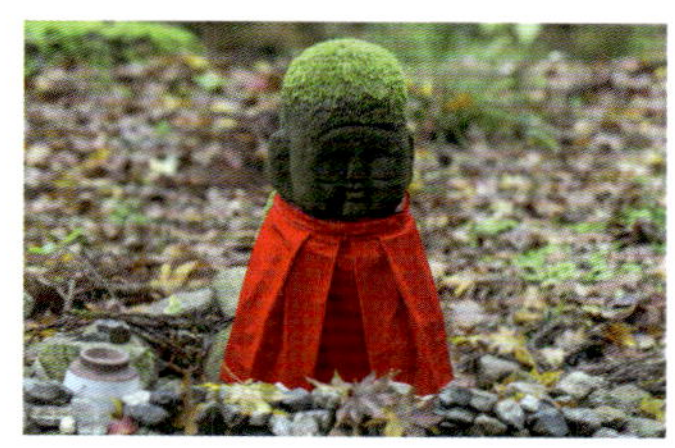

22

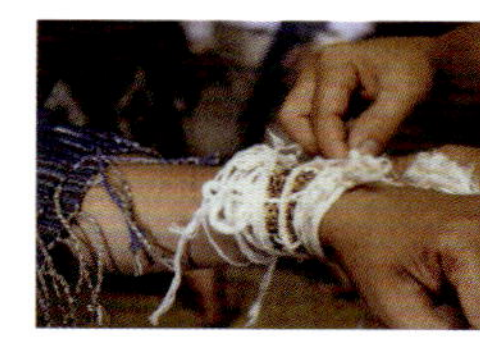

23

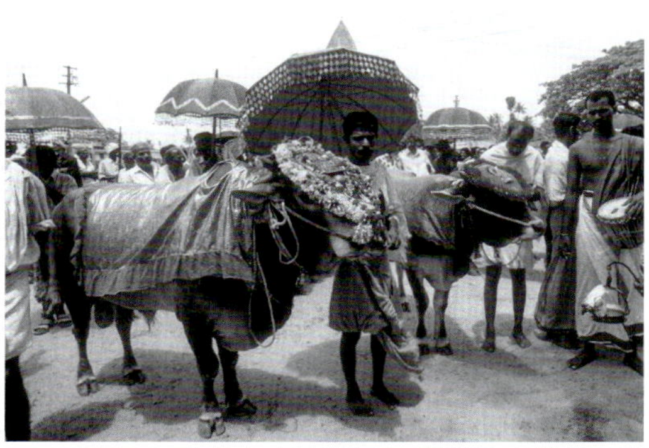

24

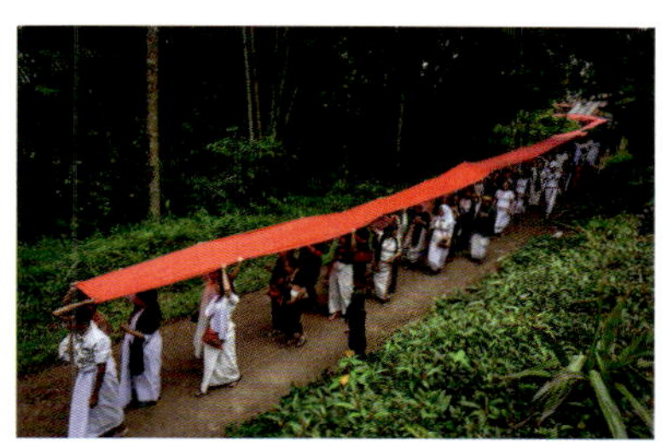

25

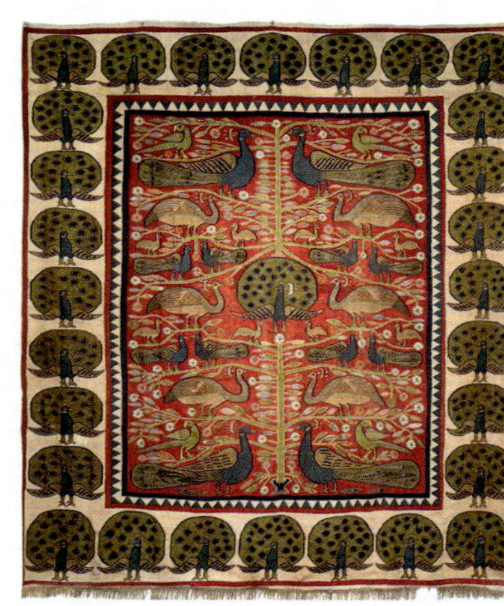

26

RITUAL TEXTILE
Across many cultures, textiles hold deep meaning in sacred rituals and ceremonies, including spiritual blessings and offerings, at the heart of which is contact between gods, ancestors and worshippers. Textiles carry or cover sacred objects, wrap or drape deities, decorate religious spaces or as prayer mats. Depending on the context, ceremonial textiles range from richly adorned silks or velvets to simple cloths that reflect austerity and humility.

18. Tibetan Prayer Flags, Himalayas, Sikkim, India.
    Usually made from rectangular cloth in five basic colours, Tibetan prayer flags are commonly strung along trails and peaks high in the Himalayas. They bless the surroundings and carry prayers to the wind. Their origin is believed to lie in the shamanistic practices of the indigenous Bon people of eastern Tibet.
19. Tibetan Lung Ta, Himalayas, 19th century.
    Block print, c. 45 × 30 cm.
    The Tibetan mythical creature 'lung ta', or 'wind horse', symbolizes the human soul in the shamanistic traditions of East and Central Asia. In Tibetan Buddhism it also represents well-being and good fortune.
20. Lamak nganten, 'wedding' lamak, Galungan festival, Ubud, Bali, Indonesia.
    Woven from palm leaves, Lamak are narrow, elongated mats used to decorated altars, shrines and daily objects, especially during the Balinese-Hindu Galungan festival. Variations in colour and motif reflect the ritual's purpose.
21. Kantha, Bangladesh.
    Made from leftover fabrics, 'kanthas', meaning 'simple stitching', are humble patchwork quilts made by Bengali women. They are often attributed with transformative properties, and kantha embroidery is seen as a meditative ritual.
22. Jizō Statue at Sainen-ji Temple, Kyoto, Japan.
    In Japan, Buddhist rituals help mourn miscarried, stillborn or aborted children. A red cloth scarf or knitted cap is placed on a Jizō statue, a guardian spirit believed to protect their souls and guide them to paradise. Red is thought to ward off evil.
23. Lao Baci Ceremony.
    Baci ceremonies in Laos invoke well-being and protection using white cotton cords tied around the wrists to symbolize connection, spiritual strength and the reunification of a person's protective spirits (khwan).
24. Decorated bulls in Oachira kali festival, Kerala, South India.
    Bulls are adorned with colourful textiles to symbolize strength and honour their role in local warrior traditions.
25. Rambu Solo funeral procession, Tana Toraja region, South Sulawsi.
    Tasked with guiding the soul to the afterlife, women pull metres of red cloth from the deceased's house to the burial site during a Rambu Solo ceremony. Red symbolizes life force and protection.
26. Dhurrie, North India, late 19th-early 20th century.
    Cotton, interlocking tapestry weave, 203 × 234 cm.

ecological time and reconnecting with everything that came before us, rather than fixating on the present or future. I see these textiles as testimonies, as visual metaphors, if you like, for how to live more deeply connected to the world around us.

CHRISTEL — Your *Tampan Tulip* series has received much praise but could also raise questions about whether you appropriated the visual language of a people who no longer exist and therefore cannot defend their cultural heritage. How would you respond to that?

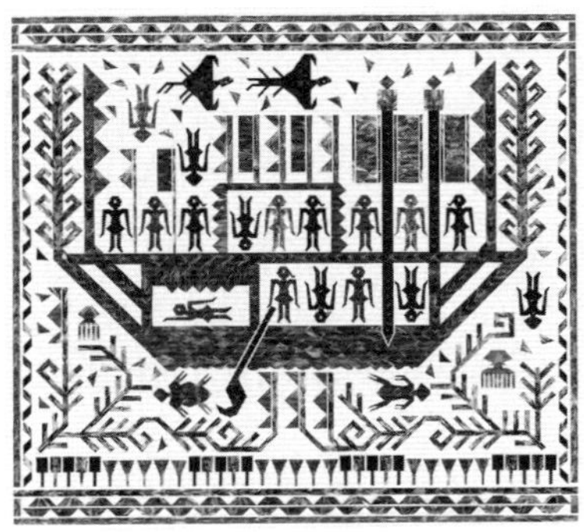

Tampan Ship of Souls #2, Jennifer Tee, 2020.

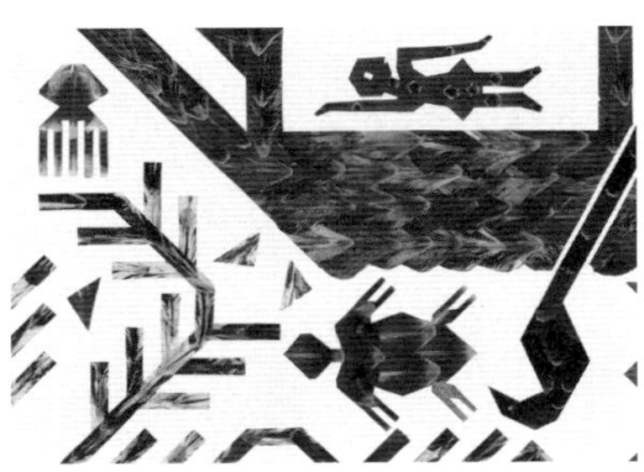

Detail, Tampan Ship of Souls #2, 2020.

JENNIFER — It's important to acknowledge the complex histories of the tampan. For me, using the motifs is not about ownership but about exploring their layered cultural connections, listening to what they might say to us today. In *Tampan Tulip*, I'm not trying to revive or re-enact the tradition. I'm engaging with its echoes — the traces it left behind — and merging them with materials from my immediate environment: tulip petals. It's about how culture transforms, migrates, and is remembered or embodied differently across time and place.

I see my work as an act of care, transformation and honouring. But I also recognize there's always tension when working with a heritage that isn't directly mine. That tension is part of the work: it raises questions about belonging, hybridity and cultural survival.

CHRISTEL — Zooming out and looking at some of your other works and performances, in which natural materials, bodily movement and presence in the moment play a key role, I wondered if you see echoes of the rituals and cosmological beliefs surrounding the tampan and palepai? I'm thinking, for instance of the performances in your 2023 exhibition 'Still Shifting, Mother Field', which featured a large series of *Tampan Tulip* as well as choreographed movement, objects and symbolic attributes.

JENNIFER — Yes, absolutely. For me, the tampan and palepai are not merely aesthetic or ethnographic objects; they carry cosmological meanings about life, death, the sea, and travel between these realms. In 'Still Shifting, Mother Field', the performances and choreographies created a space where body, spirit and material converged — a kind of ritual field where presence and movement can invoke other ways of knowing and being.

Using natural materials like tulip petals, clay or woven forms is also part of this approach: they embody their own temporalities and energies. I'm interested in how rituals structure life and connect the mundane with the cosmic, the visible and the invisible. My works don't re-enact specific indigenous rituals, but they aim to open a space where different cosmologies, gestures of care and embodied knowledge coexist. It's a way of honouring the deeper currents that move through objects like the tampan and palepai, while placing them in a new field of relations, in the here and now.

Some patterns and motifs are universal. Their form may be shaped by the society, religion or politics of a given period. Yet as archetypes they drift across time, surviving well into the present day. The ship motif is one such archetype. A symbol of voyage and passage between two worlds, it appears in prehistoric cave drawings, ancient Egyptian mythology, Christian iconography and in the eighteenth and nineteenth century Lampung ceremonial ship cloths that are the inspiration for Jennifer Tee's series of weavings that are featured here.

The recurring appearance of the ship motif at markedly different junctures, hints at a shared cosmological imagery — one that conveys movement and transition as well as ancestral connection and belonging as part of a universal language. In Lampung culture, ship cloths accompanied individuals during rites of passage. Yet, as Nico de Jonge notes in this book, the textiles themselves also witnessed a succession of passing cultural influences — each leaving its trace and turning these ceremonial cloths into an intercultural amalgam, born of centuries of migration. In her *Tampan* series, Tee carries the ship motif into the present as a universal symbol of transition, migration and, at our own time, perilous boat crossings in which thousands seek safer futures, many never reaching their destination. Yet her work also grounds the imagery in its ritual context, thereby threading ancestral wisdom into the fabric of our present lives.

If a textile's warp and weft are often likened to the inner workings of history — the warp representing the underlying structures that sustain it, and the weft infusing it with the distinctive colours and textures of a specific time and place — then the layered structure of Tee's jacquard weavings may be understood as a thought–form too: as a metaphor for apprehending the presence of deep time.

On the reverse side of the weavings, an accumulation of coloured threads drifts alongside the composition on the front. Each thread emerges only intermittently, depending on its momentum and position within the larger design. Hidden from view yet always present, this deep reservoir of dormant threads that surface only occasionally, represents 'deep time' as a woven archive in which layers of memory and meaning lie interlaced.

The idea of an all-encompassing weave (binding human and non-human, past and present, the material and the spiritual) resonates with the cosmological knowledge Tee encounters in the imagery of the historical *tampan* and *palepai*. Interestingly, this idea has been part of textiles' spiritual function from the beginning of time. Many cultural traditions understand textiles not simply as material objects but as carriers of spiritual meaning; its threads mediate contact between gods, ancestors and worshippers.

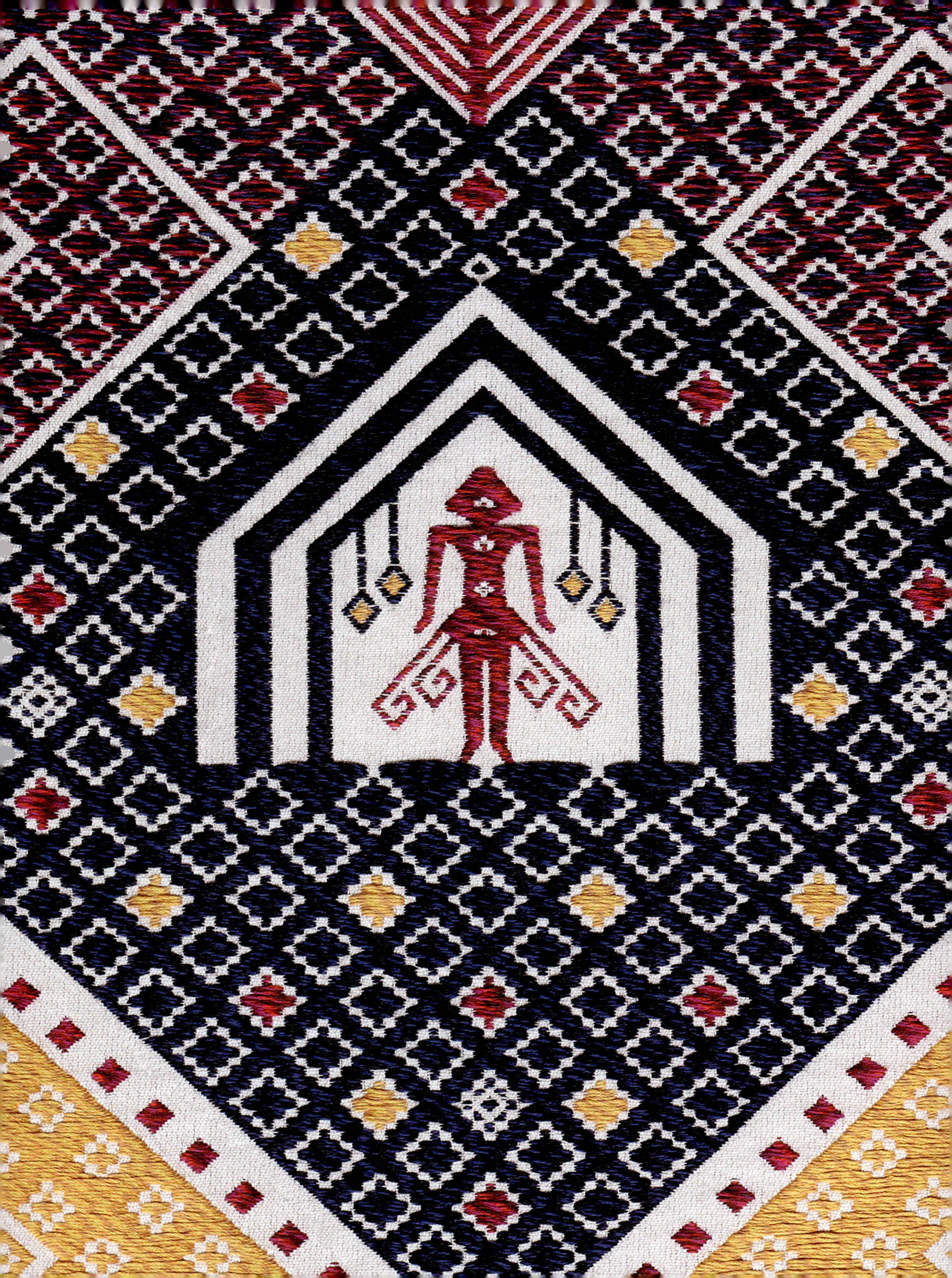

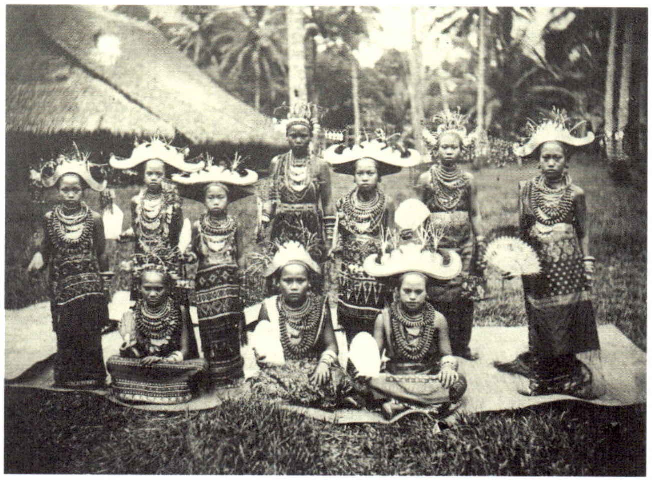

Young Lampung women from Cunungsugih-Besar, photo by C.B. Nieuwenhuis, c. 1900. Print on cardboard, 10.6 × 13.9 cm.

The young women of marriageable age wear ceremonial dress, including the 'siger', a headdress made of gold leaf, symbolizing female fertility.

The iconography of the ship cloth from Lampung has fascinated Western researchers and collectors since the early twentieth century — their gaze almost exclusively directed at the ship motif, commonly interpreted as a 'ship of death'. However, as Nico de Jonge, an expert on Indonesian art and culture, argues in this essay, such a partial interpretation leaves many other elements unexplained. By examining the function of the ship cloth within its original context, De Jonge reconnects its symbolic imagery to Lampung's ancient societal structure — including reverence for ancestors and earth spirits — and combines this with a close reading of the subsequent cultural influences that shaped Lampung society over time.

The Lampung province in southern Sumatra is known today as one of the most densely populated and poorest parts of Indonesia — a dramatic contrast to its recent past. Travellers who visited the region in the nineteenth century, for example, were often awestruck by the impressive display of wealth. It is no coincidence that during this period the inhabitants of the region, also called Lampung, were known for their 'persistent vanity and ostentation'.[1, 2]

# LAMPUNG SHIP CLOTHS
## Ancient Symbolism and Cultural Adaptation

Nico de Jonge

Lampung's former wealth was closely linked to the lucrative trade in pepper.[3] Large shipments of pepper grown in South Sumatra would enter the world market through Bantam (now known as Banten) — which was a centre of commerce on Java. However, when this trade market collapsed, Lampung was plunged into poverty.[4] This downturn in fortune was exacerbated by the 1883 eruption of the Krakatoa volcano, which caused a colossal tsunami that ravaged coastal villages, claiming thousands of lives. The downturn continued into the twentieth century, and worsened after the Lampung area was designated as the primary immigration destination for poor migrants coming from overpopulated Java.[5]

Today, Lampung objects in museum collections, including the renowned ship cloths, testify to the former exceptional wealth of the region. They also demonstrate the unique syncretic nature of Lampung's material culture. Like few other Indonesian ethnic groups, Lampung culture offers an almost complete reflection of the long history of the archipelago. All major religious and cultural traditions that reached Indonesia over the past 4,000 years left their traces in Lampung society, and by the nineteenth century, the intermingling of these different cultural influences had infiltrated all aspects of social and cultural life.

1. The original version of this essay appeared in Reimar Schefold and Steven G. Alpert, eds, *Eyes of the Ancestors: The Arts of Island Southeast Asia at the Dallas Museum of Art* (2013).
2. English biologist Henry Forbes gave an apt account of this in his writings of 1880 upon encountering splendidly adorned young girls in some villages: 'Every girl is arrayed in sinkels or necklets, of various shapes of heavy silver, few or many, according to the wealth or position of her parents; on their arms rows and rows of bracelets, and in their ears large buttonlike earrings.' See Henry O. Forbes, *A Naturalist's Wanderings in the Eastern Archipelago* (1885), p. 127.
3. From the 9th century, pepper — originally an Indian commodity — became a cash crop in Java. From the 15th to the 19th century, pepper was also grown in Lampung, Palembang, Bengkulu and Jambi, and developed into a major export from Sumatra.
4. According to Friedrich Funke, the global pepper market collapsed around 1870; as a result, many Lampung pepper gardens gradually became overgrown. See Friedrich W. Funke, *Orang Abung. Volkstum Süd-Sumatras im Wandel. Band II—Das Leben in der Gegenwart* (1961).
5. Due to the arrival of Javanese migrants, only one in ten inhabitants of Lampung province is a descendant of the indigenous population, see Roelof Broersma, *De Lampongsche Districten* (1916), pp. 228-245.

## LAMPUNG ORIGINS

The term Lampung refers to three ethnic groups living on the peninsula: the Abung in the northern highlands, the Pubian in the centre and the Paminggir along the southern coast. The three groups considered themselves related, sharing the same mythical founding father, Si Lampung. Their communities were organized in patrilineal groups, known as *suku*. Four or more of these suku constitute a so-called *marga*.[6]

As with all Indonesian peoples, the foundations of Lampung culture were laid in the late Stone Age, when Austronesian-speaking groups spread across the archipelago. Ancestor worship can be linked to these ancient roots, as can the practice of headhunting and ideas about cosmology. The tradition of the Dong Son culture subsequently developed on Sumatra in the Bronze and Iron Ages.[7] A more complex organization of labour led to a more hierarchical society, in which the pursuit of higher social status — often initiated through elaborate feasts of merit — became a hallmark of Lampung culture.

Presumably not long after the start of the Common Era, Indian merchants brought Hinduism and Buddhism to Sumatra. As early as the seventh century, Sumatra was already a key player in the trade between India and China.[8] Historical sources reveal that from the middle of the seventh century onward, South Sumatra (including Lampung) was part of the Buddhist kingdom of Srivijaya.[9] In the mid-thirteenth century, Arabian tradesmen introduced Islam. When the power of Srivijaya's kingdom weakened, and in 1550 the local ruler of West Javan Bantam converted to Islam — henceforth known as the Sultan — the 'new' religion slowly spread via the coastal regions across South Sumatra. With the arrival of Europeans in the archipelago in the sixteenth century, the Lampung were confronted with Christian ideology and a Western way of life.

In the nineteenth century, cross-cultural interactions were present in nearly all aspects of daily life within the tiny village communities. Both Lampung's art and its cultural traditions reflect these cultural exchanges to a considerable extent. To better understand the unique character of this 'amalgamation', we will take a closer look at two important pillars in Lampung society: the ascension of the papadon and marriage. As will be shown below, a close study of these two interrelated ceremonies will help us to better understand the function of the renowned ship cloths and the symbolic meaning of their designs.

## CULTURAL INFLUENCES

Receptiveness to foreign influences is generally considered one of the characteristic traits of Indonesian cultures: the new is never shut out, but invited in. Over time new influences continued to infuse old traditions, yet the underlying cultural concepts remained virtually unchanged.[10] Prehistoric Lampung traditions, as we will see, became enmeshed, for instance, with elements from Hindu-Buddhism and Islam. Of significance here is the great difference between the inland and coastal regions: the influence of Islam remained limited to the Paminggir who lived on the coast, whereas the inland-lying marga of the Pubian and the mountain marga of the Abung remained unaffected during that entire period.[11]

It is very clear that the veneration of ancestors and earth spirits, both essential strands of Lampung's Austronesian inheritance, was still at the centre of Lampung life in the nineteenth century. Even though elements of Hindu-Buddhism and Islam had been incorporated into the religion, Lampung ancestors and spirits connected to nature continued to organize daily life. The adoption of these new religions appears to have been largely a matter of applying new names to old ideas. For instance, among the Lampung, the only known creation myth deals with the origin of the island of Sumatra and Si Lampung, the collectively worshipped founding father. The entire story glorifies the worship of ancestors, fully in accordance with prehistoric traditions. With the arrival of Hindu-Buddhist cosmology, Si Lampung, the creator of all earthly things, was given the Sanskrit name *dewa*, applying a thin Hindu-Buddhist veneer while keeping its traditional character.[12] In a similar way, Islam was incorporated into the veneration of earth spirits. In the Austronesian tradition, the natural environment was often associated with spirits who asserted themselves as the true owners of the land and acted as sources of fertility. In the coastal regions, these ancient spirits were referred to by the Arabic term *jin*.[13]

## ASCENDING THE PAPADON

Nineteenth century Lampung life mainly revolved around attaining as high a social status as possible. All other matters were set aside in favour of this struggle for prestige, which, for the most successful men, culminated in the ascension to the papadon, an ancient seat of honour that represented power, dignity and prestige. Each rung of the social ladder had its own titles and privileges.[14] For example, as the status of a man became elevated, so did the bride price he could ask for the hand of his daughter: a 'value' that would be amply visible in the quantity of jewellery she would wear.[15] Every Lampung male hoped to experience the ascending of the papadon at least once in his life (despite the enormous costs), which, as we will see later, was closely linked with that other pillar of Lampung culture: marriage.

The papadon itself, the throne that represented ultimate prestige, had a long and complex history. The traditional stone version of the chair, the papadon batus, had prehistoric roots. As with other important ceremonial objects, its appearance changed frequently due to the dominant cultural influences of the time. However, its essence — as a seat of dignity — and the ancient cultural concepts it embodied were preserved. Notable adaptations concerned its physical structure and the symbolism of its decorative motifs.

Here, too, the most obvious modifications occurred in the coastal regions where the papadon was made of wood, a material that was more suited to adornment and stylistic change than the stone versions that persisted among the mountain people.[16] In the early years of contact with Islam, coastal papadon chairs began to include wooden backrests (*sesako*) with meticulously copied floral patterns in Javanese court style modelled on the state thrones that were then in vogue at the court of Bantam.[17] In the nineteenth century, Western influences also started to appear on coastal papadon, including theriomorphic legs featuring dramatic animal claws, which were almost certainly based on seventeenth and eighteenth century European chairs. Each time, a design associated with power and prestige was adopted, aligning the dignity of the papadon with these external and foreign symbols of glory.[18]

## ANIMAL SYMBOLISM

The use of animal motifs, however, was not new in Lampung culture. Older papadon frequently had legs in the shape of animal feet, for example an elephant's foot, or featured decorative carvings of animal motifs — symbolic elements that almost certainly expressed the original function of the honorary seat: the elevation in status of the man ascending the papadon.[19] What did these animals symbolize? And how did their appearance and symbolic meaning change over time? Indigenous species — such as the water buffalo, hornbill and elephant — are seen most frequently on the papadon and on other cultural artefacts. Although their appearance may vary per region, they seem to be part of a type of animal symbolism deeply rooted in Lampung culture, which probably had its origins in the tradition of headhunting.

Several researchers have shown that the ascent to the papadon was traditionally a rite of passage for young men. Before a man was allowed to sit on the papadon, he had to sever one or more heads. A young man acquired social prestige through killing, making him eligible for marriage. At the end of the seventeenth century, headhunting had already fallen into disuse in the coastal areas, but in the nineteenth century there were still reminders of this ancient custom, including a mock fight in the square in front of the *sesat*, the village community centre.[20, 21] The animal symbolism displayed on the honorary seat also served to express the prestige that had been acquired through violence. Each of the three endemic animal motifs can be linked to this practice. In South Sumatra (as in other parts of Indonesia), the elephant was known as the mount of a great warrior.[22] Some of the prehistoric megalithic monuments found in the area confirm this.[23] The hornbill was also widely associated with headhunting as well. An old report about headhunts among the Abung compares their tradition to that of the Dayak from Borneo where the hornbill was the preeminent symbol of headhunting.[24] Finally, water buffalo horns functioned as traditional trophies in Lampung culture. Until well into the nineteenth century, for example, they would be attached to the roof of the sesat in order to promote the prestige of a village.[25]

As time went on, the mythical garuda and naga must have been added to this indigenous trio, most

6. J.H. Hissink, 'Het pepadonwezen en zijne attributen...' (1904), pp. 75-76, 95.
7. Named after an excavated settlement in what is now northern Vietnam, the Dong Son culture represented an important prehistoric tradition in Indochina. Dong Son culture was widespread throughout South-East Asia.
8. Véronique Degroot et al eds, 'Early History and Archaeology of Sumatra: An Overview' (2009).
9. Ibid.
10. Reimar Schefold, et al, *Indonesia in Focus: Ancient Traditions—Modern Times* (1988).
11. C.H.M. Palm, *De Cultuur en Kunst van de Lampung, Sumatra* (1965), p. 42; Nico de Jonge et al, *Shipcloths of the Lampung, South Sumatra* (1980), p. 15.
12. The creation myth was published by J.A. du Bois in 'De Lampongsche Districten op het eiland Sumatra' (1852), pp. 330-332. In the religious and sacrificial customs, there was also a strong focus on worship of ancestors. Their graves were regularly visited, and offerings were made, especially at the grave of the founder of a marga. See, for example, Palm, *Cultuur en Kunst*, p. 62; Hissink, 'Het pepadonwezen', p. 76 and De Jonge, *Schipcloths*, pp. 27-28.
13. Oscar L. Helfrich, 'Bijdragen tot geografische, geologische en ethnographische kennis der afdeeling Kroé' (1889), p. 541.
14. For titles, see Funke, *Orang Abung, Band I*, pp. 218-219 and Broersma, *De Lampongsche Districten*, p. 43.
15. The status of *papadon marga* allowed the marriageable girl (*muli*) to wear twelve bracelets, the status of *papadon tiyuh* permitted six to eight, while the status of *papadon suku* allowed two to three bracelets, see Hissink, 'Het pepadonwezen', pp. 105-108.
16. See Funke, *Orang Abung, Band I*, pp. 86-90; *Orang Abung, Band II*, pp. 315-321; Abraham N. van der Hoop, et al, 'De Megalitische hoofdenzetel oorsprong van den Lampongschen Pepadon?' (1940), pp. 60-77 and Palm, 'Cultuur en Kunst', pp. 40-80.
17. A common misunderstanding concerns the origin of the Lampung papadon complex. Some authors have wrongly assumed it was copied from Banten. See, for example, J.A. Aeckerlin, 'De pangkat papadon in de Lampongsche Districten' (1894), pp. 1532-1542; Hissink, 'Het pepadonwezen', p. 91. In fact, the seats of honour derive from the same ancient megalithic custom practised both in Lampung and in Banten. An illustrative example is the design of one of the last *papadon* seats ever made, after the Second World War in the Abung area: its legs are carved in the shape of soldiers' boots. See Funke, *Orang Abung*, vol. II, image opposite p. 325.
18. Another illustrative example is the design of one of the last papadon seats ever made (after World War II in the Abung area): the legs of this 'throne' are shaped like soldier's boots, see Funke, *Orang Abung, Band II*, image opposite p. 325.
19. Ibid. p. 319 and image opposite p. 325 for a papadon seat with elephant's legs; for images of a sesako decorated with animal figures, see Palm, 'Cultuur en Kunst', p. 54; Funke, *Orang Abung, Band II*, opposite p. 317 and Robyn Maxwell, *Textiles of Southeast Asia: Tradition, Trade and Transformation* (2003).
20. Palm, 'Cultuur en Kunst', p. 62; Funke, *Orang Abung, Band I*, pp. 59-78.
21. Funke, *Orang Abung, Band II*, pp. 323-326.
22. See Frederic M. Schnitger et al, *Forgotten Kingdoms in Sumatra* (1939), pp. 190-191, 201-202, who refers to the role of the elephant among the Dayak on Kalimantan and among the Batak and Lampung on Sumatra.
23. Ibid. p. 202 and plate 36.
24. Cornets de Groot, as cited in Funke, *Orang Abung, Band I*, p. 61.
25. Helfrich, *Bijdragen*, p. 609. The number of slaughtered water buffalo was a key marker of the organiser's social status. Ascension to the highest *papadon* seat required the sacrifice of thirty buffalo, often exhausting one's livestock. See Hissink, 'Het pepadonwezen', pp. 100-102.

probably during the era of Hindu-Buddhist influences or even before. The mythical bird garuda, mount of the Hindu deity Vishnu, is originally from India, and the dragon-like serpent with a crowned head, commonly known as naga is a revered creature in China, with complex symbolic associations, including fertility. Exactly why these foreign mythical animals became important in Lampung culture is difficult to determine. An important reason may very well have been their frequent presence as decorative patterns on trade items exported to Sumatra.[26] Moreover, the garuda bird could naturally be associated with the indigenous hornbill, which was already a popular symbol. The same assimilation seems to have occurred with the peacock. As they were incorporated into Lampung symbolism, however, both creatures lost their original meanings and gained new ones. It is important to bear this in mind when we take a closer look at that other preeminent art form of Lampung, the so-called ship cloths.

## SHIP CLOTHS

Extravagantly decorated ship cloths from Lampung have been of great interest to the outside world since the early twentieth century, but many of their images and motifs remain a mystery. Their designs appear to be a true melting pot of Asian traditions. Along with indigenous Lampung patterns, such as ancestral houses, known as *rumah poyang*, we see Javanese wayang-style motifs, Chinese-style dragons and birds, and Hindu-Buddhist elements such as the previously mentioned garuda. The ship features as a dominant motif on nearly all cloths, which are named after it. As is the case with many traditional Lampung art forms, the production of ship cloths came to a standstill at the end of the nineteenth century, after which the fabrics gradually disappeared from society. In time, the complex techniques used also faded into obscurity.[27]

Despite their similarities, the character of these cloths varies. Based on shape and use, they are commonly divided into two categories: *tampan* and *palepai*. Tampan cloths are square and tend to be relatively small in size — their sides rarely exceed ninety centimetres in length. Palepai have a more elongated shape, usually about three metres long, with an average width of around fifty centimetres.

Decorative and symbolic motifs also vary considerably. In contrast to tampan, which are usually adorned with very delicate and in some cases abstract patterns, palepai feature rather robust, clearly recognizable subjects. The figurative language of the ancient Dong Son culture can be recognized in the decoration of both types of cloth, notably in the filling of the entire cloth with images, a tendency toward symmetry, and the decorations of the outer edges with stylized double spirals, meanders, and hook and key patterns.[28] At the same time, regional differences in style between tampan and palepai can be distinguished. Tampan produced in the coastal regions, so-called tampan pasisir, often feature maritime themes.[29]

Paminggir women living in the coastal regions were known to produce both tampan and palepai, whereas Pubian and Abung women living in the inland and the mountain regions, only made tampan. In addition to these two major categories, other types of ship cloths are known to have existed in the southern coastal regions too, such as the rare tatibin, which appears to have been a scaled-down version of palepai, and the unique and valuable tampan maju, ship cloths known for their beautiful beadwork and shells. Besides these fabrics, the Lampung created woven mats (*lampit*) and embroidered sarongs (*tapis*) embellished with many decorative patterns akin to those on the ship cloths.

Since the early twentieth century, tampan and palepai iconography has fascinated researchers and collectors. Unsurprisingly, their attention mostly focused on the meaning of the predominant ship motif. Early on it was observed that the cloths were used during Lampung death rituals. Therefore, the ships were initially viewed as ships for the soul.[30] Later, when it was discovered that the textiles were related to all life-cycle rites, the motif was seen as symbolizing transition and movement. However, the rather general nature of this interpretation has always been somewhat problematic. Furthermore, many other motifs such as the numerous animals depicted aboard the ships, were left unexplained. Very significant in this respect is the fact that the animal motifs have scarcely been investigated for their indigenous meaning but repeatedly identified as religious symbols stemming from a Hindu-Javanese tradition. Other kinds of meaning expressing concepts specific to Lampung have apparently never been considered. Moreover, little thought seems to have been given to the most relevant and most deeply rooted pillar of Lampung culture: its boat symbolism.

## LAMPUNG BOAT SYMBOLISM

A major reason for this oversight seems to have been a lack of appropriate sources, although it has long been recognized that boat symbolism is an important concept in Lampung society. Despite these gaps, a partial reconstruction is possible, aided by recent studies on boat symbolism in other parts of Indonesia.[31] Although it may manifest differently in each area, generally, the symbolism ultimately refers to the sexual union of a man and a woman. In this way a family — or, in the case of the first ancestors, even an entire society — could 'set sail and catch wind'.

In Indonesia, traditional boat symbolism was predominantly found in areas where Hindu-Buddhism, Islam and Christianity had not yet arrived or had arrived relatively late, as was the case in the Moluccas. On many of the smaller islands situated east of Timor, this symbolism has been well documented, and it consistently appears to have functioned in two ways.[32] Most significant is the ship's function as a model of society. Houses and villages were often portrayed as boats, with their inhabitants the symbolic crewmen. A more 'hidden' form of nautical symbolism referring to the creation of society underlay this; this symbolism represented the marriage of the first ancestors. In rituals, their wedding was repeated through the metaphorical 'boat of matrimony' setting sail.

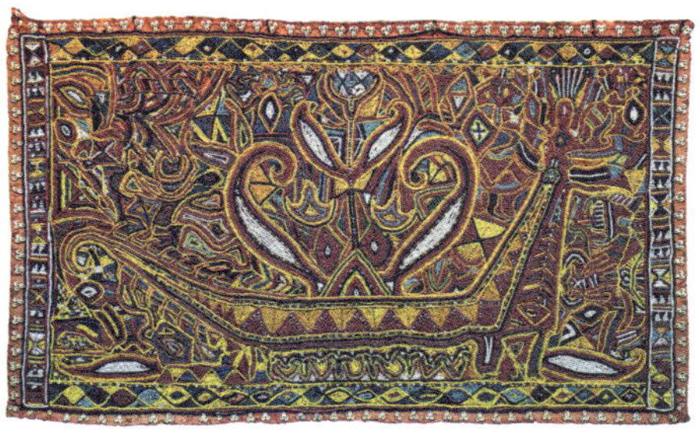

Beaded 'tampan maju', Lampung, Sumatra, before 1878. Cotton, beads, shells, rattan, 103 × 60 cm.

This rare and valuable Lampung tampan maju depicts a symbolic matrimonial boat, 'maju' meaning 'married woman'.

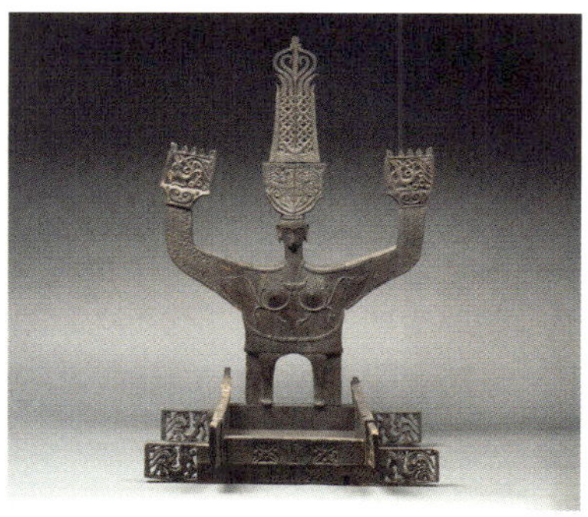

Wood-carved 'Luli' sculpture from Leti Island, South-East Moluccas, 17th–19th century. Wood, 103.7 × 70.4 × 72.6 cm.

The arms are shaped like ships, with animal figures on the hands representing symbolic prows, while the ancestress herself rises from the boat like a tree, evoking vegetation.

In this metaphor, the woman was regarded as a boat, lying on the beach, waiting for a man who wanted to go sailing. Only when the man — the helmsman or captain — boarded the boat could it set sail; that is, only then could society come into being. All subsequent marriages were regarded as a re-enactment of this primordial marriage and made use of similar symbolism.

There are many ways in which the image of the boat of matrimony figures in material culture, pointing to its omnipresence and significance. For example, the association between a woman and a boat was marvellously conveyed in Southeast Moluccan ancestor statues called *luli* (meaning holy) particularly in the position of the arms. As a result of Christian influences, these forms of art unfortunately disappeared. Likewise, this symbolism is superbly evident in the decorations of ships themselves. Splendidly adorned prows and sterns often show aggressive animal figures such as snakes, roosters and hunting dogs. These creatures were more than mere decoration; they were part of a physical construction in which the bond between man and woman — or, in other words, the founding of the family — was portrayed. Although there were considerable regional variations, one part of the boat construction was marked as a feminine 'hull' or 'keel', whereas other parts — usually the prow or stern — were marked as a masculine 'captain' or 'helmsman'. The union of these parts brought the family together in the same way that a real boat can sail because of an assembly of components.

At the same time, these references showed the traditional division of tasks in society. The female parts of the boat were associated with a vagina or uterus and suggested that giving birth to and caring for children were typically female responsibilities, while the male prow and stern showed that protecting the family and its reputation, especially by way of warfare, was viewed as a male domain. By attaching symbols to these male parts — usually the animal figures mentioned above — the groom was portrayed as a great head-hunter, famed for his capacity to kill.

Ongoing studies suggest that this form of boat symbolism was not restricted to eastern Indonesia but was in fact widespread, most likely encompassing islands in the western regions as well, such as Bali, Madura and Java. This research also shows that we are dealing with a prehistoric tradition that must have existed on the islands before they acquired their current Hindu (Bali) and Islamic (Madura and Java) identities.[33]

Everything seems to indicate that South Sumatra must have embraced this type of boat symbolism as well. The boat served as a structuring principle for houses and ceremonial processions.[34] Nautical imagery and boat symbolism also played an important role in nineteenth century love songs from Lampung. According to linguists, sentences such as 'the vessel will not sail unless you are the captain' signified an implicit marriage proposal.[35] This, together with other examples, can lead us to conclude that the association of nautical symbolism with romantic love was deeply rooted in Lampung culture.[36]

26. See, for example, Ekowati Sundari, 'Trade Ceramics from Sumatra in the Collection of the National Museum (Jakarta)' (2009), pp. 100-101.
27. Tampan and palepai were woven using the same technique: single-coloured supplementary wefts applied to a plain weave cotton foundation. The most labour-intensive and time-consuming job was counting out the threads needed for the intricate patterns, before mounting them on the back tension loom. See De Jonge et al, *Shipcloths*, p. 32.
28. Ibid. pp. 14-15.
29. A distinction is made between inland tampan (*tampan darat*) and coastal tampan (*tampan pasisir*), the latter often showing maritime details and West Javanese influence. See Robert Holmgren et al, *Early Indonesian Textiles from Three Cultures: Sumba Toraja Lampung* (1989), plates 30, 32. Tampan darat designs also show clear affinities with textiles of T'ai-speaking peoples on the Southeast Asian mainland. See Mattiebelle Gittinger, 'A Reassessment of the Tampan of South Sumatra' (1989), pp. 225-239.
30. See, for example, Alfred Steinmann, 'Enkele opmerkingen aangaande de z.g. scheepjesdoeken van Zuidsumatra' (1939), pp. 252-256.
31. For more recent studies on boot symbolism, see for example, Nico de Jonge et al, *Forgotten Islands of Indonesia — The Art and Culture of the Southeast Moluccas* (1995); *Outrigger Canoes of Bali and Madura, Indonesia* (1987) and *A Summary of Indonesian Canoe and Prahu Ceremonies* (1986), both by Adrian Horridge.
32. De Jonge et al, *Forgotten Islands*; De Jonge, *Religious Art*.
33. See Horridge, *Outrigger Canoes* and *Summary*.
34. Mattiebelle Gittinger, 'The Ship Textiles of South Sumatra: Functions and Design System' (1976), p. 219.
35. Van der Tuuk, as cited in Broersma *De Lampongsche Districten*, p. 110.
36. To our knowledge, no concrete information on Lampung boatbuilding has been recorded, and museum models offer little insight. Despite claims to the contrary, Lampung society lacked a strong maritime tradition: its people were primarily pepper farmers, and boats were used chiefly for river transport to the coast.

## FERTILITY AND STATUS

The tampan and palepai played a role in practically all rites of passage. The tampan were often used as sitting rugs for the initiate(s), often in combination with decorated mats. The palepai, on the other hand, were usually hung on a wall inside the house where the ritual was performed. The textiles were connected in an intrinsic way to the two rituals we have already discussed: the celebration of marriage and the papadon ascension. Marriage was all about fertility, while the papadon ascension obviously revolved around prestige; social values that were expressed in the designs of many of the fabrics that appear to have been produced especially for these occasions.

The ornamentation on many tampan cloths relates directly to traditional Lampung marriage. The motifs often refer in a symbolic way to the bride and groom, with a prominent role for nautical love or boat symbolism. An animal (representing the captain or bridegroom) is repeatedly shown in a sailing boat (representing the bride). In many cases, the depiction of a highly stylized hornbill is found, but the peacock, originating from the Asian mainland (China and/or India), also occurs very often. This bird was probably adopted into traditional Lampung animal symbolism in a way similar to the incorporation of the garuda. The peacock feathers and crests that are present in other animal motifs also suggest this.

Fertility is the main theme in the ornamentation of many smaller tampan; their role was mainly limited to weddings, and they were likely part of the bride's dowry.[37, 38] Before the wedding — during the marriage negotiations — substantial amounts of ceremonial gifts or food, wrapped in these tampan, were exchanged between the wife-giving and wife-taking descent groups, the *suku*. During the ritual, the tampan symbolized the bride and her role within the suku that was taking care of progeny.[39] On many islands of the Indonesian archipelago, textiles were associated with new life, because they were produced by women and were made of cotton, which is a product of the earth, the ultimate source of fertility. Likewise, weaponry was widely associated with male pursuits and represented the groom and his duty upholding the group's reputation. In Lampung society, this symbolism could be observed during the wedding ritual in which a spear, with a tampan attached to its shaft, was stuck into the ground next to the bridal couple; in other cases, a yarn reel and a spear would be used.[40]

In many designs, another primary motif besides the boat of matrimony is visible: a tree sprouting from a boat. The motif recalls the tampan maju mentioned above: a boat (the woman) that through the imagery of vegetation is presented as a source of fertility. The significance of the boat/tree motif was also visible in another way in nineteenth century Lampung society. At parties and at their weddings, the marriageable girls from the highest social class traditionally wore ship-like head decorations (called *siger*) made of gold leaf and sporting a floral motif. In this way, siger symbolized female fertility, just like the boat/tree portrayals on the tampan.[41] Although our analyses of the

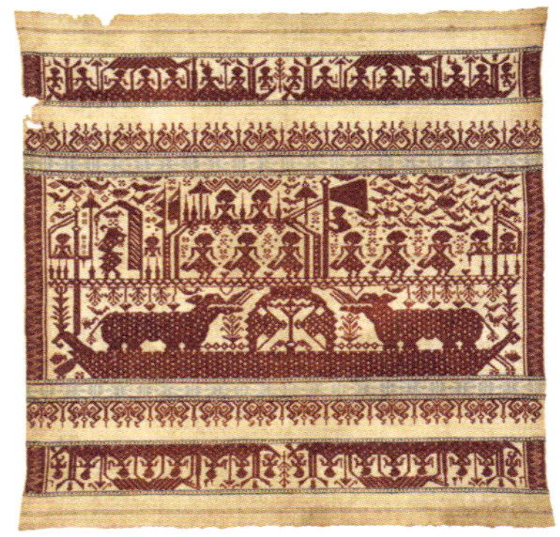

Tampan with water buffalo's, Lampung, Sumatra, c. 1900. Cotton, 72.4 × 71.1 cm.

This tampan probably depicts a wedding party. The ship with animal theme usually refers symbolically to the bride and groom. The overall design celebrates the beginning of new life within Lampung society.

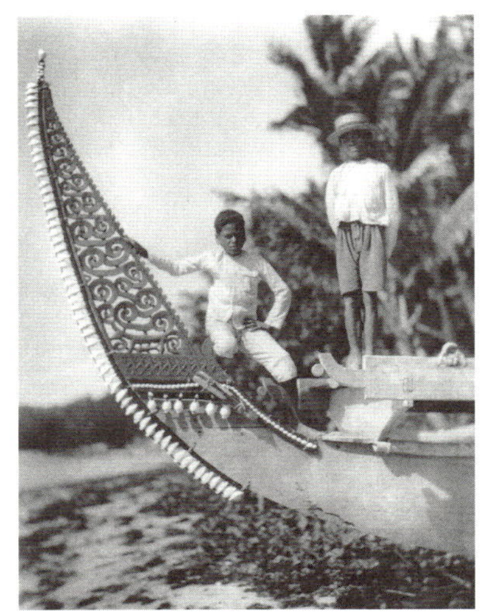

Children on the prow of a Tanimbar boat, South-East Moluccas, c. 1930. Photo by missionary Petrus Drabbe.

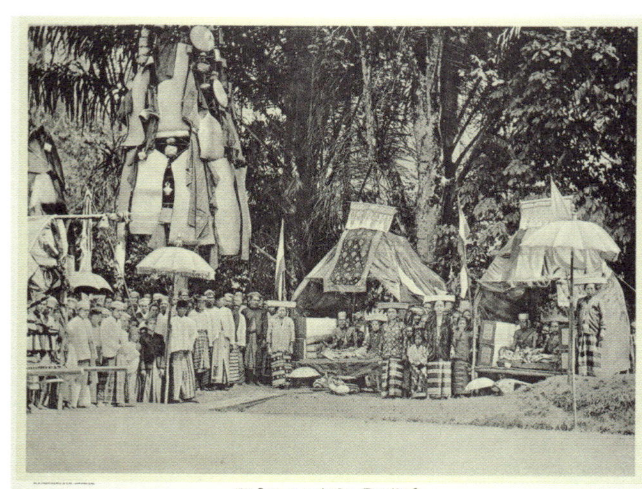


Lampung two-couple wedding, Abung region, late 19th century. Photo – probably by J. Demmeni – published in Eigen Haard (1900), Nr. 44.

Two Abung couples are seated during the 'turun mandi' ritual, which preceded the papadon ascension and the wedding ceremony. To the left stands a 'kayu ara', filled with presents for the groom's family, which included beads, shells, coins, delicacies and textiles originating from the bride's grandparents.

boat of matrimony and the tree/boat combination may leave many designs unexplained, we clearly see what the smaller tampan were all about: fertility. The use of these fabrics for various rites of passage, including birth, circumcision and death stemmed from the bond that two suku had entered through marriage.[42] This relationship was reaffirmed and strengthened on these occasions through the exchange of textiles.

## ADORNING THE THRONE

The palepai of the coastal Paminggir functioned completely differently from the tampan. These textiles, up to three metres (ten feet) in length, did not circulate through the community, but were the exclusive property of the traditional Lampung aristocracy. For them, these cloths were like regalia; owning a palepai played a major part in legitimizing the distinguished position of an aristocratic suku in Lampung society. This was expressed in the motifs on the fabrics: above all else, they had to communicate status.

There are strong indications that a palepai was made especially for a papadon ascension. A highlight of the ritual surrounding this rite of passage was the ride in the stately, ship-like carriage, called *rata*, to the community village centre where the thrones of the suku were kept.[43] The float was part of a larger procession that featured a variety of things: dancing marriageable girls wearing a siger on their heads, musicians, masked clowns, and people waving streamers, carrying umbrellas and other insignia.[44] At the head of the parade were often several women arrayed in the shape of a crescent moon and carrying a narrow band of cloth between them. The cloth was usually a piece of white textile, but according to a credible source, this could just as well be a palepai.[45] White was the colour of the highest Lampung rank, and a palepai was also closely tied to the throne.[46]

Traditionally, the white cloth and palepai seem to have been used for decorating the papadon seat during the ascension ceremony. The textiles were draped around the bottom of the seat, which might well explain their unusually extended shape.[47] With subsequent use in society, a palepai would represent the papadon seat to which the fabric had been ritually connected; as such, the cloth would, as it were, be the literal proof of the papadon ascension.[48]

It goes without saying that status was also the dominant theme in the designs of many palepai.[49] The majority of the cloths seem to portray a ship's deck with realistic, festive scenes. At its centre are two mounted animals facing each other, a symbolic representation of the papadon ascension. Here, elephants and water buffalo appear most frequently. As we have observed, these animals were strongly associated with prestige in traditional Lampung society; this also explains their appearance in the form of decorations on the ancient thrones. However, other symbols unrelated to ritual festivities are often visible on palepai as well, such as stacked buffalo horns attached to a stake. These were obviously included to convey the prestige of a suku through the display of valuable trophies.[50]

37. Based on dominant design elements, it is possible to distinguish between various categories of smaller tampan. In this manner, Gittinger classified all the tampan she investigated into six categories. See Mattiebelle Gittinger, *A Study of the Ship Cloths of South Sumatra: Their Design and Usage* (1972), pp. 95-132.
38. Regarding the dowry, see Gittinger, 'Ship Textiles' (1976), p. 213 and C. op 't Land,' Een merkwaardige 'Tampan pengantar' van Zuid-Sumatra' (1968-1969), p. 114.
39. The association of smaller tampan with fertility would sometimes also be visualized in another phase of the marriage ritual: across a symbolic bridge, composed of several tampan woven together, the bridal couple would walk to a ceremonial bedroom. See picture 165 in Maxwell, *Textiles of Southeast Asia* (2003).
40. Gittinger, 'Ship Textiles', p. 214 and Hissink, 'Het pepadonwezen', p. 144.
41. According to Funke the floral motifs of the siger represented, among other things, flower species and the 'growing waringin' (a kind of Ficus tree), see Funke, *Orang Abung, Band II*, pp. 180-181.
42. Circumcision is relatively new in Lampung culture. It was generally introduced only when Islam became widespread, at the start of the 20th century.
43. Here, and in the following discussion, we refer to the ascension of the *papadon marga*, the highest Lampung rank.
44. See, for example, Hissink, 'Het pepadonwezen', p. 106; and Schnitger, *Forgotten Kingdoms in Sumatra*, pp. 198-199.
45. Regarding the white piece of textile, see Van der Lith et al, *Encyclopaedie van Nederlandsch Indië* (1896-1905). Regarding the palepai, see Schnitger, *Forgotten Kingdoms*, pp. 199, 201. Although this author does not use the term palepai, his description and accompanying illustration (pl. 38.1) imply that such a cloth is meant.
46. The three highest papadon ranks each had its own colour: white belonged to the *papadon marga*, yellow to the *papadon tiyuh*, and reddish brown to the *papadon suku*. See, among others, Hissink, 'Het pepadonwezen', pp. 103-108; see also fig. 45.
47. See Schnitger, *Forgotten Kingdoms*, pp. 198, 201 and Funke, *Orang Abung, Band II*, p. 236. In relation to the papadon seat in Kroé, Schnitger even speaks of a *krosi bulampok*, a chair (placed on a stone) decorated with a cloth (see also Hissink, 'Het pepadonwezen', p. 91, note 2).
48. As noted, palepai were hung on the wall of the house during rites of passage, and sometimes during meetings and festivities as well. They acted as the 'visiting cards' of the various aristocratic suku present at the ceremony. It reflected the internal balance of power between individuals and groups. The representation of the thrones by means of textiles occurred in another 19th century context as well. Funke describes how the palepai, which would formerly have decorated the papadon seats, replaced these seats of honour halfway through the 19th century when the Dutch colonial administration discouraged the very expensive papadon ascensions. Instead of sitting on the wooden thrones, participants would sit on the cloths, and in this way the ancient papadon tradition continued, if less conspicuously. See Funke, *Orang Abung, Band I*, p. 253.
49. The first to note this was the archaeologist and founder and curator of the Palembang Museum of Archeology, Friedrich Martin Schnitger. He also noted that his interpretation did not exclude the increasingly popular views of Steinmann during his time, who designated the ships on the cloths as soul ships. See Schnitger, *Forgotten Kingdoms*, pp. 201-202.
50. See note 25.

How, then, do we interpret the boat motif, associated with fertility, displayed on these cloths? If the palepai are associated primarily with status, then what might the depicted boats imply? The answer may be found in the rata, the ceremonial carriage mentioned earlier, which not only carried the ascender of the papadon, but also his future wife. Commonly the wedding ceremony would take place right after the ritual ascension of the papadon, reaffirming the intrinsic connection between the papadon and the institution of marriage. If the papadon candidate was already married, the original wedding—elaborate ritual clothing included—was simply re-enacted. The reciprocity was expressed clearly in the design and labelling of the rata: shaped like a ceremonial boat on wheels almost always including a stem based on an animal form, it was denoted by the term *perahu papadon* in many regions, meaning 'papadon boat'. Depicted on many palepai, however, it was portrayed frontally, with a specific focus on the symbolism of prestige. To the left and right, rather than the boat's stern and prow, are the wings of the animal making up the 'boat on wheels' (a garuda or hornbill). And between these wings of the rata—on the ship's deck—the papadon ascension can be observed.[51]

Several details inform this interpretation, each of which concerns the spot on the symbolic boat of matrimony where the bridal couple was seated. This was usually a kind of throne, which was covered by a canopy, or baldachin. Rata models in museums show that this chair was adorned as though it were a papadon seat and included animal decorations.[52] Thus, the float clearly suggested how the entire event, including the festive wedding ceremony, was intended to be understood.

A portrayal of the papadon seat of the stately, ship-like carriage seems to be found in the middle of many palepai. A typical feature of various baldachins was their specific shape (slightly bulky and flattened out, with sloping sides), which can be readily recognized in many cloths. Beneath the baldachin, we often notice two animals, each carrying a human figure. These probably represent the bridal couple, who were the central focus. After their arrival in the sesat, both would often mount the actual papadon together. The representations on various palepai carried at the head of the procession would thus reveal to onlookers the essence of what was ceremonially yet to come.

However, it is important to note that this design did not appear only on palepai. A large group of tampan—also made by coastal Paminggir women—was decorated with highly similar designs. The slightly larger examples (with sides sometimes measuring up to three feet in length) are of particular interest; many of them originated from the area surrounding Lampung Bay (particularly Kalianda). Here, these tampan functioned in a similar manner to palepai: owning them was associated with the papadon ascension, and local suku considered these cloths to be part of their regalia.[53] Research suggests that the democratization of the papadon complex, initiated by the sultans of Bantam, most likely played a role in this. The sultans introduced a series of ranks, called *papadon pangkat*, that were purchasable by anyone, and which operated alongside the old aristocratic papadon system, where precise regulations existed regarding which type of cloth belonged to which rank and title. The palepai-like tampan most likely belonged to the common complex.[54]

## CONCLUSION

In the previous paragraphs, I have aimed to demonstrate that the boat motif on ship cloths symbolized more than just movement and transition. Traditional Lampung animal and boat symbolism offers clues leading to new insights. The symbols were combined in a unique way in the stately carriage, or rata. As a part of the joint marriage and papadon ritual, both fertility (the wedding ceremony) and prestige (the papadon ascension) were displayed by means of this float.

This is probably not the last word on the symbolic significance of the ship cloths. Various layers of meaning may once have existed, expressed through cosmic symbols of which we know little. Research in South Sumatra will probably not increase our understanding. Over the course of the nineteenth and twentieth centuries, the papadon system was abolished everywhere as a result of increasing pressure from the Dutch colonial administration; simultaneously Islam expanded tremendously.[55] Today, all Lampung people are Muslim, and there are few reminders of the old symbolic system in which boys were given animal names such as Gajah (elephant) and girls were customarily named after elements of the loom.[56]

51. Interestingly, the composition and style in which the papadon ascensions are depicted on these types of palepai may be derived from West Javanese art forms. Especially striking are the similarities with the *gunungan* used in *wayang* presentations: here, too, centre stage is often reserved for two opposing animals, and wings (as temple decoration) can be found on the sides. In her thesis (1972), Gittinger investigates this subject more thoroughly.
52. See, for example, Palm, 'Cultuur en Kunst', p. 55; Schnitger, *Forgotten Kingdoms*, p. 198 and Funke, *Orang Abung, Band II*, image opposite p. 244.
53. Palm shows an image of a tampan from Wairate (Ratai, Lampung Bay), which formerly belonged to the regalia of the owner of a papadon rank. This cloth was collected by F. Broekmans, who spent many years working as a physician in the Lampung area after World War II. Broekmans was, according to Palm a 'meticulous observer'. See Palm, 'Cultuur en Kunst', pp. 65, 70.
54. Johannes F. Snelleman, 'Nog een merkwaardig weefsel uit de Lampongs' (1910), pp. 75-76. Concerning a red-ship-style palepai originating from Kalianda, Snelleman reports that it was used exclusively by penyimbang marga who bore the titles of *pangeran*, *kria*, *temenggung*, *ngahebi* or *demang*. They would hang the cloths from the wall close to where they were seated during adat meetings, feasts, and marriage and circumcision rituals.
55. As far as we know, the last papadon ascension took place in the early 1950s (with the Abung). For a description see Funke, *Orang Abung, Band II*, pp. 235-59.
56. See Hissink, 'Het pepadonwezen', p. 147.

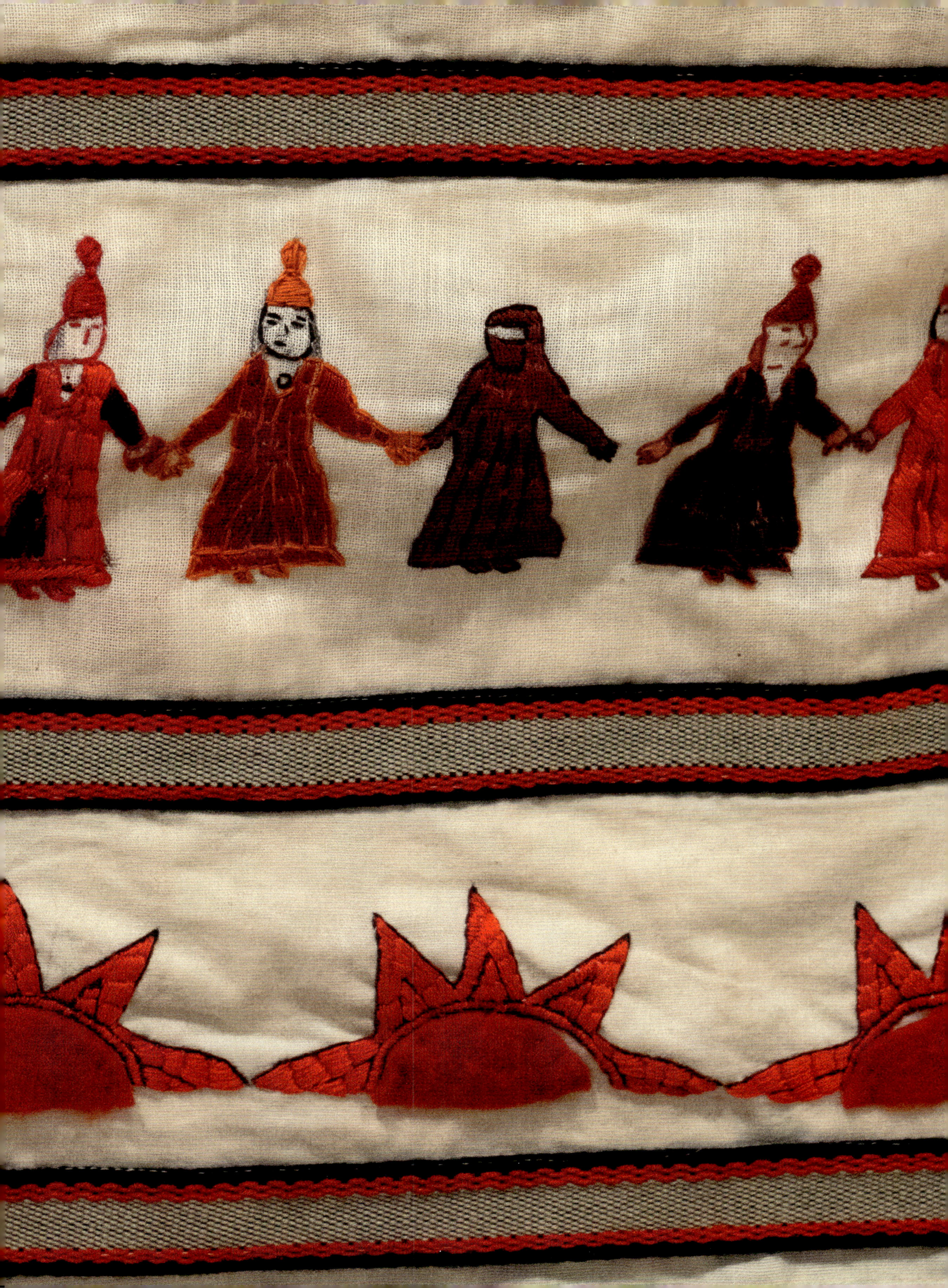

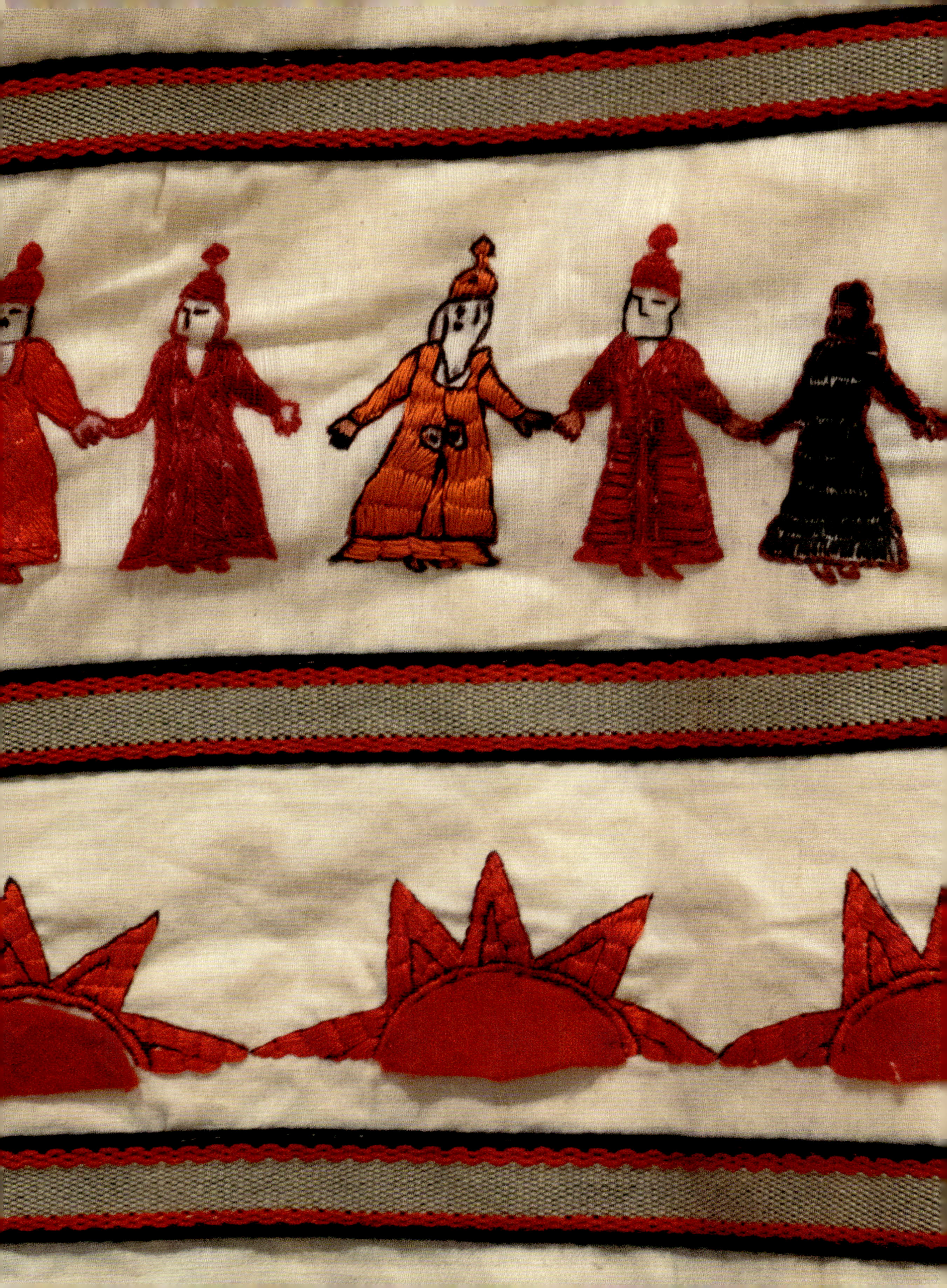

# *Sperveri*
Mounira Al Solh

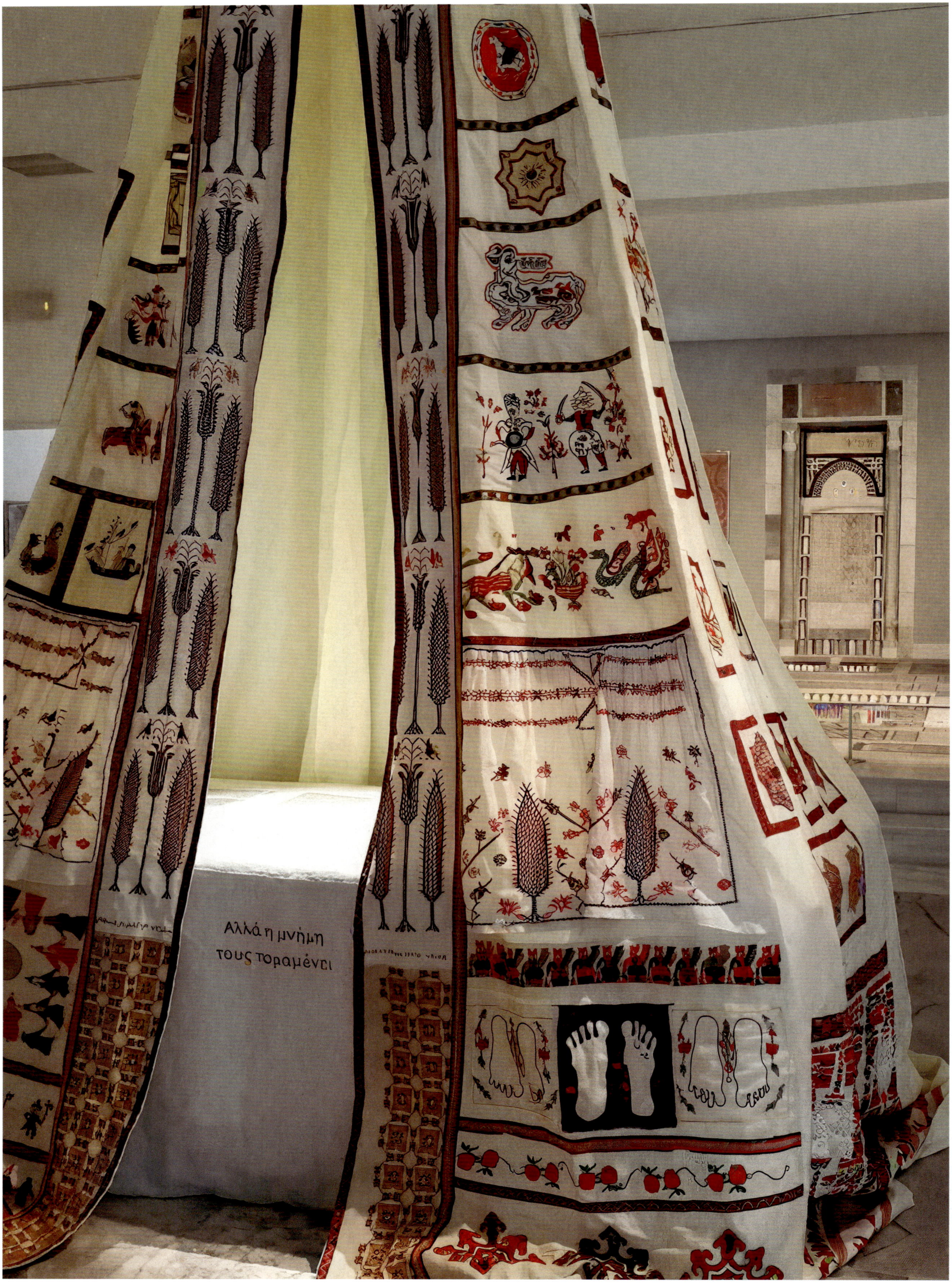
Αλλά η μνήμη
τους τοραμένει

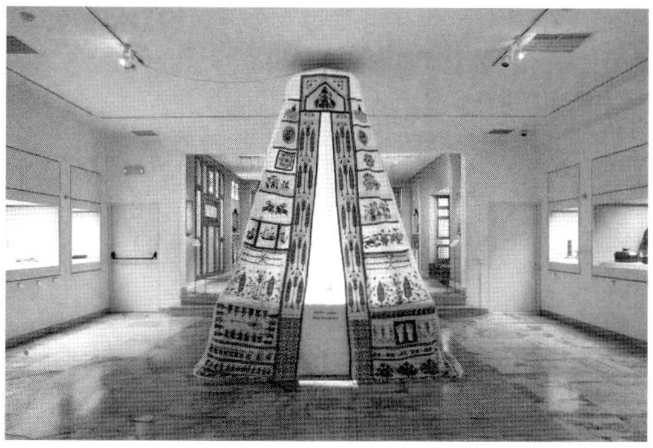

Sperveri (يريفريبس), Mounira Al Solh, 2017.

Polyester, cotton and silk threads, acrylic paint, curcuma and pencil on linen and cotton, various embroidery techniques, including cross-stitch and freestyle filling, 400 × 220 × 110 cm.

Mounira Al Solh's *Sperveri* presents a tent-shaped structure elaborately embroidered with motifs and designs. It is modelled on hand-embroidered bed tents, or *spervéri*, from the Greek island of Rhodes, which were used to cover the marital bed. *Sperveri* measures around 4 metres in height and 10 metres in diameter at the base. The structure is suspended from the ceiling and sits on a plinth, 100 centimetres high and 200 by 100 centimetres in plan — the size of a small bed. The tent is made of a pale yellow linen sewn together with an opening at the front, with multiple embroidered panels on the front and sides, and like the historical bed tents, the back, normally placed against the wall, is left empty.

Similar to the Rhodes bed tent, the embroidery on this contemporary spervéri is executed in reds and greens, with some added yellow, brown and black. There are mermaids, peacocks, people in traditional dress, a ship, a lute, rows of dancing warriors, horses with wings, octagonal stars, flowers, trees and feet. Rich in imagery and laden with symbolic meaning, the heavily embroidered surfaces conjure up an otherworldly realm inhabited by folkloric creatures and tales, triggering our curiosity and inviting close examination.

The embroidery reveals a variety of styles and techniques, including cross-stitch and freestyle filling, with polyester, silk and cotton threads. Pieces of decorated silk and cotton ribbon — the kind that can be found on markets and in haberdashery shops — frame the various panels.

The most lavishly embroidered areas border the opening. Here, two slender cypress trees flank a schematic representation of a flower, with two birds facing each other on top. They are embroidered in a fine cross-stich of dark reds and greens with additional lighter reds and yellow for the birds. The tree-flower-bird motif is repeated vertically on the door panels, which converge at the top in a pediment featuring a dancing female figure flanked by two peacocks. Trees also appear on two horizontal panels, one on each side the opening, surrounded by flowers, branches and birds.

If the embroidered exterior creates a sense of wonder and beauty, the atmosphere inside is sober, even sacrosanct. A bulb hanging from the top casts just enough light to read the roughly ten hand-embroidered texts carefully arranged on the plinth. The 'letters' are in both Arabic and English and signed with initials or a first name, place and date: 'Khaled, Kassel, 22-10-2016', or 'Samira, Tripoli, 2-12-2014'. What connects the stories told in these documents is the sense of unimaginable anguish and loss. One letter reads: 'They took my son, my husband and my brothers and they slew them in Mosul, after forcing them to play a duel on horses with swords. I wish the horses had wings to save them.' On the front of the plinth, just below the edge, is a dedication embroidered in Greek: 'Αλλά η μνήμη τους παραμένει' ('But the memory of them remains.')

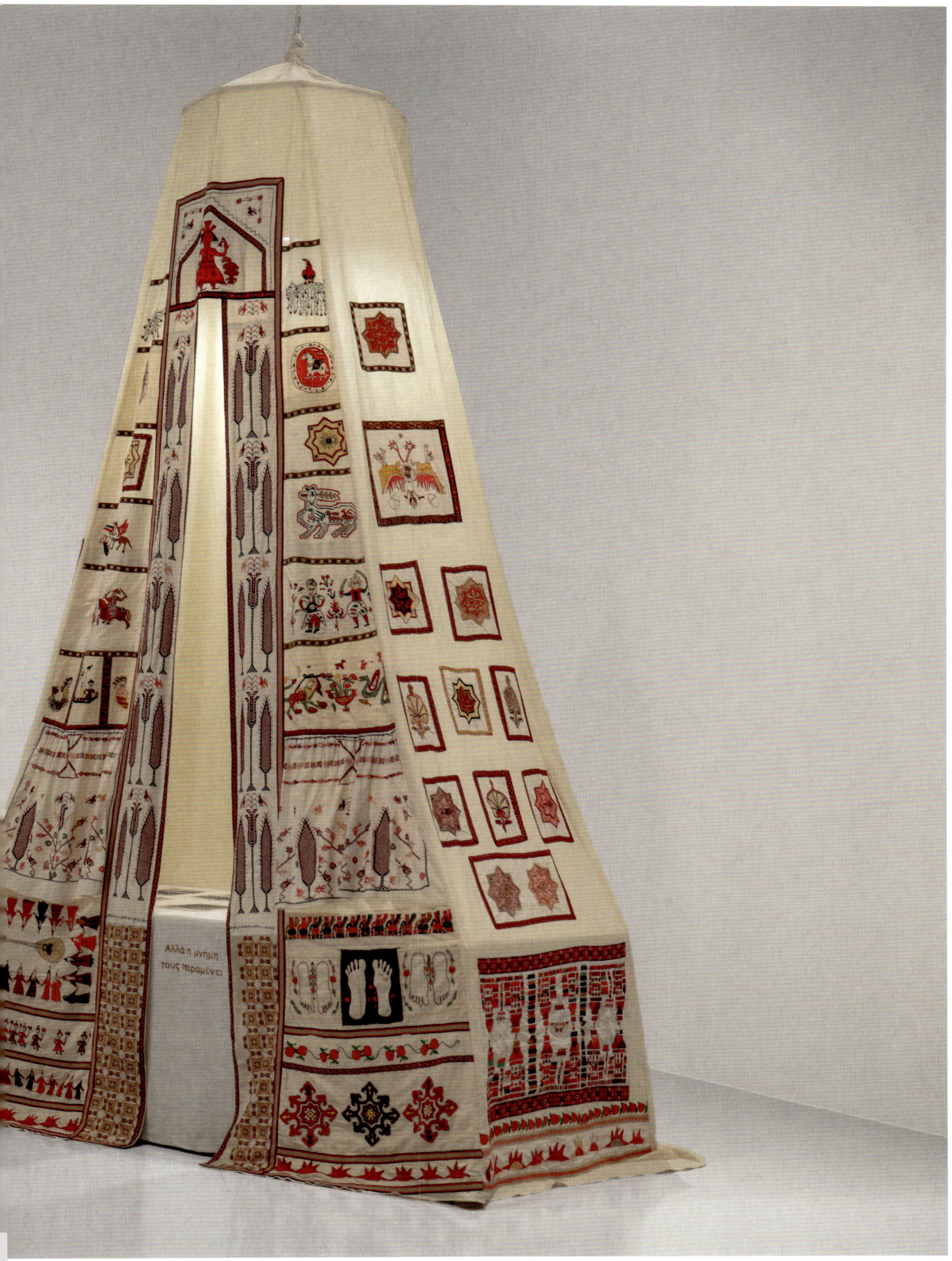
Αλλά η μνήμη
τους παραμένει

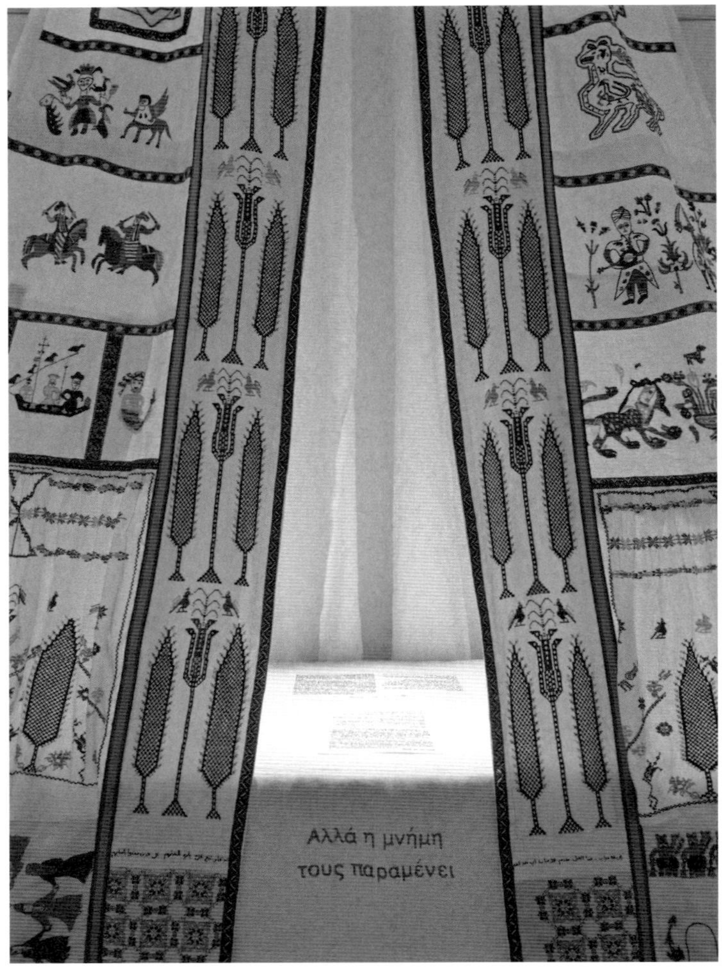


Detail Sperveri, doorpanels with cypress trees and two peacocks drinking from a fountain; inside hand-embroidered letters.

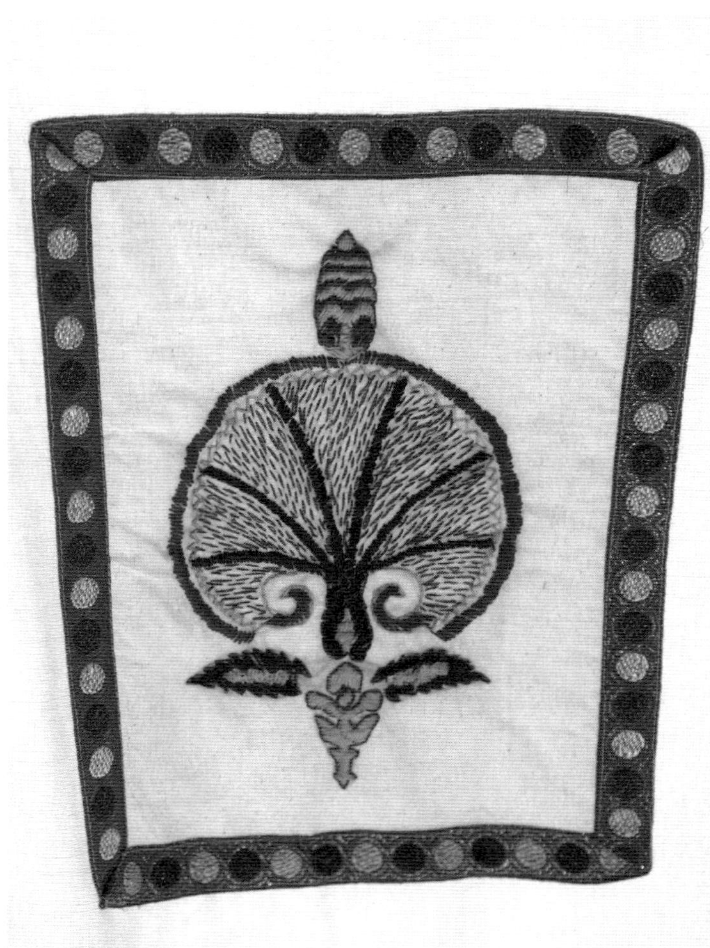

Detail Sperveri, embroidery of stylized flower vase motif typical of Bursa textiles and ceramics.

# UNRAVELLING SPERVERI
## In Conversation with Mounira Al Solh

Over the past fifteen years, Lebanese-Dutch artist Mounira Al Solh has written down and stitched, word by word, the stories of people who fled their home countries to escape oppression, violence or economic hardship. Their stories of loss and resilience, often combined with her own experience, have formed the core of her multidisciplinary practice, which encompasses painting, drawing, performance, textiles and embroidery. *Sperveri* (2017) is her first large-scale embroidery project, for which she collaborated with women embroiderers from Lebanon, Syria and Palestine. The motifs that decorate the tent are inspired by the artist's research into traditional embroidery from Greece and the Islamic Arab world.

CHRISTEL — You work in many different media. You paint, draw, perform, make large installations, and you use textiles. Do you remember when did you first picked up a needle and thread?

MOUNIRA — I remember my grandmother was always busy embroidering dresses and other things. I spent a lot of time with her when I was growing up, so she must have been the one who infected me. But one of my most vivid memories is stitching up holes in my pyjamas. That was during the civil war in Lebanon in the 1980s. As I child I was scared, dealing with the constant threat of loss. I had nightmares. Before I went to sleep, my mother let me cut holes in my pyjama and let me stitch them up. It relaxed me. Embroidering still relaxes me when I'm stressed or anxious, especially today, when these same fears are very real again, with the war and devastation in Lebanon and the Middle East.

CHRISTEL — Textiles and embroidery are an important part of your artistic vocabulary. You sew banners, stitch on drawings and create these lavishly embroidered tents, which you decorate with symbols and motifs that you find in various sources, including old Arab, Islamic and Persian manuscripts and folklore tales. For the embroidery on *Sperveri* you drew your inspiration from the rich Greek tradition. How did the research unfold? And how did you select the motifs you embroidered on the tent?

MOUNIRA — The idea for *Sperveri* was born when I was working in Athens on another project, *I Strongly Believe in our Right to be Frivolous*. It was the time of the Arab Spring and the war in Syria and the surrounding region. I was talking to people who had to flee their home country because of conflicts, people from Syria and Afghanistan. Sketching each individual helped me to get closer and to have conversations that were not only about the war or politics, but about more intimate everyday things. They all wanted to talk to me about their personal losses, the losses of loved ones.

At that same time I discovered these beautifully embroidered bed-tents — one is on display at the Benaki Museum in Athens. Women would spend years embroidering bedlinen, cushions and these bed-tents for their dowry. The more elaborately embroidered, the prouder they would be. The wedding was the most important occasion in a woman's life because it meant she would leave her family home forever, so she would embroider her hopes and dreams into the textiles using motifs

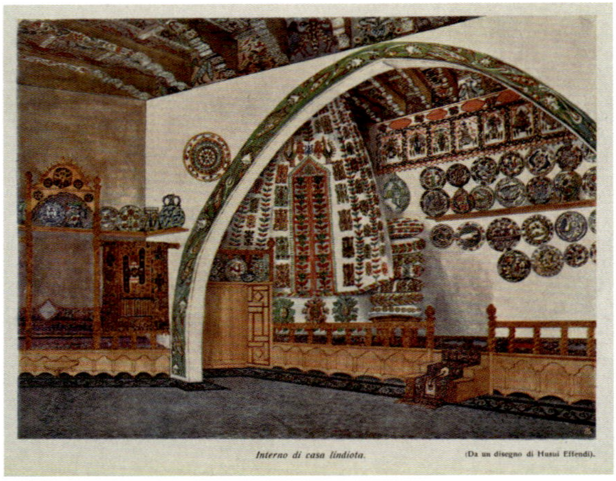

01

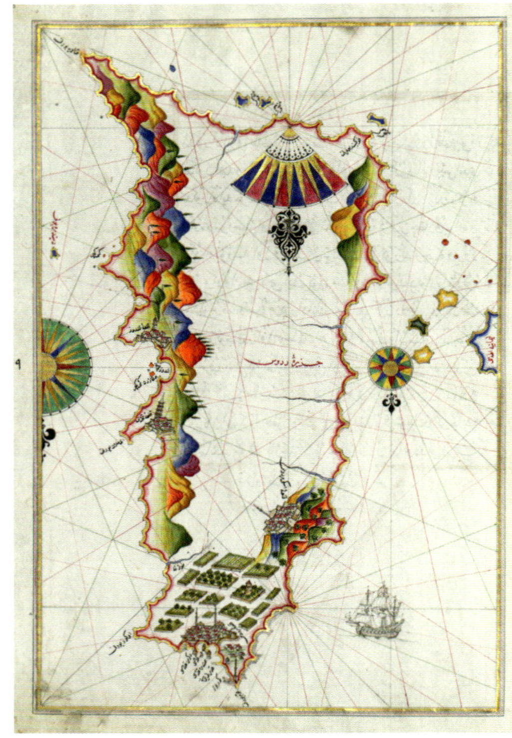

03

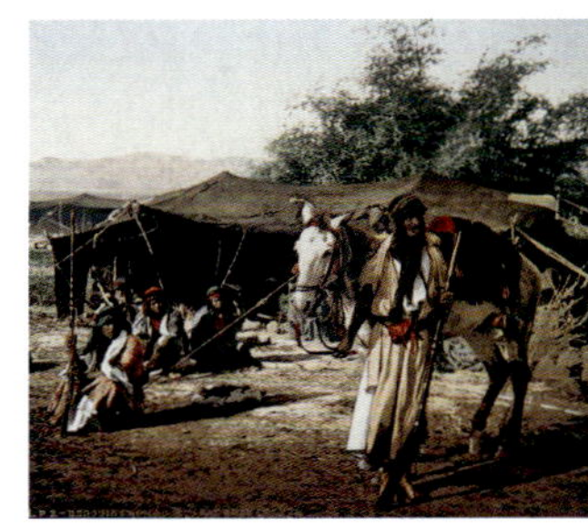

04

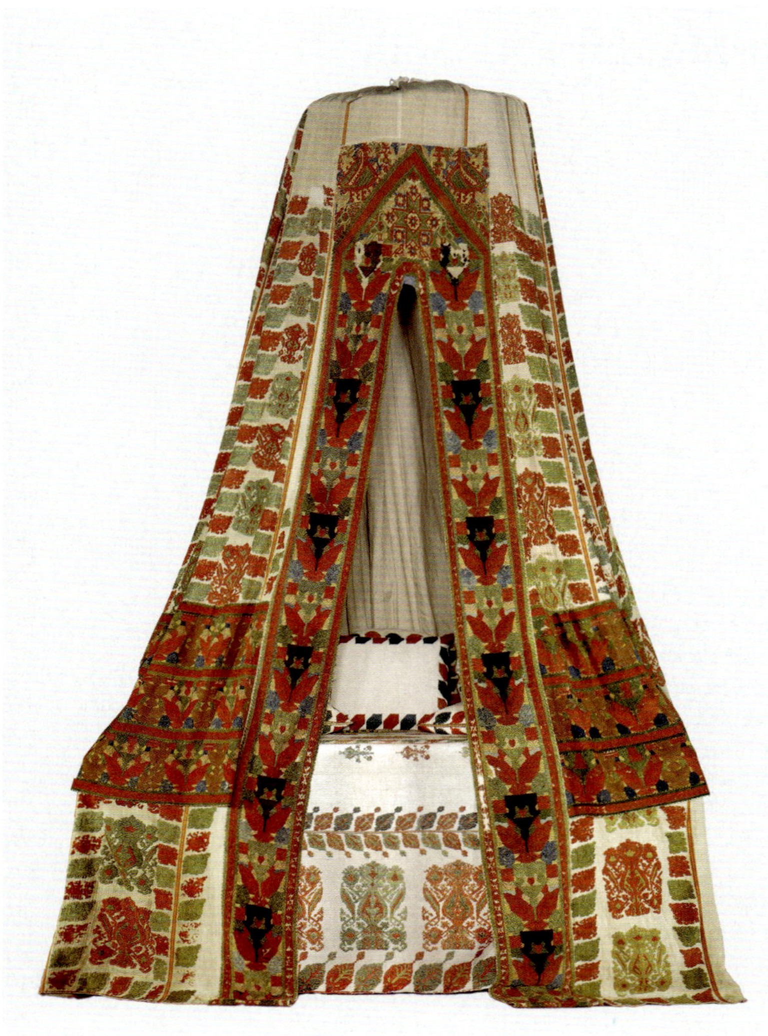

02

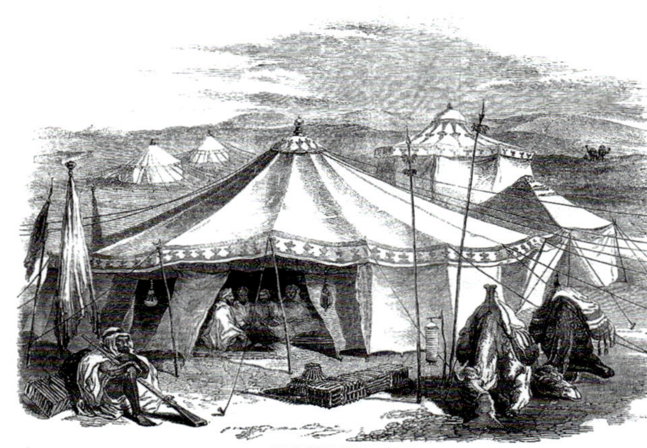

05

01. Interior of a Rhodian house with a bed-tent (after a drawing by Husei Effendi) published in Marica Montesanto's La Citta Sacra (Lindo), 1930.
02. Colourfully embroidered 'spervéri' (bed-tent) with floral motifs, flowerpots and peacocks, one of the few surviving examples. Rhodes, 17th–18th century. Height 4 m, hem circumference 10 m.

SPERVÉRI
On Rhodes, the Greek island closest to Turkey, a sperv éri was a hand-embroidered, bell-shaped tent covering the nuptial bed in one-room houses. The linen bed-tents consisted of eight to sixteen panels that taper from 40-45 cm at the bottom to 13-15 cm at the top. The seamed panels were draped over a polygonal wood piece ('milosper-véri') and attached to the ceiling. Bed-tents were probably introduced to Rhodes in the 14th century by the Knights of Saint John of Jerusalem. A sperv éri would have been part of a bride's dowry. When the women of the family came together to install the tent, they would perform a special dance. As the main decorative feature of the house, the sperv éri was a powerful statement of the socio-economic status of its owners. Only a few complete tents have survived because most were cut up and their embroidery used for cushions or bedcovers.

03. Map of the Islands of the Aegean Sea Including Chios, Cos, Rhodes and Crete, illustration from the 'Kitab-ı Bahriye', Piri Reis, c. 1521 and 1526. Ink and pigments on laid European paper, 34 × 24 cm. The Kitab-ı Bahriye ('Book of the Sea') was a navigational guide made by the Ottoman admiral, corsair and cartographer Piri Reis (1470–1553). The book contains atlases of the Mediterranean islands and coastlines, including Rhodes and the Dodecanese. Rhodes, long central to trade and crusader routes in the eastern Mediterranean, was conquered by the Ottoman Empire in 1522 and remained under Ottoman rule until 1912. In the 21st century, Rhodes has become the first stop for many people seeking asylum in Europe.

TENTS
Providing shelter and protection is one of the primary uses of textile. Tents have housed everybody from nomads to recreational campers, soldiers and disaster victims. Various styles developed over time in response to climate and lifestyles. Today, tents are often associated with homelessness and forced displacement.

04. Bedouin tent in Galilee, c. 1890. Colour photograph taken by Félix Bonfils. Bedouin tribes still use archetypical 'black tents'. Women weave the gable roof from black wool from goats. The tents provide portable and durable protection against harsh desert environments, adaptable to their nomadic lifestyle.
05. Traveller's encampment in the desert, 1857. Etching. The Arabian Desert became a popular destination for British

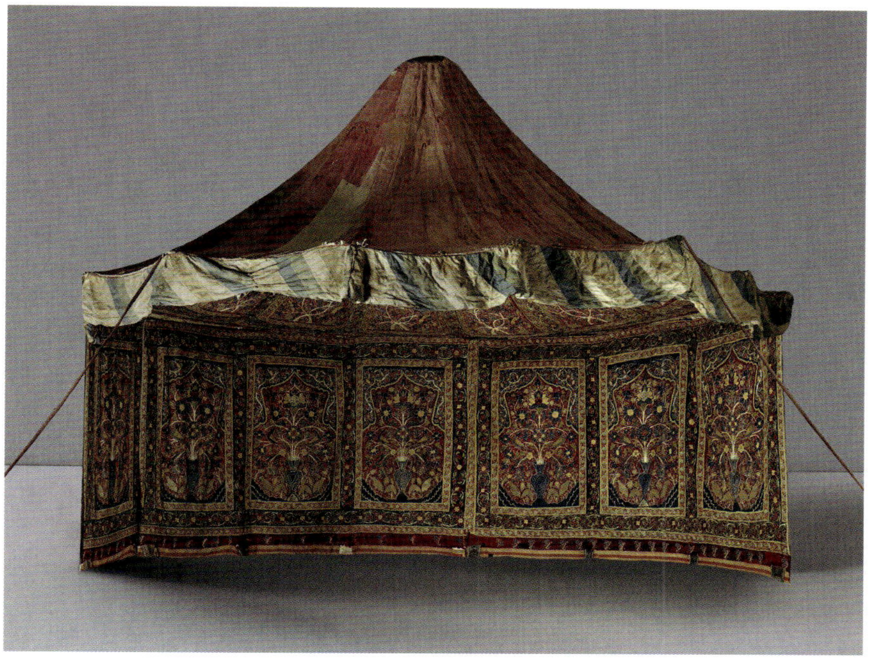

06

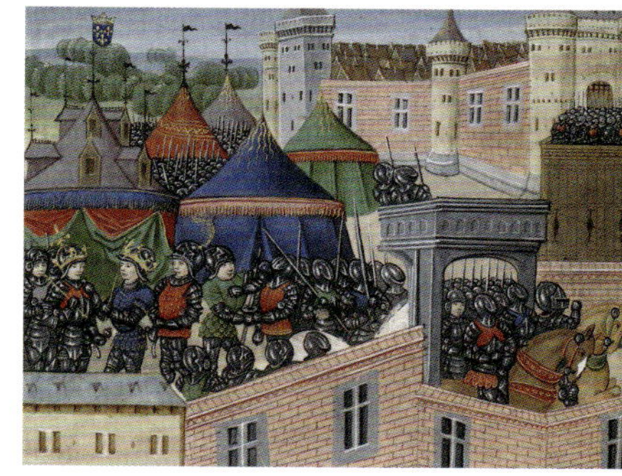

07

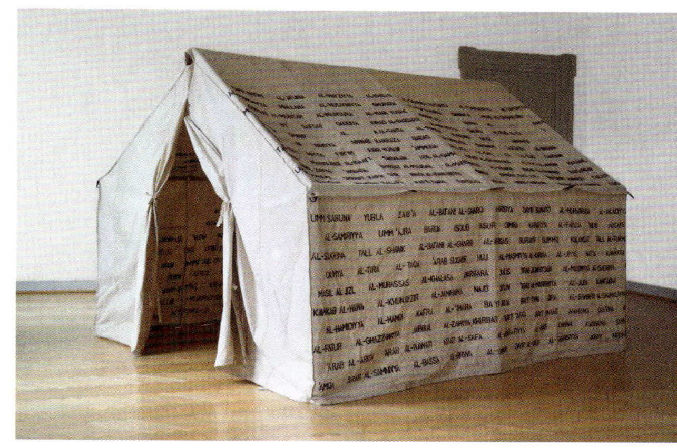

09

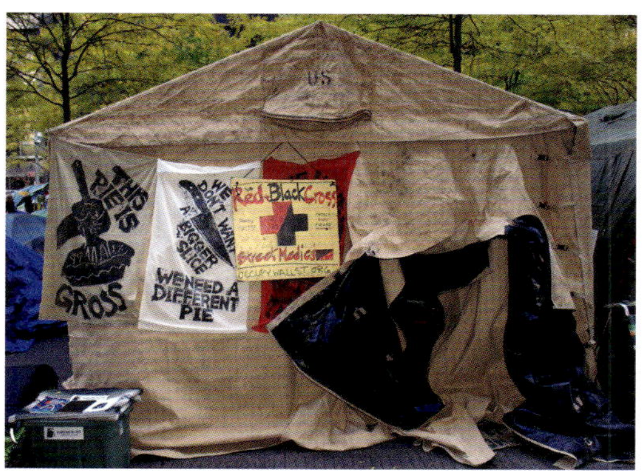

08

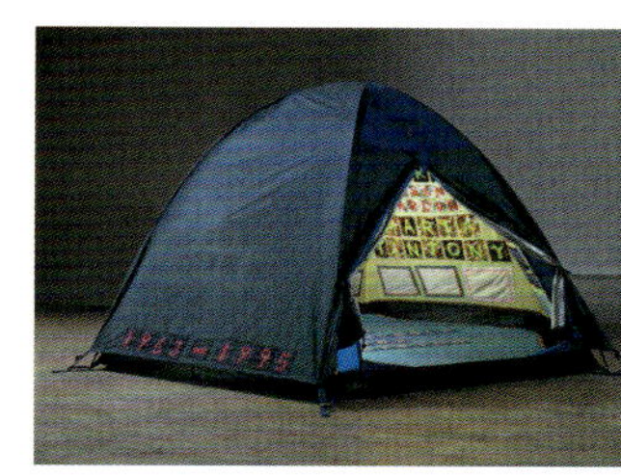

10

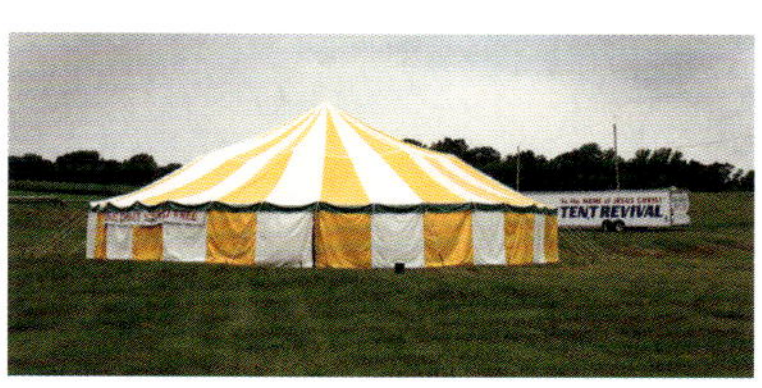

11

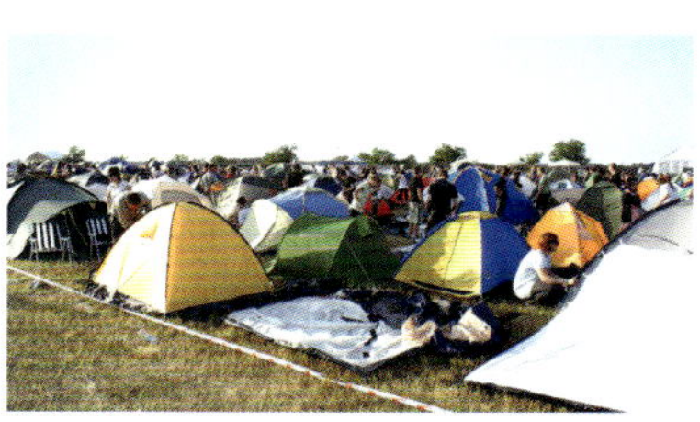

12

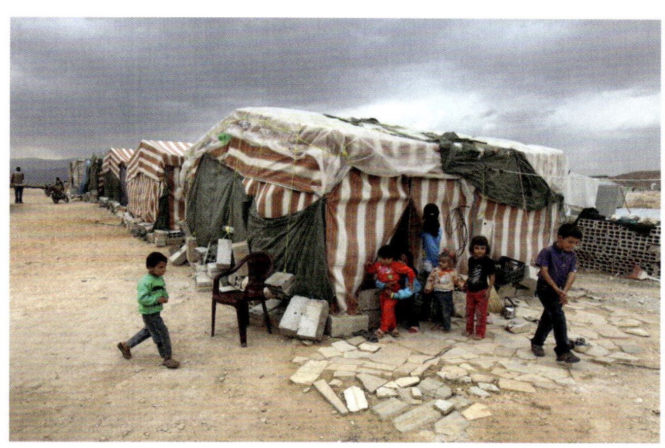

13

officers of the Indian colonial government. Later, groups of upper-class British travellers, charmed by the spirit of exploration, ventured into the desert, escorted by Bedouin guides.

06. Royal Round Tent, made for Muhammed Shah, c. 1834–1848. Iran, Rasht, Qajar period. Interior: wool, silk. Plain weave, inlaid work, embroidery, chain stitch, leather. Exterior: cotton, wool, plain weave, rope, iron ring, 360 × 400 × 400.1 cm.
Royal tents were potent symbols of authority, wealth and power throughout the greater Middle East. Rulers could own thousands of tents, some as large as castles. They were part of larger compounds and used for social functions and imperial ceremonies reserved for men only. Royal tents are elaborately decorated with coloured wool and silk-thread embroidery – the work of men and boys – showing exuberant flora, vines and birds.

07. Siege of Metz 1444 (detail), miniature from the Chronique de Charles VII (Grandes Chroniques de France), by Jean Chartier, c. 1475–1500.
The miniature shows the kings of France (Charles VII) and Sicily (René d'Anjou) with their armies before Metz in 1444.

08. Medical tent at Occupy Wall Street protest, New York, 2011.
Camps have been frequent symbols of protest, from the peace camps across Europe and North America in the 1970s and 1980s, to the anti-globalist protest in 2005, the Occupy movement in the 2010s, to the worldwide pro-Palestinian protests in 2024 and 2025.

09. Memorial to 418 Palestinian Villages which were Destroyed, Depopulated and Occupied by Israel in 1948, Emily Jacir, 2001.
Refugee tent, embroidery thread, daily log of names of people who worked on tent, 244 × 366 × 305 cm.
Artist and activist Emily Jacir raises socio-political issues such as the movement and displacement of populations, borders and boundaries. This work consists of a refugee tent with the embroidered names of 418 Palestinian towns that were wiped out in 1948, when the State of Israel was founded, followed by the forced displacement of people in what is known as the Nakba.

10. Everyone I Have Ever Slept With 1963–1995, Tracey Emin, 1995.
Blue tent with embroidery and appliqué, mattress and light, 122 × 245 × 215 cm.

11. Modern marquee tent. This tent is used for a gathering of Christians in Pennsylvania. Tent meetings, also known as tent revivals, are used for evangelic events or healing crusades in various towns that attract thousands of people.

12. Camping grounds with rows of lightweight dome tents on the last day of music festival, Germany.

13. Syrian refugee children in front of their tents at a refugee camp in Arsal, 2012. Arsal is a Sunni Muslim town in eastern Lebanon near the Syrian border. The camp has become a safe haven for hundreds of refugee families.

that had been passed down generations, like flower-pots, peacocks and ships. I started to research the meaning and the history of these motifs, not only in Greek culture, but also in ancient Byzantine, and Persian and Islamic culture. I noticed that the technique and style of this embroidery closely resembled the needlework I'd seen in Lebanon, made by Palestinian women in camps. And it made me think about how embroidery must have travelled between these regions for many centuries.

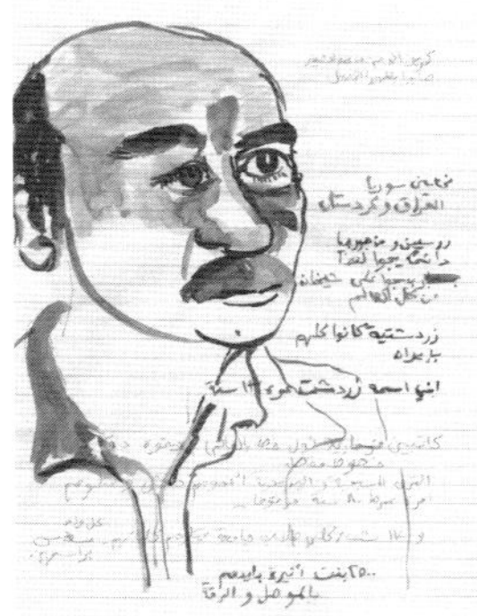

I Strongly Believe in our Right to Be Frivolous, 2012–ongoing. Hand-written conversations and drawings on yellow legal pad and A4 paper, mixed media, 28.6 × 21 cm.

But what I found most interesting was how the symbolism of these motifs still echoes the same hopes and fears I heard in the stories of the men and women I spoke to, who were forced to flee their homes. That's when I decided that I wanted to make a contemporary bridal tent using these old motifs to tell those contemporary stories, and to dedicate it to the memory of all those who were sadly lost recently.

CHRISTEL — Can you explain how those ancient motifs relate to these contemporary stories?

MOUNIRA — Well, in traditional Greek embroidery, the peacock symbolizes fertility and eternity. Women would embroider it onto the gable over the entrance of their bed-tent, with these big, curved tails and an eight-pointed star in the middle, which is used in many cultures as a symbol of unity, harmony and stability. The peacock is a very old symbol and can mean different things in different cultures. You find it on the pharaoh statues in ancient Egypt. In Greece the peacock is associated with Hera, the wife of Zeus, and the patroness of women, marriage and childbirth. But on my *Sperveri* I connect the peacock with the story of Khalit, a Yazidi man from northern Iraq, who witnessed the massacres by ISIS. You can read his story inside the bed-tent. In the Yazidi religion, which is one of the oldest in the world, the Peacock Angel is a divine being, the chief of all incarnations of God, and a symbol of immortality. So this peacock is dedicated to him, together with the sun motif that is repeated along the borders.

CHRISTEL — You have embroidered some fascinating creatures and epic scenes on the panels of the tent. In the middle panel on the left I see a man on a horse, and on the right this mythical animal, and in the gable at the top there is this flamboyant red lady, dancing, with a peacock by her side, in what looks like a schematic representation of a house. Is there a story attached to these motifs?

MOUNIRA — The woman in red is connected to the story of the bride that you can read inside the tent. The man on the horse is based on examples of Greek embroidery I saw at the Benaki Museum. You can find them on cushions or bedlinen embroidered for a girl's dowry, and they represent the groom's best man as part of the wedding procession. Just like the people dancing with the lute in the middle. The horse with wings is a very old Byzantine motif. In the Islamic tradition we have the Buraq, the winged horse-like creature that carried Muhammed to the heavens and back. But for me, the man on the horse is connected to the story of the Iraqi woman inside the tent.

Another important motif is the cypress tree, which again is an ancient symbol in many cultures in the eastern Mediterranean. In the Palestinian cross-stitch tradition, every region — Ramallah, Jaffa, Gaza — has its own variations. More recently, the tree has become a symbol of Palestinian resilience. But in Greek and Roman culture, the cypress tree is also associated with mourning. You often see it in cemeteries or on paintings depicting someone mourning the loss of a loved one.

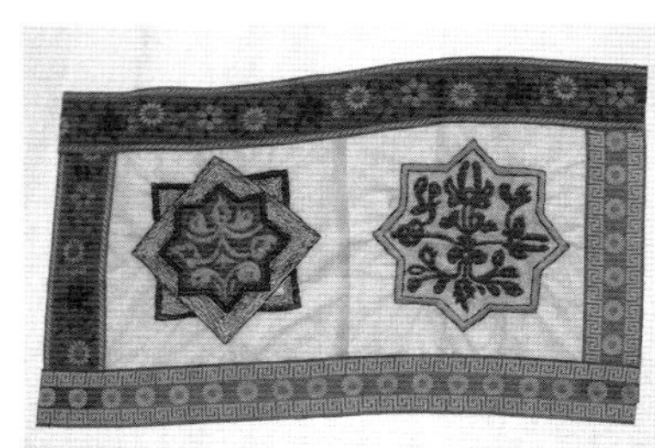

Detail of Sperveri, embroidered 8-pointed star.

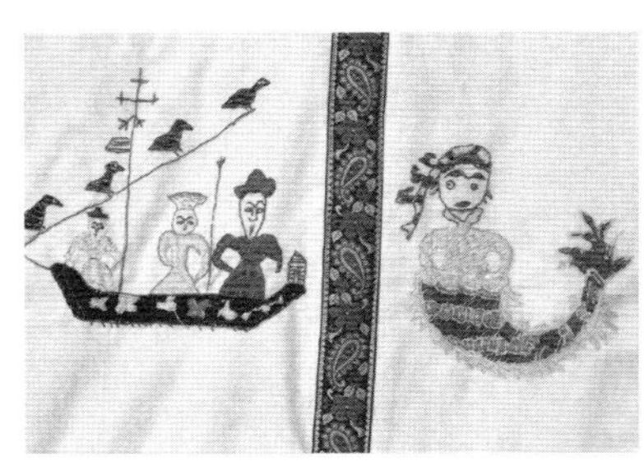

Detail of Sperveri, embroidered ship motif flanked by harpies.

I thought it was important to show how these symbols are connected in various cultures, even if their meaning might be slightly different. But also, how these symbols and motifs are still relevant today, expressing the same hopes and dreams. Take the sailing boat, for instance. It was an important element of island culture, but it also expressed the concerns a woman might have had back then, about losing her husband or son when they went out to sea to fish, hoping they would return safely. In *Sperveri* the Greek sailboat travelling across the Aegean Sea takes on a new meaning with the

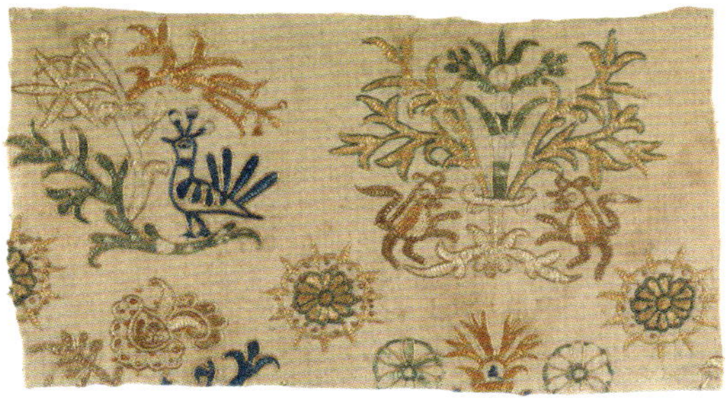

14

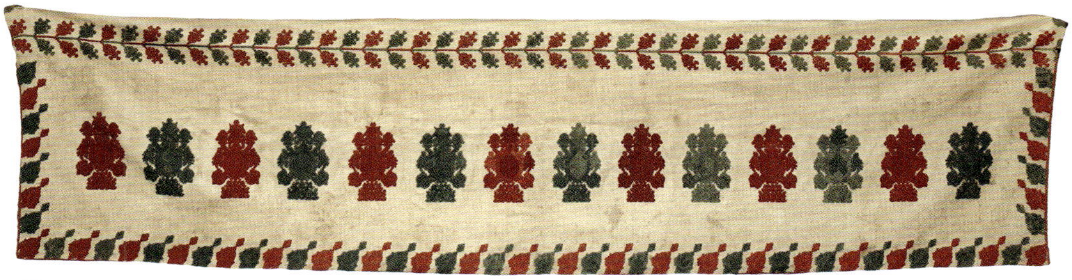

15

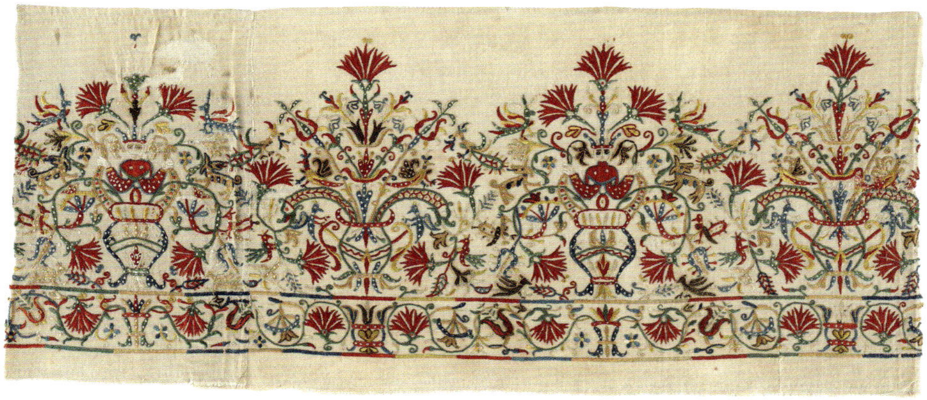

16

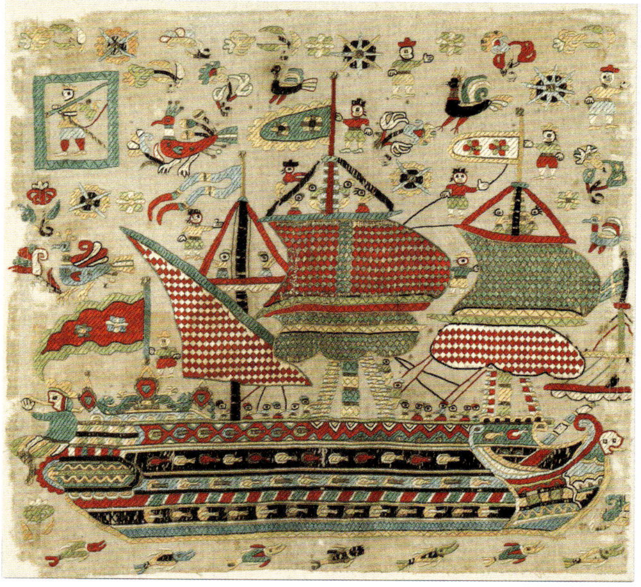

17

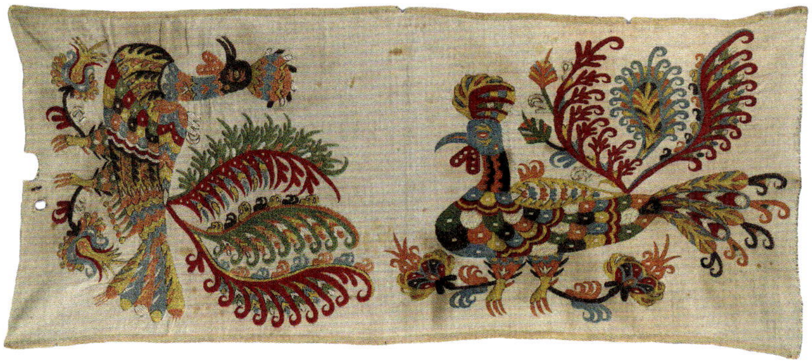

18

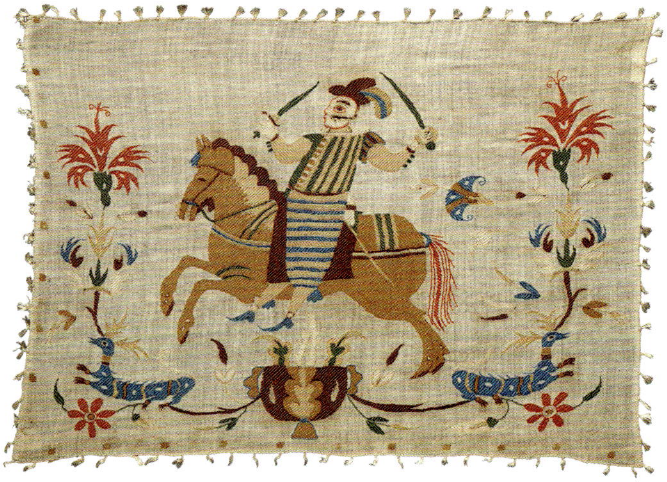

20

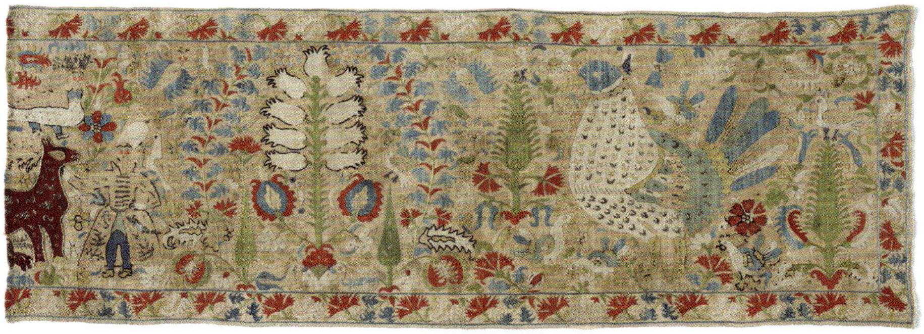

19

GREEK EMBROIDERY MOTIFS
Embroidery is more than decoration; it is a centuries-old language that conveys people's hopes and beliefs, as well as the social and geopolitical histories of a region. Traditional Greek embroidery adorned dowry textiles and festive clothing, featuring motifs inspired by nature, island life and indigenous myths and customs. Repeated stitch by stitch for generations, these motifs are imbued with symbolic meanings rooted in antiquity.

14. Fragment with mythical birds, trees, animals and medallions, region unknown, 19th century.
Coloured silk floss on unbleached cotton, stem, herringbone, satin, French knot stitch, 29 × 16 cm.

15. Bed valance with diagonal leaves and 'glástra' motif, Rhodes, 18th century.
Blue-green and red silk thread on beige linen, Rhodes stitch, 62 × 246 cm.

GLÁSTRA
The stylized vase overflowing with flowers and leaves is a common motif in many artistic traditions. On this bed valance, the vase motif is executed in a typical Rhodes stitch, a loose cross-stitch technique using thick untwisted silk, creating a compact relief surface.

16. Fragment skirt border with flower vase and two-tailed mermaid, Crete, 17th–18th century.
Coloured silk and cotton thread on linen, chain, herringbone, satin and stem stich.

GORGONA
Cretan motifs closely resemble European embroidery, particularly from Venice. The 'gorgona', a two-tailed mermaid, appears in ancient Greek mythology and medieval art, symbolizing both protector and seductress. They often appear in compositions with plants, human figures, animals, birds and imaginary creatures such as double-headed eagles and winged snakes.

17. Cushion cover with ship motif, Skyros, Sporades, 17th century.
Coloured silks on fine linen, corn, brick, chain, back and cross stitch, 43 × 46 cm.

SHIP
Ships are a common motif among seafaring cultures. This festively decorated three-masted schooner is crowded with miniature figures, fish, birds and mythological creatures and is typical for the embroidery style of Skyros.

18. Part of a bridal sheet with hoopoe, Skyros, Sporades, 18th century.
Coloured silks on fine linen, darning and double-running stitch, 91 × 41 cm.

BIRDS
The hoopoe is a popular motif in neo-Hellenic art. It was the sacred symbol of Zeus and Apollo, the sun god. In Ancient Greece, the peacock symbolized immortality, and later vanity and self-assurance.

19. Bridal cushion cover, with cypress trees, flowering stems, birds, human figures, Epirus, 17th century.
Coloured silks, metallic-wrapped thread on linen, chain stitch, herringbone stitch, running stitch, stem stitch, 40 × 109 cm.

TREE OF LIFE
Stylized trees were popular motifs. The Greeks worshipped trees and regarded them as sacred. Stylized trees are often found on bridal sheets, symbolizing fertility and longevity.

20. Pillow cover with horseman wielding two swords, Skyros, 18th century.
Coloured silks on linen, darning and double running stitch, 37 × 49 cm.
Wedding scenes, including processions, dancing guests or a bride or relative on horseback are a common feature of Greek embroidery.

treacherous journey refugees are currently undertaking across the same waters.

All the images and motifs are inspired by or are reinterpretations of motifs I saw in the incredible Historic and Islamic collection at the Benaki Museum, and in books on Greek embroidery I found in their library. I matched these images with the stories I'd heard, and then created my own interpretations. In a way *Sperveri* takes another look at the images and patterns once embroidered in celebration and joy, and are now seen in the context of those tragic stories of war.

CHRISTEL — In the historical spervéri, the entrance panels and the gable at the top are the most richly decorated parts, holding great symbolic meaning as they guide the energy brought into the tent. Many door panels are embroidered with so-called *glastras*, or flowerpots, symbolizing longevity, and bestowing a long life on the married couple. You embroidered the door panels with a pattern of cypress trees, a symbol of mourning.

MOUNIRA — Yes, I combined the cypress tree with two peacocks drinking from a fountain, which symbolizes fertility. The symbols of the cypress tree and the flowerpot derive from the tree of life; they are also a symbol of hope because they point to the sky. More importantly, I did not want to make another spervéri, I wanted to make my own one.

CHRISTEL — You collaborated with various women on the embroidery. How did that work?

MOUNIRA — I needed a lot of hands because it was a really ambitious project, and I had little time. So I recruited family members and women who knew how to embroider, like Soubhya, who lives in a refugee camp in the south of Lebanon, and she works with a team of women embroiderers. I would make the drawings, and they would embroider them, infusing them with their own embroidery tradition.

We didn't have time to finish all the panels, so Soubhya gave me a beautiful embroidered piece that was under her television in the camp. That was such a generous gesture. It also emphasizes the nomadic nature of embroidery. I mean, after some time, many traditional spervéri were cut up and their parts used elsewhere, for cushions maybe. But what's more important is that she made this piece in 1980. And in 1982 there was the Israeli invasion of Lebanon, because they wanted to destroy the PLO in southern Lebanon — just like today. Many people were killed, but this piece of textile has survived.

CHRISTEL — At the top of the two pieces, you embroidered a sentence in Arabic. Can you tell me what it says?

MOUNIRA — It reads: 'To all those we have lost'. It's an interpretation of the Greek phrase I embroidered on the bedsheet, which, literally translated, means: 'But the memory of them remains'.

CHRISTEL — Tents represent the oldest functional application of textiles, provide shelter from the weather, accommodate a nomadic lifestyle. Today, however, tents are associated with people who are forced to flee, and with makeshift refugee camps. Was this something you had in mind when you started working on *Sperveri*?

MOUNIRA — This must have been on my mind, because when I was working on *Sperveri*, we all realized that the conflict in Syria and Iraq was not going to end, and many people had to leave their homes to escape war and persecution. I was living between Athens and Beirut, and Athens was, and still is, a city where many people are stranded before they continue their journey to the north of Europe.

But I'm very wary of this association because I didn't want to make a 'refuge tent' or a tent about refugees. I wanted to make something beautiful. The original spervéri had a ceremonial function. Women spent years embroidering it, imbuing it with their love and hope, and then it was placed over the marital bed in a ceremony, with dance and music for the couple's wedding night. I'm interested in the stories that these tents tell us about the lives of women back then.

CHRISTEL — But when you look inside the tent, you don't see a marital bed. You see embroidered texts sharing tragic stories of war and loss...

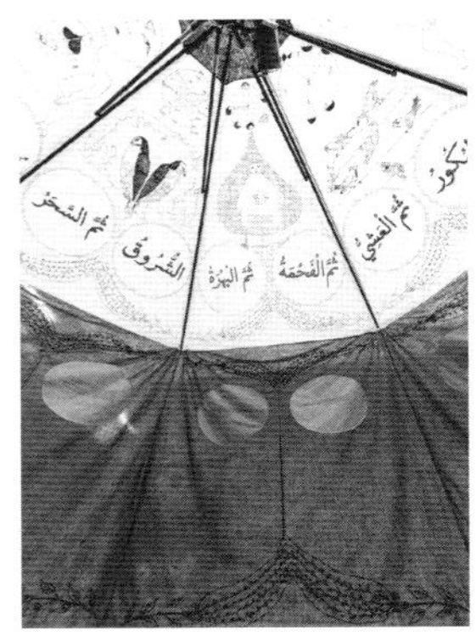

Lackadaisical Sunset to Sunset, 2021. Cotton, silk thread, wood, sound, hand-embroidered, sewing, voice recording of Lebanese singer Rima Kcheiche, 220 × 350 cm.

MOUNIRA — For me, *Sperveri* is a memorial, a breathing library, offering refuge to the stories of people who have lost a lot due to conflict and war. I think it's important that those stories are remembered too. They document an era that is deeply affected by war and displacement in the Arab world, and how it affects individual lives. But my works are not illustrations. I see them as conceptual gestures, more open and more fluid in what they might mean. Today, for instance, emotionally, I am not the same person as I was eight years ago when I made the tent. And the context we live in today is different. The situation in my country is different.

CHRISTEL — You made several tents after *Sperveri*, one more exquisitely embroidered than the other. I'm thinking of the three tents, yellow, red and taupe, *Lackadaisical Sunset to Sunset* (2018–2022), one of which we showed in the exhibition *Interwoven Histories*, which also featured

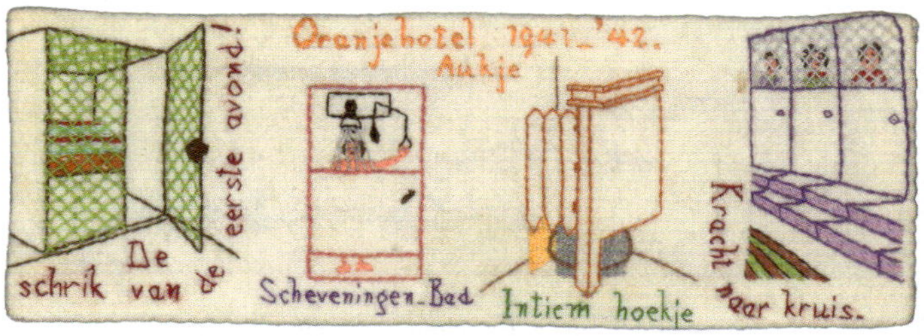


21

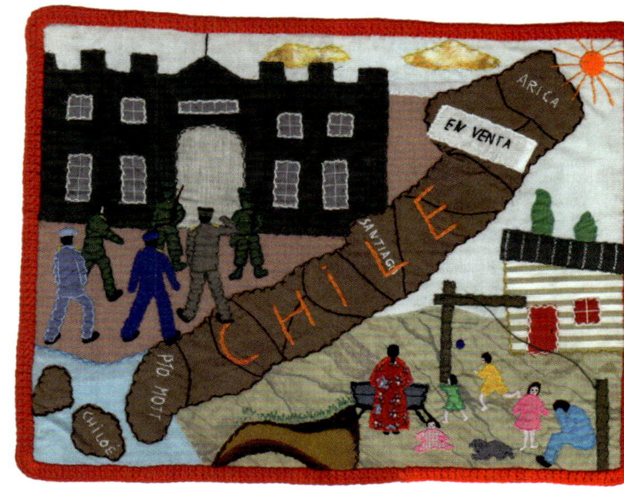


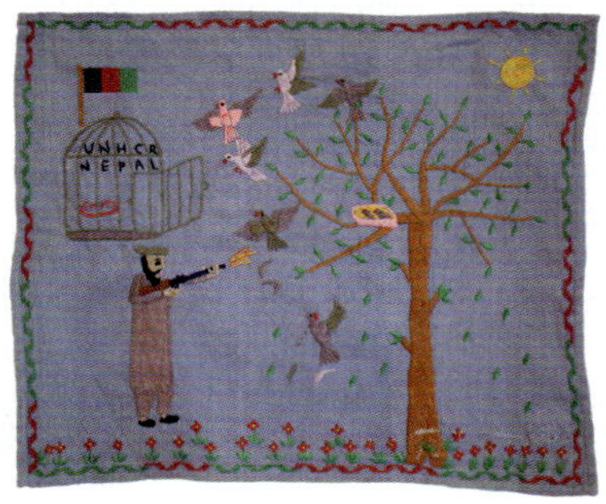


23

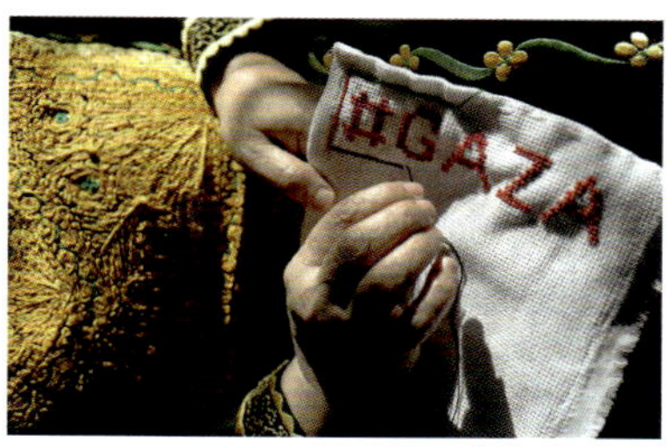


22

24

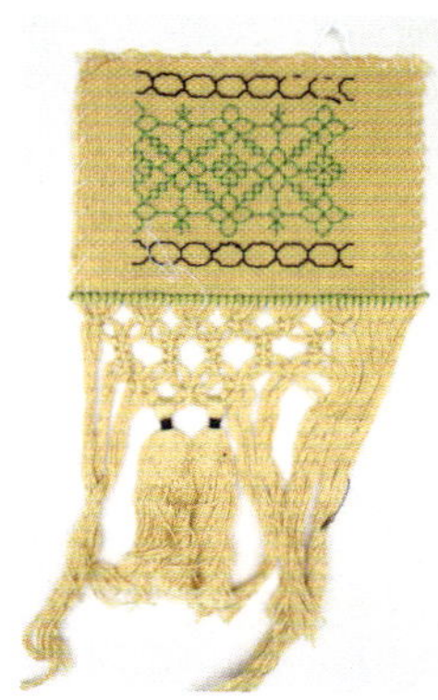

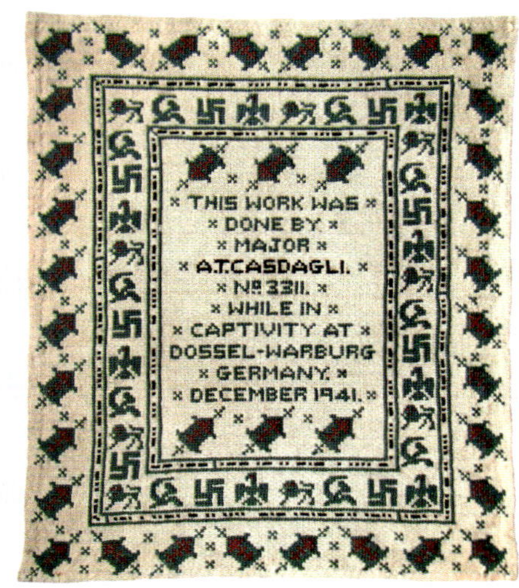


26

27

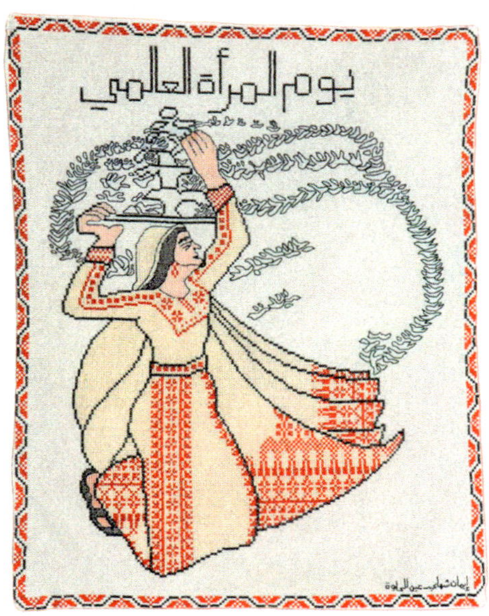


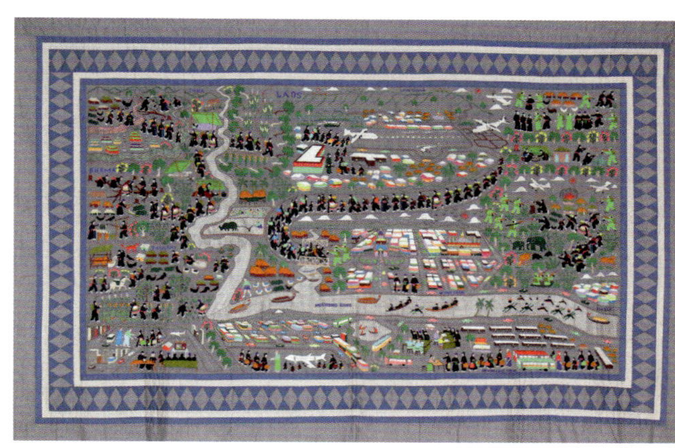

25

28

MAKING A MARK
Entrusting their hopes and sorrows to cloth, people around the world have picked up needle and thread to deal with traumatic events. Sometimes, stitching was their only means to mark their existence; other times, a way to process experiences and stay sane. Women (and men) in captivity went to great lengths to embroider, sourcing cloth from torn sheets, pull threads from headscarves and old clothes. These pieces were made for themselves, as gifts or to send coded messages outside.

21. Bookmark, Aukje Wagemaker (1895–1984), made during her incarceration at 'Oranjehotel' prison, Scheveningen, 1941–1942. She was arrested for her role in the Dutch resistance. Depicting prison life, she humorously referred to the primitive shower and toilet as the 'Scheveningen-Bath' and 'the intimate corner'.

22. Arpillera, Chile en venta, unknown artist, c. 1973. Embroidery and appliqué on jute, 38 × 49 cm.
Brightly coloured 'arpilleras' were made mostly by Chilean women during the Pinochet dictatorship in the 1970s and 1980s. With their men imprisoned or abducted, women gathered in churches and homes. These works provided the women with income but also served as outlets for expressing daily struggles. Distributed abroad through churches, arpilleras amplified their resistance and built networks of solidarity.

REPAIRING TRAUMA
In areas affected by conflict and war, creating textile works, either alone or in a group, is by many seen as a powerful way to deal with trauma. What cannot be said in words is expressed by needle and threads.

23. Birds of Passage, Shekiba Sarabi, Nepal, 2023.
A story cloth created during a Common Threads workshop in Nepal.

24. Tatreez embroidery, Umm Ahmed, 'Gaza Camp', Jerash, Jordan, 2025.
'Tatreez', a centuries-old embroidery technique, is practiced by Palestinian women in refugee camps. 'Tatreez helps us navigate our feelings. It is a way for us to honour our traditions and preserve our culture in the face of erasure', Umm Ahmed says.

25. International Women's Day, 8 March 1981, Panel 0610, Iman Shehaby, Ain al-Hilweh, Lebanon. Cotton on linen, cross stitch, 59 × 45 cm.
The Palestinian History Tapestry tells the story of Palestine through embroidered panels. It supports women living under oppression or in exile while sharing the stories, culture and heritage of their ancestors.

26. Sampler from a memory box of a Dutch woman in a Japanese internment camp, 1942–1945. Hand embroidered, tasselling, 26.8 × 13.1 cm.

27. The Casdagli Sampler, 1941. Major Alexis J. Casdagli embroidered his sampler in December 1941 while a prisoner of war at Dössel Warburg camp in Germany. The piece features swastikas and other symbols along with Morse code messages hidden within its decorative border, reading 'God Save the King' and 'Fuck Hitler'.

28. Wall hanging, Xia Xiong 5200 (refugee camp registration number), Thailand, 1980. Embroidery and appliqué on cotton, 150 × 780 cm.
Created by Hmong women after the Vietnam War, the work depicts village life in Laos, scenes of war, the flight across the Mekong River, refugee camps and settlements in Thailand.

embroidered birds. Or the red tent you made for your solo exhibition at the Baltic Centre for Contemporary Art, in Gateshead. Were your considerations in making these tents the same?

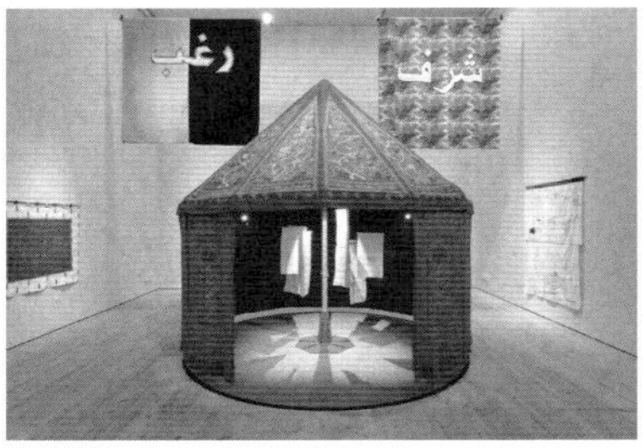

A Day is as Long as a Year, 2022. Organic hemp tinted with henna, cotton, wool, silk and polyester thread, metal and wooden tent structure, sound, collectively embroidered, 400 × 400 cm.

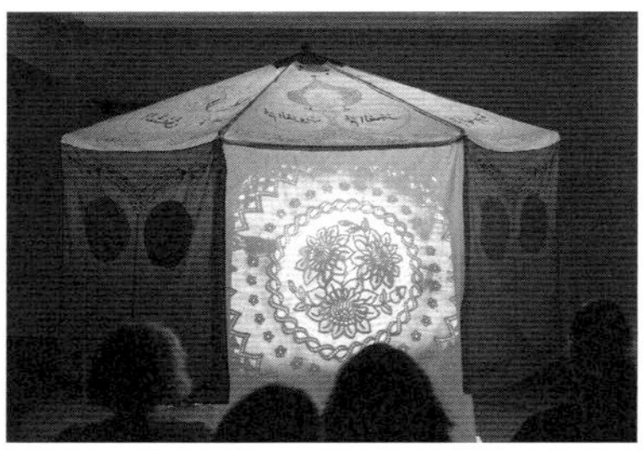

Performance of Lackadaisical Sunset to Sunset, 2021. Performers: Mounira Al Solh, Jana Saleh; transparent sheets, slide projector, base, amplifier.

MOUNIRA — Haha, yes, you can say I have a bit of an obsession with tents. Each one is unique, however. The tent I made for Norwich, *A Day is as Long as a Year*, was directly inspired by the Royal Round tent of Muhammed Shah, who was the ruler of Iran between 1834 and 1848. I saw pictures of that in a book, and I knew I wanted to make a copy of it, but have it embroidered by women.

Royal tents were potent symbols of a ruler's authority, wealth and power, and they were embroidered with flowers, blossoming vines and birds, using silver thread, appliqué and a chain stitch called Rasht work, which makes the embroidery very thick, almost three dimensional. They're really beautiful.

CHRISTEL — It was men who embroidered the imperial tents, was it not?

MOUNIRA — Yes, women were not allowed to work on these tents. That's why I wanted to work with various groups to embroider each of the panels. To give them back their power, and to feminize this very masculine symbol of power. Inside the tent people could read stories of women who have defied a system of inequality and the conditions of war while keeping some humour in the stories too.

The tent series *Lackadaisical Sunset to Sunset* is also dedicated to the resilience of women. Women from Lebanon and Syria who defy a system of patriarchy, inequality and hardship. Some of the stories I included are from my mother, others from neighbours and friends. To me, like *Sperveri*, these tents are breathing libraries. They belong to the oral traditions in which women, and men, would share stories, passing them down through the generations. I think the stories of these women need to be preserved and read in a beautifully decorated space.

CHRISTEL — On the inner surface of *Lackadaisical Sunset to Sunset*, you embroidered not only elegant birds, elongated curvy forms and some enigmatic creatures, but also the hours of the day in Arabic calligraphy. Is there a particular story connected to these images?

MOUNIRA — The names of the 24 hours of the day, which you can also hear through the speaker, are a reminder of the female body's ticking clock. It's a personal reference. The other embroidered motifs are based on drawings of an endangered species of bird that lives in the Lebanese mountains, symbolizing the divine link between Heaven and Earth.

CHRISTEL — You also use your tents to stage performances, for which you collaborate with other artists and performers, like musician, producer and DJ Jana Saleh.

MOUNIRA — Yes, these performances were inspired by the spervéri dance. I've done many public performances and gatherings in my tents. They function as social spaces, not just as beautiful objects. Doing these performances inside the tent, with the audience outside, is also a way to animate it as an intimate and safe space. We need somewhere to feel safe these days, to be able to temporarily forget the pain and terror of the devastating wars in the Middle East.

CHRISTEL — Beautiful tents as sanctuary and shelter?

MOUNIRA — As a refuge for the soul.

*Sperveri* weaves together multiple moments of migration, memory and movement in a layering of histories of passage and displacement. It does so through its adaptation of the centuries old language of Greek island embroidery, passed down from generation to generation, whose forms and symbols bear the traces of the cultures that have crossed the region where it is rooted; through the form of the bed–tent, a structure once marking a young woman's passage from her family home to married life, evoking both intimacy and departure; through its reference to tents in general, the archetype of shelter and nomadic movement; and through the bits and fragments the artist recovered from the stories of women and men who fled their homes to escape violence and oppression.

First to catch the eye are the delicate embroidered motifs, which lend a sense of wonder, beauty and meaning. Like the mermaid that sits upon one of the panels, the imagery draws us in before revealing the terror and trauma held within the stories that have found refuge inside the tent. The fragments laid out within speak to the realities of lives lived under duress. However distant or alien these experiences may seem to most of us, shared from within the sanctuary of the beautifully embroidered tent, they bring home a side of the contemporary condition that many prefer to ignore. This reality, however, is also reflected in the birthplace of the bed–tent, Rhodes. An island close to the Turkish border, Rhodes has long been at the crossroads of trade routes, pilgrimage and military expansion, and remains a first stop for many who seek refuge and a better future in Europe.

In making the work, Al Solh drew on a variety of archives of ancient embroidery motifs whose symbolic meanings have for centuries reflected the hopes and dreams, faith and fears of people, and connected them to the stories of our time. Yet *Sperveri* is as much about the lineages of its motifs as it is about the hands of the women who embroidered its surface. The creation of the tent was a labour of many hands — as the artist emphasises in our interview. It was a joint effort, rooted in craft, memory and community. Al Solh worked with Palestinian and Syrian women living in refugee camps in Lebanon, who apply their embroidery skills both to earn an income and to sustain a connection to their heritage. Here too, in these sites of exile, the displacing nature of migration leaves its material trace on the mixture of embroidery styles. As Rachel Dedman explains in her contribution to this publication, as women from across Palestine came together in refugee camps, so too did their embroidery techniques and the traditional repertoires of motifs.

*Sperveri* gathers these different stories of migration — temporal, material, symbolic and human — into a single embroidered surface where memory, movement and making intertwine.

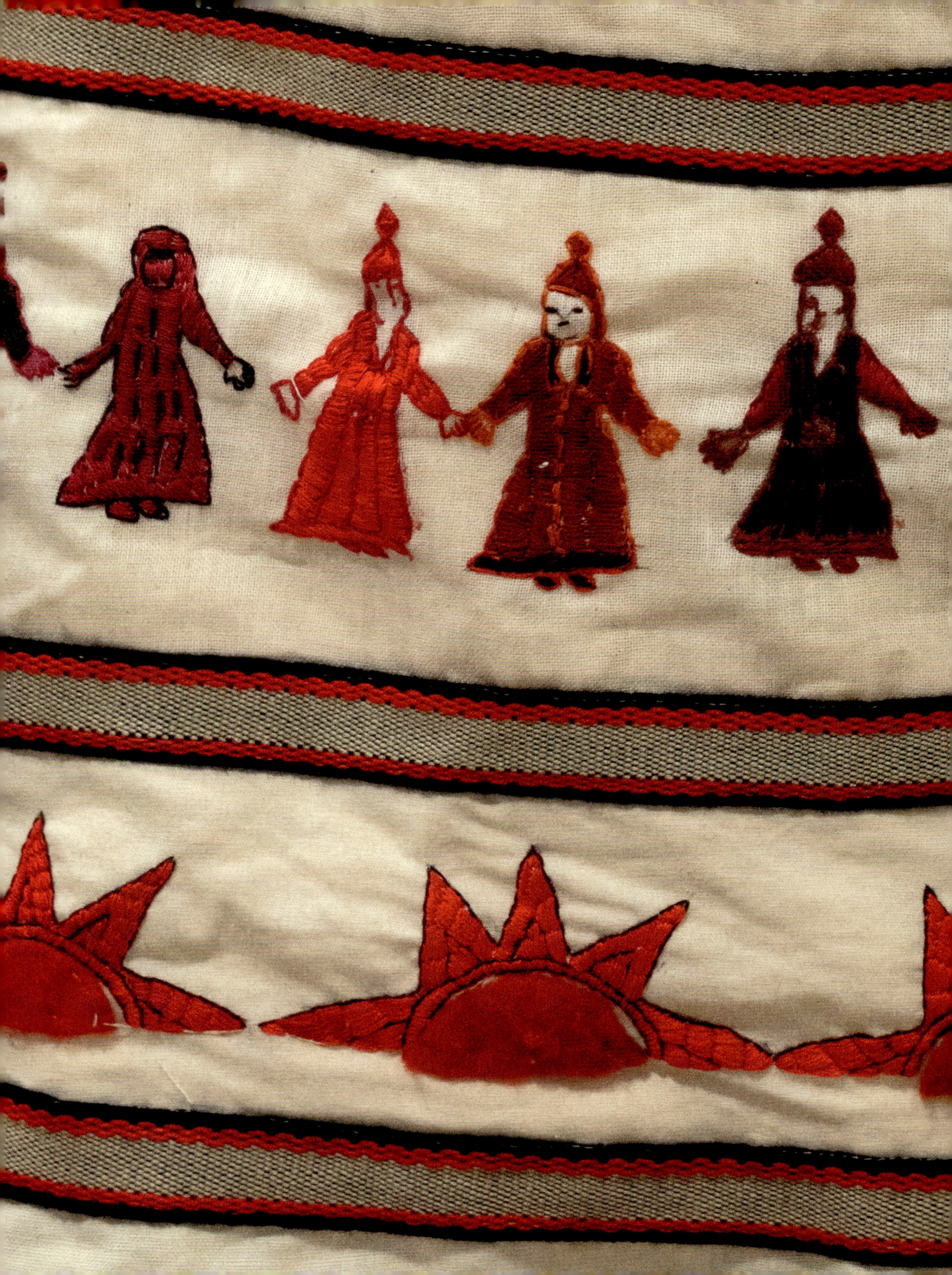

Every dress tells a story. In the following essay, curator and writer Rachel Dedman draws on her decade-long engagement with the art and cultural heritage of the Middle East. A specialist of the history and contemporary significance of Palestinian embroidery—*tatreez*—she tells the stories behind five dresses made by Palestinian women across the course of a century. These garments attest to embroidery's role as a symbol of nationhood, a form of resistance, and a practice reflective of collective memory and the trauma of displacement. Embodying Palestinian creativity and resilience, tatreez offers an intimate vehicle for unfolding a human history of place.

Clothing's connection to the human hand and body means that where people travel, so too do textiles. The effects of migration and displacement, often recorded in statistics or documented through oral histories, are also written in intimate ways upon objects and places. Examining the tangible, personal and creative traces of migration and its experience offers a powerful complement to macro perspectives on history.

Palestinian embroidery and notions of migration are closely intertwined, not only because Palestinians

# MIGRATION'S MATERIAL TRACES
## Embroidery and Palestine

Rachel Dedman

have been in exile and under occupation since 1948, but because embroidery is, like many ancient crafts, an inherently mutable practice. Across the twentieth century alone, embroidery has transformed from an historic craft practiced by rural women for their own use, to a politicized symbol of Palestinian nationalism, and a commodity circulating in a global marketplace. Woven into the social, economic and political fabrics of its time, Palestinian embroidery tells stories of movement and change.

There can be a reluctance, however, to think of heritage in terms of change. In the case of Palestinian crafts, this hesitation is understandable. Palestinian heritage is relentlessly subject to Israeli appropriation and foreign commercialization. The mere existence and continuation of traditional practices in Palestine are threatened by over seventy years of Israeli occupation, with its routine physical and economic violence. For those safeguarding tradition, it feels essential for Palestinian heritage to simply survive, let alone evolve. However, few crafts—of any kind, from any context—remain static over long duration. Creative practices closely connected to the expression and daily lives of people are intrinsically responsive to change within those communities.

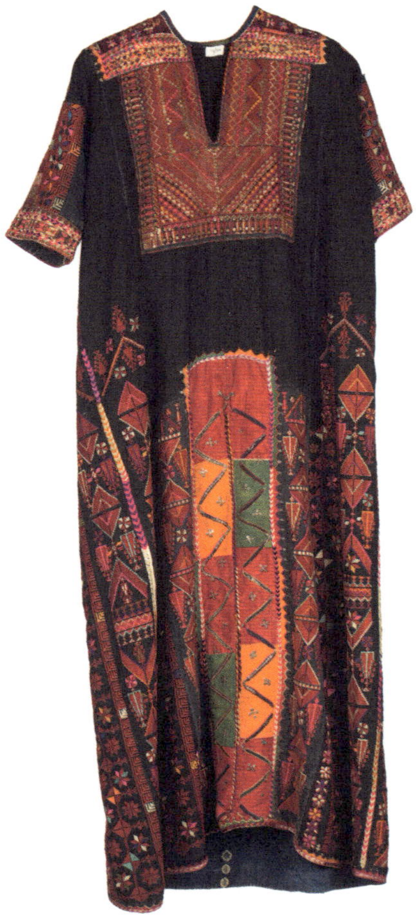

Jellayeh dress from Hebron in Beit Dajan style, 1900–1915, from the collection of The Palestinian Heritage Museum, Dar Al-Tifel Al-Arabi.

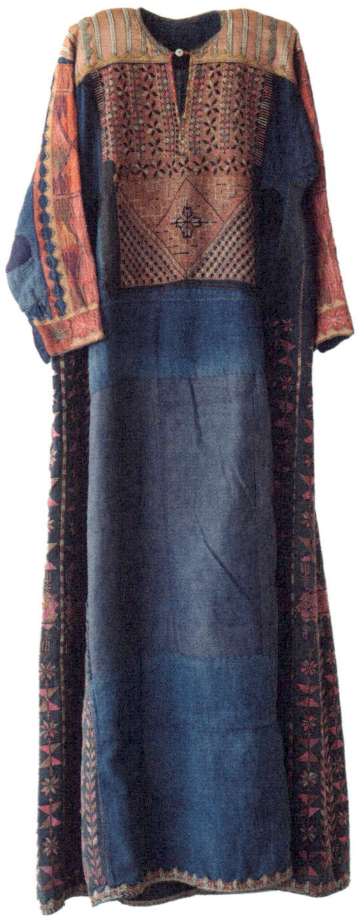

Everyday dress from Hebron, 1930–1935, from the collection of Tiraz: Widad Kawar Home for Arab Dress.

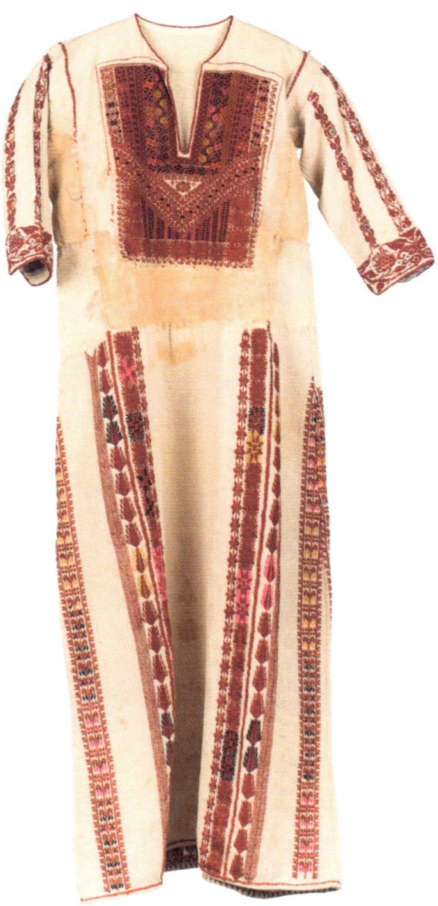

Dress from Ramallah, 1930s, from the collection of Maha Abu Shosheh.

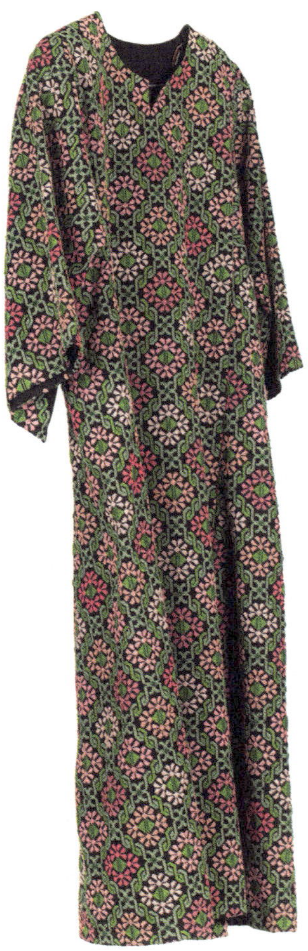

Dress, 2014, embroidered by Raja El-Zeer, from the collection of the Palestinian Museum.

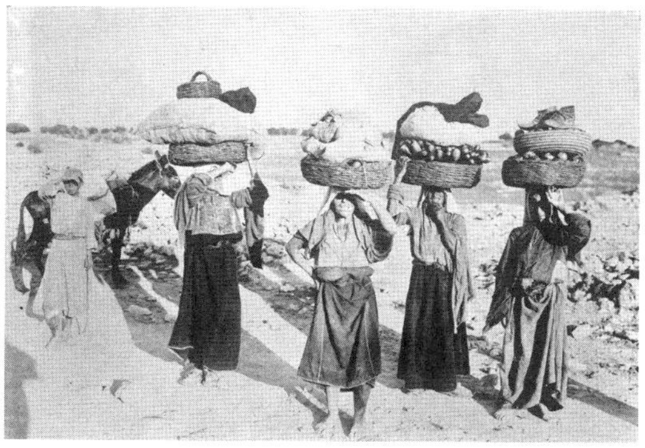

Postcard showing a group of rural Fellah women in Palestine on their way to the market, c. 1889–1914.

The five dresses discussed in this essay carry the intimate marks of women's lives across time, and reflect the changes Palestinians have endured for over a century. They record the human experience of displacement and resistance in Palestine, and the ripple effects of colonialism and global trade. They speak to the craft itself as a migratory bird, with motifs and designs moving across territories, and garments transforming materially over time. Embroidery is made to pass into other hands: a craft inherited, adapted, and bequeathed again.

## JELLAYEH DRESS FROM HEBRON IN BEIT DAJAN STYLE, 1900–1915

Embroidery in Palestine was traditionally a rural convention, practiced by village women for centuries. Before 1948, girls would learn to embroider at the age of six or seven, taught by their mothers and grandmothers. As she grew up, a young woman would prepare her bridal trousseau — the chest containing clothing and cushions she took into marriage — whose embroidery reflected its maker's natal village as well as her stylistic choices. Palestinian embroidery is characterized by significant regional diversity, with individual villages across Palestine known for distinct stitches, motifs, fabric and styles of dress. Embroidered clothing was a language, with a vocabulary and grammar, which enabled women's dress to be 'read' and interpreted by others.[1]

Based on the structure and embroidery of this dress, we can determine that its maker was from the Hebron area, with influences from the area of Beit Dajan. Hebron in particular was known for its *jellayeh,* a split-front coat-dress, which was worn over an underdress. The richness of the embroidery and use of gold thread and sequins suggest this was a special piece, perhaps for a wedding. The silk and taffeta patchwork on the central panel is typical for the area, and may have been applied by a professional embroiderer for a fee. Women found inspiration for embroidery patterns in flora, fauna, daily life and local political events. The embroidered motifs on this dress include the *khayam al-basha*, or Pasha's tent, a motif which was used frequently in the Hebron area, along with motifs of the grape vines that grew on local hillsides. Designs were handed down from mother to daughter, with subtle changes and additions made by each generation, reflecting the organic evolution of fashion.

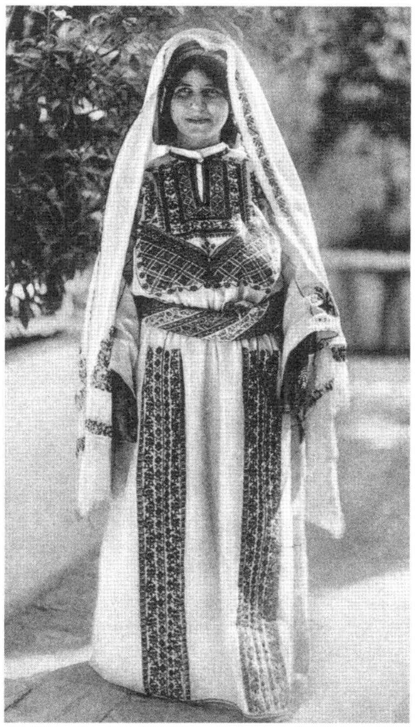

Postcard of a Ramallah woman, early 20th century.

Inspiration also came from beyond the village, as market days brought women into contact with those from different areas of Palestine. Women might spot an unusual motif on someone else's dress, commit it to memory and rush home to embroider it. Mismemory and/or creative licence would turn it into something new: a novel design now specific to her village, with a name of its own, which she might in turn pass on to her friends and daughters. This evolution of embroidered motifs was expedited by the introduction of cars and buses into Palestine in the 1920s. Mechanised transport meant women could travel further afield for market days than they had before, and meet women from areas that were previously inaccessible. Contact with

1. Shelagh Weir, *Palestinian Costume* (2004), p. 20.

clothing of different styles prompted greater migration of design across Palestine.[2]

Broader political and economic changes also left a mark on local dress conventions. With the beginning of the British Mandate period in 1918, social norms around modesty changed and attitudes became more conservative. Women in Hebron, for instance, who had worn their jellayeh with open fronts, sewed up their skirts from the inside or — as in this example — used buttons to hold the garment closed. Subsequent generations made their dresses with solid front panels, or with the long slit permanently fastened, to retain the local style without compromising contemporary taste. As such, the changes absorbed into the garment's design speak to the ways in which colonial norms, technology, and shifting tastes in fashion prompted the evolution of tradition.

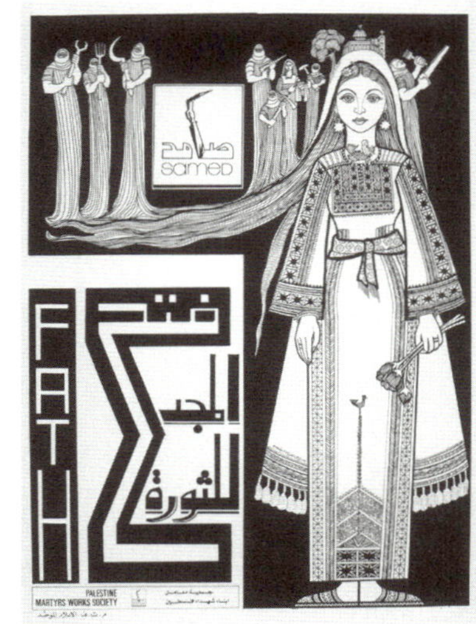


Glory to the Revolution, poster with artwork by Abdel Rahman Al Muzain, c. 1979. Issued by the Unified Information Office of the Palestine Liberation Organisation (PLO).

## EVERYDAY DRESS FROM HEBRON, 1930–1935

Dresses such as the Hebron jellayeh are the pieces for which Palestinian embroidery is renowned: richly-decorated and spectacular, worn at the most important events of a woman's life. The garments that women wore most frequently, however, were known as 'everyday dresses'. These quotidian garments are often humble and well-worn, but offer intimate insight into the lives of Palestinian women in the late nineteenth and early twentieth centuries.

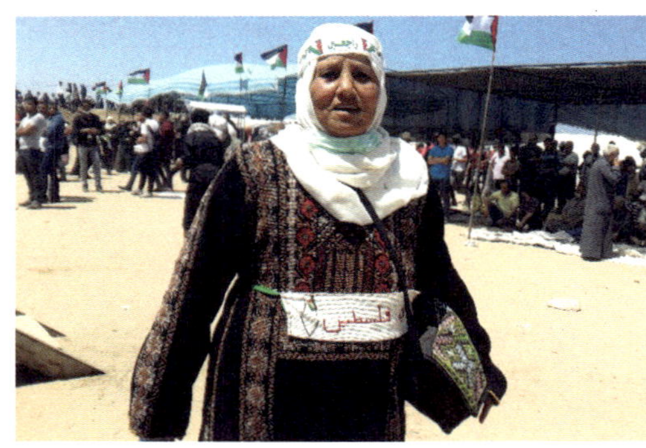

A Palestinian woman wearing a traditional 'thobe' during the Great March of Return in Gaza, 2012.

The everyday dress shown here carries traces of motherhood, and tells us about its maker's daily work, both domestic and agricultural. The holes on either side of the chest panel indicate how she would have breast-fed her babies without changing her dress, through flaps that have been sewn closed once the children were weaned. Large patches at her knees hint at how she may have sat, day in and day out, to prepare food or clean clothes — wet hands wearing away the hand-woven linen over time as she got up and wiped them dry. When viewed inside-out, this dress reveals a patchwork structure of blue fabric. Cotton and linen were dyed with indigo to create the blue garment base typical across Palestine. The darker the blue, the more costly and prestigious the clothing, having required several rounds of dye.[3] Everyday dresses often used cheaper light blue fabric, with areas bleached from extended time working in the fields in the sun. In places where fabric wears easily, women would use their husband's shirting to shore up delicate areas under the arms or at the elbows.

One hallmark of these garments is the presence of more than one embroiderer's hand. A dress in formation was embroidered in sections, which were sewn together at the end. Everyday dresses might incorporate sections of embroidery from dresses a woman inherited from her mother or grandmother. The result here is an historical, layered object that bears the traces of many hands' work. In this way, Palestinian embroidered dresses resist notions of the definitive museum object. Few can be pinned to a single maker or specific moment of origin: embroidery is slow work, an individual pursuit embedded in the communal, connected to social ritual and matrilineal history.

2. Widad Kawar, *Threads of Identity* (2011), p. 114.
3. Weir, *Palestinian Costume*, p. 26.
4. See Tina Malhi-Sherwell, 'Embroidering the Motherland: The Fabric of Palestinian National Identity' (2001), pp. 117-130 and Rachel Dedman, *Labour of Love: New Approaches to Palestinian Embroidery* (2018), pp. 27-32.
5. The First Intifada began in 1987 and ended in 1993, with the signing of the Oslo Accords.

Despite embroidery's status as a domestic handicraft, technological innovations and the international textile trade also left their traces on Palestinian garments. From the mid-nineteenth century, hand-woven cotton, linen and woollen cloth were produced in the main towns of Palestine, alongside textiles coming from Syria, Egypt and Europe. During the British Mandate era an increased import from Europe and Asia brought new fabrics into Palestine. Foreign cottons were enjoyed for their novelty, so some dresses included panels of European cotton or scraps of precious velvet in eye-catching positions — as a jacket lining, or at the hem of a dress — as a sign of wealth and fashion. On this dress, the sleeves carry distinctive zigzags in running stitch, a sign of machine-made embroidery. Although today the hand-made is prized above the industrial, in 1930s Palestine the sewing machine was a novelty, and access to one would have been a mark of social status, which the maker of this dress wore prominently on her sleeve.

### DRESS FROM RAMALLAH, 1930s

The events of 1948, which Palestinians call the *Nakba*, or catastrophe, changed the lives of everyone in Palestine. Hundreds of thousands of Palestinians were forcibly displaced from their homes by Zionist forces, and many were killed or injured in the battle to keep their land from occupation and their villages from destruction and ethnic cleansing. Today, Palestinians within Palestine remain subjugated and controlled, living under the violence of military occupation and apartheid; those in diaspora have become permanent refugees, exiled from their homes for over seventy years, unable to return.

This dress embodies the realities of the Nakba. It is clear from its cut, colour and motifs that it was made by a woman from Ramallah. However, according to Maha Abu Shosheh, the collector who owns the dress today, the original maker of the dress donated it to another woman in 1948. The woman who inherited the dress had been displaced from her home in central Palestine during the events of the Nakba, and walked into the West Bank carrying perhaps nothing to wear but the clothing she had on. The woman who inherited the dress must have been taller and broader than the original embroiderer, as the garment has been enlarged: panels have been added at the sides and around the waist. The material used for the panels is hessian sacking from a bag of flour issued by UNRWA, the United Nations Refugee Works Agency, which gave out provisions to refugees in the aftermath of the crisis. The Arabic letter *nuun* (n), from the word for flour, *tahin*, is visible on the side of the dress, stamped onto the sack in familiar UN-blue. The materiality of this garment speaks not only to the urgency and trauma of the situation in which Palestinians found themselves in 1948, it attests equally powerfully to the generosity and resilience of women at one of the most difficult moments of their lives.

After 1948, women lost access to the Damascene silks, natural dyes, and French thread they had embroidered with previously, as the economic networks and cottage industry that had supported embroidery was shattered. Instead, Palestinians found themselves living in makeshift refugee camps without income, or as exiles in the West Bank, Jordan, Lebanon or Syria. For many women in the 1950s, machine-embroidered dresses became a popular, inexpensive alternative to hand-embroidered garments, and durable synthetic fabrics predominated from the early 1960s, embroidered with motifs inspired by fashions seen in foreign magazines. For many women, their hand-embroidered wedding dress was one of the few things they took with them when they were displaced in 1948, and cherished for the rest of their lives. Others were forced to sell these precious items to make ends meet. This particular garment is a testament to the multiple women who have worn it, and a witness to their experiences. It offers a poetic and practical opening to conversations around the intimate realities of displacement.

### INTIFADA DRESS, 1987–1993

The 1970s saw embroidery become a key tool in the revival of Palestinian heritage and the articulation of Palestinian nationalism. An image of idealized Palestine, embodied by the rural peasant women — at once earth mother, wife and fighter, toiling the earth, producing children, always wearing embroidered dress — circulated on paintings and posters.[4] Embroidery featured heavily in such imagery, and shifted into a symbolic register. The politicization of embroidery, and its attendant associations with Palestinian history, authenticity and legitimacy, has informed its use until today.

This politicization of embroidery reached a zenith during the First Intifada, a mass, popular uprising against the Israeli military occupation of the West Bank and Gaza.[5] The Intifada was characterized by strategies of resistance and civil disobedience, boycotts, strikes, refusal to pay taxes, refusal to participate in the Israeli economy, and clashes involving stone-throwing and violence. The Israeli authorities made it illegal for Palestinians to show their national colours in public, or to fly the Palestinian flag, so women began to stitch explicit symbols of resistance onto their dresses. Embroidery became a place in which it was possible to articulate Palestinian nationalism in public.

'Intifada dresses', such as this one, mingle traditional motifs embroidered in Palestinian colours with a new symbolic vocabulary that speaks to resistance. Here doves sail across the chest panel, flanked by rifles; on other examples, important architectural sites such as the Dome of the Rock or Al-Aqsa Mosque are given prominent positions. The flag and map of Palestine is a repeated motif, running in bands down the skirt and around the cuffs. Allegiance to Fatah or the PLO is made explicit on some Intifada dresses, on others the Ship of Return sails along the back hem.

Such dresses render women's bodies sites of explicit political resistance. Unlike flags or signs, a dress could not be confiscated by the Israeli military, so it acted as both medium and message. The

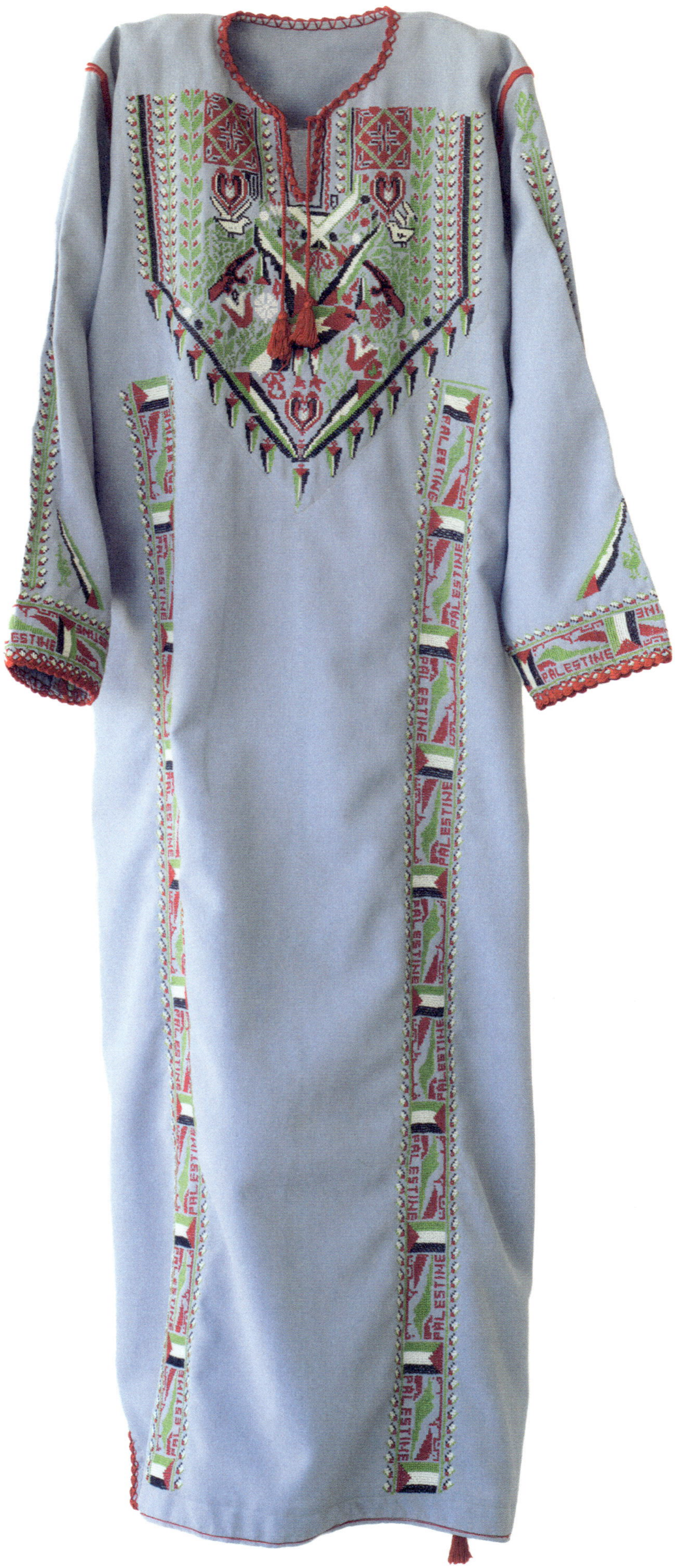


Intifada dress, 1987–1993, from the collection of Tiraz: Widad Kawar Home for Arab Dress.

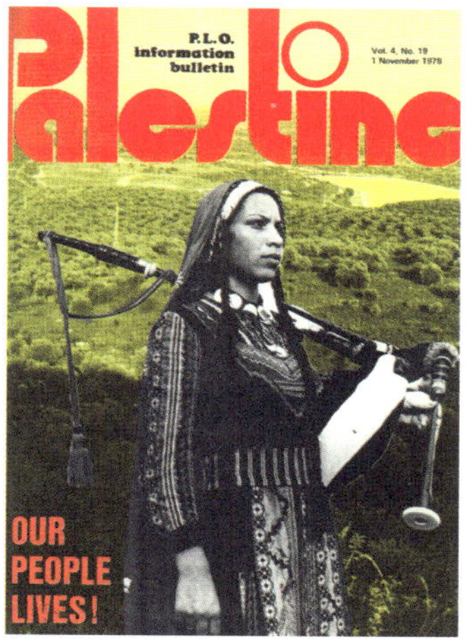


Cover of PLO information magazine, vol. 4, no. 19, 1 November 1978.

use of English stitched alongside Arabic speaks to the public role such garments were perceived to play — an awareness of the international media's documentation of the realities of the Intifada, and a desire for the dresses' narrative to be parsed by sympathetic audiences abroad.[6]

What is also important about such garments is that they feel different to the typical material culture of protest. Demonstrations are usually accompanied by scrawled signs, painted banners and graffitied walls, creative gestures that are relatively spontaneous and ephemeral. Intifada dresses are the antithesis: embroidery is slow and pain-staking work, and embroidering full garments requires months and years of work. These were likely stitched in secret under difficult and dangerous conditions. This is partly what makes them so extraordinary — they speak to the *sumud,* steadfastness, of the Palestinian people, and the idea that resistance in Palestine is a process, not an event.

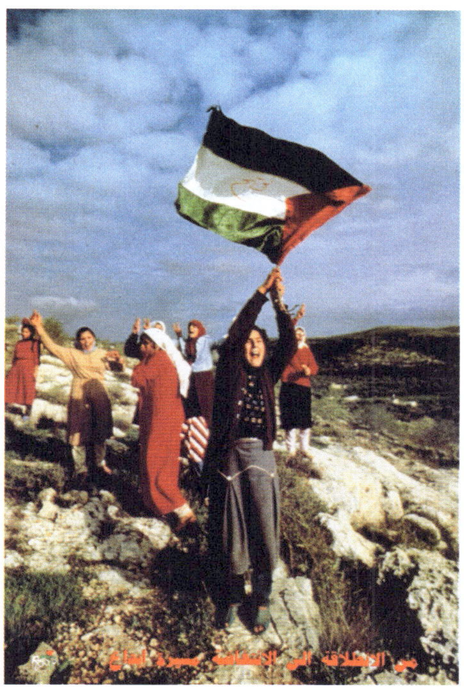

'From the Revolution to the Intifada, a Long Way of Innovation', poster by the Roots Foundation, 1988.

## DRESS, EMBROIDERED BY RAJA EL-ZEER, 2014

Today in Palestine, embroidery is still worn on a daily basis by a few members of the oldest generation, and on special occasions by women of all ages. Embroidery is most commonly encountered, however, as product or commodity. From cushions and shawls, to phone cases, laptop covers, handbags and keyrings, a plethora of embroidered goods are available in shops and online, in Palestine and abroad. Many of these items are produced by Palestinian women working for NGOs and charities, which in the decades following the Nakba were founded locally and internationally to support women impoverished by exile and occupation. Embroidery shifted from a labour of love to labour for pay.

Embroidery-producing organizations provide women with important opportunities to work and support their families, and for those living as refugees in Jordan, Lebanon and Syria the chance to feel connection to their homeland. However, the impact of embroidery's commodification has been mixed and complex. This is an industry that fuels embroidery's class divide, and in many cases involves exploitative labour conditions. By virtue of the politicization Palestinian embroidery has undergone since the 1970s, embroidered objects today act as shorthand for the Palestinian cause, as touchstones for abstract notions of solidarity or female empowerment. These powerful associations can make it difficult to criticise the infrastructural conditions that underpin embroidery's production and circulation today. Respect for tradition is understandable and important, but the romanticization of embroidery's making and the veneration of selective aspects of tradition can hamper innovation in a craft that is naturally mutable.[7]

This dress was made by Raja El-Zeer of Selfit, Palestine. Raja works as a professional embroiderer, earning an income by making dresses to order for others. This particular dress is one she embroidered for herself, to wear at her son's wedding. For a purist of Palestinian embroidery, little about Raja's dress would be considered

6. Kawar, *Threads of Identity*, p. 429.
7. For fulsome exploration of the ethics and problematics of contemporary Palestinian embroidery production, see Rachel Dedman, *At the Seams: A Political History of Palestinian Embroidery* (2016) and Dedman, *Labour of Love,* pp. 32-49.

traditionally Palestinian. The cut reflects the style of the 'camp dress' or 'new dress' which became ubiquitous following the Nakba, as women from across Palestine mixed in refugee camps and the form of dresses homogenized. Its repeated pattern and all-over embroidery is unusual, and Raja's use of two-tone thread reflective of an innovation that has been popular since the 1980s.

The repeated motif on this dress is not necessarily traditionally Palestinian either. Raja shares inspiration for motifs with her embroiderer friends via Facebook and WhatsApp, experimenting with patterns that are more contemporary than conventional. In the 1930s, when the French thread company DMC (Dolfus, Mieg & Cie) introduced industrially dyed thread into the Palestinian market, the company circulated pattern books along with the thread. These books exposed local embroiderers to techniques and designs from elsewhere in the world, prompting adaptation and innovation in local practices.[8] In much the same way, Raja and her friends today draw inspiration from each other, the internet and social media.

Despite not looking conventional, by virtue of being made by Raja, this dress remains as strong an example of Palestinian embroidery as any of its hundred-year-old sisters. Dresses such as Raja's are evidence that Palestinian embroidery continues to preserve itself, evolving in step with the women who make it, and that embroidery is an active, living craft, one that has always reflected and responded to the changing dynamics of life in Palestine.

This text was written in 2022.

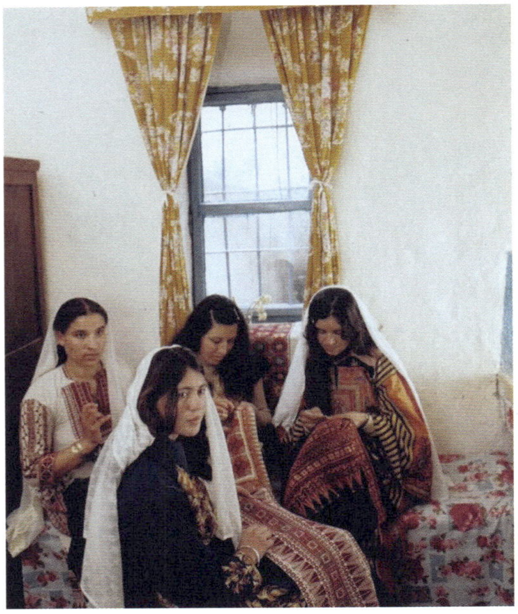

Palestinian women in Qalandia refugee camp participating in Qalandia Camp Women's Handicraft Society, Palestine, 1974.

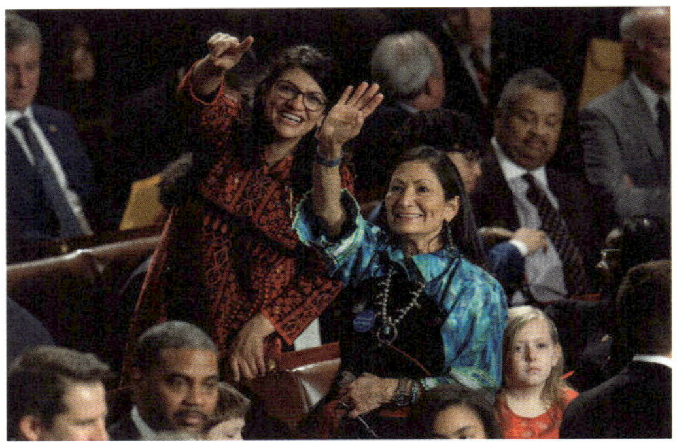

Michigan Democrat Rashida Tlaib is sworn in as representative into the United States Congress wearing a traditional thobe. Next to her the first elected Native American congresswoman Deb Haaland, 2019.

8. Margarita Skinner, *Palestinian Embroidery Motifs: A Treasury of Stitches 1850-1950* (2007), p. 12.

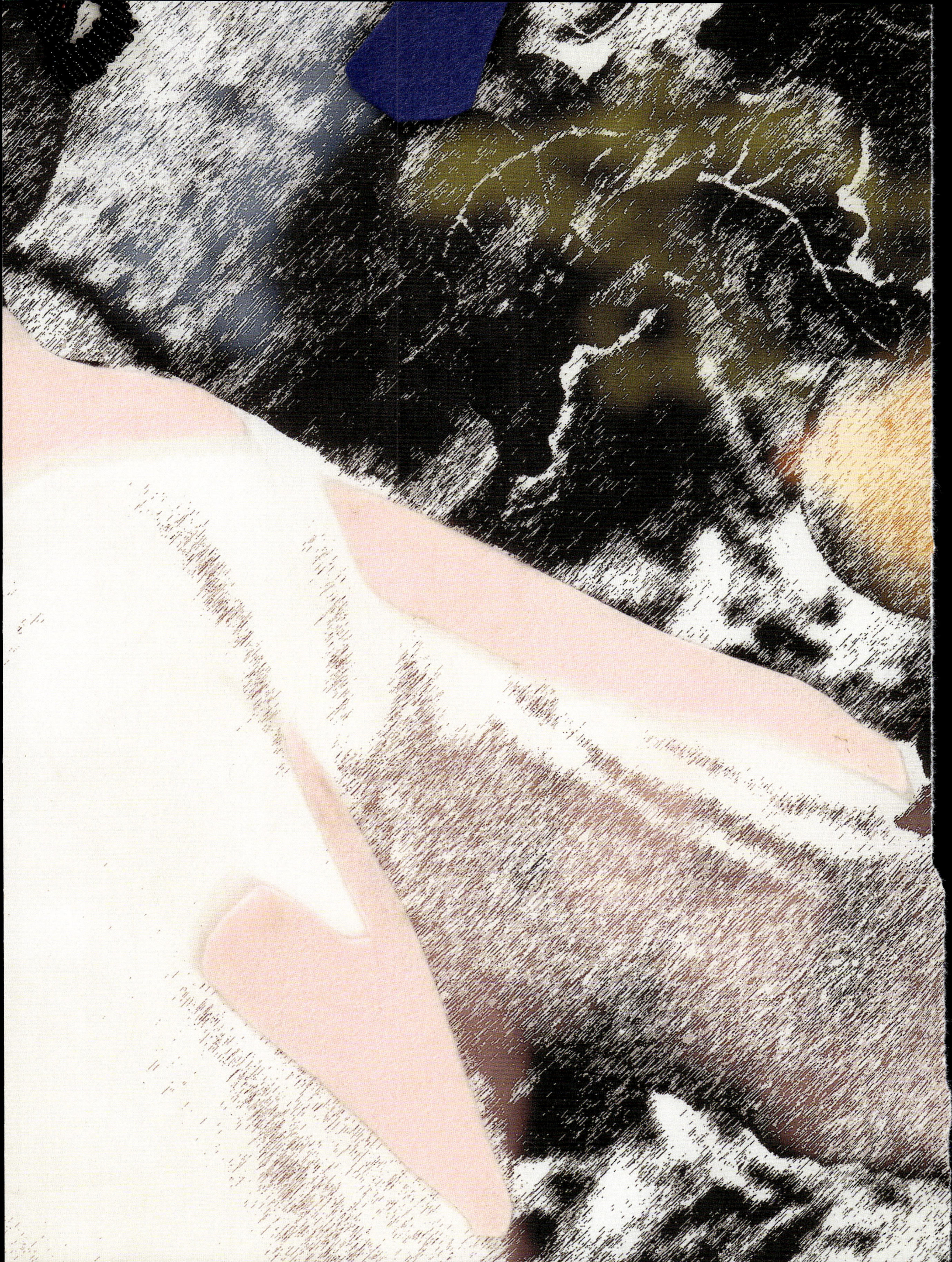

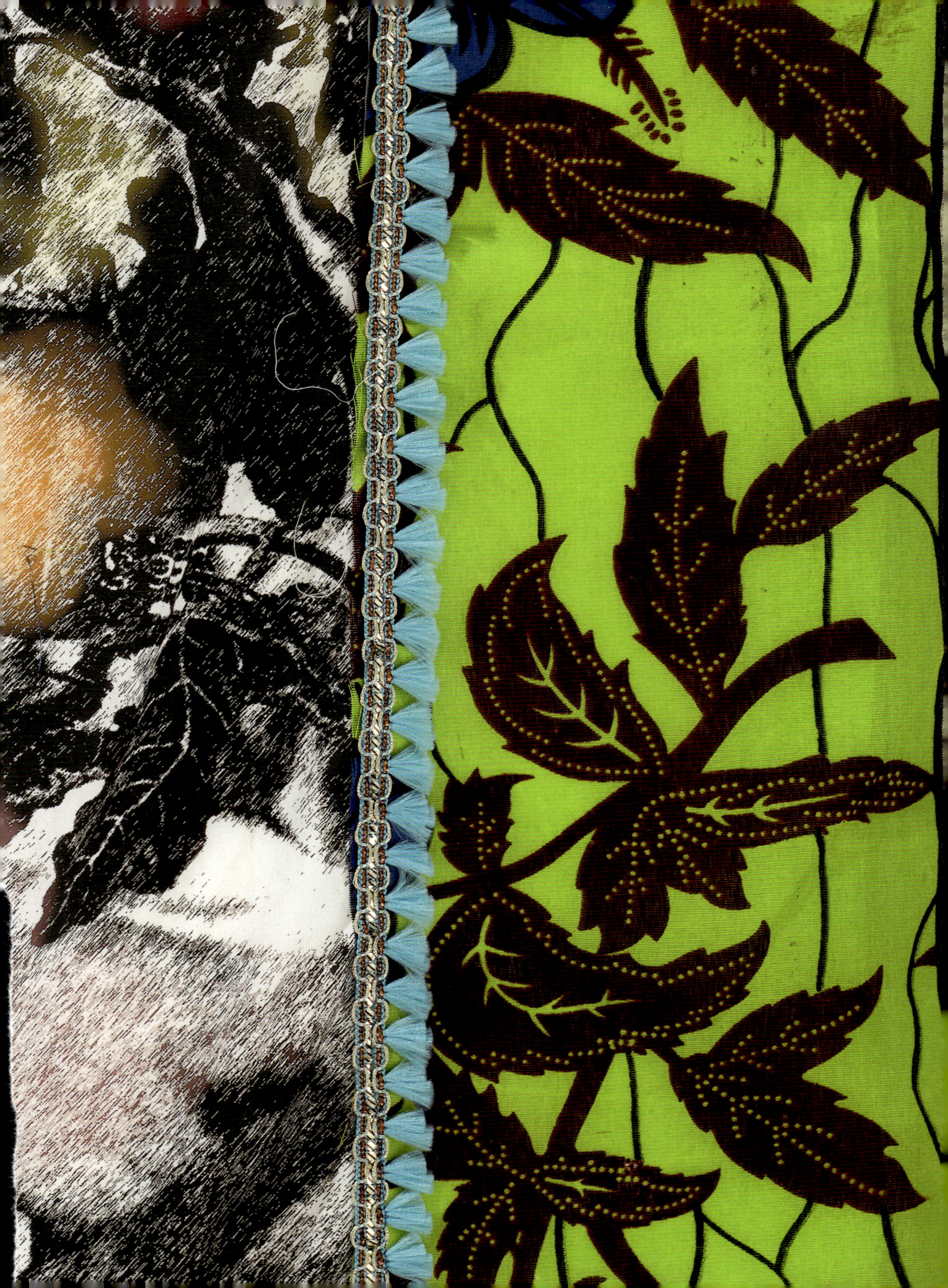

# *Vrouwen van VOS*
patricia kaersenhout

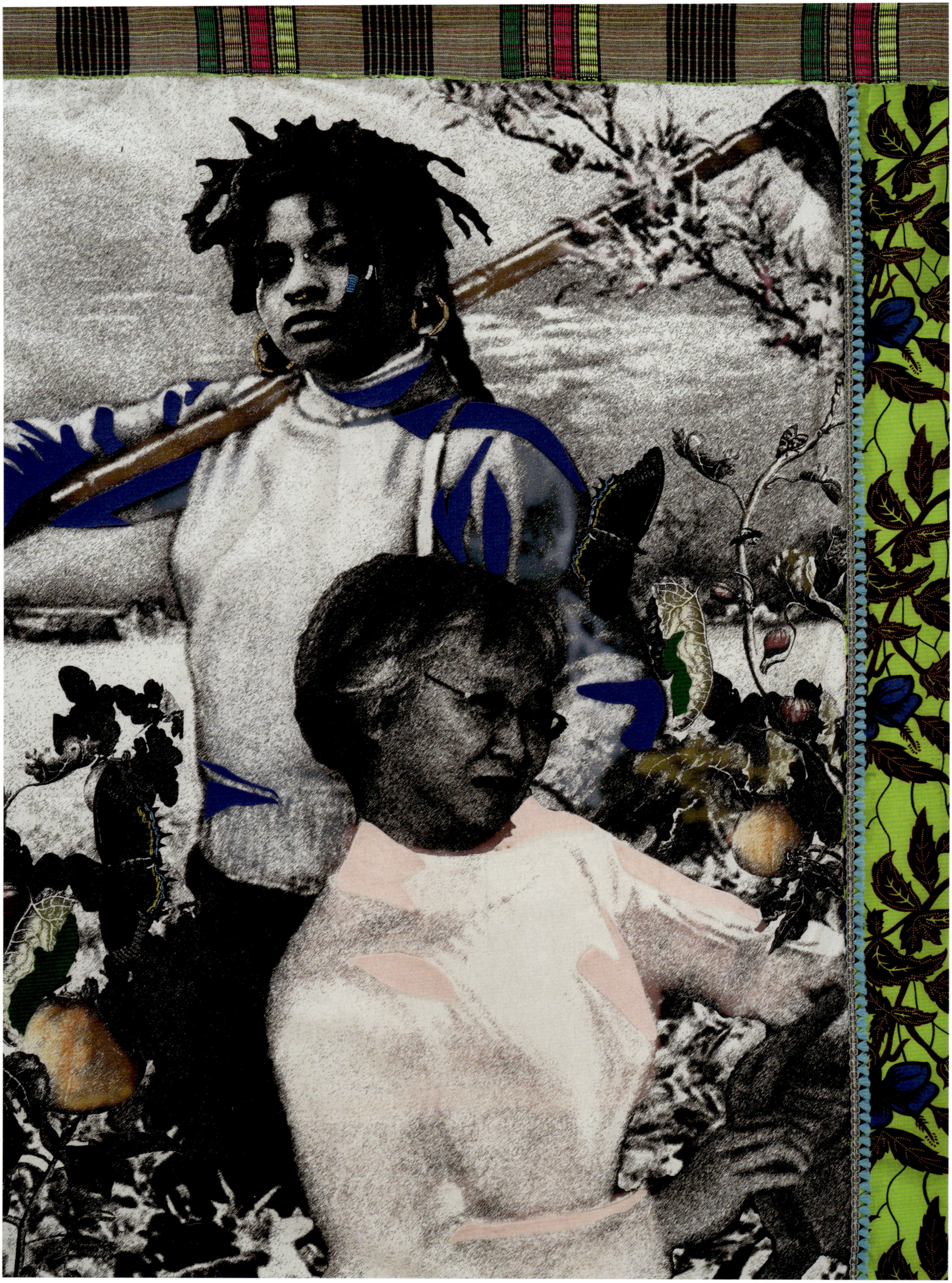

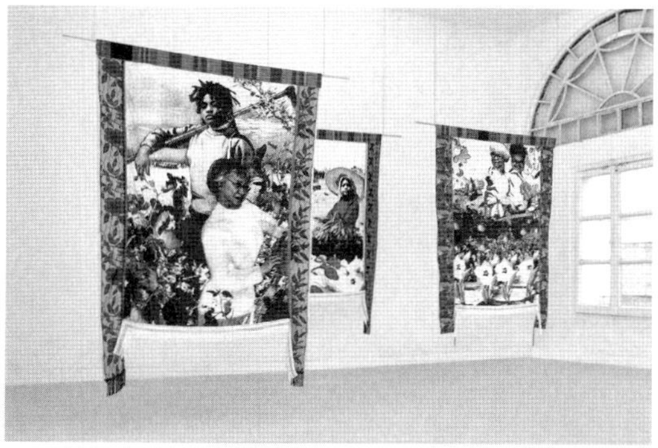

Vrouwen van VOS, patricia kaersenhout, 2020.

Digital print on cotton, beads, felt, African wax fabrics, wood, hand and machine embroidery, appliqué. Naomie Pieter & Twi Tjoa, 200 × 140 cm; Jessica D'Abreu & Polly Levens, 180 × 130 cm; Camille Parker & Mevr. Weels, 200 × 140 cm.

*Vrouwen van VOS* is a series of three textile banners, each depicting two women standing side by side. The black and white images are digital assemblages of photographs and various motifs, including leaves, flowers, and butterflies. They are framed by strips of colourful patterned fabric, colloquially known as African or Dutch wax print, and are embellished with pink, orange, blue and white ribbons, ruffles and tassels.

The women are pictured in pastoral settings: in a field of large flowers, between vegetable crops, on a farmyard. On the middle banner, two women wearing conical hats resembling traditional Asian rice hats pose with a basket in their arms filled with plants; behind them are two pigs in front of a barn. The women look steadfast, self-assured, empowered. On the banner to the left, the younger woman carries a scythe over her shoulder, as if ready to work. The older woman beside her has a softer look and is inspecting what look like gourds. There is a sense of heroism and strength here that, in combination with the fabrics and ribbons, make the banners a celebration of female power.

The photographic images look grainy, with black and white areas contrasting sharply, as if they were stencilled or photocopied multiple times. Colour has been added in places: a subtle green to leaves, light orange or pink tints to accentuate vegetables or flowers. Other elements are highlighted with pieces of coloured felt: blue appliqué patches on a blouse, creamy white on petals, or bold yellow in the folds of the *angisa* worn by one woman. Some details are embellished with small glass beads, including shiny black beads to highlight eyeglasses, earrings and lips, pink and white ones to add lustre to a butterfly and the voluminous flower corsage worn by one woman. Across all three banners, flowers with large, heart-shaped petals appear as a recurring motif.

The images are printed on plain white cotton. For the borders, the artist used different African fabrics, mixing high-quality and mass-produced textiles available at markets. A repeat pattern of blue flowers and brown leaves adorns one bright green border, while a classic patchwork-inspired design consisting of a plethora of multi-coloured patterns forms another one. Printed along the edges are selvedge labels featuring the name of the manufacturer and reference number: GUARANTEED REAL WAX 16356, or VERITABLE REAL WAX D.NO.997554. Each banner is lined by crochet fringes made of synthetic white yarn and silky ribbons sewn across the seams.

The banners are sewn by hand and by machine. In some places the machine creates a straight line of stitches, but most stitching is jolty and irregular. Looking closely, we can see more 'imperfections', such as fabric pulling at a seam, stitching gone askew, or loose threads hanging from the back. The protest banners are clearly not intended as a demonstration of the artist's sewing skills. Instead, their makeshift appearance adds to their directness and subversive character.

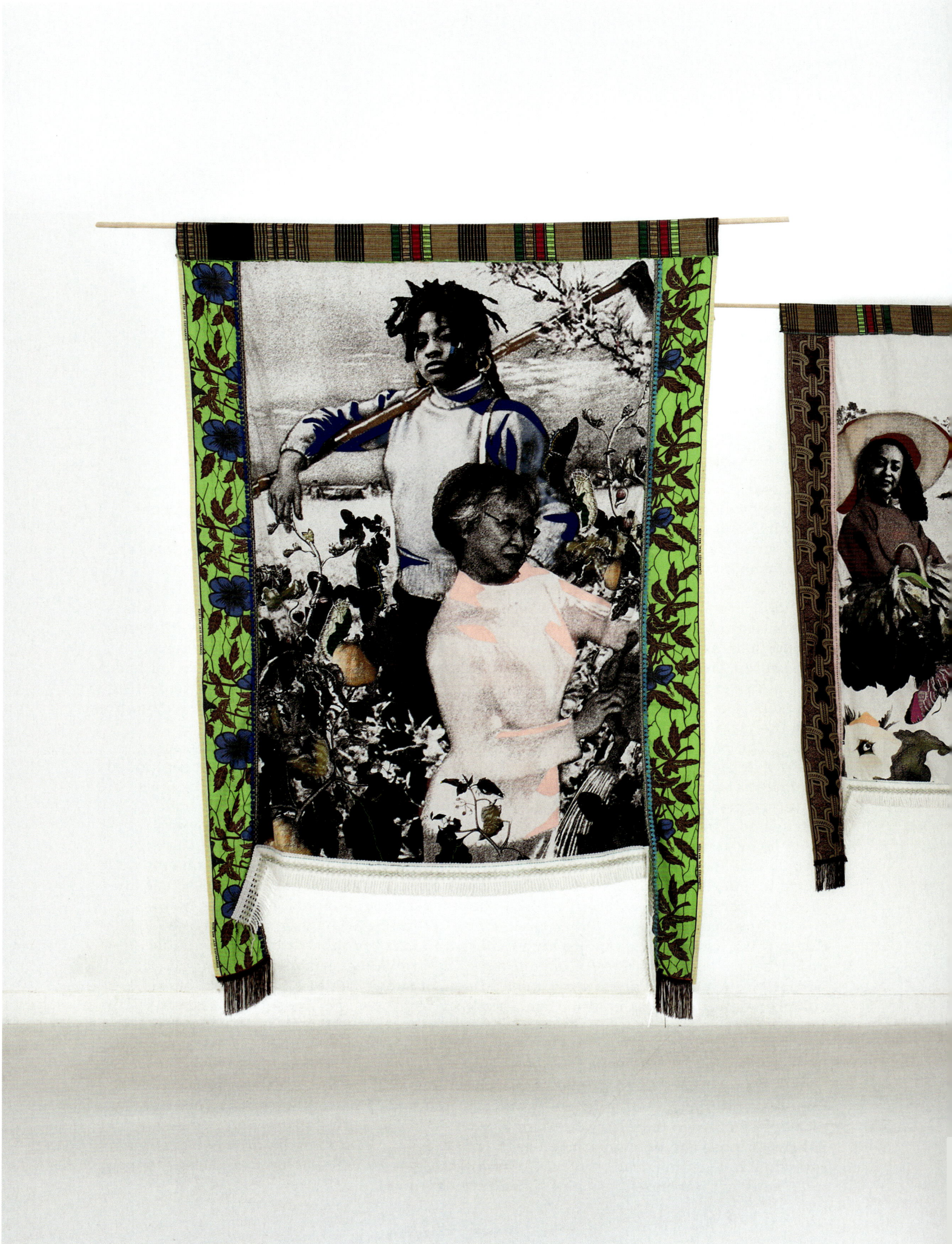

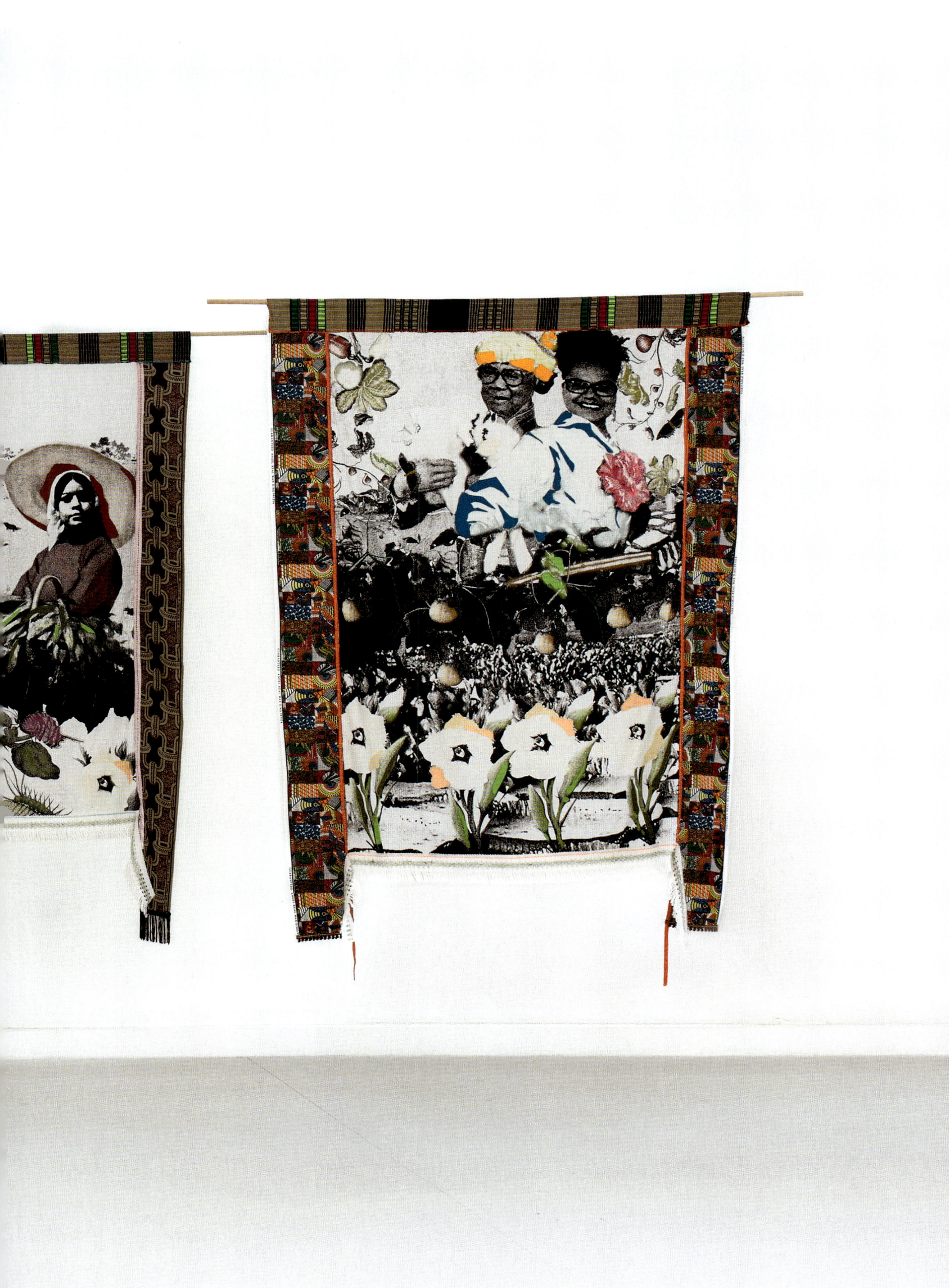

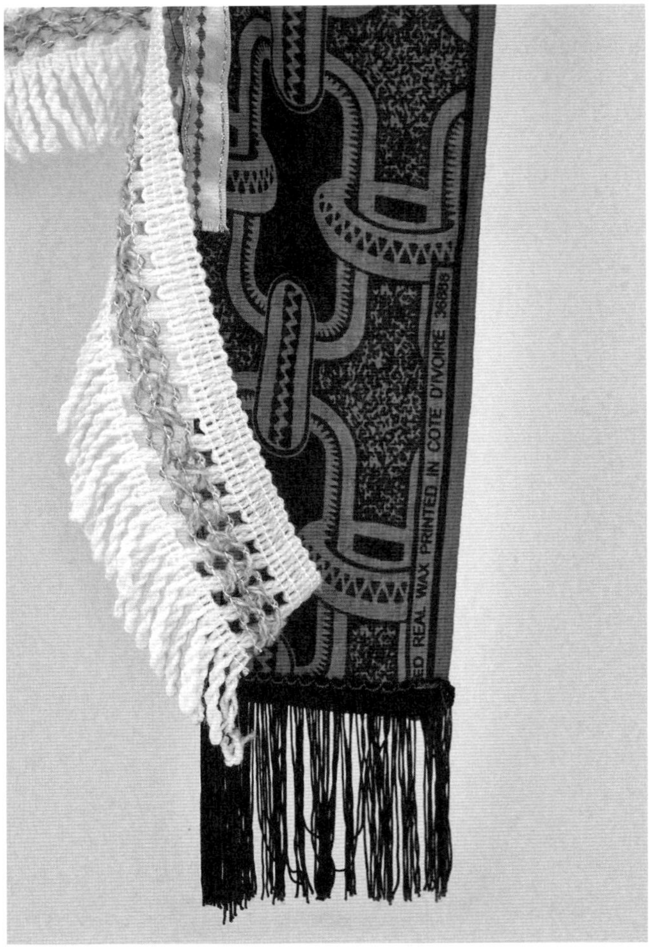


Detail Jessica d'Abreu & Polly Levens, African wax fabric border and fringes.

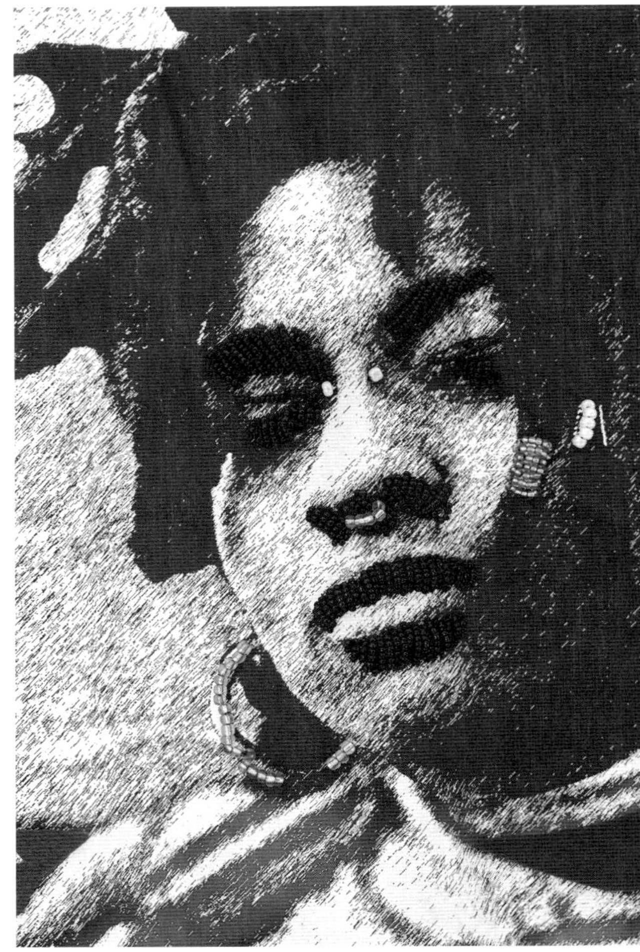

Detail Naomi Pieter and Twi Tjoa, bead work.

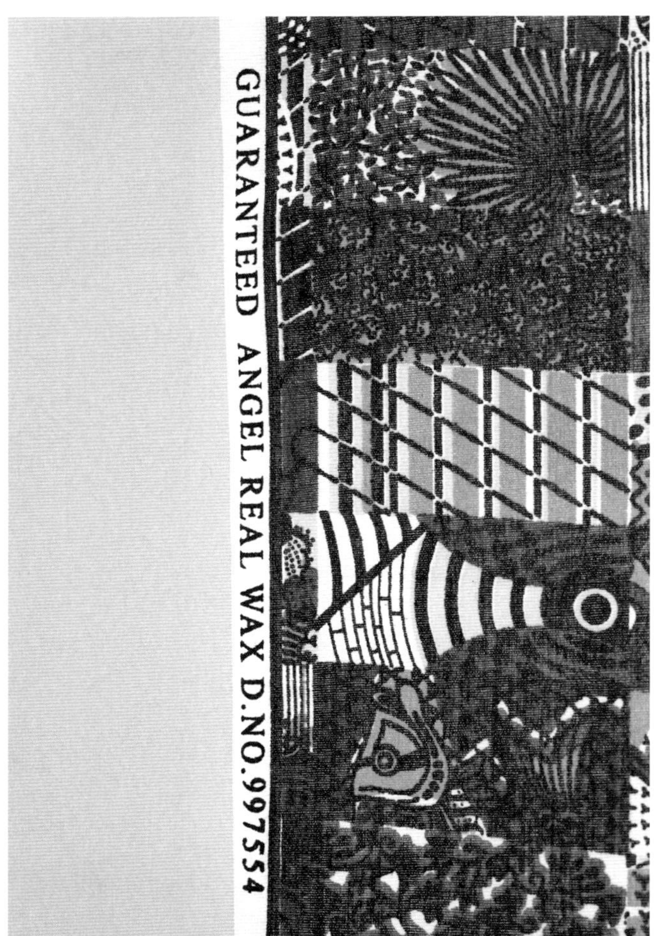


Detail Camilla Parker & Mevr. Weels, African Wax fabric with quality mark and design number in selvedge.

# UNRAVELLING VROUWEN VAN VOS
## In Conversation with patricia kaersenhout

*Vrouwen van VOS* is the third series of textile banners in which visual artist patricia kaersenhout brings important Black women poets, academics and activists out of oblivion. The banners honour six women who played a vital role in the struggle for social justice for Surinamese women in the Netherlands. Born in the Netherlands to Surinamese parents, kaersenhout investigates their background in relation to their upbringing within the culture of Western Europe. Working across a wide range of media, including textiles, they explore the movements of the African diaspora and its relation to feminism, sexuality, racism and the history of slavery.

CHRISTEL VESTERS — What draws you to textiles?

PATRICIA KAERSENHOUT — For each project, I choose a medium or material that is connected with the content of the work, not necessarily because of its aesthetic or stylistic quality. I often work with cotton because the fabric relates directly to the history of colonial exploitation and the transatlantic slave trade. In many textile-based works, I use so-called African wax textiles, which I bought on my travels through West Africa.

CHRISTEL — I noticed that you didn't cut off the selvedge labels printed along the edge of the fabrics. Markings such as 'Guaranteed Real Wax', 'Authentic African wax', or 'True Original Wax Hollandais' are tell-tale signs of a history scarred by colonial expansion and appropriation. To what an extent does the history of African wax fabrics play a part in these works?

PATRICIA — Vlisco fabrics are part of Dutch colonial history. I remember reading about it and suddenly realizing why I'd been collecting them all those years. In my culture we believe in embodied history, meaning that history is not only communicated in written or oral form, but that it becomes part of our bodies, and can therefore be transmitted between bodies, between spirits. Somehow these fabrics spoke to me about this history of appropriation and extortion. So yes, the history of the Real Dutch Wax fabrics, and the capitalist operation of manufacturers like Vlisco, influenced my choice to use African textiles in my work.

CHRISTEL — Do you use them to critique the cultural appropriation that took place under colonial regimes? As reminders? I mean, African wax fabrics are incredibly popular amongst young people in West Africa and North America, even in Surinam.

PATRICIA — Appropriation is not necessarily a negative thing. After all, culture exists because of mutual influencing and exchange. Take the use of chintz textiles in the traditional clothing from the small Dutch town of Hindeloopen. Today these wax-coated fabrics are described as vernacular culture, whereas they were originally made in India, imported to the Netherlands, and adapted to reflect local tastes. The same kind of cultural exchange occurred with African wax fabrics. Dutch designers modified them in response to the local tastes in West-Africa in terms of colours, symbols and motifs. Vlisco later started to collaborate with local designers.

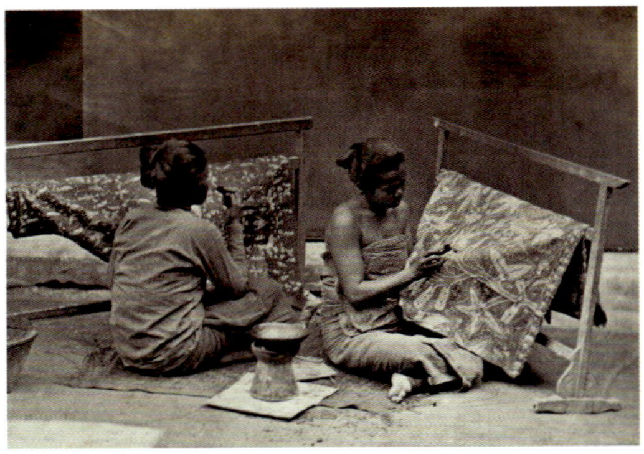

01

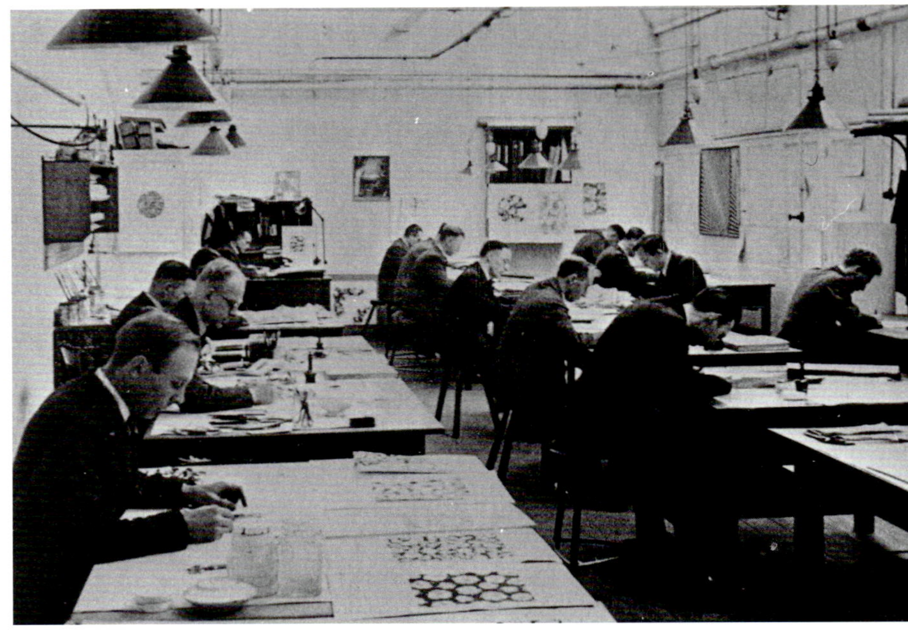

02

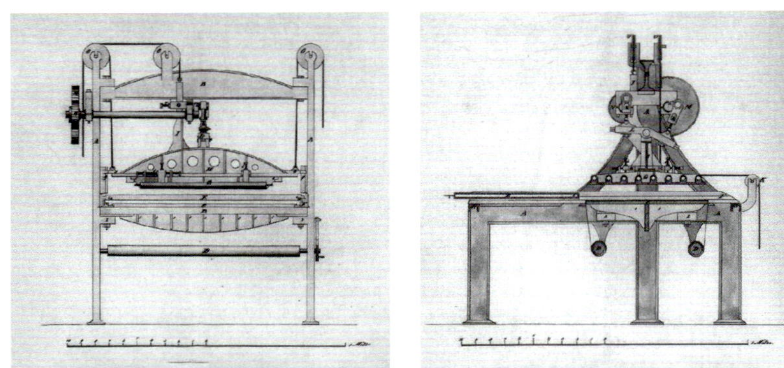

03

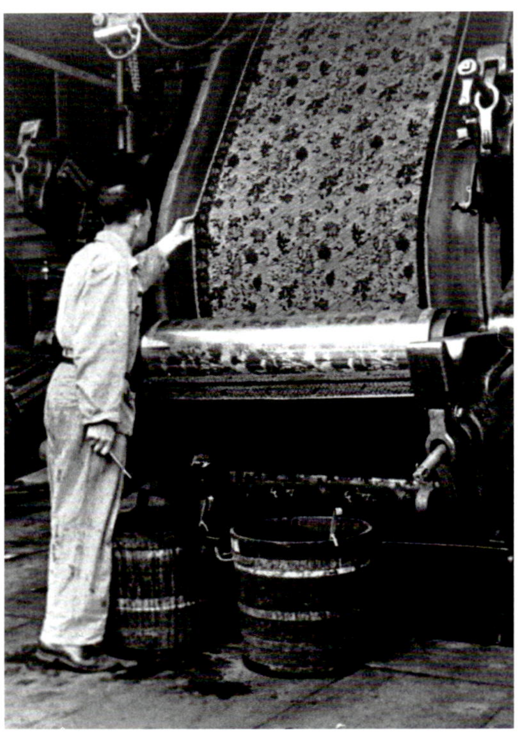

04

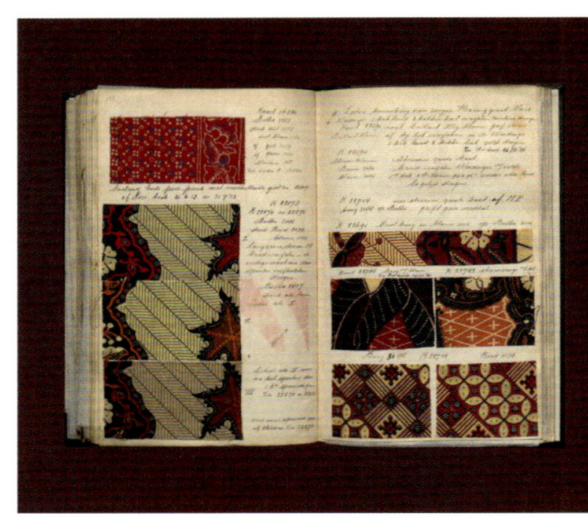

05

BATIK
Batik, from the Javanese 'bathik', is a resist-dye technique where patterns are drawn by hand with warm wax on both sides of cotton fabric, applied with a pen-like instrument called a 'tjanting', or a printing block known as 'tjap'. Once the wax solidifies, the cloth is dyed in a single colour. The wax is then removed, revealing the white pattern. A second or third colour can be applied by repeating the process. It could take months to create one sarong. Batik has been practised since ancient times across the world. The most refined batik is found on Java, Indonesia, where symbolic imagery blends Hindu-Buddhist, Chinese, Islamic and European influences. By 1840, several Indo-European and Dutch women had set up batik workshops on Java. Unbound by local traditions regarding the use of motifs and colours, they created modern batiks for local and European markets.

01. Studio portrait of Women making batik, Java, Indonesia. Photograph by O. Kurkdjian & Co., c. 1870–1900.

IMITATION BATIK
Spotting a business opportunity, textile mills in the Netherlands began experimenting with industrially printed batik fabrics. However, the printing machines caused cracks in the designs, and the cloths were rejected by the Javanese as inferior. Seeking new markets, mills such as Vlisco and the Haarlemsche Katoenmaatschappij began exporting imitation batiks to West Africa. By 1950, Africa had become Vlisco's primary market, where its wax prints remain symbols of luxury and cultural identity.

02. Vlisco Design Studio, Helmond, the Netherlands, c. 1930–1950.

VERITABLE WAX HOLLANDAIS
Since 1946, Vlisco has created over 350,000 original textile designs, each marked with a unique number. Some designs have been archived, while others remain in production or are reissued in new colours palettes. To distinguish authentic Vlisco fabrics from cheap knock-offs, the selvedge bears the quality mark 'Veritable Wax Hollandais Vlisco' and the design's number.

03. Drawing of La Javanaise, submitted by J.B.T. Prévenaire jr. with his patent application in 1854. Reproduced in G. P. J. Verbong's 'Katoendrukken in Nederland vanaf 1800' (1988).

04. Printing machine at Vlisco, Helmond, c. 1930–1950.

LA JAVANAISE
Today, imitation batiks are cheaply made with digital printing, lacking depth and texture. Imitation batiks were initially produced through labour-intensive hand block printing. The introduction of machines such as the Perrotine and the Javanaise industrialized the process, increasing the scale and speed while reducing costs. Over time, different printing techniques created distinct visual effects.

05. L. Driessen, Bewerking der artikelen 1911–1930. Sample book with dye instructions, Leidsche Katoenmaatschappij, c. 1924. Sample books were used to document the specifics of each patterned fabric, including dye and printing instructions. They also served as catalogues or as production ledgers.

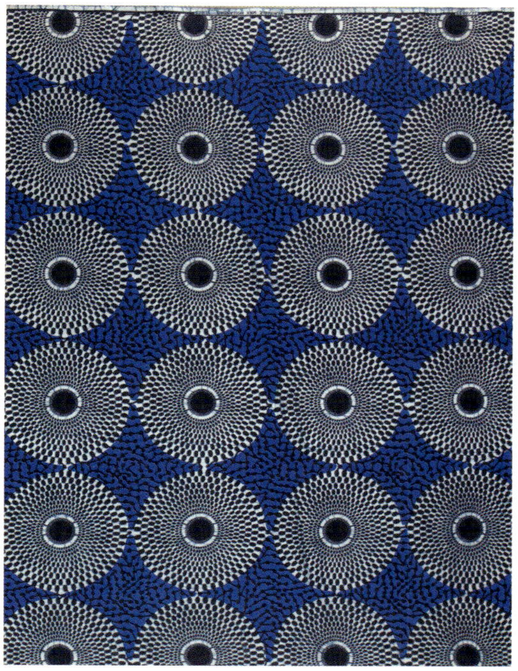

06

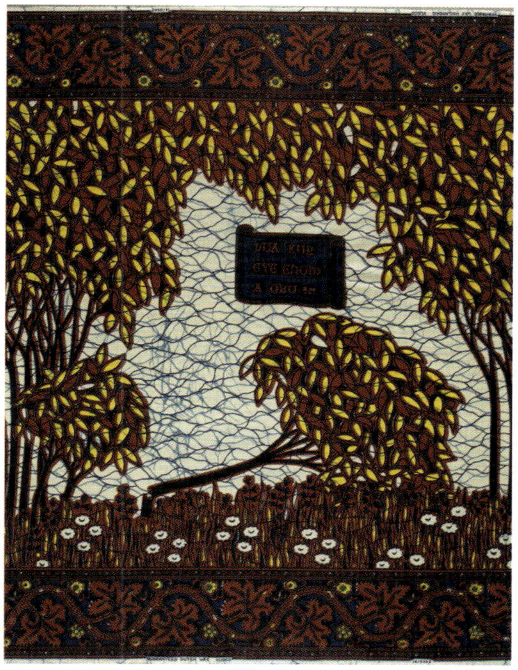

07

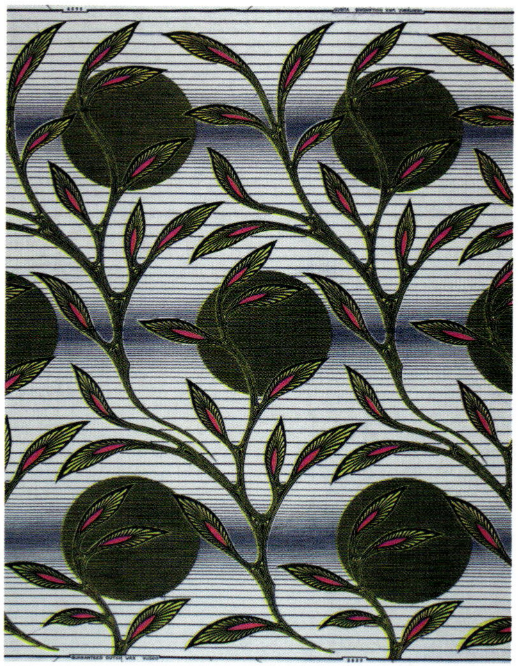

08

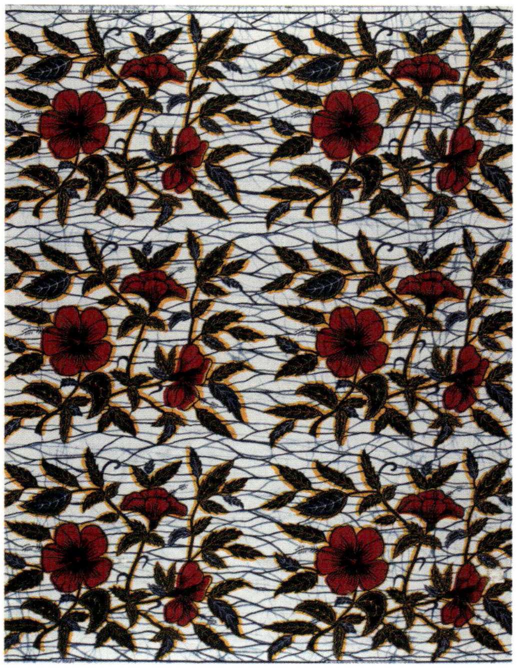

09

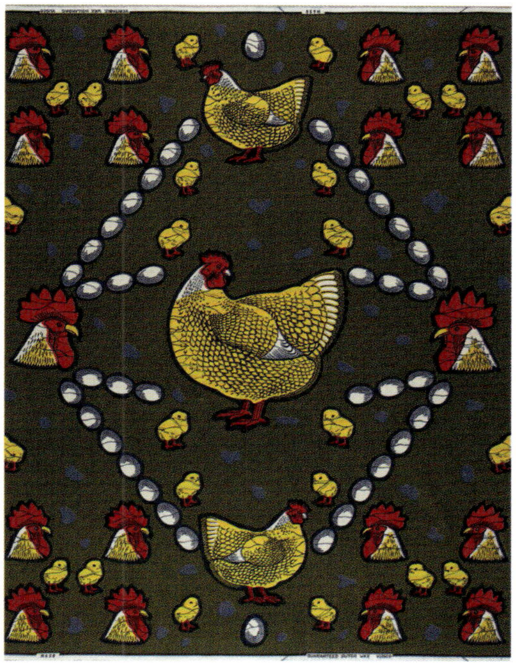

10

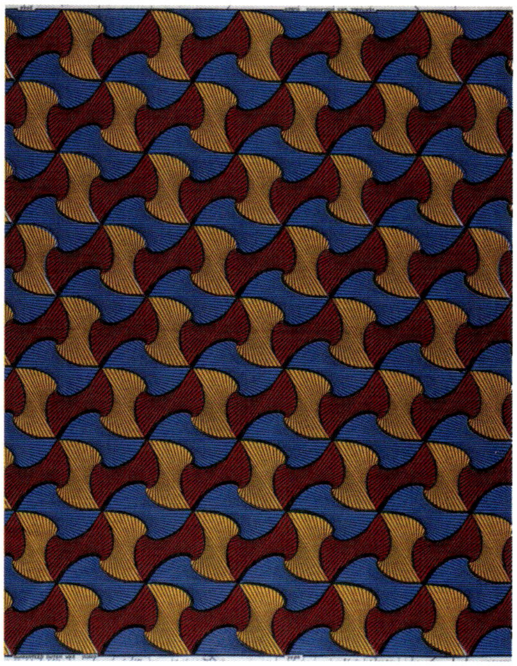

11

STORIED DESIGNS
Until 1930, no European designer had travelled to the African continent. Designs were created from imagination, based on written descriptions or on graphic elements borrowed from Indonesian textiles, such as the garuda bird. The fact that white European men designed wax prints for Black African ladies explains the gap between the intention behind a design and their interpretation by the African market. Around 1934, Vlisco began consulting with local traders, such as the Nana Benz in Togo, on regional colour and pattern preferences. These saleswomen became a vital link between the European manufacturer and local customers and are responsible for naming many patterns and assigning symbolic meaning. Some names reference local proverbs, notable figures or events; others reflect daily concerns. Names and stories often vary between regions, embedding themselves into the vernacular traditions of each place.

06. Vlisco, VL00633.296, Wax Block. Design by Piet Snel, 1936. Given names include: Record, Target, Plaque-Plaque, Nsu Bura, Gbédjégan.
This design has different names in different countries. In Ghana it is called ‘Nsu Bura’, which means ‘water well’, referring to the ripple effect after throwing a stone in a well, meaning that whatever you do, good or bad, it will have an effect on everyone around you. In Togo it is called ‘Gbédjégan’, after the traditional straw king’s hat, and in Nigeria it is known as Record, after old vinyl records.

07. Vlisco, VL00662.125, Wax Block. Designed for Haarlemsche Katoenmaatschappij, a company later acquired by Vlisco, 1933. Given names: Fallen Tree, Zaïre.
The Twi proverb ‘Dua kur gye enum a obu’, shown next to the broken tree, translates as ‘One tree alone cannot stand the wind’ – a reminder not to carry burdens alone. Zaïre, its other name, alludes to the wealth Ghana and the Ivory Coast amassed through cacao trade with present-day DR Congo.

08. Vlisco, 14/3639, Wax Block. Design by Jan Mollemans, 1982. Given names: Grotto, Pomme de Discorde, Mirror in the Sun.

09. Vlisco, VL00921.204, Wax Block Design by Dries van de Ven, 1952. Given names include: Hibiscus, Hibisque Florba.
This pattern is especially popular in Guinea and Ivory Coast. Twelve yards are essential in every dowry: ‘No Hibiscus, no wedding!’

10. Vlisco, VL0H628.139, Wax Block. Design by Ted van de Ven, 1952. Given names: Happy Family, La Famille.
This design represents the archetypical African family: the maternal figure in the centre, surrounded by chicks and eggs – future children. The father is seen as troublesome, shown only by the rooster’s head.

11. Vlisco, 14/3686, Wax Block. Design by Johan Sleegers, 1984. Given names include: Santana; Chérie, ne me tourne pas le dos.
Marital issues are often symbolized through Vlisco designs. This pattern is based on a sketch provided by female vendors and is said to represent an angry woman turning her back to her pleading husband.

However, cultural appropriation becomes a problem when people claim something as only and uniquely theirs — when culture is conceived as something monolithic, or when people don't recognize or don't want to acknowledge that many influences from other cultures have shaped their culture over time. To me, Hindeloopen chintz and Real Dutch Wax fabrics are prime illustrations of how interaction with other cultures lies at the root of Dutch culture. By including African wax textiles I want to raise critical questions about authenticity, and what it means to call something authentically or Real Dutch. I think there's something perverse about stealing something from someone else's culture, and then identifying it as authentically Dutch. It's only when we recognize that both all cultures exist by virtue of mutual influencing that we can tap into the beauty and power of it. Then we're not talking about appropriation, but about interaction and exchange.

Something else I find interesting about the story of African wax fabrics is how new designs immediately take on meaning when they appear on markets in Benin, Nigeria, Togo or Ghana. The batik technique is imported from Indonesia and its designs are created in Helmond, but it's the women selling the fabrics in local shops and markets who think up their names, interpret their designs with stories and attach symbolic meaning to the patterns and motifs that have significance to the local community, literally embedding them into the oral culture of West Africa. This kind of synergy and interplay between cultures fascinates me. Moreover, the same fabric can have other connotations in other regions.

CHRISTEL — How is the story of these African textiles connected with the theme of *Vrouwen van VOS*?

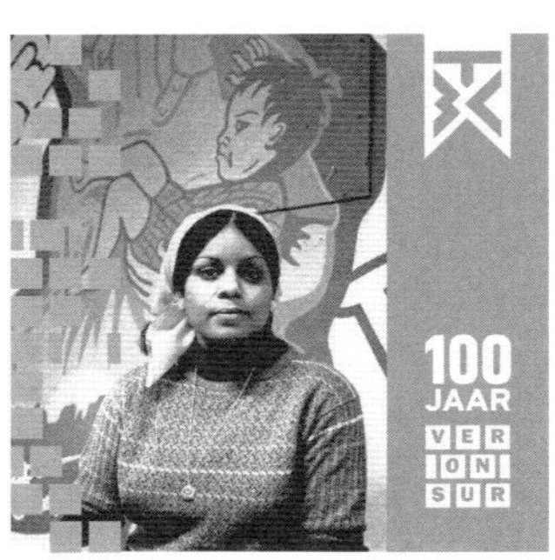


Poster for the exhibition Vereniging Ons Suriname: 100 Years of Emancipation and Struggle, The Black Archives, Amsterdam, 2020–2021.

Founded in 1919, the Vereniging Ons Suriname is the oldest society in the Netherlands dedicated to the emancipation of Surinamese people and recognition of their culture.

PATRICIA — In *Vrouwen van VOS* I portrayed six women who are or were active in the Vereniging Ons Suriname and who all contributed to the emancipation of the Surinam community in the Netherlands. I based the images on the visual language of communist propaganda posters because I wanted to show them as heroines. Combining them with African wax fabrics was an intuitive decision, but with hindsight, I see that these things are connected — the colonial histories embodied in the fabrics and the fight for social justice these Black women were involved in.

CHRISTEL — In earlier works, such as *Food for Thought* (2019) and *Proud Rebels* (2015), you portrayed key Black female scholars, journalist, poets or activists individually. Why did you portray the six women from VOS as duos?

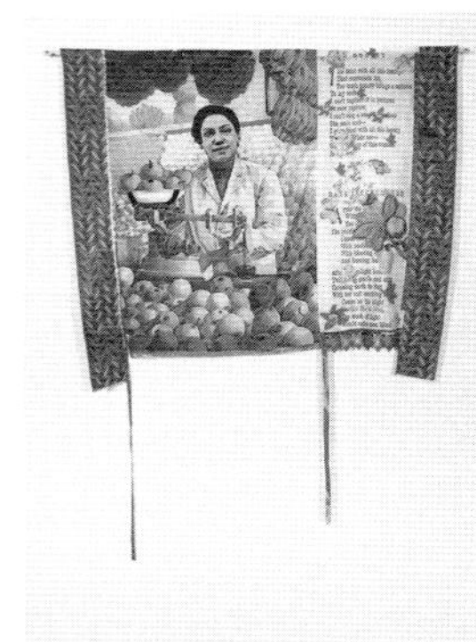

Food for Thought: Hermine Huiswood #3/4, 2021.
Andiye, digital print on cotton, beads, felt, African fabrics, wood.

PATRICIA — In *Vrouwen van VOS* I combined a younger generation of activist women, such as Naomie Pieter and Jessica de Abreu, with an older generation, like Mrs. Wheels and Twie Tjoa. I wanted to show that every generation of activists stands on the shoulders of their foremothers. Twie Tjoa, for instance, has been fighting for the rights of Black, migrant and refugee women, as well as for members of the LHBTIQ+ community for almost four decades. The younger woman standing behind her, Naomie Pieter, is an anti-racism and queer activist, and the driving force behind the Black Lives Matter demonstrations in the Netherlands. We cannot view any of these women or their achievements as separate from each other. I also want to address that the fight for emancipation and against racism in the Netherlands has always been part of a broader, international movement. Take Otto and Hermina Huiswood, for example, who were both involved in the civil rights movement and were members of the American Communist Party before they moved to Amsterdam and became involved with VOS People were internationally connected and organized themselves, even before the internet.

CHRISTEL — Like an invisible fabric?

PATRICIA — Yes, like a communal body fuelled by a common fight for equal rights — workers, Black people, women. What many people don't know, or have forgotten, is that Black women were instrumental in the Pan-African movement and the anti-racism movement. Especially Caribbean women. They helped to set up the National Association for the Advancement of Colored People, one of the oldest civil rights movements in the Unites States.

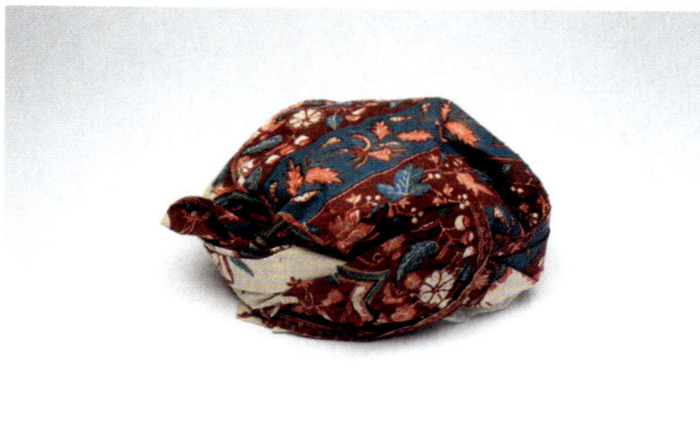

12

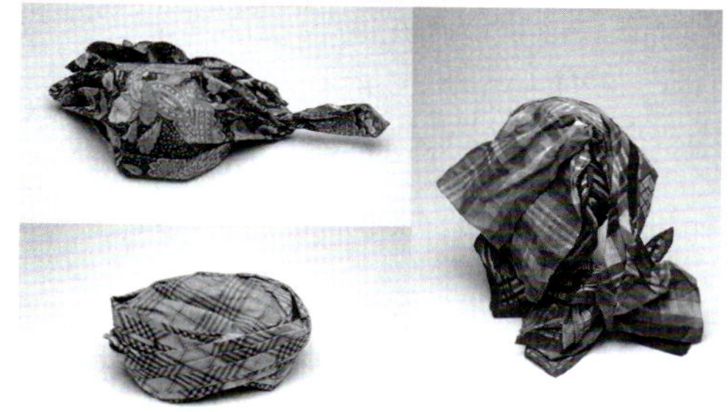

15

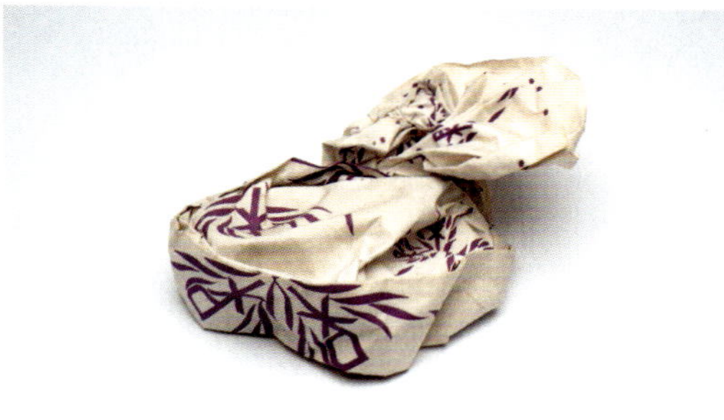

13

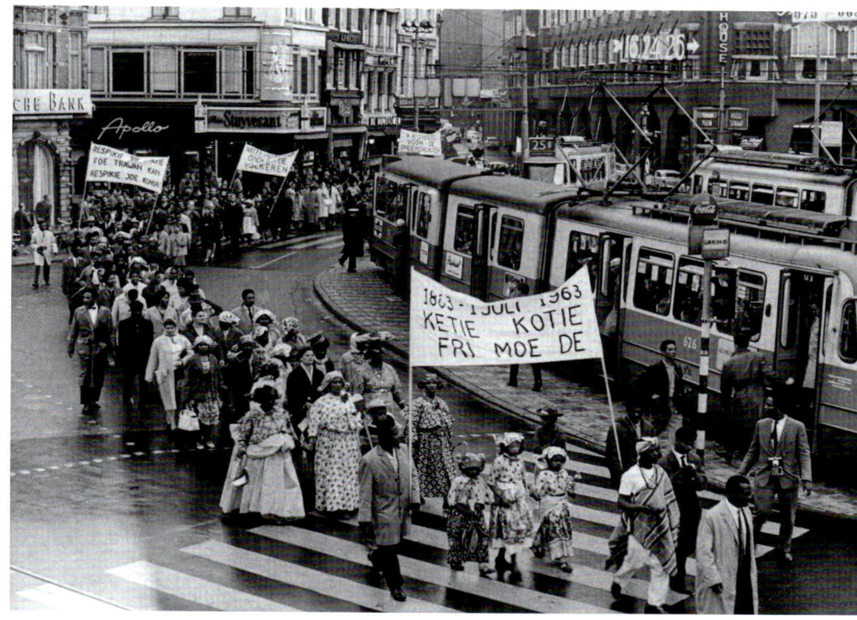


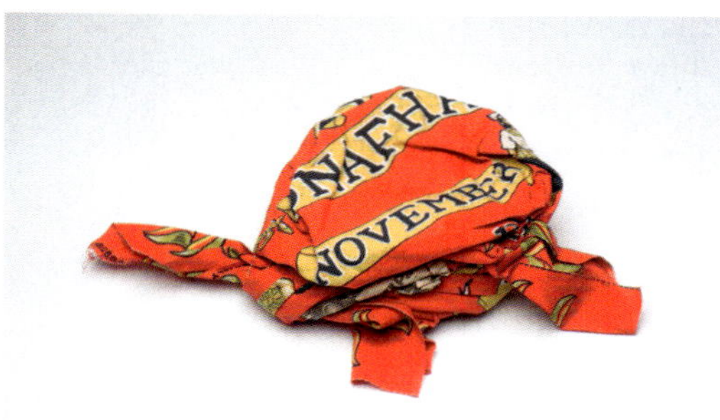

14

16

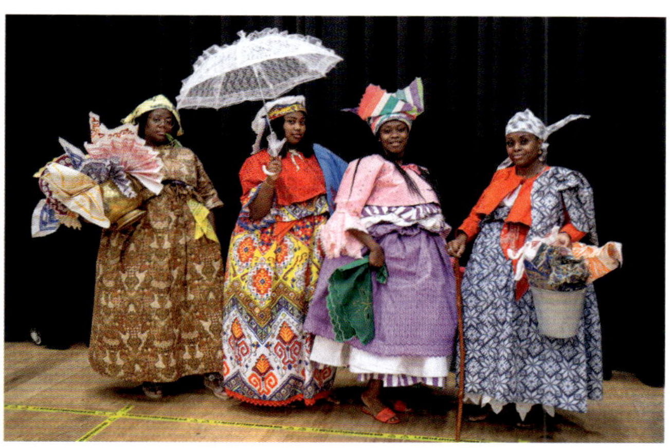

17

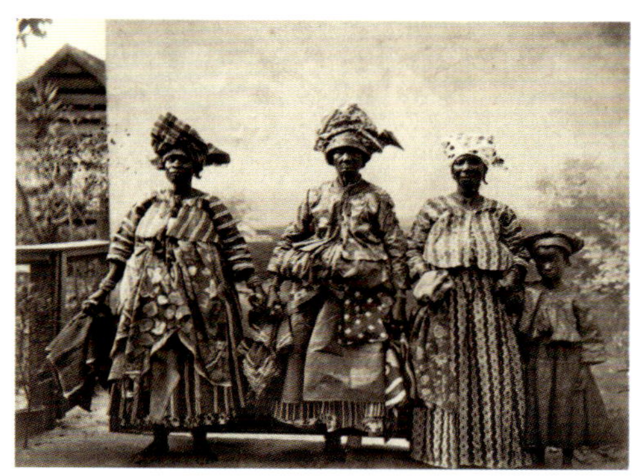

18

FOLDED MESSAGE
Dress communicates mood, social standing and identity. It can also relay coded messages – visibly through motifs or hidden in folds. The 'angisa' is a patterned and distinctively folded headscarf worn by Afro-Surinamese women as part of their traditional dress, the 'koto'. Each folding style has its own name and meaning. Through the choice of pattern and fold, women express their state of mind or signal intentions. Unfolded, an angisa measures 90 × 90 cm.

12. Angisa, Surinam, before 1988. Batik cotton, Yampanesi, 'strek'ede' fold, c. 35 cm. The 'strek'ede' fold, meaning a bow tied head, signifies confidence and pride. Made of batik cloth from Java, this angisa is also known as Yampanesi.
13. Angisa, Suriname, before 1966. Printed cotton, 'waaier ede', c. 20 × 20 cm. This headscarf, featuring the Christian P and X symbols, was likely worn on religious holidays. The 'waaier ede' fold means a fan-shaped head.
14. Angisa, Suriname, 1975. Printed cotton, 11 × 33 × 28 cm. Special cloths commemorate key social or political events. This angisa was worn to celebrate Surinam's independence in 1975.
15. Different folding styles including 'wakti mi na tap uku' (top left), a signal cloth meaning wait for me on the corner; 'lontoe ede with fini ploi' (bottom left), worn during mourning; and 'lantji angisa' (right), believed to be worn by market women before 1899.

KETI KOTI
On 1 July, Surinamese and Caribbean communities in the Netherlands celebrate 'Keti Koti', marking the formal end of slavery in the Dutch East Indies in 1863. Women wear full regalia and join the vibrant 'kotomisi' parade through the streets.

16. 1 July 1963, Keti Koti parade in Amsterdam marking 100 years since the abolition of slavery. In 1963, only a few walked the streets to commemorate the abolition of slavery in the Dutch colonies. A banner reads '1863–1 juli 1963, Ketie Kotie, fri moe de' (meaning broken chains, free but exhausted). Before Suriname's independence in 1975, its colonial past drew little attention in Dutch society. Today, several public institutions, including the Royal Family, have issued formal apologies.
17. Kotomisi dressed by Andy Arduin for 'Winti Na Rutu', a film by Jaasir Linger, Rotterdam, 2020. Traditional and modern koto attire includes a multi-layered skirt, jacket and headpiece, worn at public events, weddings and dance parties known as 'koto-dansi'.
18. Kotomisi in front of a backdrop, 1880–1900. Photograph by J.E. Julius Eduard Muller, Dutch Colonial Parliament member in Suriname. For some, the koto symbolizes pride in heritage and identity; for others, it recalls colonial oppression, when plantation owners' wives forced Black servants to wear loose costumes to cover their bodies.

CHRISTEL — You mentioned that you based the portraits of the women on communist propaganda posters. What was your reason for choosing that particular imagery?

PATRICIA — In the 1920s and 1930s, but also later, many Black activists turned to communism because they believed it would give them a voice, grant them more rights, and because racism was less immediate. I decided that the visual expression of the banners should be similar to communist propaganda posters, especially those dealing with agriculture and food production. For me, women working the land, growing their food, is a metaphor for the way they have nurtured the world and the fight for social justice with their intelligence. At the same time, these images commemorate all those women who were enslaved in the Caribbean, and the economic role they played during slavery by growing vegetables on their provision plots, generating a little income by selling them at markets. It was a subversive act, because by doing so they undermined the economics of the plantation system. The banners are portraits, but they are also monuments. They bring these women, whose existence has long been erased from history, out of the shadows and commemorate them.

CHRISTEL — Many artists use textile banners to make political statements. Banners are a surface that merges textiles and activism. They have literally carried messages of protest on the streets for centuries. What attracted you in the format of the banner?

PATRICIA — The form initially appealed to me because you can exhibit banners in all sorts of ways — attach them to a wall or hang them in space. They also relate to flags, which are symbols of national identities, and of power. It was only later that I made the connection with protest banners.

CHRISTEL — Is it important for you that people can see the back sides of the banners?

PATRICIA — I think it's great that people can see all the stitching at the back. I like this analogue look. It corresponds with the way you associate black-and-white photographs with the old stencilling we uses for our zines. I wasn't really interested in perfect sewing or dexterous needlework. I don't mind that the works look unpolished and rather crude. I once made a banner and neatly finished the back side, but that somehow killed the spirit of the work.

CHRISTEL — Talking about the connection between textiles and activism, I had to think about the work you made in collaboration with Rolando Vázquez, *Our Light Will Outlast Their Flags* (2023), in which you ask visitors to pull the floating threads from the top layers of a Jacquard woven tapestry. By doing so thread by thread, they reveal the black-and-white image hidden underneath. Why did you invite people to participate like this?

PATRICIA — That work consists of three tapestries for which we collaborated with the TextielLab in Tilburg. We wanted to create works that would literally unravel and deconstruct symbols of power — in this case the war flags of the three main colonial trading companies that operated from the Netherlands: the Dutch East India Company (VOC), the Dutch West India Company (WIC) and the City of Middelburg. We used black-and-white images from early twentieth century postcards depicting people from the colonies who were put on display at World Fairs in so-called 'human zoo's'. In the tapestries, the coloured stripes of the flags were superimposed on these images as free-floating threads, some of which we left hanging loose, as a metaphor for unravelling these symbols of colonial power and returning some dignity to the people portrayed by making them visible again. Each time the tapestries are exhibited, we ask the audience to help us to physically deconstruct these symbols of power by pulling threads from the weavings. Not only changing strength into vulnerability, but also empowering people to take part in this process of healing and repair. When we first exhibited the three works, we invited a Winti priest to perform a *wasi prati* ritual to allow our ancestors' souls to find peace. It was a beautiful and powerful experience for everyone who was present and participated in this communal body of healing.

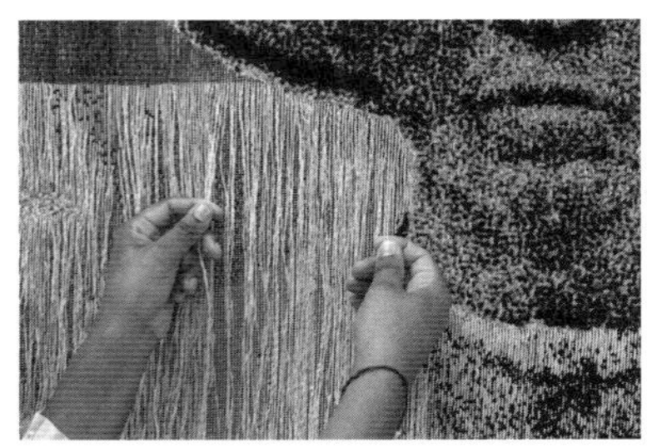

Detail Our Light Will Outlast Their Flags, 2021.
Jaquard woven tapestry, wool, polyester, with rolando vazquez.

CHRISTEL — In the three *Vrouwen van VOS* banners, and in your other textile-based works, you stitch, sew, patch, embroider… What do needle and thread represent to you, other than traditionally being seen as items associated with a female activity?

PATRICIA — Embroidery has many different connotations. It has been used to decorate linen and repair clothing, yes. But the act of embroidering also has this violent and subversive quality of piercing a surface, which I find interesting. My performance *Stitches of power. Stitches of Sorrow* (2015–ongoing) couples that subversive quality with the violence that has been inflicted on the bodies of Black women over centuries. I invite people to wash their hands and together embroider a piece of white cotton. They are unaware that the image they are embroidering is a Black female body. To me, penetrating that image with a needle is a re-enacting of that violence, but at the same time it allows for some sort of healing whereby the audience becomes a communal body and together we are stitching up colonial wounds, visible and invisible, that have been — and still are — inflicted on Black (female) bodies through slavery, colonialism and racism.

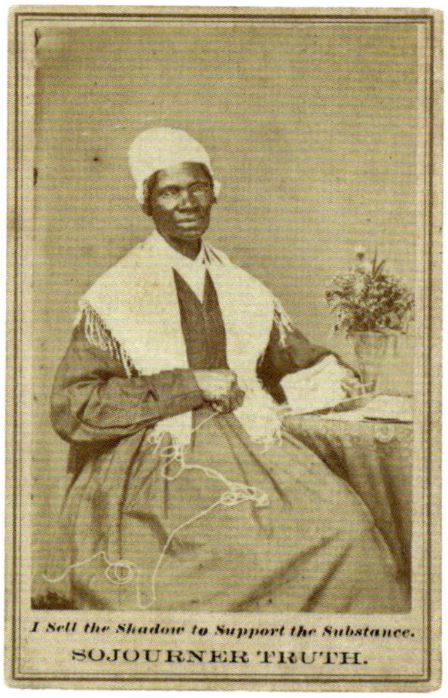


19

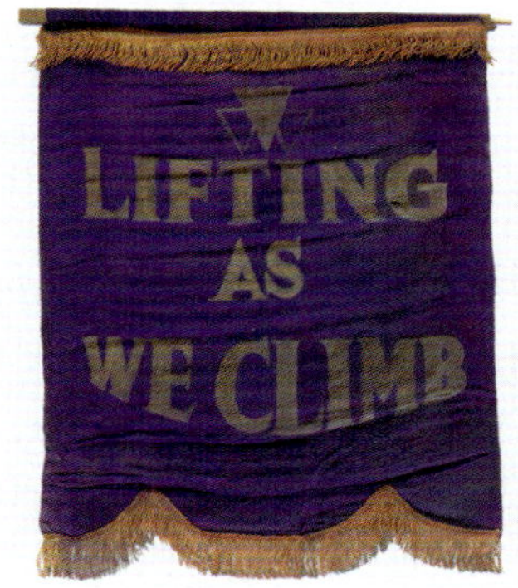


20

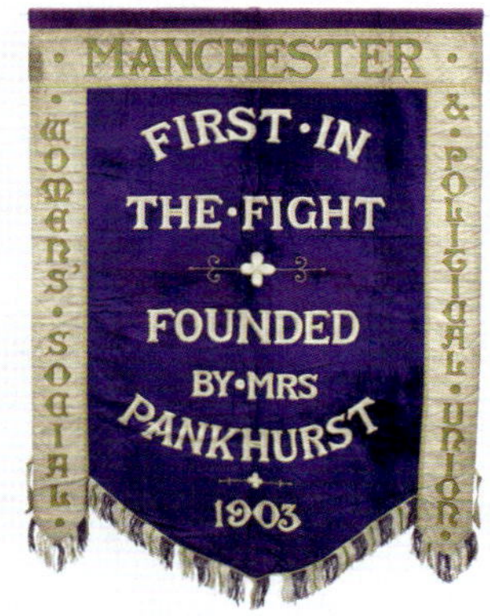


21

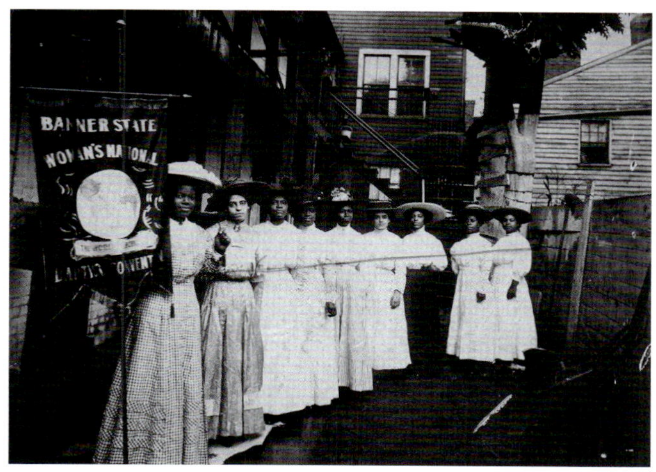

22

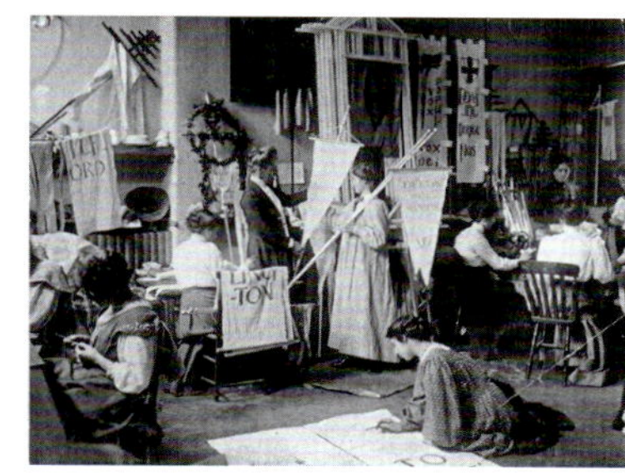

23

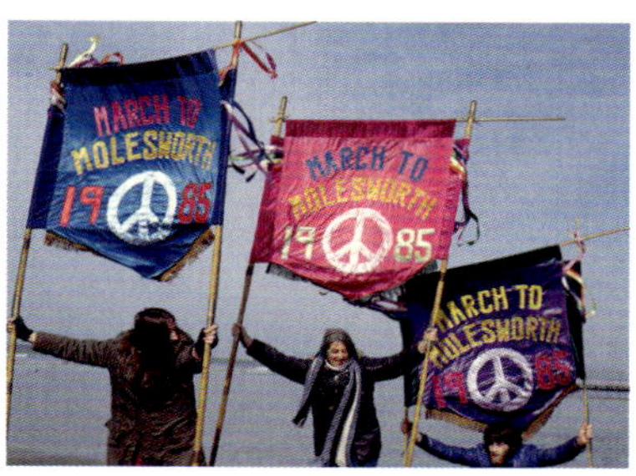


24

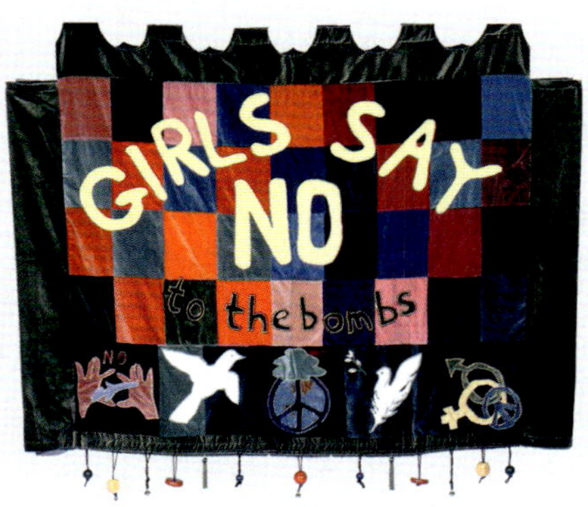


25

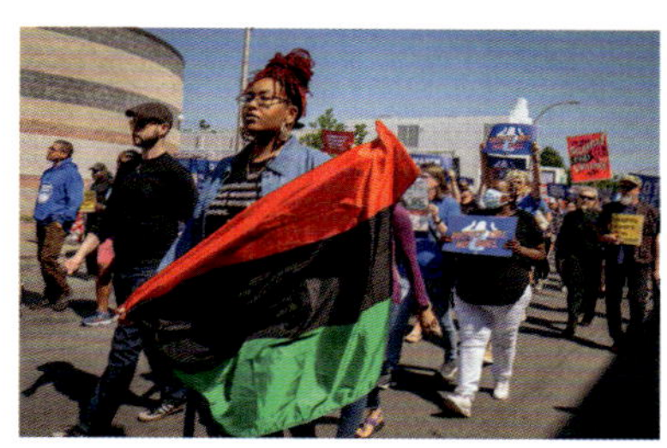

26

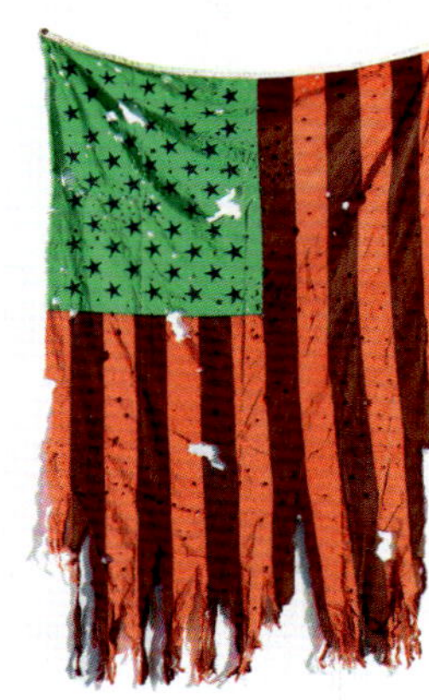

27

ACTIVIST THREADS
Many histories of struggle and emancipation are stitched with textile. Transportable and light, textiles are ideal for carrying messages of protest onto the streets, unifying people 'under one flag' and forging new bonds of solidarity. Challenging stereotypes around women's work, both women and men have picked up needle and thread to express dissent in creative, peaceful ways.

19. Cabinet card of Sojourner Truth, 1864.
Photographic print, 16.5 × 10.8 cm.
Sojourner Truth (1797–1883) was an American abolitionist, preacher and women's rights activist. Born into slavery, she escaped to freedom in 1928 and spoke at rallies across the US. Her famous speech 'Ain't I a Woman?' challenged racial injustice in the feminist debate. Truth is often depicted knitting, referencing her work teaching formerly enslaved people needlework skills to support themselves.
20. Lifting As We Climb, banner with motto of the National Association of Colored Women's Clubs, c. 1924.
Silk, wood, gold paint, 94.6 × 80 × 3.5 cm.
21. First in the Fight, Founded by Mrs. Pankhurst, 1903, banner with motto of the Manchester's Women's Social and Political Union, 1908.
Silk and cotton. Appliqué and embroidery, 185 cm × 135 cm.
Every women's club owned a unique banner in the official Suffragette colours (white, purple and gold), either ordered from specialist workshops or made at home. This one was made by a church banner manufacturer, hence its ecclesiastical design.
22. Nine African-America women holding a banner reading 'Banner State Woman's National Baptist Convention', c. 1905–1915.

BLACK SUFFRAGE
Black women played an active role in the fight for universal suffrage, but their contributions have long been overlooked. In the US, they were excluded from committees and forced to march separately. In the late 1800s, Black women founded their own clubs to address issues affecting them directly.

23. Making banners for a WSPU rally, 1910.
24. March to Molesworth, 1985, banners by Thalia and Ian Campbell for the Campaign for Nuclear Disarmament.
25. Girls Say No to the Bombs, banner by Thalia Campbell for the Greenham Common Women's Peace Camp, 1983.
Velvet, yellow and black lettering, tassels. Patchwork, appliqué, sewing, 117 × 156.5 cm.

WOMEN'S PEACE CAMP
From 1981 to 2000, thousands of women from all walks of life camped at RAF Greenham Common in Berkshire, UK, to protest the arrival of cruise missiles. Banner making, songs and poetry became part of daily life.

26. Woman carrying Pan-African flag at the 'March for our Lives', 11 June 2022, Buffalo, New York.
27. Oh Say Can You See, David Hammons, 2017.
Cloth, two metal grommets, 242.6 × 154.2 cm.
In 1920, Marcus Garvey and the Universal Negro Improvement Association created the Pan-African flag to symbolize Black liberation, pride, and unity – green for land, red for blood and black for skin colour. In 1990, artist David Hammons re-imagined the US flag in Pan-African colours to create the African-American flag.

CHRISTEL — It makes me think of Roszika Parker's *The Subversive Stitch* from 1985. She argues that embroidery, historically seen as a feminine craft, has been both a tool of oppression and a form of resistance.

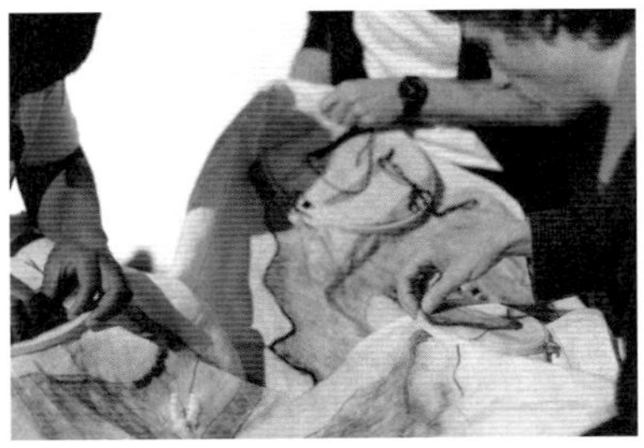

Stitches of Power. Stitches of Sorrow, 2014–2020.
Performance, various locations.

PATRICIA — Yes, but Parker focusses on the context of white, European women. I want to add a different perspective and juxtapose this image of a white woman leisurely embroidering a pristine white cotton fabric with her clean hands with the image of Black women forced to pick cotton on plantations, their hands coarse and dirty. Understanding that these white histories are built on the labour and bodies of Black women is crucial in healing some of the wounds.

CHRISTEL — You also frequently embroider glass beads and little shells into your works. How do these materials tie in with stories of colonialism, activism and resistance?

PATRICIA — The beads are a bit smaller than historic trade beads, but I use them as a reference to colonial history and the transatlantic slave trade. Glass beads, or slave beads as they were also called, were used as barter by Europeans in their dealings with local kings and tribesmen in Africa. Most of the glass beads were made in Venice, but they were also made in the Netherlands. Later, they were used as token money in exchange for goods, services and slaves. Glass beads were so popular in Africa that tons of them were produced. They were used as ballast in trade ships and then exchanged for human cargo, gold and other goods. That's how European glass beads ended up across the world: replacing the beads made from bone, shell or stone in the jewellery of indigenous Americans and the embroidered clothing in West Africa. All these materials, beads, shells and fabrics echo the migration and forced displacement of West Africans as a result of colonial transatlantic trade. There's a strong affinity between Black culture in Surinam and in the southern colonies of North America, because the African people who were kidnapped and put to work came from the same African region. They share the same ancestral heritage.

CHRISTEL — Coming back to the idea of mutual cultural influencing, I noticed that flowers are a strong motif in *Vrouwen van VOS*. Why did you chose those particular flowers, besides the fact that they are beautiful and decorative?

PATRICIA — One of the flowers I often depict is the Okra flower, which is used in rituals and ceremonies in many West African cultures, where it symbolizes survival and resilience, but also gratitude for the richness of the earth. When women were kidnapped in West Africa and transported to plantations in colonies, they would hide its seeds in their hair. So the plant travelled with them to their new land. Okra also means 'soul' in the Yoruba language. The idea that women under those circumstances would take a piece of their motherland, of their culture, of who they are, with them, braided in their hair, so that they would have something of home that they could grow and nurture — that really touched me. That's how lots of grains and seeds travelled from Africa to the Americas.

CHRISTEL — That's such a powerful image of resilience — and resistance. You often speak of the need for solidarity and communality. How does this translate into your textile works?

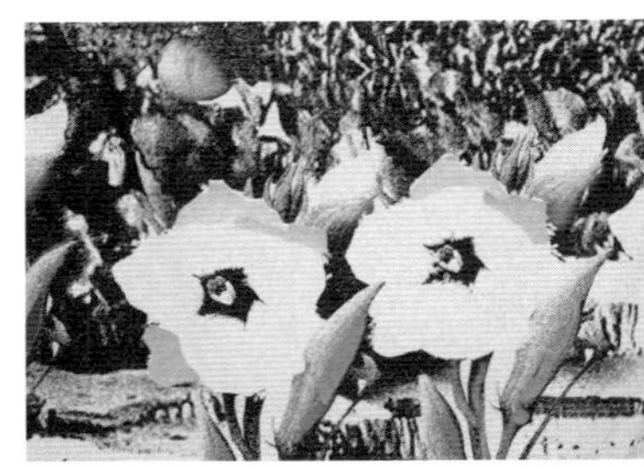

Detail Vrouwen van VOS: Camilla Parker & Mevr. Wheels, 2020.
Digital print on cotton, machine and hand embroidered, appliqué, beads, felt, African fabrics, wood.

PATRICIA — I'm interested in creating a communal body, and textile is the perfect medium to achieve this. It brings people together, but it's also a spiritual way of connecting with the world, and what was here before us. I really believe that there's something spiritual about weaving. Just think of the Mammo's in Colombia who weave their own clothing and bags. They start in the centre and move upwards in a circle until the bag is there. And the fabric weaves a story linked with the universe. They believe that the bag is alive. I always have one of those bags with me. It's close to my soul; I'll never throw it away. It's beautiful.

*Vrouwen van VOS* echoes histories of migration in its use of wax-printed fabrics and glass beads. More specifically, the three banners echo the movement of the African diaspora and the violence and racism that befell Black women. However, rather than portraying the latter as victims of these histories, kaersenhout portrays them as heroines, highlighting their important roles in the fight for social justice and the emancipation of Black women across the world.

Pieced together from different materials — propaganda images, African wax prints, felt, crocheted fringes and glass beads — the three banners pull together different threads of resistance: the fight against the Western colonizer, Black women's struggle for full recognition in the campaign for women's rights and the call for Black men to acknowledge women's contribution to the struggle against racial discrimination. The activist tone of the work is amplified by its makeshift appearance — its irregular stitching and loose threads hanging from the back — fraying any notion of these histories existing as neat, iron-pressed surfaces and disrupting the gaze that seeks tidy closure.

But this is not where the story ends. The works also speak to the life force and strength of women; their resilience and power to heal and repair what's been broken in our societies. The story kaersenhout tells in the interview, of the okra seeds smuggled across the Atlantic Ocean and planted in new soil to provide food for survival, offers a poetic example of new life emerging under dire circumstances. It also points to renewal and cross-pollination as vital to the survival of a culture.

Like the okra seeds adapting to new soil, when textile patterns enter a different aesthetic tradition, fresh hybrid designs and new styles often emerge — as is the case with the type of wax-printed fabrics that frame each banner. When the manufacturer Vlisco introduced its textiles to the African market, the colourful fabrics were quickly adopted into local cultural vernaculars. Their patterns were given names by the women in the markets and infused with symbolic meanings that reflected the everyday customs and lore of the place. With time, their designs were modified and adapted to reflect local tastes, colours, symbols and motifs; it was years before Vlisco began to collaborate with local designers.

As Ananya Jahanara Kabir proposes in her essay on Vlisco's famous Angelina print, we can read the surface of pattern as the work of memory, viewing the pattern itself as a repository of aesthetics, taste and the history of cultural exchange. Being based on three distinct lineages — Javanese batik, West African taste and Dutch industrial production — Vlisco fabrics are often considered the epitome of cultural exchange, though not without having been criticized for the cultural appropriation and the exploitation of an indigenous craft. However, without dismissing the contested aspect of cultural appropriation and the forces that drive it, these exchanges and mutual influences between cultures are, as kaersenhout points out, what keeps them alive too.

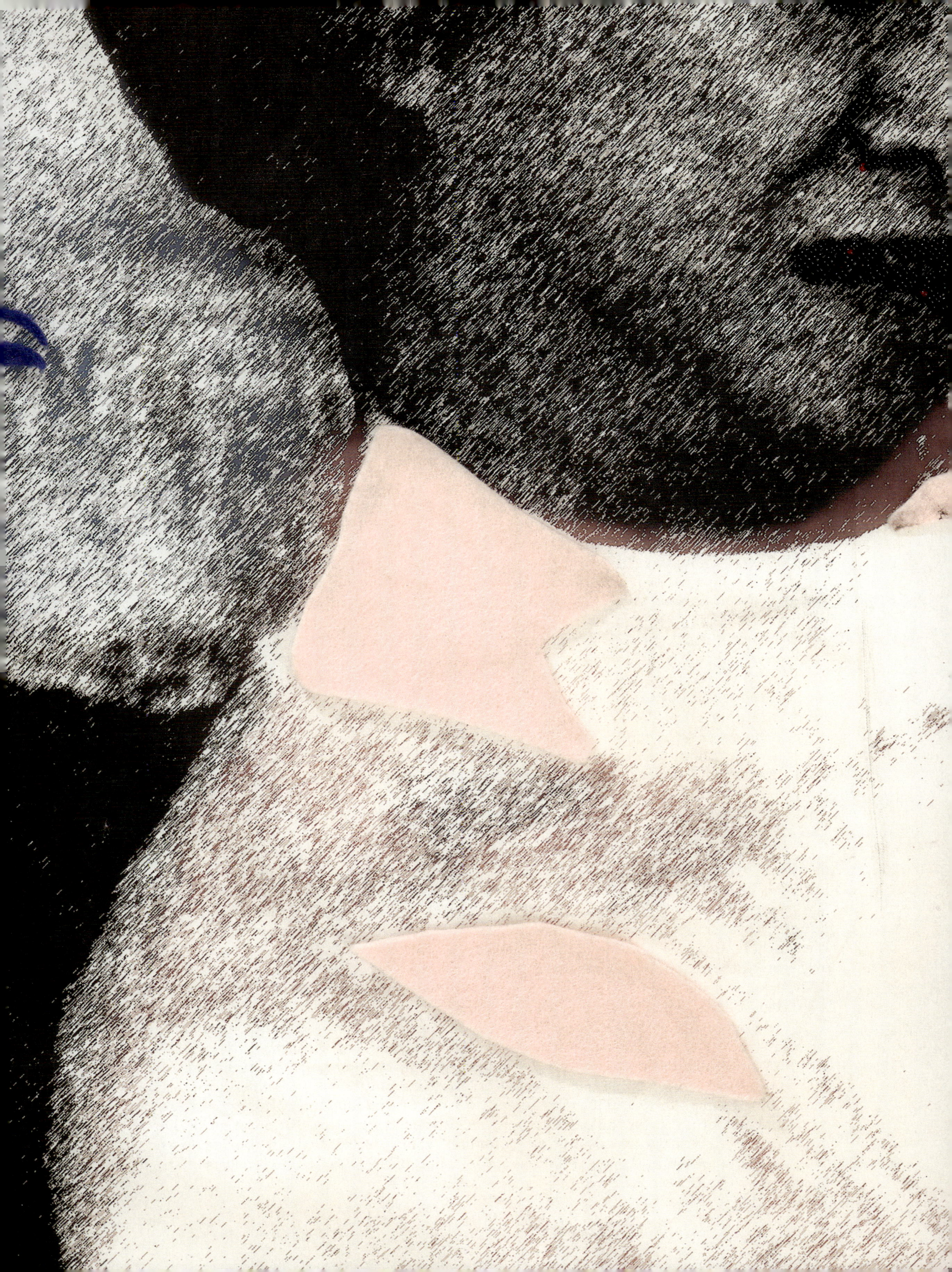

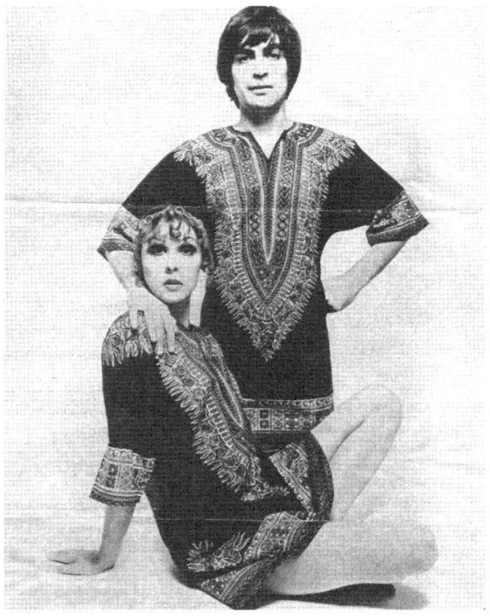

Two models showing the Dashiki. Promotional material from the Vlisco Archive, c. 1960–1970.

Ananya Jahanara Kabir's research combines creolization across the Atlantic and Indian Oceans, critical philology, and the relationship between literary texts, embodied and material culture, and memory. In addition to dance, music, film and visual art, textile is one of the forms of cultural expression that, according to Kabir, can be read as an archive of memory. In the following essay, she offers a close reading of one of the most popular African wax fabrics, the Angelina by Vlisco, reading its surface pattern as a repository of aesthetics, taste and the history of cultural exchange within the Indian Ocean world.

# VLISCO'S ANGELINA
## Indian Ocean Memory on the Surface of Pattern

Ananya Jahanara Kabir

The textile pattern known throughout West Africa as Angelina, with the variant names Addis Ababa, Java, and Dashiki, has a complex history that awaits detailed study and narrativization. The wider history of which it is part — the development of African print textiles known as Dutch Wax — has certainly been researched enough to yield a coherent narrative about the movement of batik patterns from Indonesia to West Africa through the interventions of European mercantilism in the late eighteenth and early nineteenth centuries: the story of how, in the nineteenth century, Dutch agency brought together Indonesian designs, West African tastes and textile industries in Northern Europe, has been the subject of various publications, exhibitions and artworks.[1] Indeed, 'the story of Dutch wax print is (...) a continuation of a longer history' — that of Dutch transoceanic mercantilism from the sixteenth century onwards, and its shaping of modernity through the creation of both commodities and a taste for them across continents and cultures.[2] Yet within this general story, the specific one of the Angelina print, from which the well-known tunic called the Dashiki is tailored, has not received much attention thus far. It is this gap that my research has been addressing and which I will present a glimpse of here.

I come to Angelina through my analysis of pattern as Afro-Asian taste transfer accelerated by the Dutch, in a manner that reveals a haunting by colonial guilt, the melancholia of modernity, as well as co-creation of newness by groups that are economically, socially and politically antagonized to each other or placed in relations of inequality.[3] My methods combine research in Vlisco archives, interviews with designers and administrators both at the Vlisco headquarters in Helmond, the Netherlands, and at the Ghanaian headquarters of

1. Megan Vaughan, 'Africa and the Birth of the Modern World' (2006), pp. 143-162. See also John Picton, 'Laughing at Ourselves' (2004), pp. 45-63. P. F. van Vlissingen and Co emerged in the decades between 1844 and 1880, from complex competition between Belgian, Swiss, British and Dutch textile entrepreneurs that involved a.o. intra-European technical innovation, and the management of business interests through mechanisms of incorporation. There are divergent accounts of these early years. See the company's own narrative on the 'About Vlisco' page on their website and in the essay by Anja Aronowsky Cronberg, 'The Story of Vlisco and Real Dutch Wax: From Helmond to Accra to Paris and Back Again' (2012); *Van Vlissingen and Co's Gedenkboek, 1846-1946* (1948) and a more critical account by Nina Sylvanus, *Patterns in Circulation: Cloth, Gender, and Materiality in West Africa* (2016). For African textiles in general, in the context of which Vlisco's printed textiles should be placed, see John Picton, *African Textiles, Routledge* (2021).
2. Vaughan, 'Africa', p. 150. See also Ruth Nielsen, 'The History and Development of Wax-Printed Textiles Intended for West Africa and Zaire' (1979), pp. 467-69.
3. I theorize this co-creation as 'creolization': see, for instance, Ananya Jahanara Kabir, '*Rapsodia Ibero-Indiana*: Transoceanic Creolization and the Mando of Goa' (2021), pp. 1581-1636. On Vlisco's designs as reflecting the melancholia of modernity, which I trace back to the repressed memory of religious wars in Europe during the Reformation, which drew iconophilia underground and eventually made minimalism part of 'good design', see Ananya Jahanara Kabir, 'Crypt, Cornucopia and the Surface of Pattern: Vlisco's Designs' (2023), pp. 193-206.

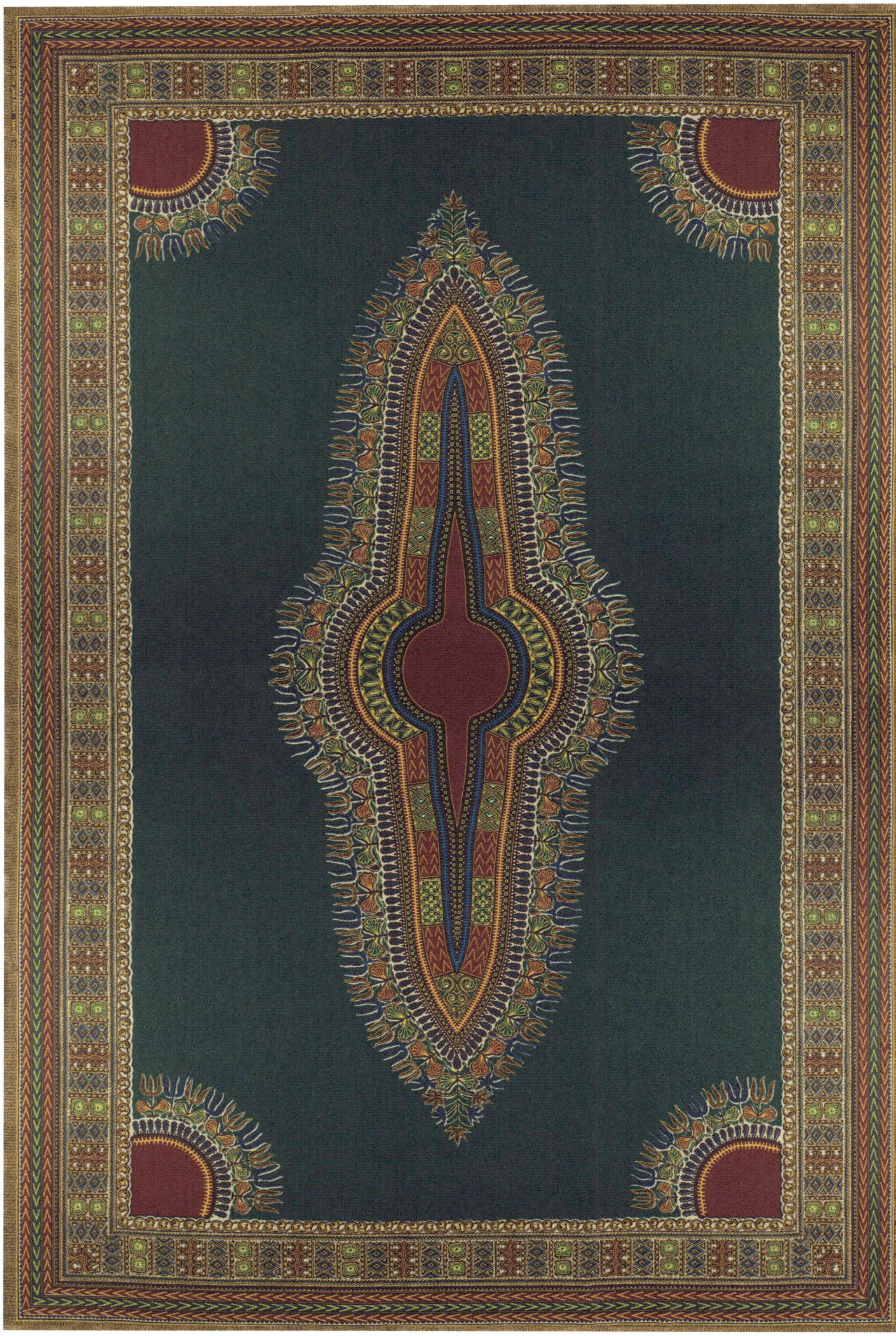

Vlisco, VL2961R.001, 120 × 180 cm.

Vlisco's Java Angelina
'Our most popular Java design is the Angelina, which was created over 50 years ago by Vlisco's designer Toon van de Manakker and is therefore a true original Vlisco design. In the 60s and 70s, the Angelina inspired shirt – the dashiki – was born and adopted by African Americans as a symbol of pride, awareness, affirmation and power. The Angelina and Dashiki have recently made a comeback in fashion and pop culture and are frequently worn by world-famous African-American singers.' (Source: Vlisco website, accessed May 2024, no longer available)

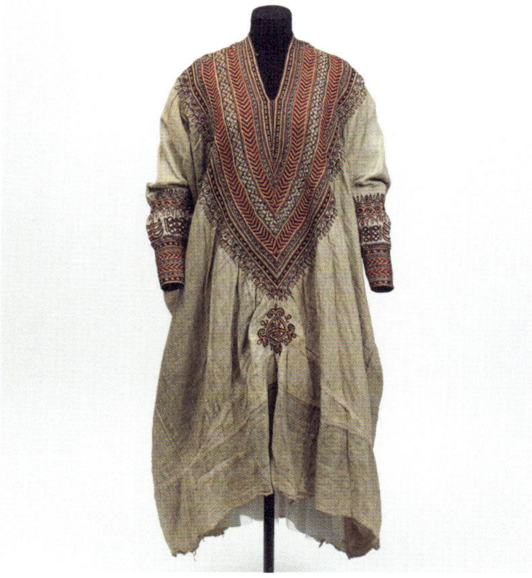

Woman's dress ('kamis') belonging to Queen Terunesh, Ethiopia, c.1860.
Plain weave cotton embroidered with silk, 124.5 × 157.5 cm.

This Ethiopian kamis belonged to Queen Terunesh, the second wife of Emperor Tewodros II and mother of Prince Alemayehu. It is made from two layers of soft cotton extensively decorated with embroidered bands around the neck, appearing to hang down the front like a large piece of jewellery. Queen Terunesh died about a month after the 1868 siege of Maqdala, while being escorted by the British army to her home province. Her possessions were sent to England.

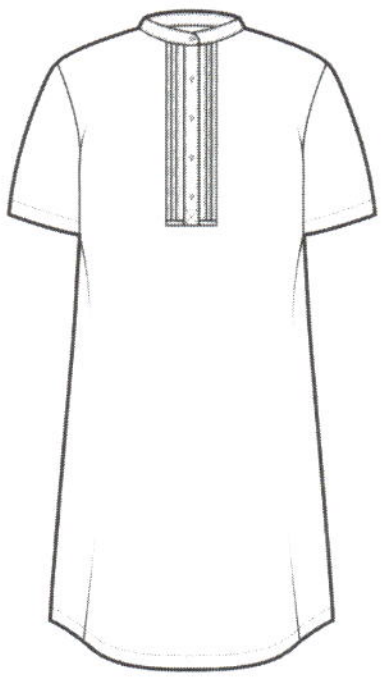

Technical drawing of kurta shirt with short sleeves, embellished henley neck.

GTP Textiles in Accra, interviews with Ghanaian designers and models, close reading of Vlisco factory premises and the spatiality of the textile as picture plane—and mapping this data against Indian Ocean textile history and memory studies, and my theorization of transoceanic creolization.[4] I thereby read the surface of pattern as the work of memory, and argue for pattern itself as a repository of aesthetics, taste and the history of cultural exchange within the Indian Ocean world and also between the Indian Ocean and Atlantic worlds. It is this methodology and approach that I bring to bear on the surface of Vlisco's Angelina.

If the Angelina pattern is an archive of memory, what is being remembered through it? Amidst the plethora of repeated patterns that march across Dutch Wax, the Angelina stands out because it is the only one where the pattern predetermines the shape of the tailored garment: a tunic with a long yoke in contrasting colours and quarter-circular sections of the same pattern that are repeated on what would form the hem. In addition, there are contrasting bands which define the hemline and the sleeve edges. These horizontal bands echo those that follow the line of the yoke through rows of small stylized floral motifs. The entire pattern is repeated in a mirror image so as to fall from the shoulders across the front and back of the would-be wearer's body. A single, contrasting colour block occupies the space of an imagined circular opening for the neck with two narrow V-shaped continuations oriented down the wearer's chest and back. If cut and sewn in fidelity to this pattern, a tunic results (which, in an African-American context, came to be called the Dashiki). This tunic resembles in shape the *kurta* of South Asia, although the patterns on the kurta's yoke are woven, embroidered or appliqued rather than printed onto the fabric.[5]

How did this 'Indic' touch enter a patterned textile that became one of West Africa's most loved and versatile fabrics, and also played, via the Dashiki, a stellar role in pan-Africanist identity assertions from the late 1960s onwards?[6] The Angelina's designer Toon van de Mannaker was declaredly inspired by Ethiopian garments.[7] This Ethiopian connection is orally memorialized in another name for the Angelina in Francophone West Africa: Addis Ababa. Be that as it may, the textile trade between India and Ethiopia well preceded European incursions into the Indian Ocean.[8] Several questions thus arise. Did the 'Ethiopian' prototype for the Angelina draw on yoke-embellished kurtas that had already entered the Horn of Africa through, for instance, Gujarati merchants who traded across the Arabian Sea? Alternatively, looking to the equally robust textile trade between India and Indonesia, was it through that route that South Asian floral motifs sedimented into the Indonesian features that Vlisco subsequently incorporated into the Angelina?[9] And where did Van de Mannaker first come across the Ethiopian sources?[10]

These questions cannot be answered in detail within the scope of this essay. But raising them alerts us to textile as an archive of transoceanic taste creation, where 'taste' becomes an index of a globalizing modernity. They also reveal pattern as

4. Ghanian Textiles Printing Company Ltd. was the first indigenous Ghanaian textile and fashion brand launched on the Ghanaian market in January 1966, by the late Osagyefo Dr. Kwame Nkrumah, Ghana's first President. GTP inherited the wax-printing process from the Vlisco company based in Helmond and is a member of the Vlisco Group. For more on its history and current orientation, see their website.
5. For an excellent gallery of possibilities for this Indic yoke, see, for instance, 'yoke pattern' on Pinterest. See also the discussion in S. S. Khar et al, 'Looking Backwards to Go Forward' (2013), pp. 181-189.
6. On the Dashiki's popularity in the 1960s and 1970s, see Tanisha Ford, 'The "Afro Look" and Global Black Consciousness' (2015), pp. 28-37 and 'The amazing history and evolution of the Dashiki'.
7. 'Angelina' page on the Vlisco website.
8. Richard Pankhurst, 'Indian Trade with Ethiopia, the Gulf of Aden and the Horn of Africa in the Nineteenth and Early Twentieth Centuries' (1974), pp. 453-497.
9. Om Prakash, 'The Dutch and the Indian Ocean Textile Trade' (2011), pp. 145-160.
10. The Vlisco website (see fn. 3) stated that 'Angelina was inspired by a 19th century Ethiopian noblewoman's tunic as seen in the book African Textiles Today by Chris Spring.' However, in another post, a slightly different origin is ascribed (see fn. 13)

a mechanism whereby the memory of historical trade relations between East Africa and Asia, facilitated by the Indian Ocean space, becomes constitutive of a semiotics of Africanity. Through the Dashiki, the Angelina pattern became a potent signifier of diasporic and pan-African identity, as well as solidarity with pan-Africanism. Hence the Dashiki is a channel for linking pan-Africanism with taste creation in the Indian Ocean world, as crystallized in patterns that emerged through exchange between Africa and Asia, and between different parts of Asia. At the same time, its 'post-Dashiki' uses in contemporary West Africa confirm the Angelina's efficacy as a motor of postcolonial self-fashioning (where 'self-fashioning' can be read both metaphorically, in the manner first coined by Stephen Greenblatt, as well as literally in the context of the fashion industry).[11] Today, individual dressmakers and fashion houses across West Africa play with and tease the inherited pattern of the Angelina in various ways to make dresses, blouses, suit jackets and even trousers. In the course of this migration of the classic pattern from the tunic to other items of clothing, the Angelina's design elements are distorted, fragmented and reassembled in surprising and inventive ways.[12] Yet, this confident playfulness is always conducted in dialogue with the most distinct and indeed constitutive feature of the Angelina: what I am calling its 'Indic yoke'.

This persistence illustrates how the transoceanic past that undergirds the postcolonial present can be memorialized collectively, by those who, in different spaces and at different times, have appreciated, and continue to do so, the pattern of the Angelina. When people tailor, experiment with or wear the Angelina, they continue a centuries-long process that reveals the thorough interpenetration of the global and the local in the course of European expansionism and empire. The flat plane of the textile thus compresses a complex narrative of this interpenetration, even as contemporary sartorial play with the Angelina unfolds this narrative's potential for absorbing and reflecting new social trends and aspirations. It is for this reason that I grounded the initial phase of research in Ghana, where the pattern first found a local name: purportedly, from the song *Angelina*, a classic of the Ghanaian genre Highlife, which became a massive hit around the same time as the pattern's gathering popularity.[13] This anecdote, which would need verification, reveals the circulation of music, textile and other commodities within the framework of an aspirational postcolonial modernity, on which the colonial and precolonial past retain a shaping force. It also urges us to analyse the relationship between popular music and textile as an extension and, possibly, complication of the fairly well-understood relationship between Dutch Wax and the oral culture of the ethnic groups who would become postcolonial Ghanaians.[14]

Yet, as already noted, this relationship is also one between the transoceanic and the postcolonial, as captured in the fabrication of the Angelina. It is enshrined in the category to which it belongs: the so-called Java prints within the Dutch Wax

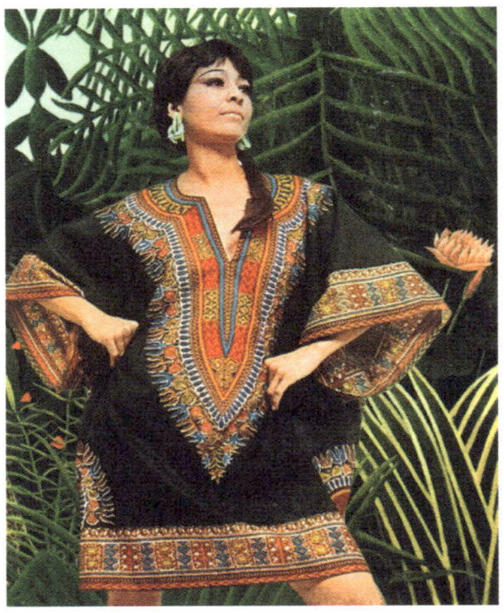

Woman showing a green Dashiki against the backdrop of a painting by Henri Rousseau. From the Vlisco archive, c. 1960–1970.

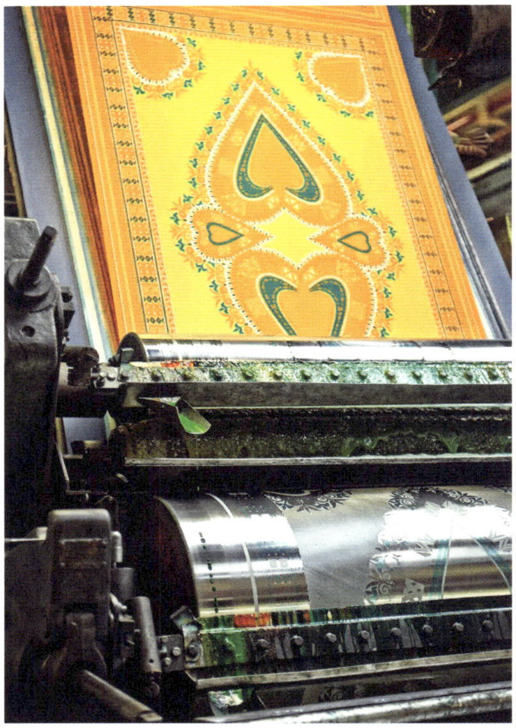

Angelina on printing machine.

'Java fabrics carry up to nine different colours, which are traditionally vivid in style and the printing of the fabrics is characterized by its precision.' (Source: Vlisco website, no longer available.)

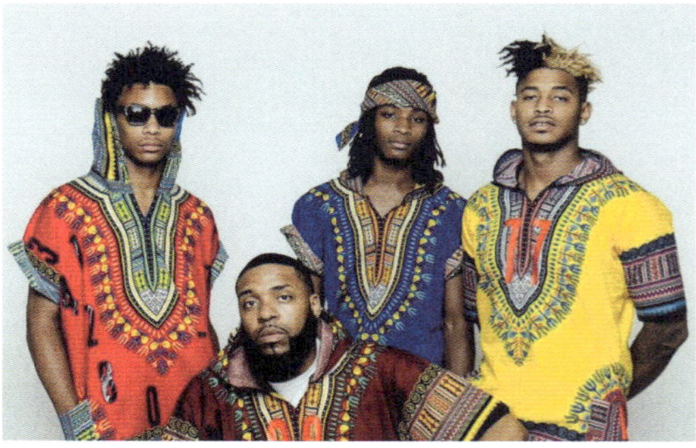

Revival of the Angelina pattern and Dashiki in contemporary fashion and pop culture.

repertoire.[15] On Vlisco's website, Java prints are given a prominent section of their own under the tab 'heritage':

*'Vlisco started in 1846 with a handful of Dutch illustrators who created interpretations of batik prints to homage the ancient Indonesian design. Java was, and still is, renowned for its intricate details and spirited floral illustrations. Java fabrics carry up to nine different colours, which are traditionally vivid in style and enriched by the special sheen and soft surface of the fabric. The process of creating Java fabrics is characterized by its precision. By applying high pressure on engraved and punctured screens and rollers, the ink and dye are rigorously pressed on to the fabrics, enabling the smallest details to be printed.'*[16]

For our purposes, we need to note an important pattern distinction between Java (including Angelina) and other forms of Dutch Wax. Dutch Wax patterns in general layer the memory of Indian Ocean materiality with West and Central African aesthetics. The space between motifs is filled with crackle and bubble effects (the famous 'defects' made by the Dutch in trying to mechanize batik production) and the patterns are densely fractalized. Java prints, including the Angelina, are, however, clear of these 'imperfections'. I interpret the chromatically clear plane of Angelina as the retention of Indian Ocean memory within Africanity, which then opens out beyond the affective circuit of the Black Atlantic. Wearing the Angelina on different kinds of tailored garments is to 'ritually activate' that memory through the prominence given to the 'Indic yoke' within tailoring processes.[17]

How Africans tailor the Angelina in a variety of inventive ways, the reasons behind their preferences for certain chromatic combinations that have survived the journey from the Indian Ocean to the Atlantic world via Europe, and their play with the inherited 'strong' design of this print are all ways in which we can see the Angelina and its uses as an index to memory work around Indian Ocean aesthetics.[18] Whose decisions have passed into local lore as legendary and pioneering? It is important to note that sources for the Angelina as a barometer of Ghanaian taste in the past fifty years include both non-elite market women who are the traditional sellers of Dutch Wax fabric and who are the repositories, therefore, of information regarding the evolving preferences of Ghanaian men and women (chromatics, popularity vis-à-vis other prints), and style-setters who encountered the Angelina in its early years and their recollections about its use then and now. These would include politicians, musicians, fashion icons and people from prominent families. In Ghana, at least, the Angelina has been a barometer of postcolonial self-fashioning since 1967. While its historical starting point can be excavated through the Vlisco archives, tracking its tailoring over the decades helps us pay particular attention to responses to the Indic yoke. The full transoceanic sweep of this textile trail thus has implications for a history of global modernity through entanglements of oceans, tastes and textiles.

While following the trail of its transoceanic affiliations, therefore, we cannot lose sight of the ubiquitous identification of the Angelina with Africanity. Since 1967, the Angelina has functioned as a visual and sartorial marker of African identity, even while its variant names and very shape proclaim this identity as shaped by dialogue with other cultures and material histories, and not merely the European. The Angelina across Africa thus also 'provincializes Europe'.[19] Angelina is a durable commodity formed out of a long cultural and mercantile conversation across the Indian Ocean, between South East Asia, South Asia and East Africa, which preceded European expansionism. Yet European intervention in the Indian Ocean waters took that conversation to the Atlantic littoral of the African continent and ultimately forged a transoceanic trail linking Asia, Africa, Europe and the Americas. The Angelina sheds light on how the transoceanic circulation of textiles, patterns, garment templates and, ultimately, taste was constitutive of a global history of modernity whose reverberations shape aspirations to authenticity and cosmopolitanism that underlie the self-fashioning of postcolonial Africans, who play so inventively with its design possibilities.

11. Stephen Greenblatt, *Renaissance Self-Fashioning: from More to Shakespeare* (2012). The work of the Nigerian-British artist Yinka Shonibare has been much discussed as an example of postcolonial self-fashioning through Dutch Wax. See, in this context, Rachel Kent, 'Time and Transformation in the Art of Yinka Shonibare MBE' (2008), pp. 12-23; John Picton, 'Yinka Shonibare: Undressing Ethnicity' (2001), pp. 66-95 and also Picton, 'Laughing at Ourselves.' (op. cit.)
12. As fashion blogger Raliat declares on the Vlisco website: 'It was so much fun trying to cut and match the centerpiece print on the Angelina fabric' (webpage no longer available).
13. Vlisco's historical page on Angelina wax print is inaccessible at the time of writing. It is replaced by a new page accessible at the Vlisco website under 'Angelina'.
14. Paulette Young, 'Ghanaian Women and Dutch Wax Prints: The Counter-appropriation of the Foreign and the Local Creating a New Visual Voice of Creative Expression' (2016), pp. 305-327.
15. 'Angelina' page on the Vlisco website.
16. The quote was taken from Vlisco's historical page on Angelina, currently inaccessible.
17. Andrew Apter et al (eds), *Activating the Past: History and Memory in the Black Atlantic World* (2009).
18. The assessment of the Angelina as a 'strong pattern' was made by Ghanaian designer Oheneba Boamah, founder of the men's fashion brand Abrantie for Gentlemen, in an interview with me in Accra on 22 May 2017.
19. Dipesh Chakrabarty, *Provincialising Europe: Postcolonial Thought and Historical Difference* (2000).

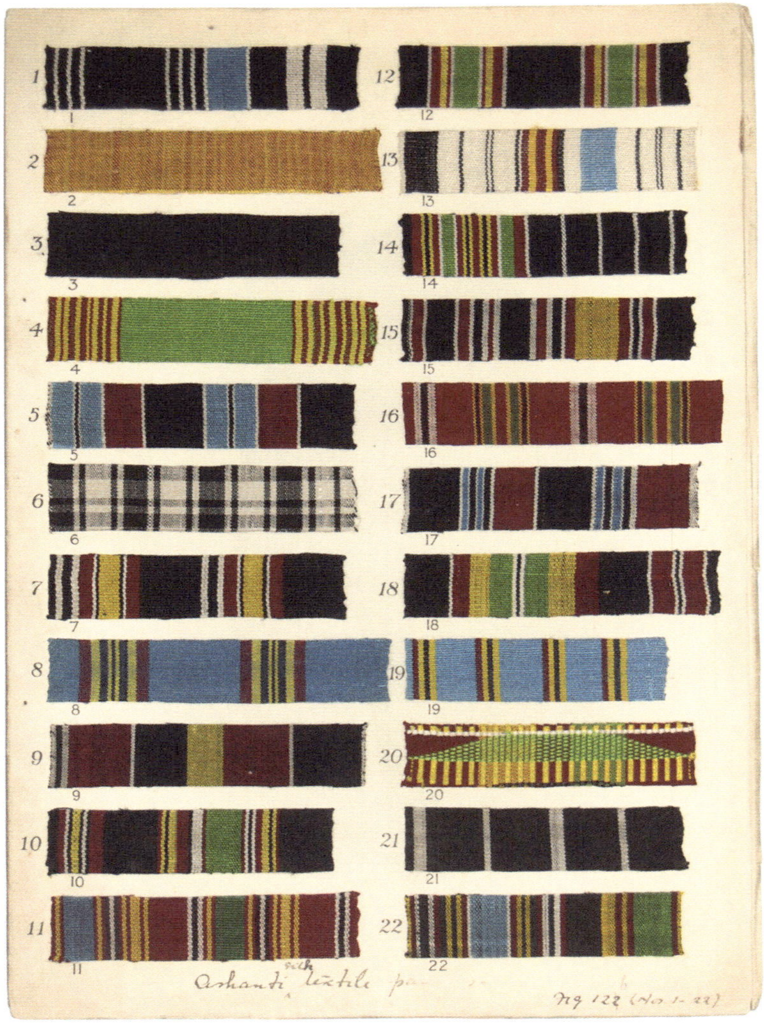

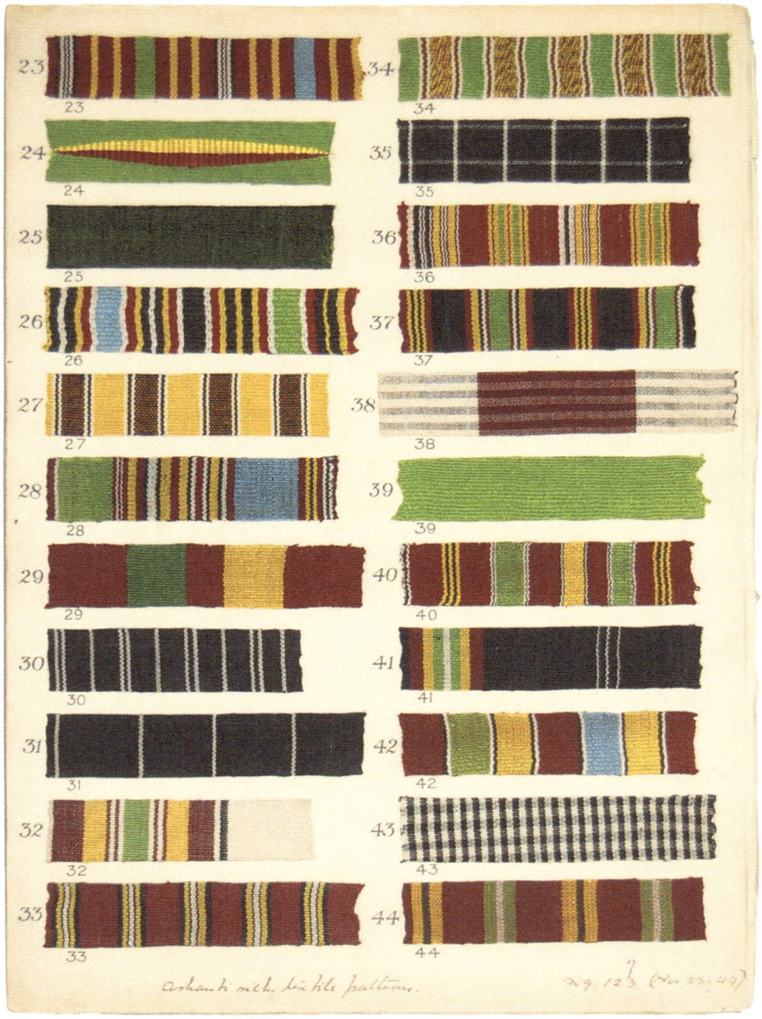

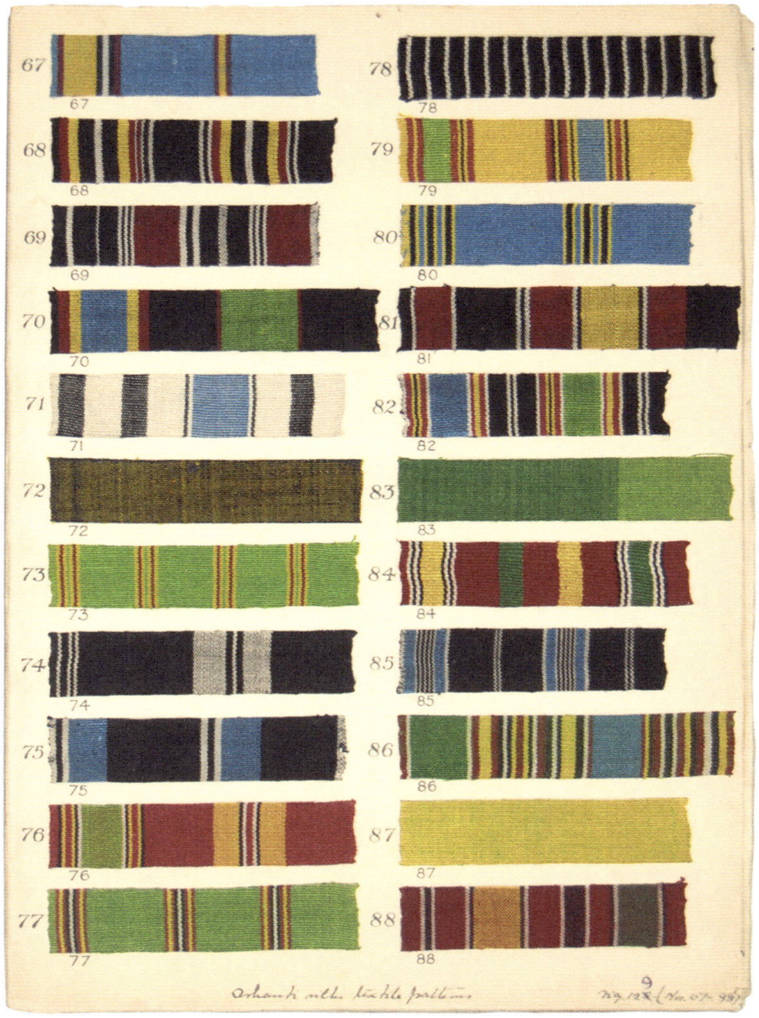

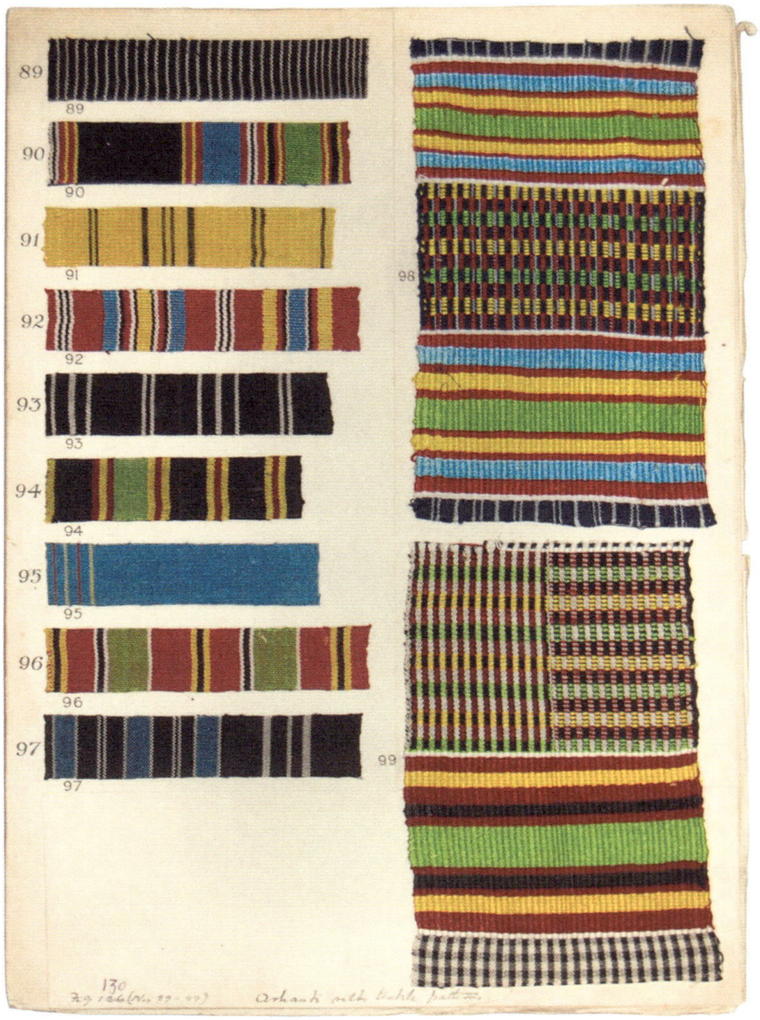

Four pages with samples of warp patterns collected and described by R.S. Rattray in his book Religion and Art in Ashanti, 1927.

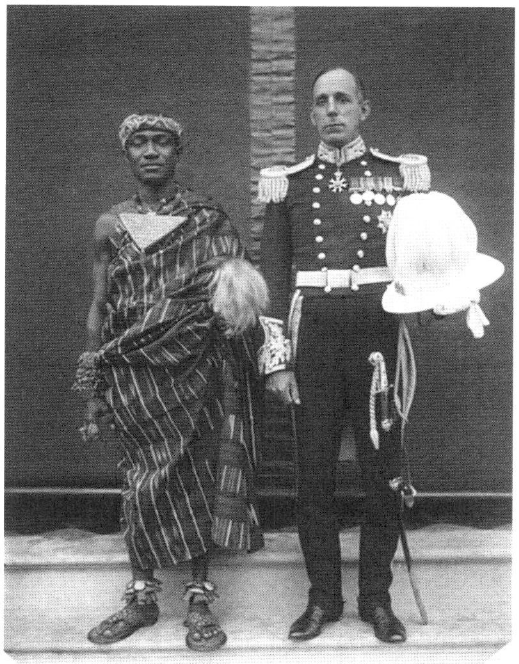

The Asantehene King Perempeh II of Asante and His Excellency the Governor, Sir Arnold Hodson at the reinstatement of the Asante dynasty in Kumase. Photographer unknown, 30 January 1935.

# KENTE CLOTH
# Mastering the Variables, Unravelling the Mystery

## Christel Vesters

Known for its vibrantly colourful and intricate designs, kente cloths are strip-woven textiles rooted in the traditions of the Akan-Ashanti and Ewe peoples of West Africa. Once reserved for Ashanti royalty, they now symbolize 'Africanness' and are widely worn by the African diaspora. However, their politicization and commodification as a symbol of a universal Afrocentric identity have not been without critique.

The magnificence of kente cloth lies in its construction and appearance. Composed of narrow woven strips sewn side by side, its grid-like patterns obscure any visual logic or organisation. Kente strips, which can measure up to ten metres, are created by stacking one pattern block onto the next. The most basic pattern sequences consist of a single-colour warp (for instance, undyed cotton with indigo threads) and a neutral weft. By manipulating the rhythm of the weft, weavers produce different pattern blocks.

With limited means — two wooden sticks and one coloured thread — and simple interventions such as altering the warp's composition, weavers can generate an endless variety of strip designs. Adding a second colour to the warp multiplies the possibilities exponentially.[1] Once woven, the strips are cut and sewn together, adding another layer of visual complexity. In some cloths, identically patterned strips are placed in a half-drop repeat; in others, different patterns are combined into rhythmic, dynamic compositions.

Traditionally, weaving in Ashanti culture was the domain of men. There were no written instructions; the skills and patterns — along with the stories they conveyed — were passed down from father to son. Women were excluded from the weaving process. In early times, kente was reserved for kings, who wore the colourful fabrics during ceremonies — moving in fast, powerful dances or slow, majestic processions. In both cases, kente cloth was made for movement, creating visual vertigo that dazzled the audience.

The visual complexity and symbolic meaning of kente fabric also captivated the attention of Western anthropologists, including Robert Sutherland Rattray, who was one of the first Westerners to study and document Ashanti art and culture.[2,3] From 1906 to 1930, Rattray was stationed in the British Crown colony of the Gold Coast — present-day Ghana — where he headed the newly established Anthropological Department of Ashanti. During his time there, Rattray compiled

1. Basic kente strips are plain-woven, though more experienced craftsmen may employ advanced techniques. An Asante man's cloth requires 28 strips sewn together, measuring approximately three metres in length and two in width. A typical female cloth consists of up of 24 strips. Commonly used colours are maroon, gold-yellow, green, red, black and blue.
2. Robert Sutherland Rattray, better known as Captain R.S. Rattray (1881-1938), was born in India to Scottish parents. He studied Law and Anthropology at Oxford University and served with the British forces in South Africa before being stationed in the Gold Coast. Rattray learned local languages and formed close relationships with Ashanti chiefs and community members, whom he acknowledged extensively in the prefaces of his books on Ashanti culture, including *Ashanti Proverbs: The Primitive Ethics Of A Savage People* (1916); *Religion and Art in Ashanti* (1927) and *Ashanti Law and Constitution* (1929).
3. Rattray, *Religion and Art*, pp. 234-235. Rattray describes kente weaving in the chapter entitled 'Technology', alongside woodcarving, stamped cloth, pottery and metal casting. Other chapters include 'Religion' and 'Rites de Passage'. The structure of Rattray's book echoes that of Diderot and d'Alembert's *Encyclopédie, ou dictionnaire raisonné des sciences, des arts et des métiers* (1751-1772), which aimed to systematically disseminate knowledge across disciplines. Like Diderot and d'Alembert, Rattray distinguishes between art and craft, and separates them from their cultural and ritual contexts.

the influential volume *Religion and Art in Ashanti* (1927), in which he provides detailed descriptions of Ashanti rituals, customs and crafts, including kente weaving. The book contains black-and-white and full-colour reproductions of various kente patterns.

R.S. Rattray catalogued over two hundred kente patterns, documenting their names, origins and meanings. He concluded that 'each design was standardized, and that they were not flights of colour-fancy run riot. Each pattern has its name and in many cases also represents the clan, social status, or even sex of the wearer; or it may also refer to some proverbial saying.' Pattern number 20, for instance, is called Adweneasa, which translates as 'my skill is exhausted' or 'my ideas have come to an end'. According to Rattray, 'This pattern is one of the best known in Ashanti, and weavers who can make it are considered masters of their craft. In older times only the Kings of Ashanti might wear this pattern.' Other patterns are named after notable people or animals or plants — such as number 71, Higya, meaning 'the lion'.[4] The index is followed by several pages of technical specifications in which Rattray meticulously deciphers the composition of each pattern, recording each manipulation of every single thread into alphabetical and numerological sequences — text that, to the untrained eye, reads like computer code.

Rattray's effort to uncover the inner logic of kente weaving reflects the modern philosophical mindset that prevailed in European academic circles at the time. Like the natural philosophers before him, nineteenth century anthropologists believed that mastering variables led to a deeper understanding of the divine order of things. Echoing Enlightenment ideals of 'proper method' and 'true knowledge' — and the belief that all natural phenomena could be explained through mathematical principles — the modern anthropologist's task was to collect empirical data and systematically describe and classify all known varieties. Today, Rattray's undertaking underscores a fundamental schism: between a modern Western worldview — rooted in science and reason, drawing distinctions where they may not exist — and the spiritual, holistic understanding of the natural world that characterizes Ashanti thought.

Over the last century, *Religion and Art in Ashanti* has become a standard reference for students of kente weaving, both in Ghana and abroad. However, its colonial origins should not be overlooked. Anthropological research conducted under colonial authority often served an imperialist agenda: understanding local customs, laws and constitutions helped colonial regimes maintain control of their subjects. Although Rattray conducted his research with genuine respect for the Ashanti and their culture, his life's work remains shaped by the colonial gaze. His scientific quest to systematically describe Ashanti kente weaving meant subjecting it to a Western rationalist system of knowledge — one that demystified its mythical origins, and reduced their intricate, vibrant designs — meant to whirl and dazzle — into flat surfaces that could be studied and fixed.[5]

Today, kente cloth serves as a token of 'Africanness' and pan-African unity — a symbol of collective heritage and a shared history of oppression. However, its commodification as a universal emblem of Afrocentric identity is not without critique, especially in political contexts. Reflecting on the now-infamous photographs of U.S. Democratic Party politicians wearing identical kente stoles, writer Doreen St. Félix argues that the gesture, intended to signal solidarity with the Black community, reinforces the 'myth of the Black monolith' — the reductive notion that African Americans constitute a single, homogeneous group. According to St. Félix, this narrative is central to the Democratic Party's strategy. 'Internal divisions within the race are not tolerated; they must be drowned out with bright colours.'[6]

No textile tradition can represent an entire ethnic group — let alone a whole continent. Cultural identities are never homogeneous or uniform; they are, in fact, profoundly diverse. Paradoxically, the history of kente resists essentialism. Its composite structure and material history reveal a hybrid textile shaped by centuries of cross-cultural exchange: weaving techniques introduced by North African nomads, and silks from Asian and European merchants, which brought the reds and blues that became key symbolic markers. To appropriate such a hybrid textile as a stand-in for the entire Black diaspora not only reduces its complexity to a visual cliché, but also erases the varied identities that fall under the single label 'Black'.

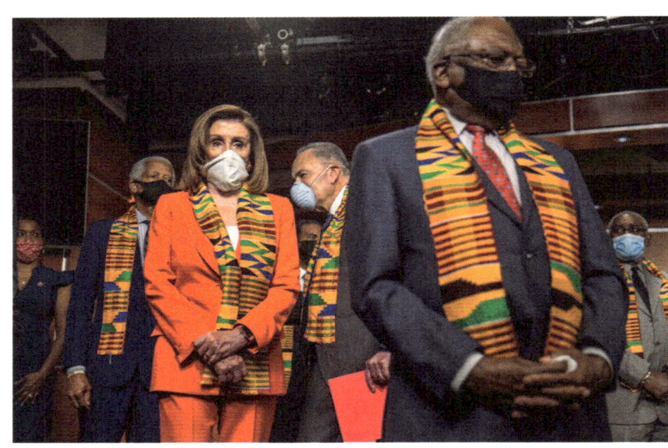

U.S. House Speaker Nancy Pelosi and other Congressional Democrats during a news conference to unveil police reform and racial injustice legislation, U.S. Capitol, Washington, June 8, 2020. To convey their solidarity with their Black constituents, the Democratic politicians wore identical kente stoles.

4. Ibid, p. 237.
5. Though they may be less visible than the colonial occupation of land or the seizure of cultural artefacts, the effects of such epistemic appropriation run deep. As kente specialist Doran H. Ross notes in *Wrapped in Pride: Ghanaian Kente and African American Identity* (1998), it is not uncommon for kente weavers in Bonwire, Ghana. Today to consult Rattray's book as a reference for standard patterns. Rattray's index of 'standard patterns' has become normative, raising critical questions: when does a description become prescriptive? And what happens when written records replace oral traditions?
6. Doreen St. Félix, 'Embarrassment of Democrats Wearing Kente-Cloth Stoles'.

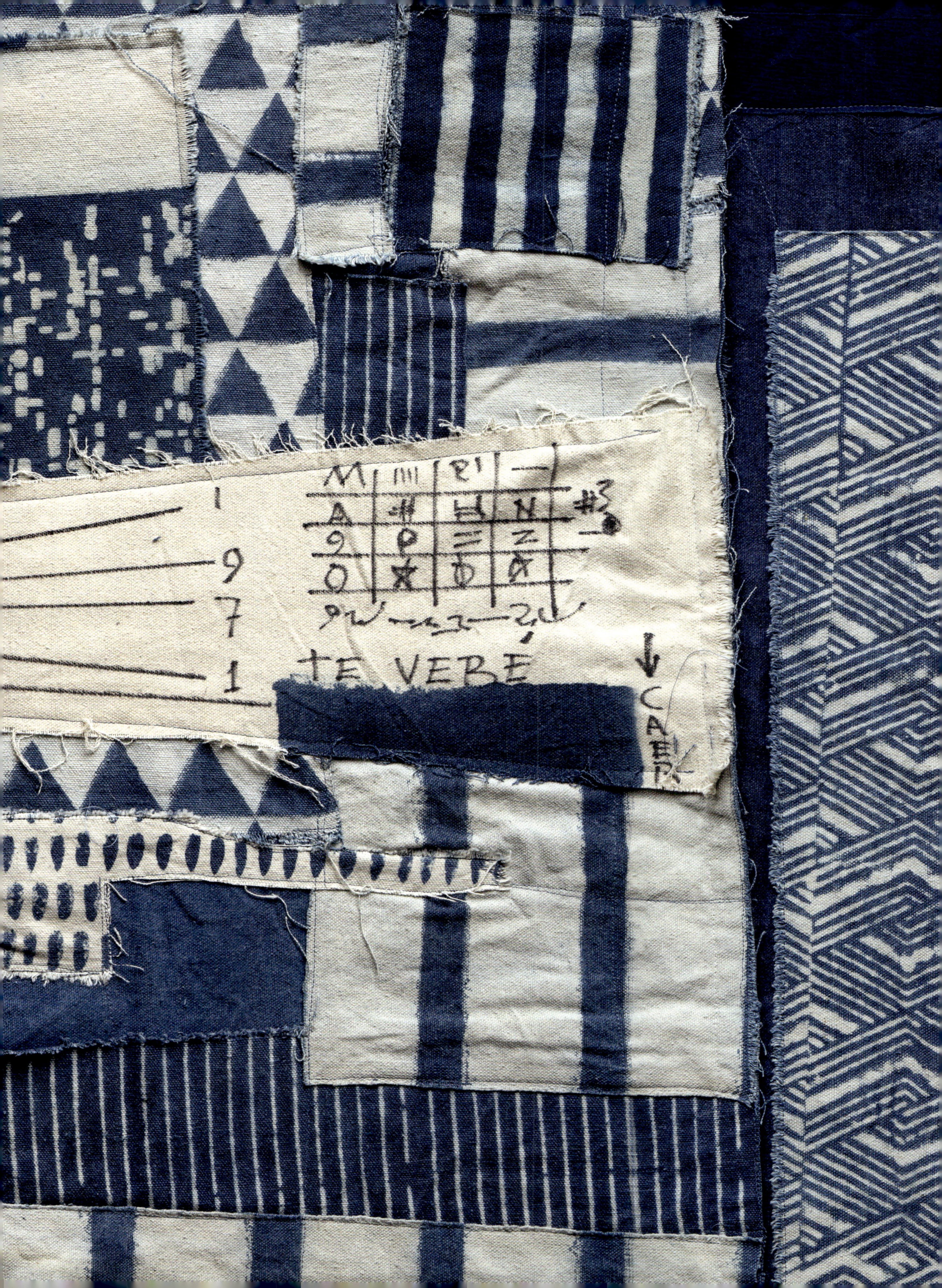

1
9
7
1
TE VERE

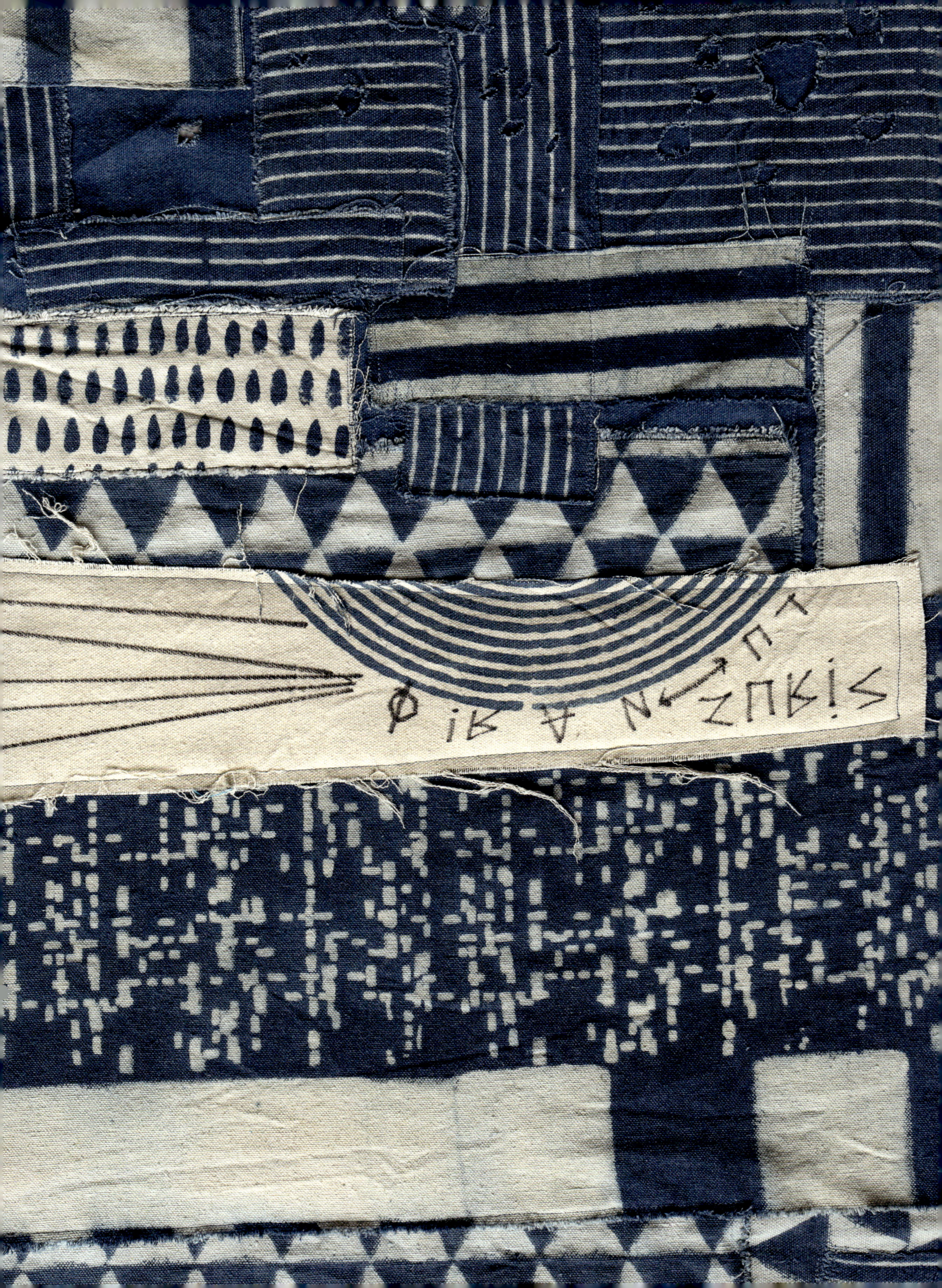

# *The Rise of the Prophet*

Antonio Jose Guzman &
Iva Jankovic

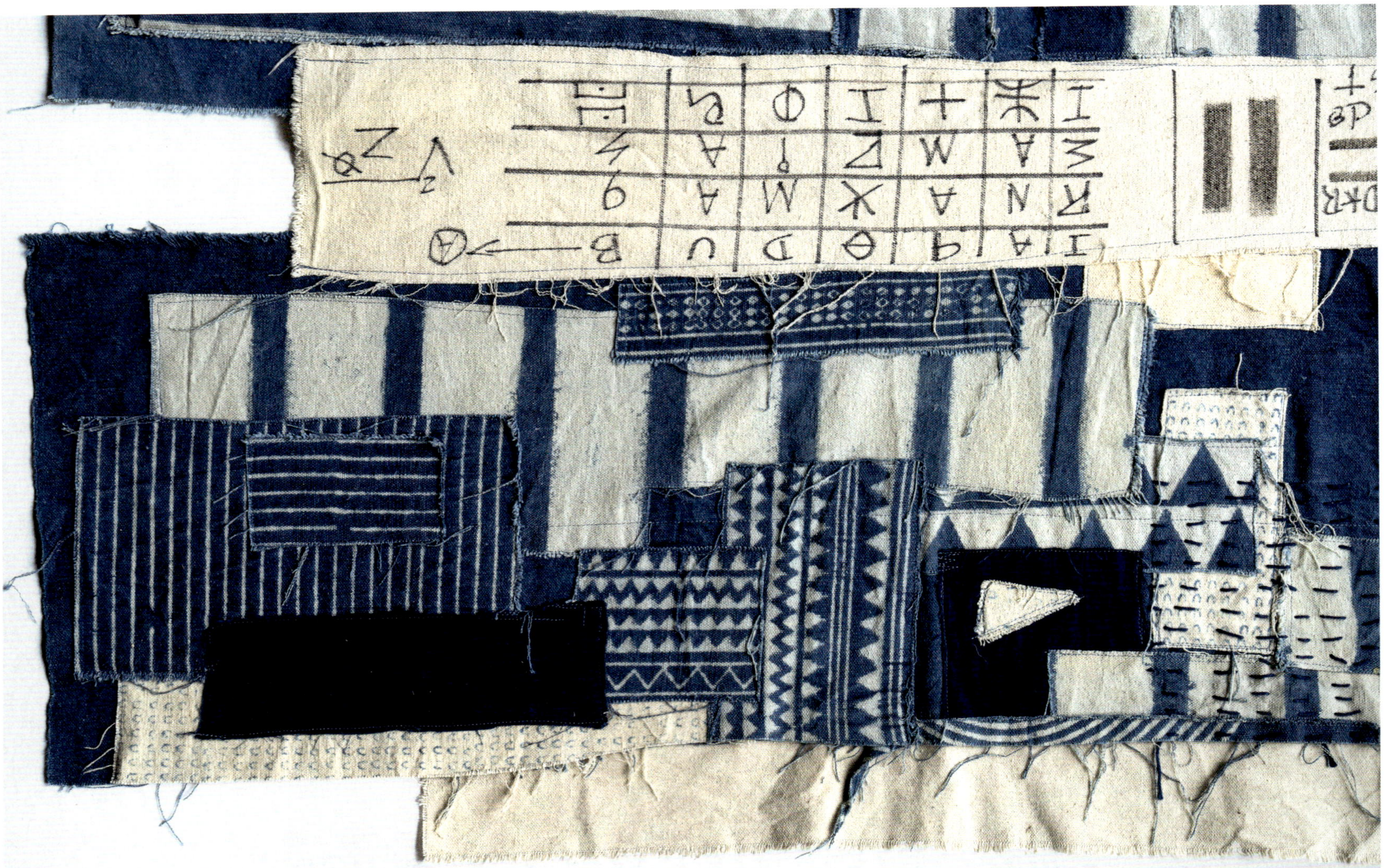

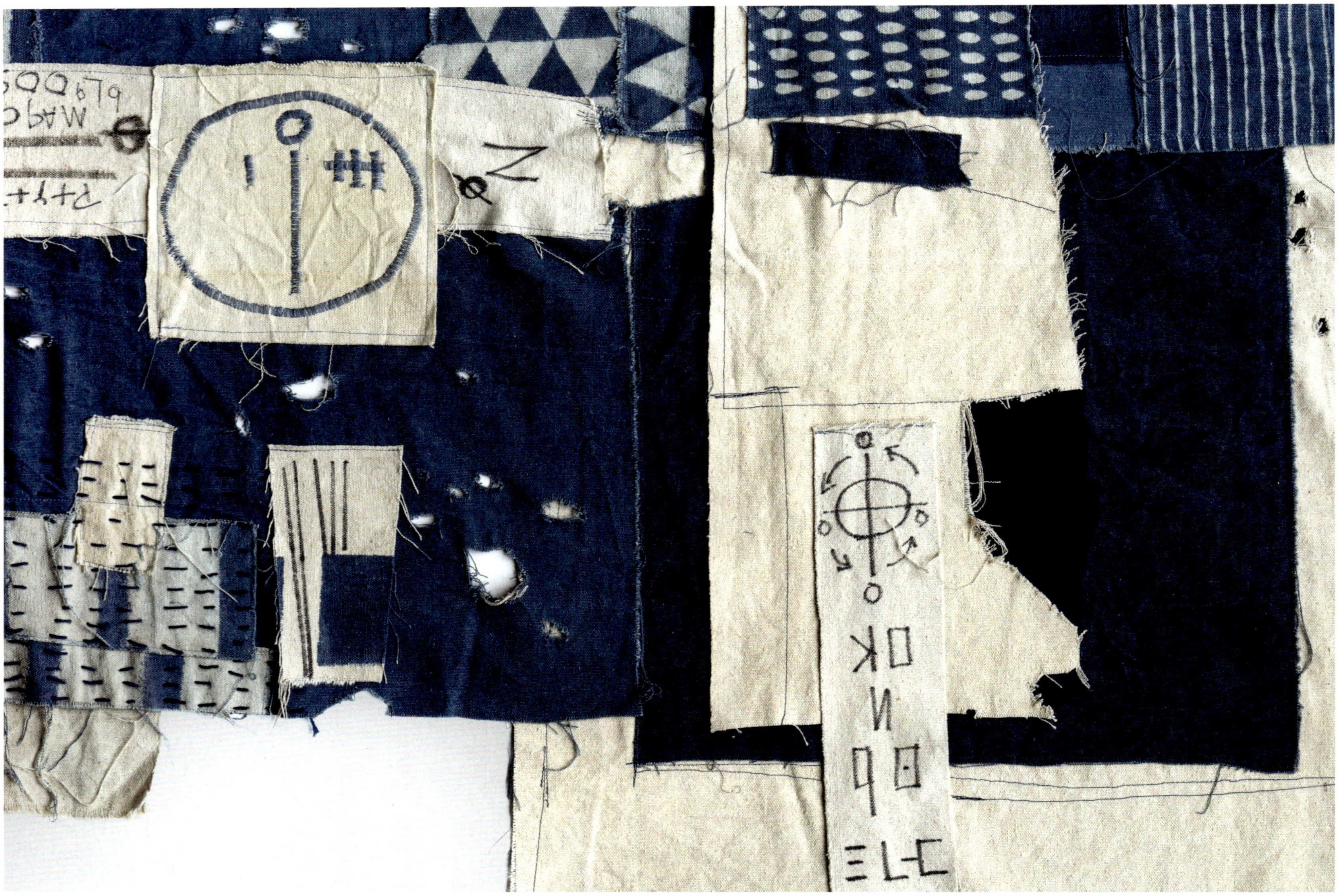

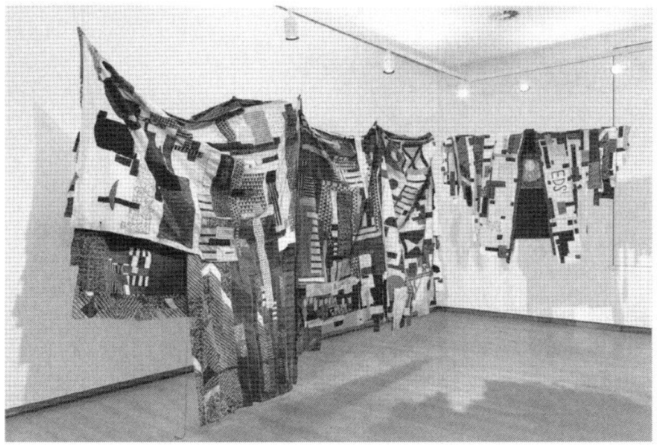

The Rise of the Prophet as part of Messengers of the Sun, Antonio Jose Guzman & Iva Jankovic, 2022.

Patchwork with Ajrakh block-printed, indigo-dyed-cotton, black marker, wood, hand and machine sewing, machine embroidery, sashiko stitching, various sizes.

*The Rise of the Prophet* is a patchwork of pieces of blue-and-white fabric sewn together to form a large variegated landscape. There are longer and shorter strips, medium-sized squares, small triangular fragments, and patches with no distinct shape. Just as the shape and size of each piece varies, so do their designs. Some feature simple patterns of dots or stripes spaced at regular intervals. Others show a seamless repeat of alternating triangles, or a maze pattern of interlocking angular and wavy lines. In between are patches of monochrome blue, and strips of unbleached cotton featuring cryptic signs.

The pieces of fabric are seamed together in a makeshift fashion, without any apparent layout or design and with all stitching in full view. Some fragments overlap or are stitched on top of one another, others float freely, only seamed to the canvas at one end. Some are stitched by hand, whereas others have multiple lines of machine stitching running across—again seemingly without any apparent plan or overall design. This sense of randomness in the composition is enhanced by the frayed edges and the many loose threads that stick out from the sides or hang down the surface, as none of the patches are hemmed. Some patches have holes in them or show other signs of wear and tear. However, *The Rise of the Prophet* does not only evoke a sense of chaos and chance: the irregularity of the composition is offset by the even rhythm of the block-printed patterns, in which the repeated motifs connect seamlessly into a single design.

While each unique patch invites detailed examination, a few jump out immediately: the white sections and strips bearing symbols reminiscent of hieroglyphs or alchemical formulas written with what appears to be black marker; the *sashiko* embroidery on the far right and the embroidered circle in light blue. Some of the fabrics are used in more than one place, others only appear once. Yet it is the unmistakable indigo blue that holds all fragments together and makes the patchwork a unified whole.

*The Rise of the Prophet* is part of Antonio Jose Guzman and Iva Jankovic's ongoing research project titled *Electric Dub Station* (2018–ongoing). Like other indigo resist-dye textile objects that are created within its scope, *The Rise of the Prophet* has been presented in various settings and installations, sometimes displayed horizontally, sometimes vertically, sometimes draped over a wooden pole, part-concealed behind other objects, thus mirroring the patchwork ideology of reuse and sampling.

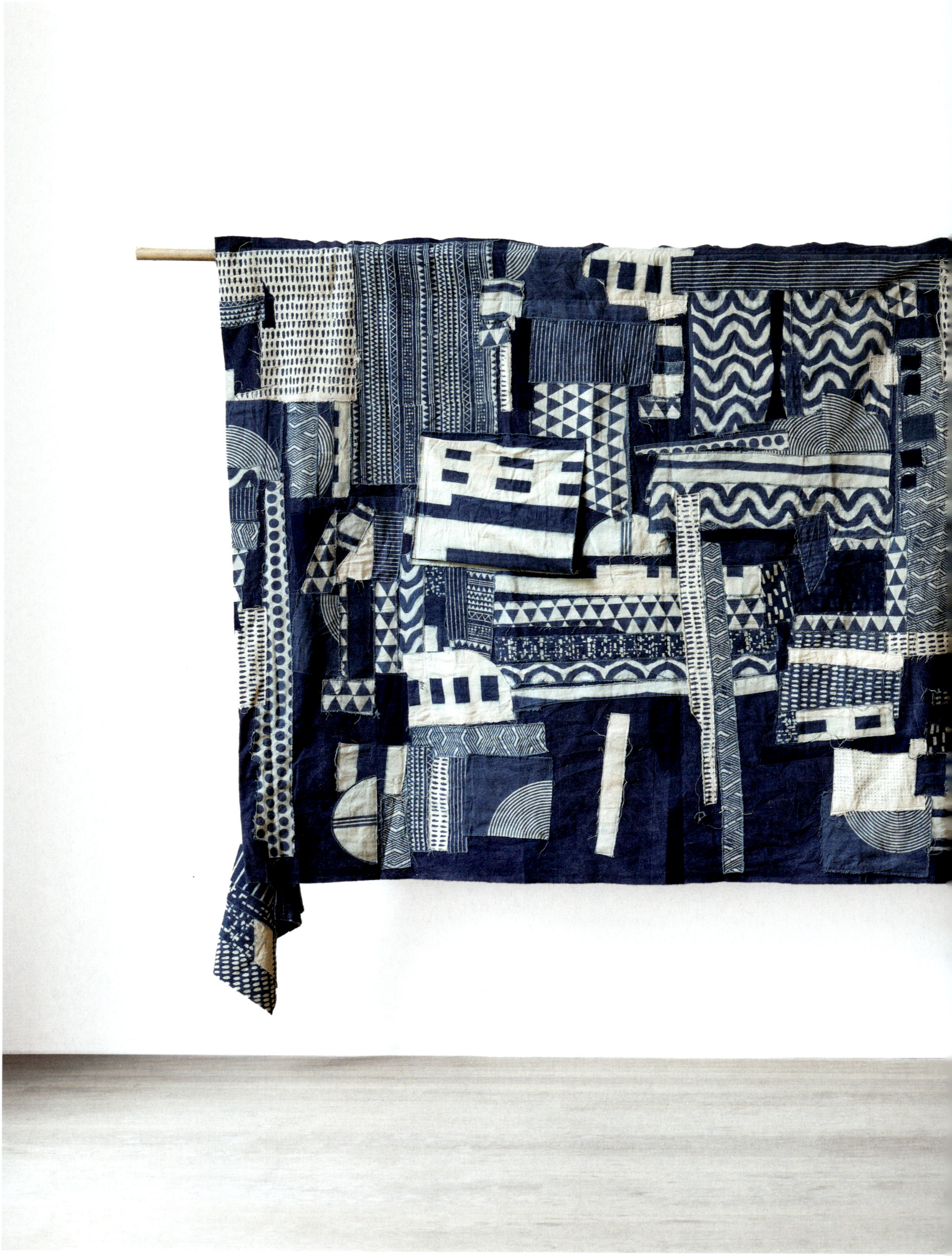

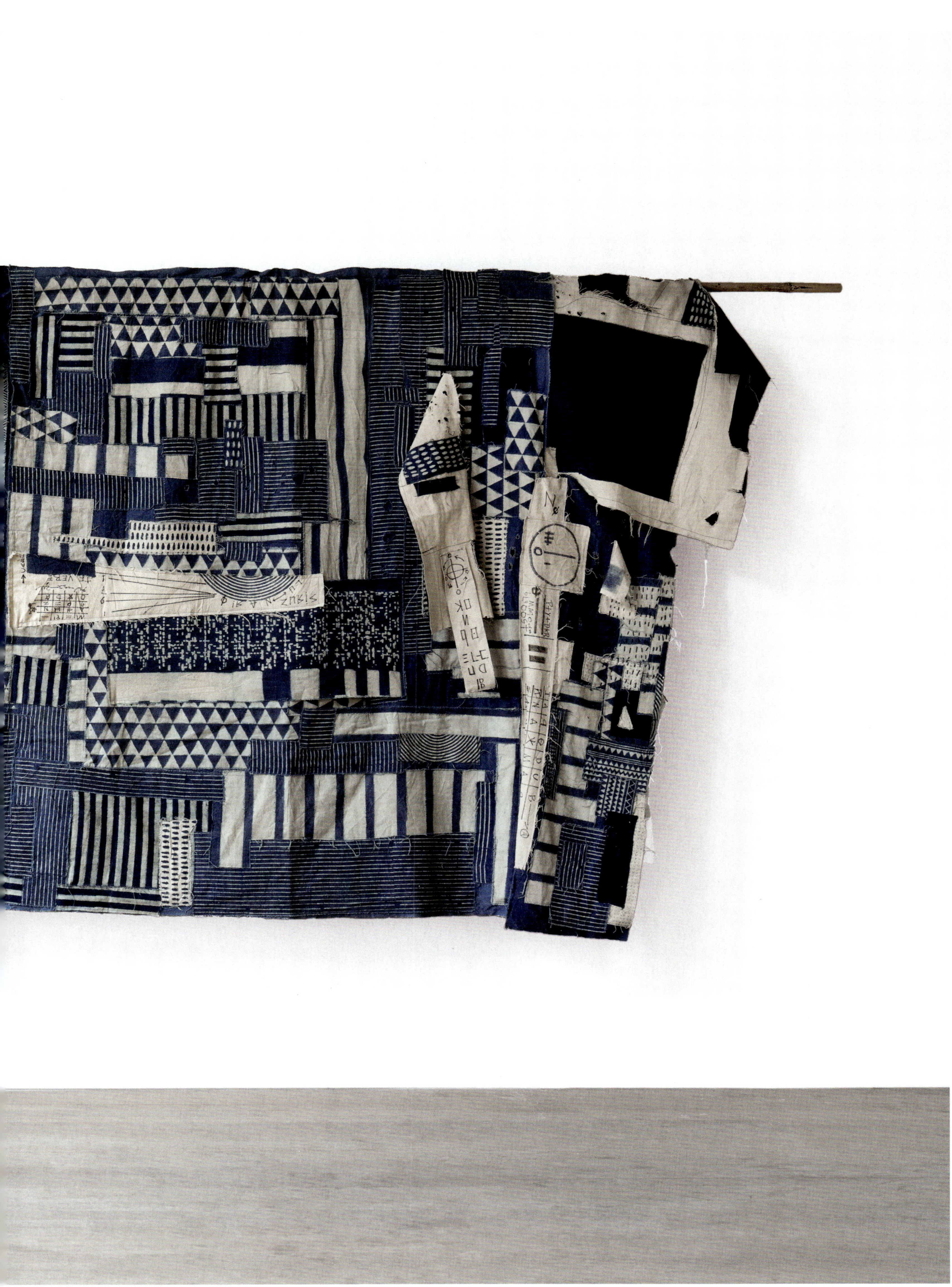

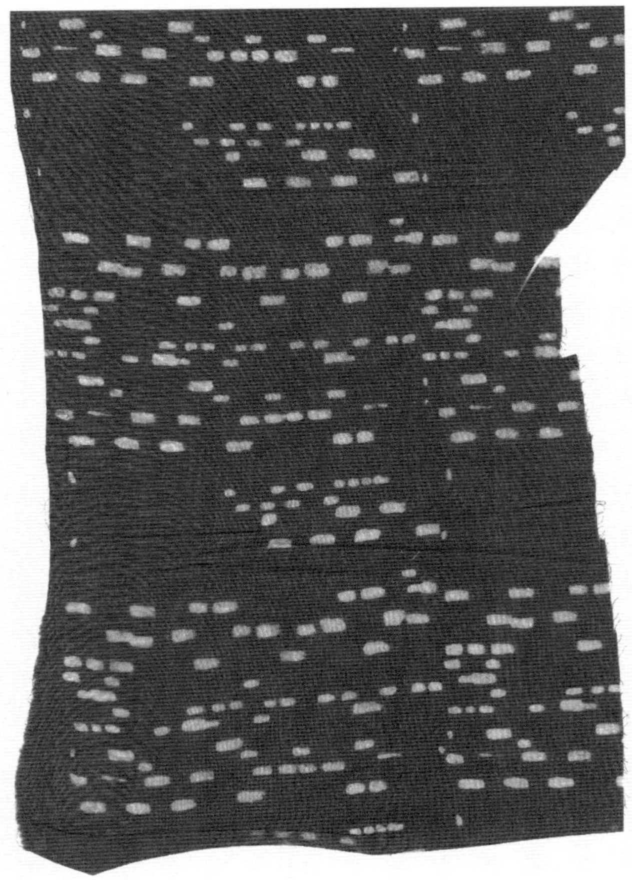

Ajrakh resist-dyed indigo fabric with block-printed DNA pattern.

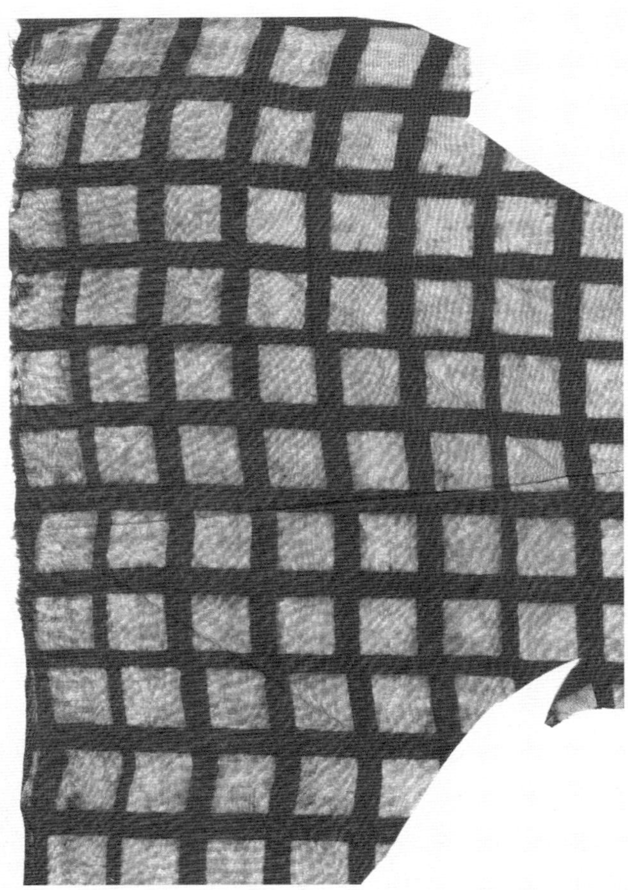

Ajrakh resist-dyed indigo fabric with block-printed pattern.

# UNRAVELLING THE RISE OF THE PROPHET
## In Conversation with Antonio Jose Guzman & Iva Jankovic

In 2019, the Dutch-Panamanian artist Antonio Jose Guzman and Dutch-Serbian artist Iva Jankovic started their multidisciplinary project *Electric Dub Station*, which takes various forms, ranging from monumental textile installations and performances to sonic happenings and photography. The project is based on their extensive research into the transatlantic and colonial history of indigo. One key element is block-printed, resist-dye indigo textile. Echoing the paths of human migration created by transatlantic trade in colonial times, indigo fabrics have become a vehicle for reflecting on cross-cultural networks and diasporic identities while reanimating the deeply spiritual meaning of indigo blue.

CHRISTEL VESTERS — The textile work *The Rise of the Prophet* is part of your research into the history of indigo. What sparked your interest in indigo blue?

IVA JANKOVIC — When we met at the Ajrakh workshop of Sufiyan Khatri in Gujarat, in 2017, we were both fascinated by the magic of dyeing with natural indigo. You have this blue pigment that comes from green leaves. When mixed into water in a vat, the water turns this light-green colour. But then, over time, the fabric becomes deep blue. You never know what the outcome will be; each bath produces a different tint of blue, depending on the fermentation of the leaves, the water temperature and so on. That's why they call it a 'living colour' and why, in some countries, knowledge of indigo dye is a cultural treasure. Later, when we started to research the history of indigo, we learnt that indigo is truly global. I mean, the indigo plant is indigenous to different regions across the globe — India, Guatemala, Senegal — and in each of these places, independently of one another, people discovered a process to extract the pigment from the leaves and turn it into a dye. Recently they found a 6.200-year old striped fabric with indigo dye in Huaca Prieta, in Peru. I think that's magical. Although many still believe that the Spanish imported indigo from India into the Americas. But we also learnt about the role indigo played in colonial trade.

ANTONIO JOSE GUZMAN — Indigo was the hidden commodity of the transatlantic slave trade. When colonizers discovered the value of indigo, they imported the plant to their colonies. To the Southern Colonies in America and the West-Indies, to Surinam, and later to the Dutch East-Indies. To work those plantations, they shipped millions of people from the African continent. Africans knew how to extract dye from the indigo leaves, and they were cheap labour. At one point, indigo was in such high demand that an enslaved person was worth his or her weight in indigo. In the nineteenth century, plantation owners dyed low-grade cloth with indigo and used it for slave uniforms, calling it 'Negro cloth', which is the precursor of blue jeans. So, you see, indigo is very much entangled with histories of colonialism.

CHRISTEL — These days we are more aware of the dark side of indigo history and the key role it played on the triangular trade routes between Asia,

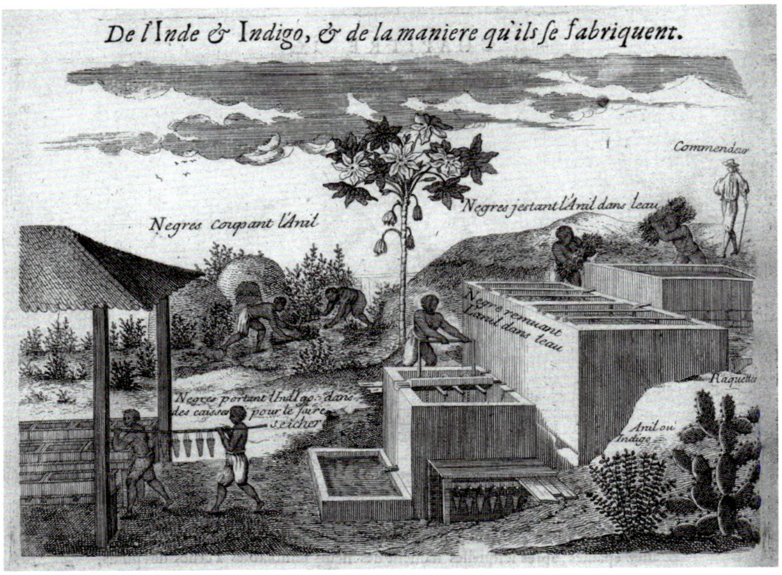


01

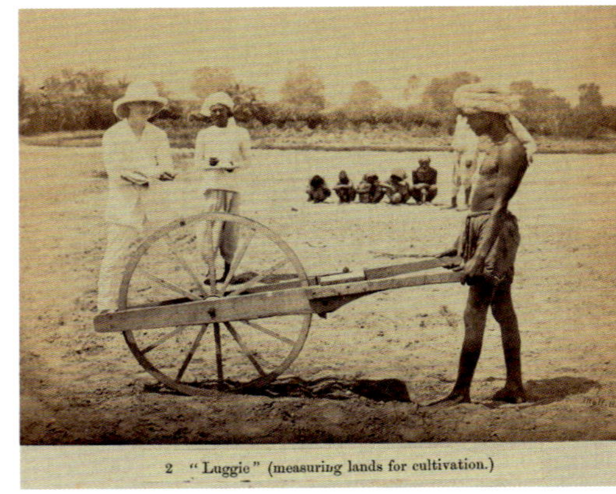


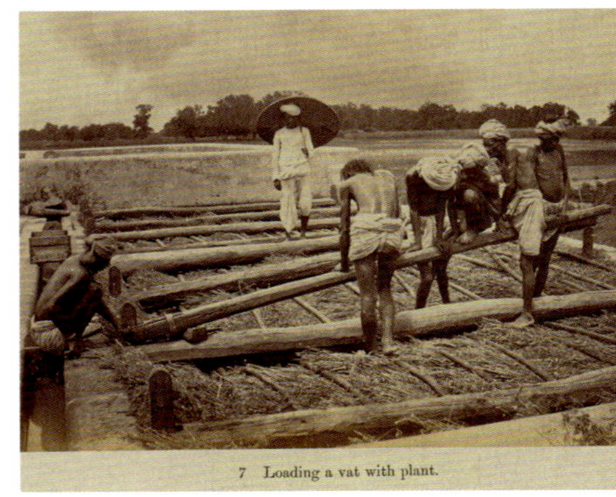


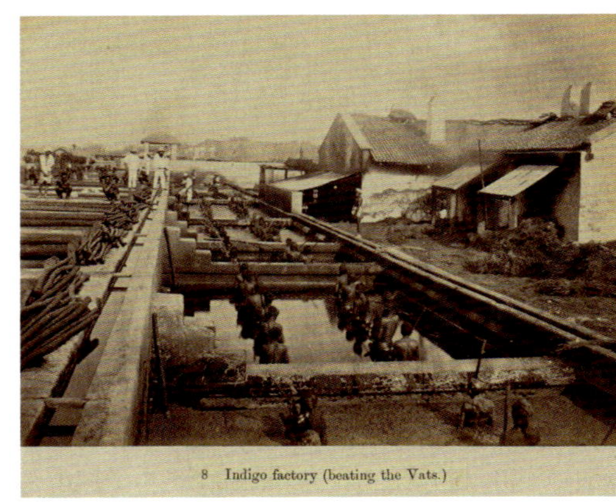


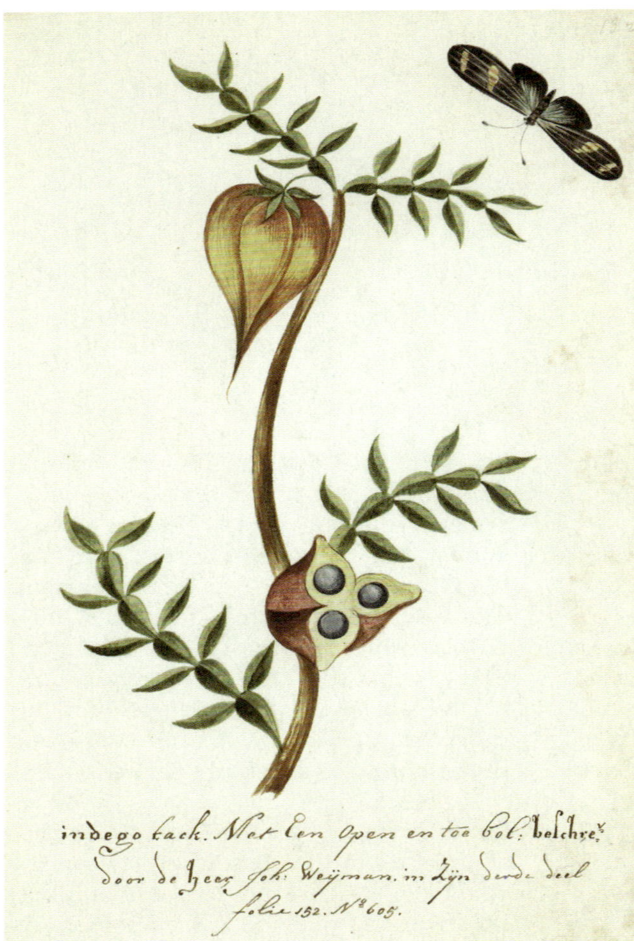

02

01. Woodcut from Pierre Promet, Histoire generale des drogues, traitant des plantes, des animaux, et des mineraux..., Paris: J.-B. Loyson & A. Pillon: E. Ducastin (1694).
02. Indigo branch with open and closed ball, Cornelis Markée, brush drawing, 'described by Mr. Joh. Weijman in his third volume, folio 152, No. 605', c. 1763.

INDIGOFERA
There are a variety of blue-dye plants, the best known of which is the Indigofera family. Thriving in tropical climates, species of the Indigofera are native to parts of Africa, India, South-East Asia and Central and South America. In the Americas the local species is called Indigofera suffruticosa, also known as 'anil', and in India the most common species is Indigofera arrectia, also known as 'natal' indigo. Long before European botanists gave the plants their Latin names, ancient indigenous cultures, thousands of miles apart from one another, had developed recipes for extracting the pigment and fixing the colours in the fibres of a textile. Indigo-dyed fabrics have been found in Peru, Guatemala, the Indus Valley, West Africa and India. The oldest patch containing indigo-dyed yarn was recovered at Huaca Prieta in Peru and is estimated to be 6000–6200 years old.

03. The Planting & Manufacture of Indigo in India: 29 Photographic Views, Allahabad, India, by Oscar Mallitte, 1877. Album with albumen silver print.
    (2) 'Luggie'(measuring lands for cultivation).
    (7) Loading vat with plants.
    (8) Indigo factory (beating the Vats).
    (15) Pressing the fecula.
    (17) Cutting indigo into cakes.

INDIGO PROFIT
It wasn't until the beginning of the 16th century, when Portuguese merchants imported the first consignment of indigo to Europe, that indigo-blue became a symbol of status and power, replacing the much paler blue dye from woad plants and making indigo dye a much sought-after and very profitable commodity. To convince potential investors back home of the profitability of the plantations, local governors and colonial companies such as the Dutch East India Company (VOC) and the East India Company (EIC) documented their findings in botanical studies, including drawings of the various species they cultivated, and sent samples of their produce back home.

04. Indigo Factory Model, 1886. Wood, clay, 200 × 150 cm. The model depicts the production of indigo dye in India and was commissioned from Indian artist Rakhal Chunder Pál by the British authorities in India for the Colonial and Indian Exhibition held in South Kensington in 1886. The model later went on display at the Museum of Economic Botany at Kew Gardens. It consists of wooden buildings and 100 clay figurines, including four oxen pulling a cart that delivers raw indigo plants, one European manager wearing a pith helmet standing on top of the vats, and 95 Indian workers occupied

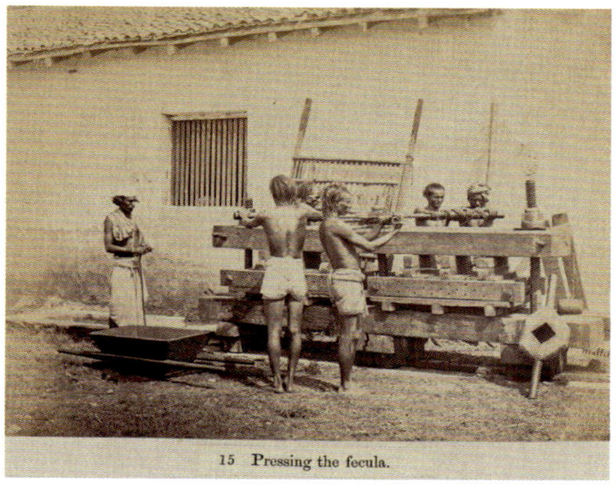


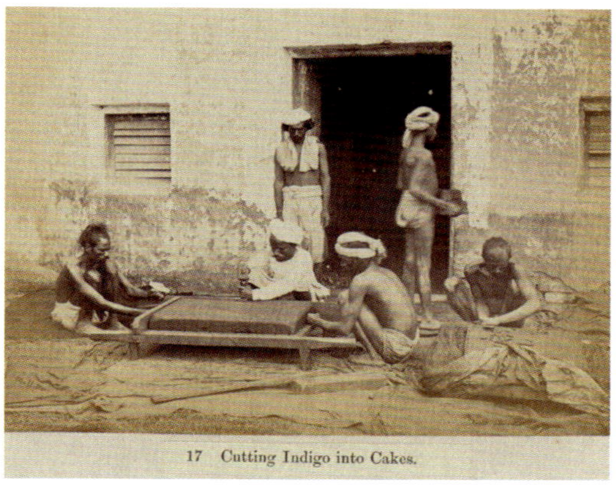


03

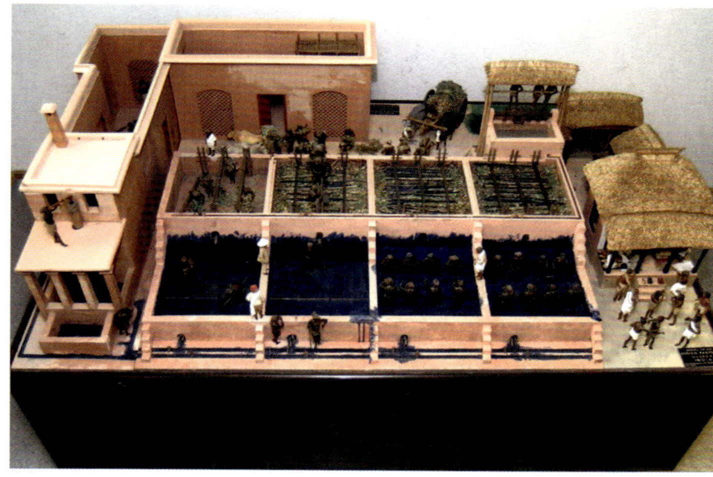

04

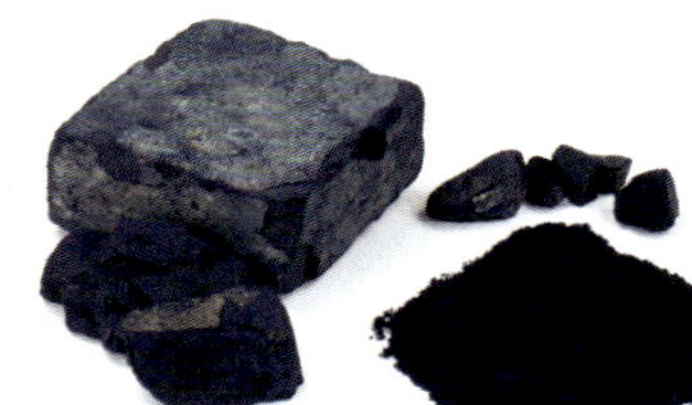

05

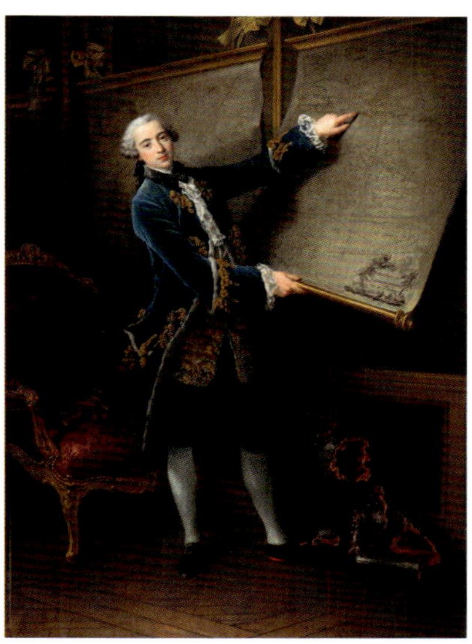

06

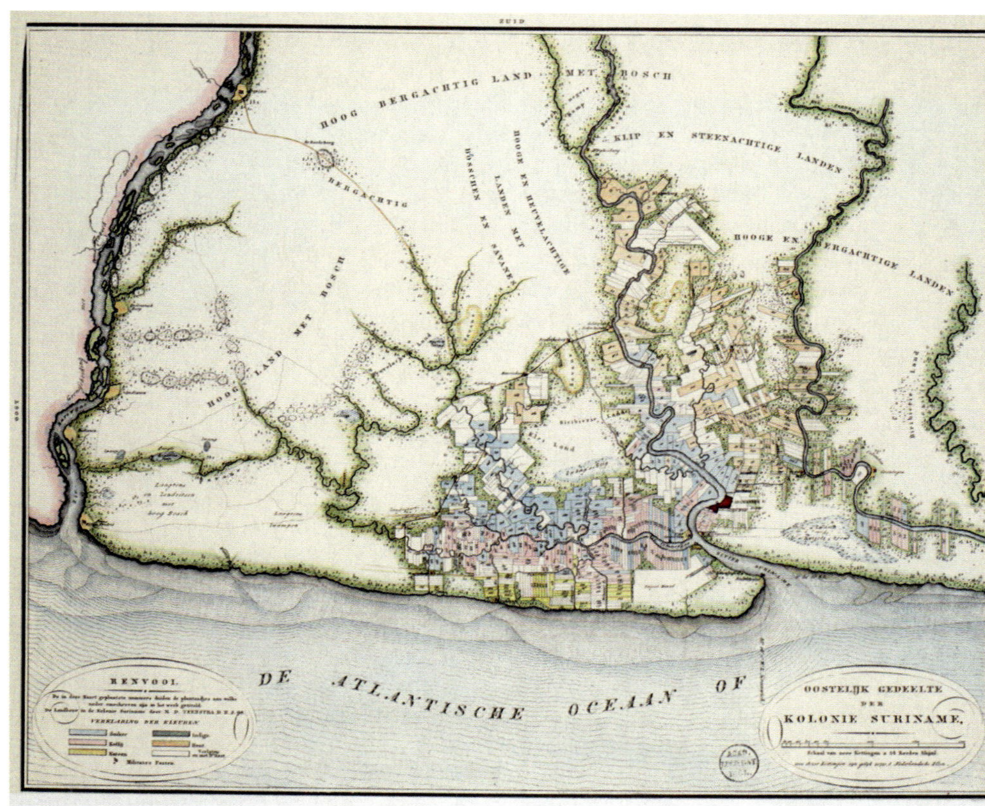


07

in various stages of the process by which indigo was converted from fresh green plants into blocks of dye. The miniature scale of the diorama turns the harsh working conditions and violent reality on indigo plantations into a doll-house-like curiosity. By entering the Museum, the model became part of a 19th century global network of knowledge production that catered not only to the scientific botanist and general public, but also to the merchant, the manufacturer, the physician, and artisans of every description.

05. Indian blue indigo dye in block and powder.

06. Portrait of the Comte de Vaudreuil, François-Hubert Drouais, 1758.
Oil on canvas, 225.4 × 161.3 cm.
Joseph-Hyacinthe-François de Paule de Rigaud, Comte de Vaudreuil (1740–1817), the son of the governor of Saint-Domingue, present-day Haiti, points at a map of the then French colony. The family owned many sugar cane and indigo plantations in Saint-Dominique, and the count earned substantial revenue from enslaved labour on his plantations without lifting a finger. Instead of a uniform, Vaudreuil wears a blue velvet coat, blue being the colour of aristocracy. In 1791, a rebellion by the enslaved population broke out on Saint-Domingue. Known as the Haitian Revolution, it led to the abolishment of slavery in the French colonies, and the independence of western Hispaniola as Haiti in 1803. The successful revolt was a defining moment in the history of the Atlantic World and its effects were felt throughout the Americas.

07. Generale kaart der kolonie Suriname: hoofdzakelijk voorstellende de tegenwoordige bebouwing dier kolonie: Oostelijk gedeelte der kolonie Suriname. Landmeter: Mabé, 1835, 48 × 53.5 cm.
This map forms the eastern half of a bigger map of Surinam that was originally part of the book De landbouw in Suriname (Agriculture in Surinam) by M.D. Teenstra, an agricultural expert posted to Surinam in 1828. The publication devotes particular attention to the decline of the plantations. The map shows the area of the 'old colony'. Although it still indicates the largest extension to the cultivated area, it is hard not to notice the many abandoned plots. Plantations in Surinam were capital-intensive agricultural companies that grew produce for the world market. Profit mattered more than anything. They were usually financed by Dutch trading firms that oversaw the sale of the produce in the Netherlands and elsewhere. Most plantations specialized in one particular product to maximize returns. The legend lists the crops grown on the various plantations, with blue representing indigo. Owing to intensive cultivation and the polluting production process, much of that land could not be used for growing other crops for a long time.

Europe and the Americas. How do these histories of extractive colonialism resonate in your works?

ANTONIO & IVA — These histories of exploitation are part of our works because they are an intrinsic part of the material history of indigo. As artists, we believe that you cannot work with indigo without engaging with these histories. We believe that the contemporary indigo fabrics we work with bear witness to these histories of forced displacement, oppression and exploitation. But our work doesn't stop there. We are more interested in the legacy of these histories today. *The Rise of the Prophet* and *Electric Dub Station* emerge from the diasporic and transcultural spheres that emerge as a direct result of forced migration across the Atlantic. They are a product of what Paul Gilroy calls the Black Atlantic. According to Gilroy, there is no such thing as a typical Black African, Black Caribbean, Black American or Black European culture, there is only a hybrid transatlantic Black culture.

IVA — Another aspect of indigo blue we are interested in is its spiritual and cultural significance across the world, its use in rituals and ceremonies. The longer we work with indigo fabrics, the more we discover. People tell us stories about what indigo means in their culture. For instance, when we did a project in Amsterdam South-East, someone told us about *blauwsel*, which is one of the things produced on the indigo plantations in Surinam. Women add blauwsel to their laundry to make it white, but in Afro-Surinamese communities they also use it in rituals to protect newborn babies against evil, by adding it to the bathing water.

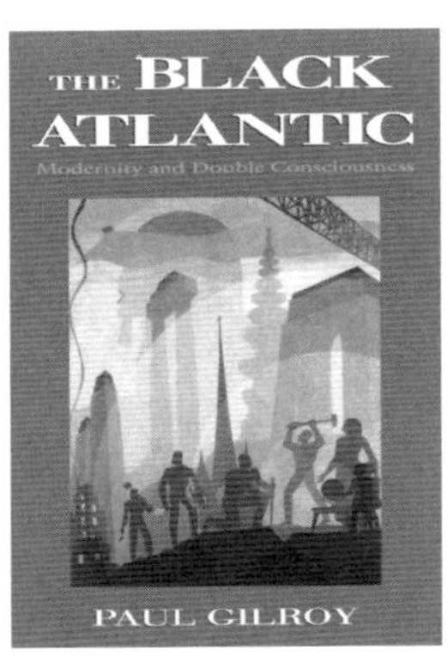


Cover of Paul Gilroy's seminal book The Black Atlantic: Modernity and Double Consciousness, 1993.

ANTONIO — These customs are very old and can be traced back to the symbolic meaning of indigo blue in various African cultures. The Yoruba people, for instance, use indigo in ceremonies and rites of passage and believe it has medicinal powers. This just shows how everything is connected.

CHRISTEL — I want to circle back to what Iva mentioned earlier, about indigo not having one unique point of origin, and that indigo knowledge and indigo textile traditions have their roots in various cultures across the globe. To me, the multi-rootedness of indigo offers a thought form to think about diasporic culture. I mean, in its natural form, indigo defies the Western, essentialist idea that all things can be retraced to their singular point of origin, which has led to such Western values as originality and authenticity.

ANTONIO — It's about the connecting threads. Everything is connected, and people look for these connections. It's not just about the transatlantic or transoceanic connections between cultures, but for us, living in Europe, coming from Panama and from the Balkans, we are always searching for things that connect us to our motherland *and* to the place we are living now. Sometimes it's a pattern in a textile, a sound or rhythm, a way of talking, or some specific food. You look for this mix of your own culture and the one that surrounds you; that's what creolization and the Black Atlantic look like to me. But for Iva, coming from the Balkans, the concept of the Black Atlantic can be something different.

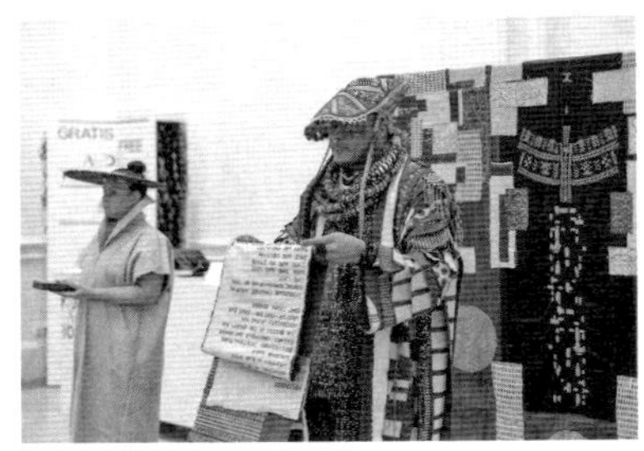

Messengers of the Sun, performance at Stedelijk Museum Amsterdam, November 2022.

Part of the project Messengers of the Sun, the performance took the form of an Afrofuturistic ceremonial procession, infused with music and dance, referencing a fictional story in which the lost children of the prophet Sun Ra, who live in the Sirius-B galaxy, are 'messengers of the sun'.

IVA — The Balkans are defined by a mix of cultures. It's where East and West meet, and clash. We have three religions: Catholic, Orthodox Christianity and Islam; we are between Africa, Asia and Europe. We are in Europe's backyard, but we don't belong to Europe. When I was growing up, Yugoslavia was part of the Non-Aligned Movement, which included many former colonies in Africa and East-Asia that had fought against imperialism, neo-colonialism and racism. For me, the mix of those cultures is where I feel I belong.

ANTONIO — What we're looking for, and what we want to create with our works and our performances, is a liminal space where various countercultures come together and connect. In Amsterdam, the Kwaku Festival or the Roots festival can be considered liminal spaces. People from various minority groups gather to be part of a bigger community. In a way it's like a fabric where threads from different backgrounds intertwine. When we exhibit our works or stage our performances, we want to insert the energy of these kinds of environments into the Western, white-cube museum. And we see, from Instagram posts for instance, how people who identify with Black Atlantic culture engage with the

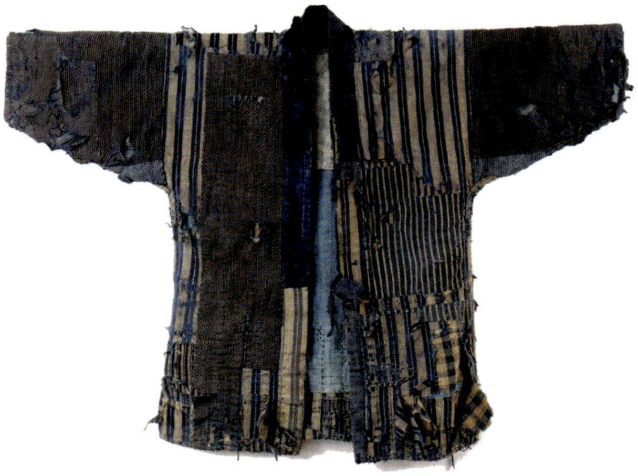

08

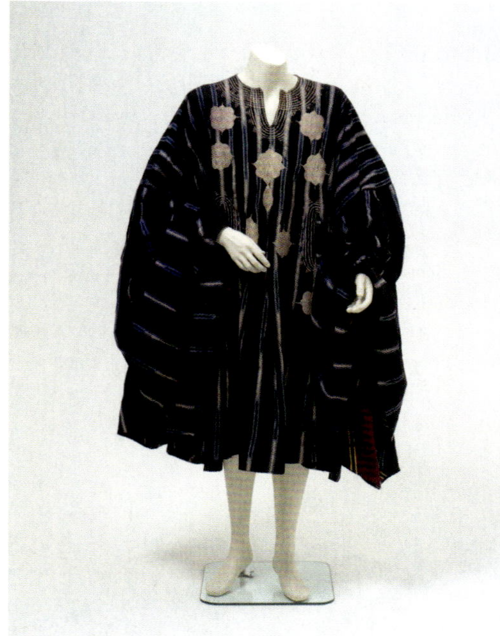

09

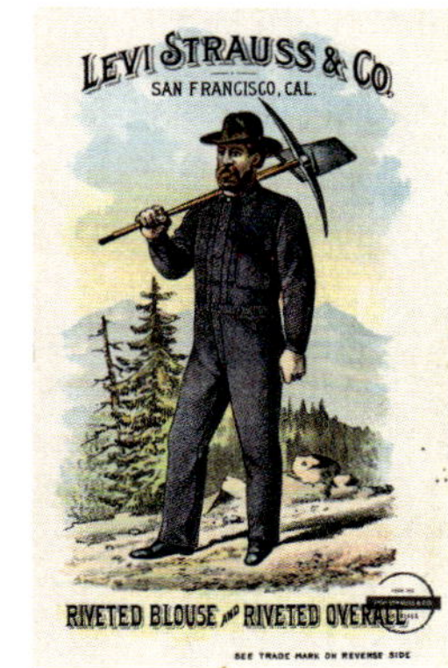


10

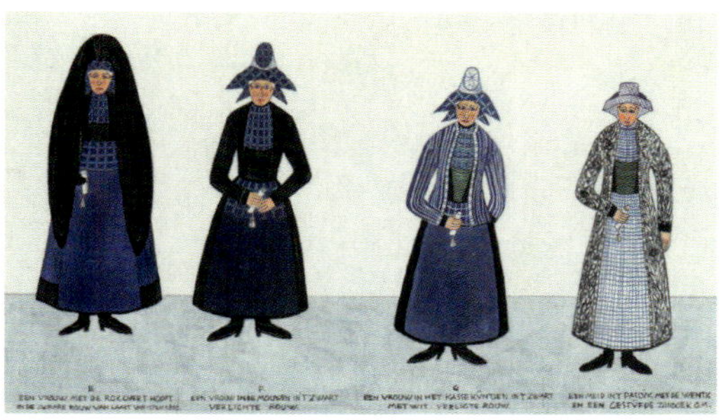

11

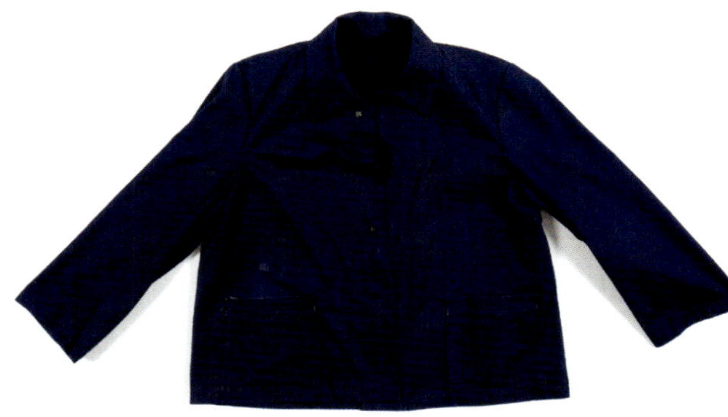

13

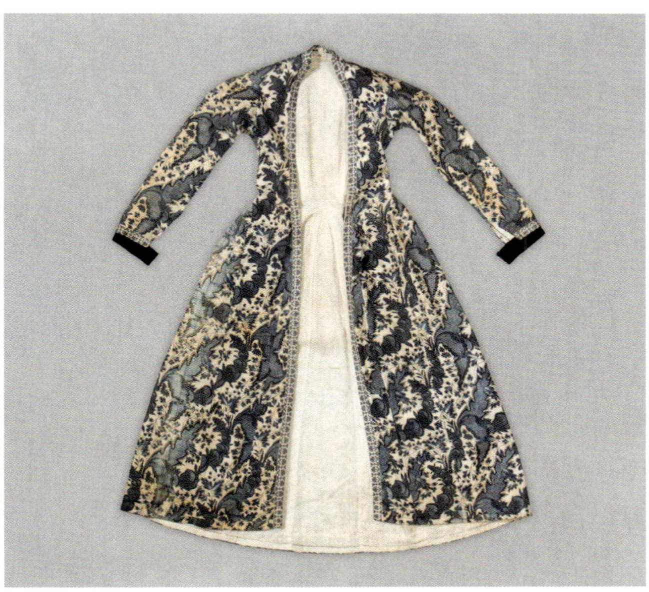

12

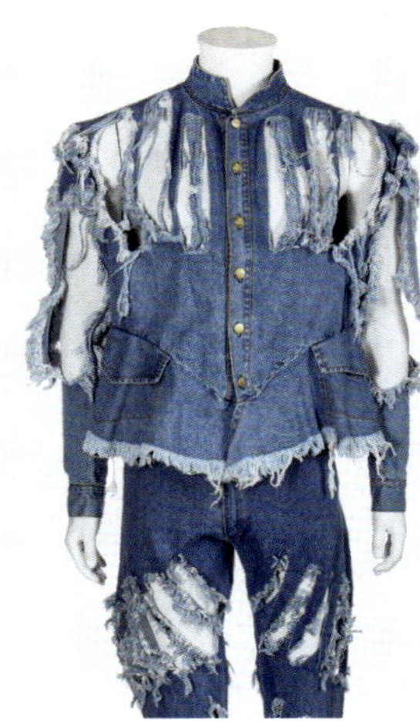

14

INDIGO WORLD
All shades of blue emerge from natural indigo dye, forming the foundation of diverse textile traditions rooted in cultures worldwide.

08. Boro Noragi, Japan, mid-1900s.
Farmer's jacket, several layers of indigo-dyed cotton, shashiko stitching, 90 × 125 cm.

BORO
From the Japanese 'boroboro', meaning something tattered or repaired. Boro technique combines patches and shashiko stitching. Farmers and fishermen favoured indigo dye for its insect- and reptile-repelling scent. Now sought-after collectibles, these garments inspire young designers interested in recycling and sustainability.

09. Men's tunic, Yoruba, Nigeria, c. 1950–1960.
Cotton, embroidery.
In Yoruba culture, indigo symbolizes wealth, stability and wisdom. It is a hallmark of Adire (tied and died) cloth, traditionally made by women. Indigo-dyed garments are worn at weddings, naming ceremonies and funerals. The dye also has medicinal uses and is painted on houses to ward off sickness.

10. Trade card Levi Strauss & Company, San Francisco, USA.
Levi Strauss & Co. patented indigo-dyed denim in the 1870s, revolutionizing workwear worn by plantation labourers and California goldminers. By the 1890s, the company started using synthetic indigo dye. In the 20th century, blue jeans became a symbol of freedom and equality.

11. Three women and a girl in Hindeloopen folkore dress, Nicolaas Huppes (after an original by Hendrik Lap), 1949.
Gouache on paper, 18 × 30.8 cm.
The four figures wear folklore dress appropriate to various stages of mourning, with descriptions below the image. The woman on the right wears a traditional 'wentke' coat.

12. Wentke, Hindeloopen folklore dress, the Netherlands, c. 1750–1850.
Cotton, linen, 32 × 140 cm.
The Hindeloopen wentke is a traditional coat from the Frisian town of Hindeloopen, renowned for its richly patterned chintz fabrics. These fabrics are historically linked to resist-dyed and block-printed cotton textiles imported from India, similar to the indigo dye that replaced the blue hues once derived from natural woad. The colour blue holds deep significance in Frisian culture and mourning customs, with darker shades symbolizing the earliest stage of mourning.

13. Zhifu, China, 1950s.
Blue cotton, blue plastic button, metal.
Recognizing the symbolic power of uniforms, Mao Zedong introduced the Zhifu (Mao jacket) in 1949 to project nationalist and communist ideology. The blue jacket became the everyday uniform of most Chinese people, connecting to China's artisanal heritage while signifying unity and rejection of Western influence.

14. Cut, Slash & Pull ensemble, Vivienne Westwood, S/S collection, 1990, England.
The collection channels punk culture through its deconstructed and rebellious aesthetic, featuring torn fabrics and raw edges. It challenged traditional fashion norms, cementing Westwood's reputation as a pioneer of anti-establishment fashion.

work. That's what we want to create with our works and performances, even if we know that, in reality, only a certain elite will come and see the work.

CHRISTEL — In terms of materiality and aesthetics, your practice is inspired by an eclectic mix of cultural traditions. For instance, for the performance *Messengers of the Sun* you created necklaces based on the traditional attire of the Baye Fall from Senegal, using a traditionally handwoven, resist-dye *jaspe* cloth from Guatemala. Is this mixing of materials and textile traditions one of the things that represents Black Atlantic to you?

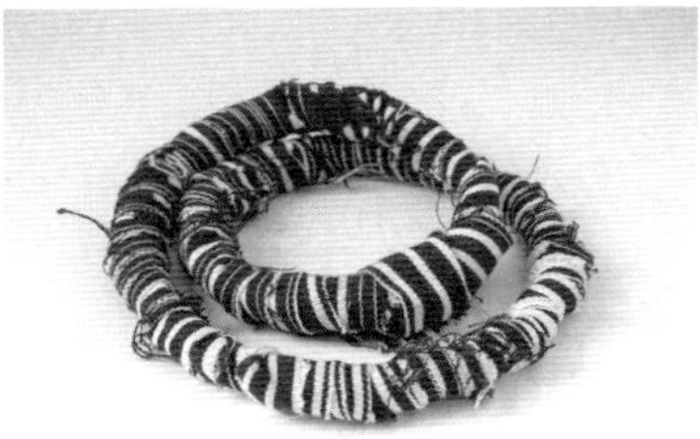

Necklace made with the traditional jaspe technique by Trama backstrap weavers and used during various performances, including Messengers of the Sun, 2022, and Orbital Mechanics, staged in Venice in 2024.

ANTONIO — For that performance we looked at the Baye Fall from Senegal, at the way they dress, their ritual chants and dances. The Baye Fall and Yaye Fall are the men and women of the Sufi-Muslim order of the Mourides, followers of Cheick Amadou Bamba, who was an important spiritual leader in Senegal. They have these locked braids that look like dreads, wear heavy leather necklaces with talismans and prayer beads, and long patchworked garments, made from indigo and resist-dyed fabrics. We mixed elements of that culture with clothing, music and dances from elsewhere. But our research started with the afrimono, which is a popular item of clothing made with block-printed fabrics, based on a Japanese kimono. The costumes are a variation on those afrimonos for which we used the Ajrakh block-printed textiles made by Sufiyan Khatri, the Ajrakh master in Gujarat we often collaborate with. We embroidered these fabrics with boro stitches and added the abstract geometric signs and symbols inspired by the *gris-gris*.

CHRISTEL — Not so long ago, this practice of 'borrowing' or sampling visual material and aesthetics from various cultures would, at least in western art discourse, be criticized as cultural appropriation, which when done by a western artist or fashion designer would be viewed as another moment neocolonial disownment. What is your take on this?

ANTONIO — I don't perceive these cultures as not being us because today cultures *are* colliding. What's more, if you look at our DNA, we are all composed of multiple ethnicities, going back thousands of years. Many people in Panama have Yoruba, Mandinka, Ashanti or Mbebe ancestry in their DNA, because they are descended from African people who were enslaved and brought to the southern colonies to work on the plantations. But even before that, groups of people travelled, crossed the ocean and mingled with locals.

CHRISTEL — You use the pattern of your own DNA in your textile works as well, like a signature almost. How did this come about?

ANTONIO — Yes, a while back I did one of those commercial DNA tests, which showed that I have Senegambian, Indigenous American and Sephardic Jewish ancestry. I used the image of the result, that abstract hieroglyphic code that sums up who you are, as the basis for various projects. One of the first things Iva and I asked Sufiyan Khatri, was to craft different traditional printing blocks based on this DNA pattern, and to produce indigo resist-dyed fabrics with it. I think by now Sufiyan and his co-workers must have produced at least 1000 metres of fabric featuring my DNA pattern.

IVA — It's a collaboration with Sufiyan. We don't copy or steal his craft, his tradition. We do use and copy things that inspire us and influence our thinking and creativity, but we experiment and create interpretations based on the originals. These things, whether it's a textile pattern, a dance, a ritual object, or a costume, they become symbols in the story we want to tell. For instance, in *The Rise of the Prophet*, you can find drawings with signs and symbols that are inspired by the writings on the pieces of cloth the Baye Fall men would carry with them in their amulets, that they wear on leather necklaces, the gris-gris Antonio mentioned earlier.

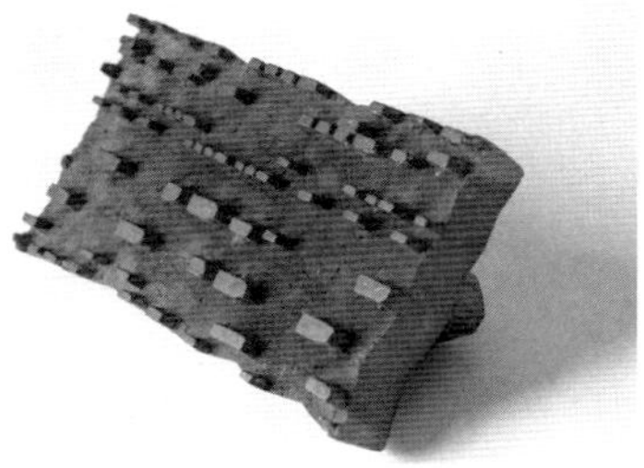

Ajrakh printing block with a pattern based on Antonio Jose Guzman's DNA, crafted by Ajrakh master Sufyian Kahtri.

ANTONIO — For us, using this reference to the gris-gris is a reminder of how ancestral knowledge and spiritual traditions travelled from the west coast of Africa to the United States with enslaved Africans, and how they were condemned and forbidden there because they were regarded as 'black magic'. That's another vital aspect of colonial history that has been forgotten: the prohibition and denial of people's native culture and beliefs.

CHRISTEL — You often you refer to your projects as 'decolonializing indigo'?

IVA — It simply means that we don't use toxic materials, but natural, organic dyes instead, so that we stop damaging our ecosystem and start to live more sustainably, and we can start to reverse some

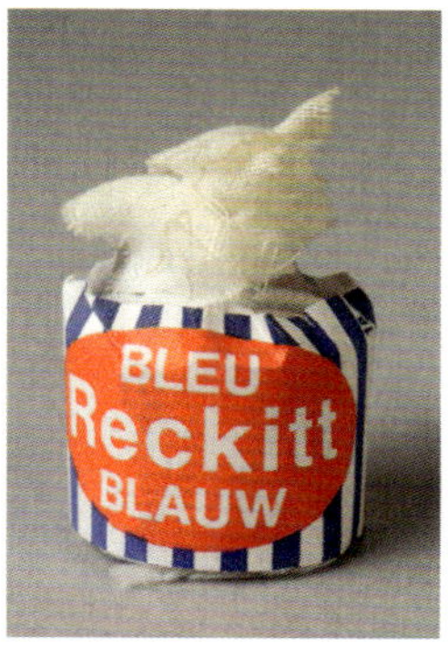


15

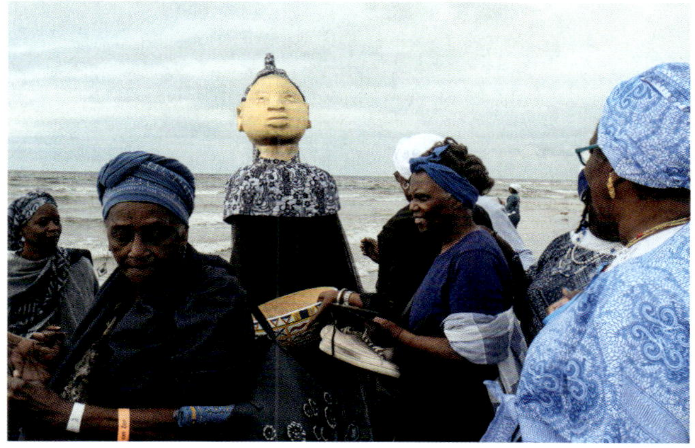

16

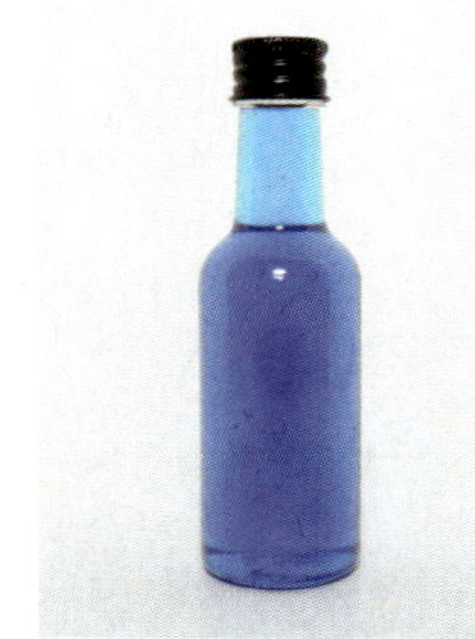

17

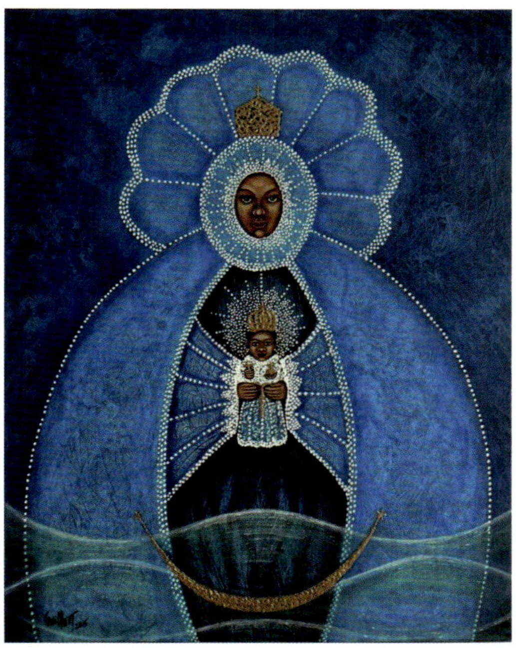

18

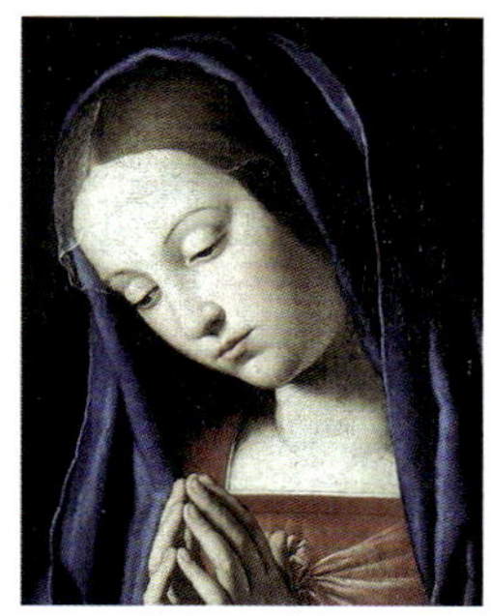

19

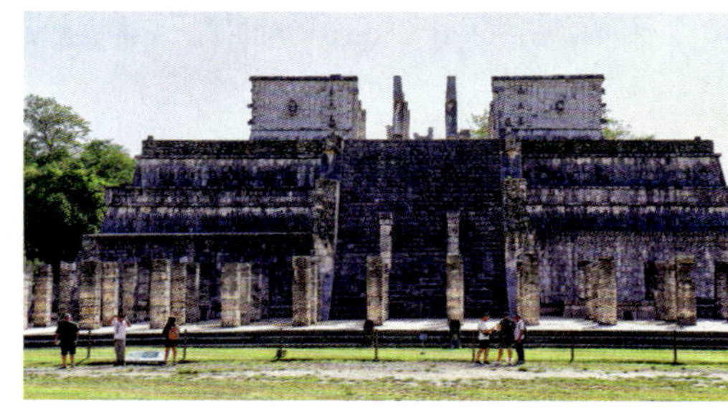

20

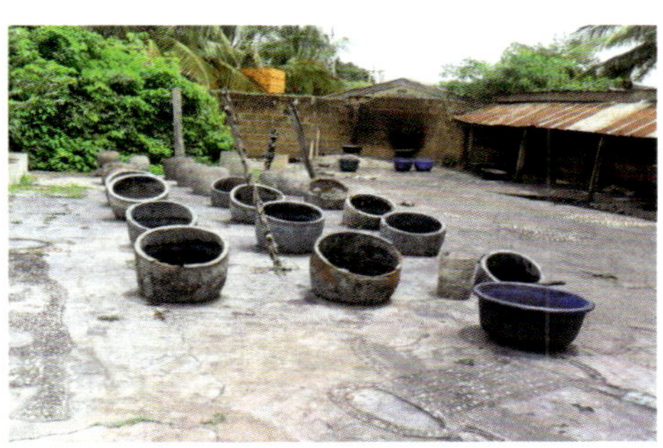

21

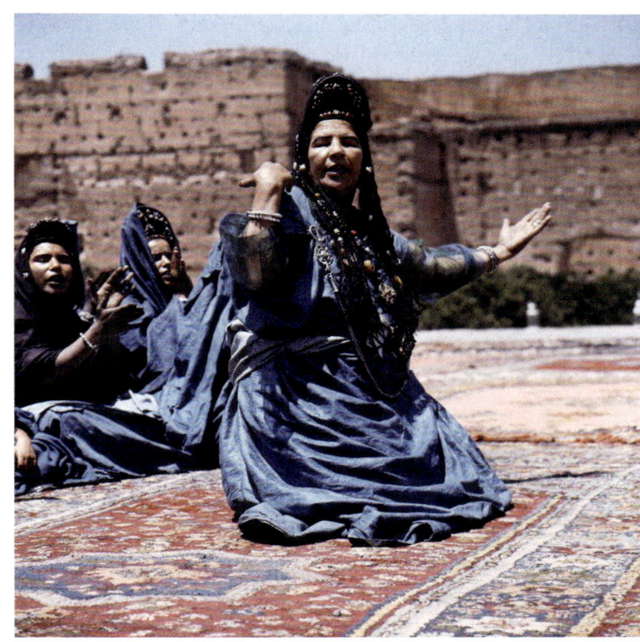

22

THE DEEP OF BLUE
From Asia to Africa and South America, extracting blue dye from indigo leaves is considered a sacred affair, requiring ancestral knowledge and divine intervention. This mystical aspect is reflected in the symbolic use of indigo blue during rituals through which communities express their religious experience. When millions of Africans were forcibly displaced during the transatlantic slave trade, these rituals endured, adapting to new environments or being forced underground.

15. Bag of Reckitt Blue, 1950–1960.
Paper, linen, 25 × 30 cm.
Blauwsel is a blue powder used by Afro-Surinamese communities in childbirth rituals. Applied to a baby's skin or bathwater, the blue symbolizes purity and is believed to cleanse and protect against evil spirits.
16. Kabra Dei aan Zee, Kijkduin Strand, 2023.
The 'Kabra', or ancestral, mask is worn in a ceremony led by Winti priestess Nana Efua (Marian Markelo) to honour ancestors who died at sea during the Transatlantic slave trade. The mask was created by artist Boris van Berkum in collaboration with Markelo.
17. Bottle of natural Indigo Water.
Made according to a traditional Hoodoo formula using herbal extracts and essential oils, indigo water is used for spiritual protection, to ward off the evil eye, cleanse the aura or for more practical purposes such as floor washing.

YEMAYÁ
Yemayá, the Yoruba orisha of the sea, survived in the Afro-Cuban diaspora as the Virgin de Regla. Typically depicted with black skin, the Virgin de Regla is a synthesis of African spirituality, Santeria and Catholicism. Yemayá is associated with fertility, motherhood and the protective, nurturing powers of water.

18. Javier Martinez, Virgin de Regla, 2015.
Oil on canvas, 40 × 50 cm.
19. Vergine Annunciata, Salvi Giovan Battista detto Sassoferrato, c. 1680–1685.
Oil on canvas, 33 × 45 cm.
In Christian iconography, the blue of Mary's mantle symbolizes her divinity, innocence and humanity. Blue articulates her role as Mother of God, bride of the Holy Spirit and mother of the Church.
20. Temple of Warriors with Chac Mool statue, Chichén Itzá, Yucatán, Mexico, 800–1050 CE.
The Chac Mool statue is believed to have been used in rituals dedicated to the Maya rain god Chaac. Ceremonial offerings – including humans – were painted with indigo and clay, a mix known as Maya Blue. This vibrant pigment was associated with the sky, water and the divine.
21. Indigo dye pots, Osogbo, Nigeria, 2013.
Yoruba women are known to seek guidance from spirits through rituals performed before fermenting a new pot of indigo dye.
22. Female dancers performing the Guedra dance, Marrakech, 1970.
Slide, photo by F.M. Cowan, 6 × 6 cm.
Named the 'blue women' after their blue veil-like dress, or 'melfa', the dancers belong to the Reguibat, an Arab-Berber nomadic tribe from the Western Sahara. Traditionally, blue has both religious and spiritual meaning, and signifies diginity.

of the damage inflicted on the land by the extractive colonialism of the past. But that's just one aspect of it. We still live in a colonial world, in terms of labour, mining and extracting raw materials, and we're still dumping our toxic waste from textile and fashion production. I believe that if we lived more sustainably, practiced fair trade and used local products, we could shift the balance and truly decolonize the world. That's why we choose to work with Sufiyan, because he uses natural materials that don't pollute the planet, and we don't exploit his skills, his labour or his cultural traditions. We pay him fairly and name him as a collaborator.

CHRISTEL — So for you decolonialism means restoring the balance and repairing the damage that has been inflicted by colonial powers in the past?

ANTONIO — That's one part of our mission. We use indigo-dyed fabrics because they carry the weight of the history of colonialism and the transatlantic trade. Amsterdam would not be Amsterdam if it hadn't been for the indigo trade. At one point, indigo was more valuable than sugar, so plantation owners in Surinam decided to replace their sugar production with indigo. But because indigo production was so toxic — it literally turned the soil blue — the land was too polluted to grow vegetables for a long time. There's still an area in Surinam called Blauwe Grond (Blue Land). But again, that's just half of the story.

To decolonize indigo also means that we want to restore the meaning indigo had for our ancestors, whether they are Yoruba, or Maya, or Indian. In my original culture in Panama, indigo has a spiritual and ceremonial meaning and is deeply connected with our animist and ancestral beliefs and rituals. Indigo is something liminal, something extraordinary, something connected to God, to mother nature, mother earth. It is deeply connected with who we are. But when the Spanish, or the British or the Dutch started to capitalize on indigo and turned it into a commodity, they killed its spiritual essence. And then later, when Adolf Baeyer and Viggo Drewsen introduced the synthetic indigo blue, the origins of indigo culture were forgotten.

So when we use indigo in this traditional and, for us, ancestral way, we *are* detoxing the material from its colonial past. For us, it's a form of resistance. We believe that all indigo textiles are animated; they have a life of their own and are a reflection of something divine. Even if they are exhibited in an art space, indigo can connect people with something more profound, in a way that other materials maybe can't.

CHRISTEL — I want to talk about the aesthetics and the scale of your textile works. In *The Rise of the Prophet*, you push the patchwork technique to a form that says punk more than it says refined craftsmanship. The loose threads, the holes, the seemingly chaotic and disorganized composition... How does this punk aesthetic connect with your decolonial agenda?

IVA — In our performances we like to connect and combine the magical aspects of indigo with the subversiveness and rebelliousness of punk culture.

ANTONIO — We both grew up in societies where punk is a counter-culture, like hip-hop, dub music and breakdance. They are anti-establishment and share a resistance to mainstream culture. Many animist religions in Latin America that are marginalized today are part of a counter-culture too, so 'fight the power' means speaking up for the rights of indigenous communities. And don't forget that many of the revolts against colonial oppressors in former colonies, like Haiti and India, started on indigo plantations. That's another connection.

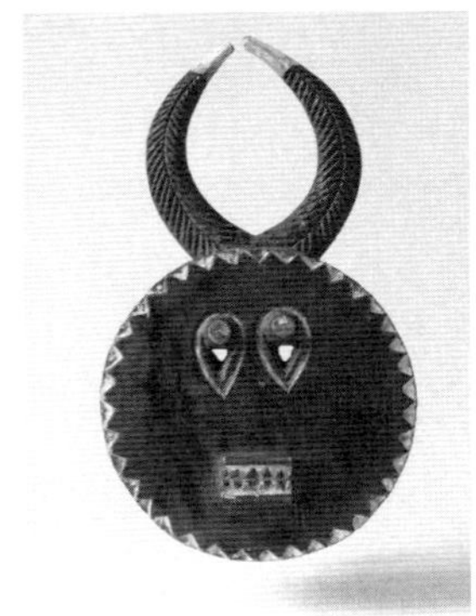

Baule Goli mask ('kple kple'), carved and painted wood, 25 × 50 cm. Purchased by the artist in Dakar in 2009.

The mask is worn by the Baule people during 'Goli', a ceremonial dance that lasts an entire day. Masks allow for closer contact with ancestral spirits and the supernatural world.

CHRISTEL — About the patchwork technique you use in *The Rise of the Prophet* and other works. The essence of a patchwork is that it unifies hitherto unlinked fragments into a new whole. In *The Rise of the Prophet* the fragments vary in pattern and shape but share the same blue colour. With a bit of poetry, can we read the work as blueprint for an ideal society where all sorts of people co-exist with space for fringes and friction?

ANTONIO — Yes, all our work is about creating spaces in which people, things, cultures coexist, about exploring the fringes, combining and connecting things to create something new. But it's also important to keep the fluidity. The western idea of monoculture doesn't exit. Nothing is fixed. We sample and remix various cultural traditions and fabrics, even our works. We borrow and collage, like in Dub music, which originated on plantations where people would sing and chant in rhythm with their movement while working.

IVA — It's also about reusing and recycling. We recycle leftover pieces from other works to make new works, and sometimes reuse a complete work, incorporating it into another installation, or vice versa, like we did with *The Rise of the Prophet*. We don't want to throw away anything.

Among the different conceptual layers of *The Rise of the Prophet*, the colonial history of indigo stands out most prominently. A mark of wealth, status and power, as well as a symbol of divine love, purity, spirituality and protection from evil across cultures worldwide, the history of 'the king of dyes' is closely tied to the exploitation of natural resources and the forced displacement of millions of people. As artists Antonio Jose Guzman and Iva Jankovic state, 'you cannot work with indigo without acknowledging its past as currency in the transatlantic slave trade'. But acknowledging indigo's colonial history is not enough: Guzman and Jankovic seek to actively 're-member' those elements that have been forcibly detached. They aim to reconnect indigo with the spiritual meaning it held in various cultural practices before these were driven underground together with other forms of indigenous knowledge and beliefs.

The knotty issue of the commercial success of indigo as a commodity in the triangular trade and, the parallel transplantation of the native Indian *neel* plant (Latin name *indigofera tintora*) into the realm of Western colonial botany are unravelled in art historian Romita Ray's essay 'Unruly Indigo? Plants, Plantations and Partitions', in which she considers the etymological roots of the word diaspora. Stemming from the Greek *dia*, meaning through, across or apart, and *speirō*, meaning to sow or to scatter seeds, the term diaspora, which in modern use has become synonymous with the movement and mobility of people, has its origins not only in idea of dispersal and displacement, but also in the ontologies of taking root, renewal and regeneration. *The Rise of the Prophet* embodies this restless, dialectical dynamic between past and present, here and there, reflecting the contemporary realities of diasporic existence.

Cultural thinkers such as Paul Gilroy, Homi K. Bhabha, James Clifford and Gayatri Chakravorty Spivak have defined diasporic cultural spheres as fluid, hybrid and relational as well as referring to them as creative formative spaces in which communities both transform and preserve their multiple cultural legacies. It is the heterogeneity and 'unruly energy' of these liminal spaces that *The Rise of the Prophet* — and the larger 'Electric Dub Station' project of which it is a part — seek to evoke. They materialize in the patchwork's makeshift aesthetic: in its disparate fragments, mismatched shapes and patterns, in the holes and traces of wear and tear, in the crooked stitching and loose hanging thread. Rather than presenting a precious, seamless surface in which every piece falls into its proper place according to a grand design, the work embraces the aspects of disorder, chance and improvisation. However, despite its irregularity and punk spirit, the patchwork holds together visually; its seams are proof that even the most disjointed fragments can be joined together to form a shared surface.

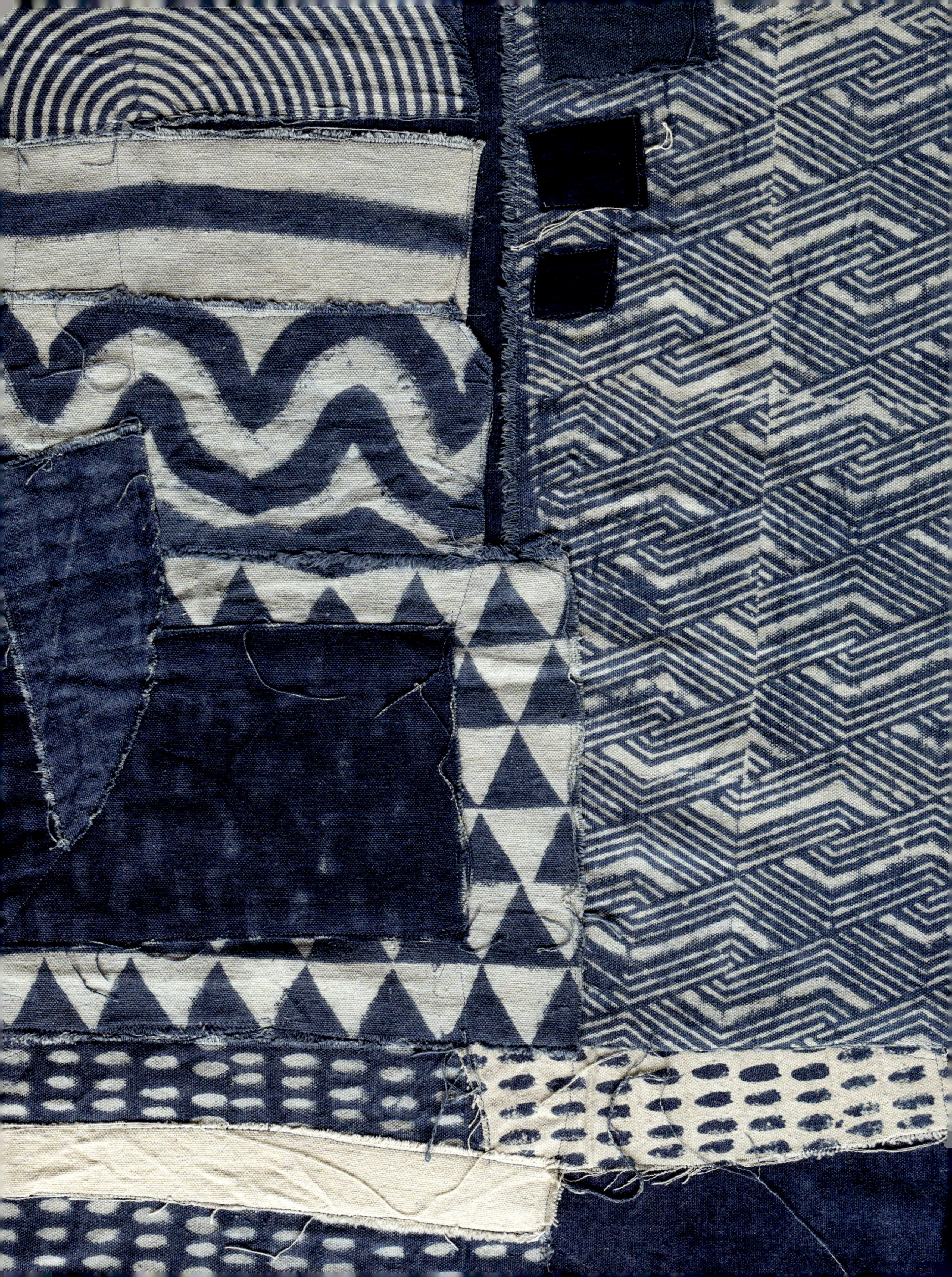

The commercial success of indigo is inextricably linked with the cost-effective management of plantations. It is also marked by the violence inflicted on the *ryot*, the peasant worker who extracted indigo blue from the plant. In the following essay, art historian Romita Ray looks at indigo plantations in colonial Bengal as dynamic sites of negotiations between plants, land and human bodies. Analyzing how material, spatial and corporeal engagements with indigo rendered plantation landscapes unruly, she tracks the disorderliness they unleashed, from their rural enclaves to the colonial city of Calcutta.

# UNRULY INDIGO? Plants, Plantations and Partitions

Romita Ray

Can landscapes be unruly?[1] Colonial documents, memoirs, and newspapers are filled with accounts of disobedient natives, 'lazy' coolies and reluctant officials. But landscapes were seen as no less recalcitrant sites ripe for surveying, improving, cultivating and profit-making. And no other landscape exemplified the orderly taming of plants and bodies as the colonial plantation whose very purpose, in S. Max Edelson's words, was to change 'a place of wild generation' into 'a space of refined cultivation'.[2] Plantations often hark back to the dense forests that once cascaded across their cultivated expanse: quintessentially unruly spaces filled with plants and animals that challenged the limits of human intervention. By transforming this wilderness into monoculture landscapes, planters cordoned themselves off from what they perceived as the savage, positioning themselves instead as civilized entrepreneurs who were 'remade and refined' by 'harness[ing] nature's abundance for profit'.[3] But were plantations truly tamed landscapes? Or did their plant and human occupants continue to resist, challenge and dismantle their cultural ecologies and political economies?

Tightly managed systems of capitalism, plantations disclose the human desire to commoditize nature on an ambitious scale. Here, plants and people submit to technologies and cultivation practices to create productive landscapes and generate commercial profit. To disrupt the orderliness upon which they rely is to render their landscapes unmanageable, not in the sense of the wild and unpredictable jungle, but rather, as contested sites of unrest and revolt where existing borders, rules, laws, structures, frameworks and ecologies are destabilized and dismantled. In effect, the unruly plantation exposes the fragility of what cultural theorist Raymond Williams once described as 'the whole complex of social and natural relationships

1. This essay was first published in Christine Göttler and Mia M. Mochizuki eds, *Landscape and Earth in Early Modernity: Picturing Unruly Nature*, (2022) which examines landscape as a mutable entity whose potential for change is rooted in nature's unpredictable elements, the disruptive patterns and flows of human and non-human interventions, and the weight of its past, present, and imagined histories.
2. Max S. Edelson, *Plantation Enterprise in Colonial South Carolina* (2006), pp. 23-24.
3. Ibid. p. 24.

which is at once our product and our activity'.[4] I am particularly interested in how these 'relationships' open up new ways of reading colonial plantations through the lens of ownership. After all, plantations are fundamentally rooted in the idea of territoriality, their visual thresholds defined by a proprietary gaze, and their physical expanse delineated by property lines and physical boundaries.

This essay focuses on indigo, a plant cultivated on colonial plantations in Bengal to produce a dye whose blueness spilled into the port city of Calcutta, where indigo became embedded in the global circuits of commerce.[5] By the end of the nineteenth century, indigo blue had built immense fortunes; triggered the *Nil Bidroho* (Blue Revolt or Indigo Revolt) of 1859; resulted in a play critiquing the tyranny of British indigo planters (*Nil Darpan*); and unleashed a wave of fierce debate in Calcutta.[6] Quite simply, indigo exposed the plantation as a deeply flawed landscape whose disorderliness was rendered starkly visible by the violence inflicted on the ryot (peasant worker). It also revealed the extent to which plantation landscapes were entwined with metropolitan sites of science, commerce, law and sociability.

These entanglements and fissures urge us to follow the unruliness of the colonial plantation back to the indigo plant whose capacity to produce colour, a lucrative one at that, preoccupied colonial scientists, government officials and indigo planters throughout the eighteenth and nineteenth centuries. Yet such a useful plant managed to unravel the tightly woven lines of race and class that separated the ryot from the planter on a plantation. How then did indigo transform plantations into contested sites of labour and territoriality? And what do its own transformations from a botanical curiosity to a blue dye tell us about the paradigm of unruliness on plantations? This last question pulls us into the geographies of rebellion and unrest that expanded far beyond the plantation to the city, bringing us to the last and final section of my essay, which analyzes how and why the violence of plantation life made its way into the social spaces of Calcutta's elite. Plantations were not just isolated pockets of cultivation in rural land; they were inextricably linked with the urban trajectories through which indigo travelled as a plant commodity destined for 'distant markets'.[7]

Disciplined in tandem with one another, plants, land and peasant bodies were bound up with the profit-making goals of monoculture farming. But while both ryot and planter were involved in the shared business of manufacturing indigo, their physical labour, social status and monetary gains were scaled along radically different lines, splintering them apart during the Indigo Revolt that saw their stark inequalities play out in the courtrooms and courtyards of Calcutta. If the plantation produced the rebellious ryot, then the latter exposed the troubling figure of the autocratic planter. By disrupting the harmonious visions of industrious labour promoted in contemporary newspapers, drawings, photographs and dioramas, this indigenous agent of landscaping and cultivating created powerful counter memories that dismantled the 'civilized' figure of the planter, further

4. Raymond Williams, *Culture and Materialism: Select Essays* (1980), p. 83.
5. Indigo blue was used to paint clay figurines from Krishnanagar and Bardhaman, and to dye cotton Neelambari saris from Shantipur and patterned silk fabrics from Cossimbazar (Kasim Bazar). It was also found in pigments used by Bengali artists in Calcutta's Kumortuli and Kalighat neighbourhoods. The Bengali term nil or neel refers to both the colour blue and the indigo plant. See Ruby Palchoudhuri, 'Neel in Bengali Culture' (2014), pp. 163-170 and Michael Wheeler et al, 'Materials and Techniques of Kalighat Paintings' (2011), pp. 173-185. Calcutta's name was changed to Kolkata in 2001.
6. Subhas Bhattacharya, 'The Indigo Revolt of Bengal' (1977), pp. 13-23; Partha S. Nandi, 'One Mirror, Myriad Reflections' (2016), pp. 48-55 and Ranajit Guha, 'Neel-darpan' (1974), pp. 1-46. *Nil Darpan* (Indigo Mirror) was first published in Bengali in 1860.
7. Kavita Philip, *Civilizing Natures: Race, Resources, and Modernity in Colonial South India* (2004).
8. Prinsep's friend Warren Hastings (1732-1818), the first governor-general of Bengal, helped him win a Company contract to cultivate indigo, see Rosie Llewellyn-Jones ed, *A Man of the Enlightenment in Eighteenth-Century India: The Letters of Claude Martin 1766-1800* (2003), p. 268 and Padmini T. Balaram, 'Indian Indigo', p. 139.
9. Maya Jasanoff, 'Passage through India' (2011), p. 125.
10. 'The cultivation of the cinnamon and pepper seems practicable, and we are sanguine in our expectations of *greatly improving the indigo plant*, as well as of introducing the date and sago trees. These *may prove an infinite service to this country* should it ever experience a failure in the crops.' Governor-General John Macpherson, 'Extract from a Public General Letter...' (1893), p. viii. Emphasis added.
11. Donal P. McCracken, *Gardens of Empire* (1997), p. 6.
12. Indrajit Ray, 'The Indigo Dye Industry in Colonial Bengal' (2004), pp. 202-203.
13. The French were responsible for introducing European indigo growing techniques in Bengal but were outrivalled by the British. See Jayati Gupta, 'The Travels and Travails of Indigo in Bengal' (2020), pp. 178-185.
14. The Company Raj refers to British rule in India under the aegis of the English East India Company.
15. Lucille H. Brockway, *Science and Colonial Expansion* (1979), p. 56.
16. Jenny Balfour-Paul, 'Indigo: From Bengal to Blue Jeans' (2013), p. 42.

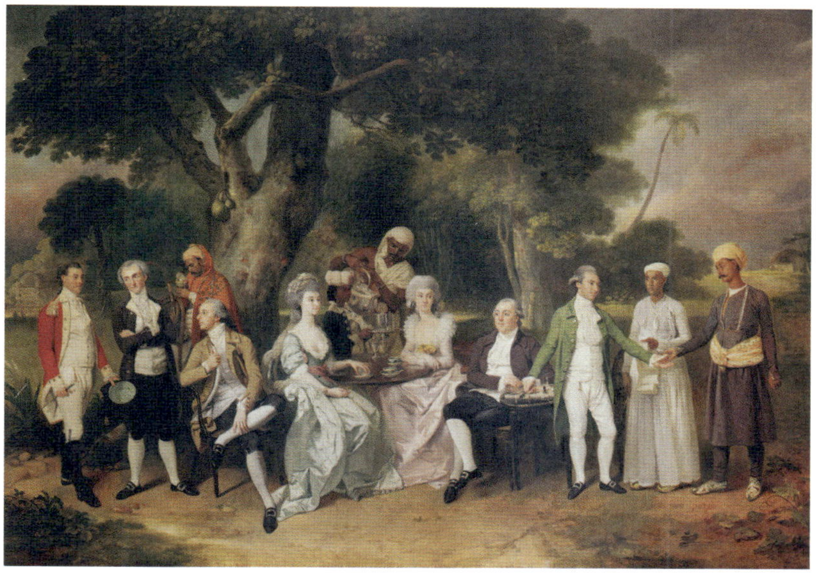

The Auriol and Dashwood Families, Johan Zoffany, c. 1783–1787. Oil on canvas, 142 × 198 cm.

revealing the seams of violence that long held together plantation landscapes. In short, the ryot unmasked both the plantation and the city as unruly landscapes.

## A USEFUL PLANT

In his portrait of the Auriol and Dashwood families (1783–1787), Johann Zoffany (1733–1810) depicts the pioneering indigo planter John Prinsep (1748–1830) as a fashionable gentleman smoking tobacco in a hookah. A prosperous resident of eighteenth century Calcutta, Prinsep earned vast wealth through the indigo plant in Bengal where the English East India Company had expanded its political and commercial foothold for over a century.[8] Portrayed alongside high-ranking Company officials and their spouses, military officers and servants, he appears with his wife Sophia Auriol (in pink) who is seated nearby at a tea table laden with porcelain teacups, while Chinese tea is served by Indian servants. Although invisible to the eye, tea, tobacco and indigo hover in the picture as colonial products associated with the colonial body. Prinsep, in particular, invokes *Indigofera* or Bengal indigo that ensured his status as a member of the Calcutta elite into whose ranks the acclaimed artist Zoffany had inserted himself to seek out his Indian fortune.[9] Plant commodities therefore urge us to look more closely at the sitters portrayed here, not just as subjects connected through social bonds, but as colonial citizens with deep links to landed wealth — mirrored no less by the sprawling garden in which they appear to socialize.

As it so happens, indigo's endorsement as a Company commodity also took place in a garden: a botanical one laid out on the outskirts of Calcutta in 1787, whose primary goal was to cultivate useful plants that would benefit Britain's empire in India.[10] The plan to improve and deploy plants as economic resources stemmed from the horrors of the 1769 Bengal famine that jolted Company administrators into realizing that they had to take a more strategic approach to agricultural practices in India.[11] There was also the devastating failure of Britain's indigo plantations in North America and the Caribbean, while stiff competition from Spain and France, who monopolized the global trade in high-quality indigo, had edged out their English rivals.[12]

Not surprisingly, attention shifted to India where the Company's robust foothold in Bengal ensured that plenty of fertile land was available for cultivating and manufacturing indigo.[13] Moreover, the port city of Calcutta, the capital of the Company Raj, was positioned near the Bay of Bengal from where indigo could be ushered to domestic and international markets.[14] European planters, many of whom had left behind impoverished indigo plantations in the West Indies to try their luck at planting indigo in India, were not disappointed.[15] By the end of the 1700s, the best quality indigo was flourishing in the districts of Lower Bengal.[16] By this time, British botanists were also exploring the economic potential of plants like indigo, tea, cotton and tobacco. When Sir John Macpherson (1745–1821), the governor-general, proposed cultivating indigo in Bengal, the Calcutta-based army engineer

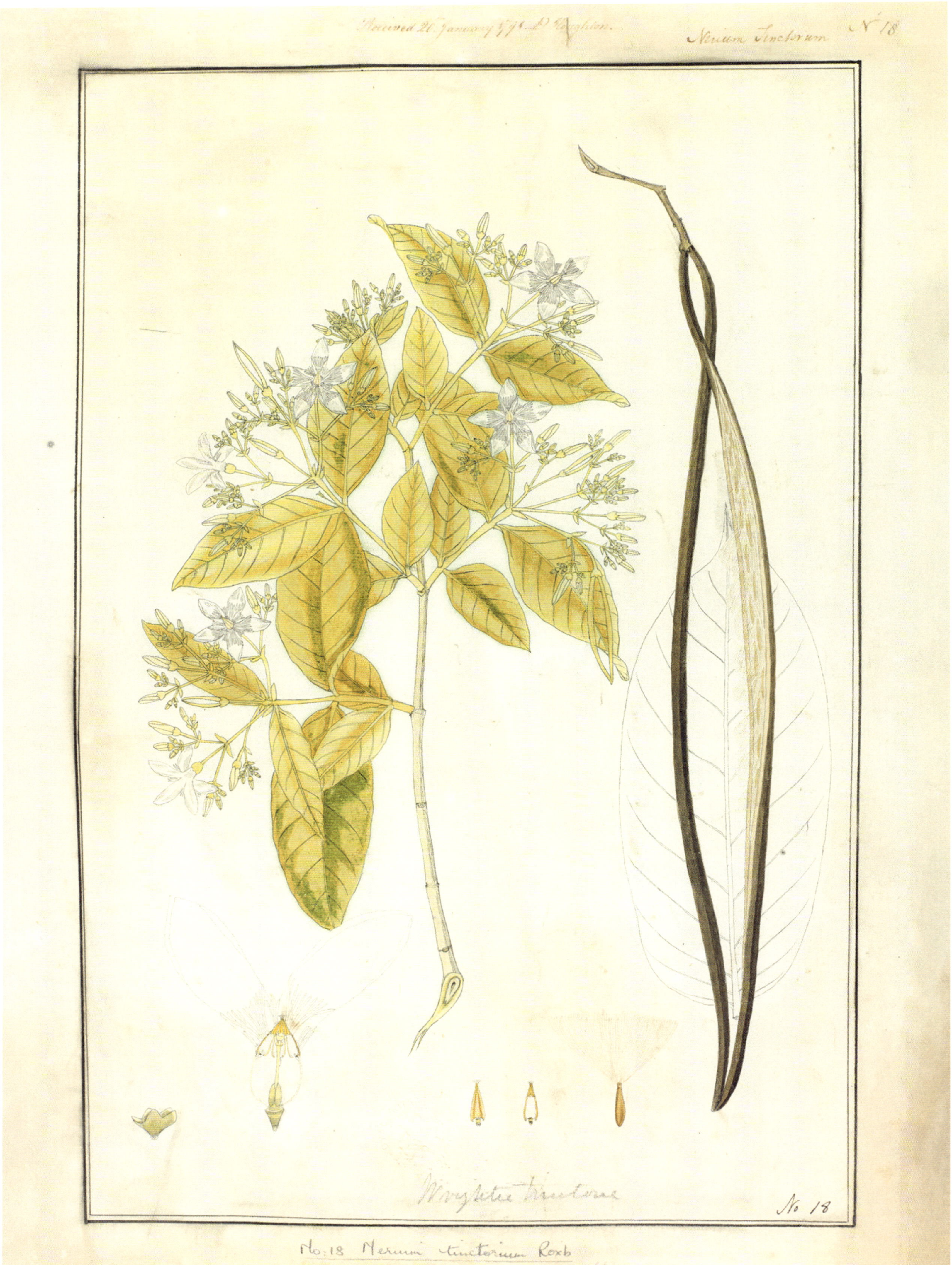


Botanical illustration Nerium tinctorium, Company School, in William Roxburgh, Icones Roxburghianae or Drawings of Indian Plants (1785–1791), plate no 18 (K). Watercolour, graphite and ink on paper, 51.5 × 35.7 cm (sheet), 47.2 × 30.5 cm (image).

Lieutenant-Colonel Robert Kyd (1746–1793) suggested that a botanical garden be used as a testing ground for growing plants as 'articles of commerce'.[17] Kyd's proposal laid the foundation for the Calcutta Botanic Garden where the relationship between useful plants and colonial commerce was first formalized on an expansive scale in British India.[18]

Botanical practice shaped the very foundation of indigo experiments in colonial India. Far south of Calcutta, on the Coromandel coast, Scottish botanist William Roxburgh (1751–1815) observed that the indigo 'plant [was] well worth cultivating' and yielded a 'deep green' colour tinged with 'violet coloured scum'.[19] Such mediations of colour and material transformations of plant matter reveal an intimate understanding of how indigo might behave if it were grown commercially.

Healthy plants require good soil. As such, they direct us to read landscapes both horizontally (across the land) as well as vertically (beneath the surface of the land). As Roxburgh would discover, the quality of soil could impact the quality of colour extracted from the indigo plant. 'The leaves of the plants raised from seed in my garden, did not yield colour till several years old, and then but in a trifling degree, and of a quality inferior to *what the old wild plants do in their natural soil*', he wrote, further remarking that '[it] is the same with the young plantations in Bengal. If the leaves are culled, and only the best chosen, the Indigo is considerably more beautiful than when taken promiscuously.'[20] Keenly aware of the importance of cultivating indigo for its botanical *and* commercial value, Roxburgh identifies indigo as both a plant and a colour, while assigning superior tonal values to the dye extracted from the 'wild' variety.

Such an understanding of the wild or the natural had to be reconciled with the need to manufacture the best quality indigo in (human) controlled landscape environments. A cosmopolitan body of knowledge built by generations of planters and indigenous indigo-makers in the Caribbean, India and elsewhere now made its way into Bengal through published texts, planters' diaries, lived experiences and oral histories. After all, indigo had been grown in India since antiquity and was exported to Europe from the twelfth century onwards.[21] Diverse technologies and methods of knowledge transmission could only benefit indigo cultivation in a place like Bengal with no prior history of commercial indigo planting, while scientific discoveries like Roxburgh's added to an already rich corpus of place-based knowledge and praxis.[22] In 1790, Roxburgh would send the results of his research to both the Company's directorate in London and the governor-general in Calcutta. His findings would be published later along with instructions to produce indigo from the 'common' indigo plant, (*indigo fera tinctorea*), as practiced at Singatollah, near Malda'.[23] By 1795, Sir William Jones (1746–1794), the late founder-president of the Asiatic Society in Calcutta, which was the leading society of scientists, collectors, linguists and so on in colonial India, had added 'Nili, *Indigofera*' to his list of Indian plants.[24] As these nodes and networks of exchange crystallized between Bengal and Britain, indigo became embedded in conversations

17. Macpherson, 'Extract', viii.
18. Adrian P. Thomas, 'The Establishment of Calcutta Botanic Garden' (2006), p. 174. The Calcutta Botanic Garden remained actively involved in indigo cultivation well into the 1800s, with one of the most fruitful collaborations taking place between its curators, directors, and scientists associated with the Indigo Improvements Syndicate (IIS) established by Calcutta's indigo traders to improve the quality of indigo seeds, plants and colour. See Prakash Kumar, *Indigo Plantations and Science in Colonial India* (2012), pp. 180-189.
19. Robert Kyd, Letters to Government (1790), pp. 368-369.
20. William Roxburgh, 'Account of a New Species of *Nerium*' (1811), p. 263. These observations were part of Roxburgh's research on the chromatic potential of the indigo plant. They were published during his tenure as the Superintendent of the Calcutta Botanic Garden, in *Transactions* of the London-based Society for the Encouragement of the Arts, Manufactures, and Commerce. The aesthetics and materiality of colour extracted from indigo preoccupied Roxburgh for two decades after he took over the supervision of the garden upon Kyd's demise. See I.M. Turner, 'William Roxburgh and the Names of Some Indian Indigos' (2014), pp. 21-25.
21. Lotika Varadarajan, 'Indigo: The Indian Tradition' (2014), pp. 83-85; Indrajit Ray, *Bengal Industries and the British Industrial Revolution* (1757-1857), (2004), pp. 207-208 and Balaram, 'Indian Indigo', pp. 140-144.
22. Prakash Kumar, 'Planters and Naturalists' (2014), pp. 740-744. Kumar notes that in comparison to Bengal, the 'Coromandel region' in South India had a well-established history of indigo production.
23. Roxburgh, 'New Species of *Nerium*', p. 252.
24. William Jones, 'A Catalogue of Indian Plants' (1795), p. 234. Founded in 1784, the Asiatic Society was a prestigious institution devoted to science, art, and literature. Jones's list was published posthumously in the Society's journal, *Asiatick Researches*.

about colour, plants and commerce, joining other plants like cotton and tea to shape the Company's 'wide-ranging' portfolio of business investments in Asian plant commodities.

At the heart of these conversations were botanical fragments and drawings of the indigo plant that travelled from Calcutta to London. Material evidence of the taxonomic diversity of Indian landscapes that now entered—and indeed built—some of the most prominent botanical collections in Britain, they included a watercolour drawing of *Nerium tinctorium* made by a Company artist in Calcutta for *Icones Roxburghianae* No. 18, a copy of which was received in London in 1791 and deposited in the botanical gardens at Kew, and a specimen of *Indigofera caerulea Roxb.* collected in Patna in 1812, also deposited at Kew via the Calcutta Botanic Garden.[25] Vivid examples of the 'exotic, inexhaustible array of Indian plants' and images that contributed to British science, art and profit, these representations transpose the leafy components of the indigo plant, its minutiae intact, onto blank sheets of paper. Reconstituted as a botanical curiosity through European pictorial and scientific conventions, indigo is altered into a familiar artifact far removed from its natural surroundings in India. Flattened out, its form invites close looking, engendering an intimacy of vision. In an era of heightened empirical scrutiny and documentation facilitated by repositories like herbaria and by the new and exciting optical technologies of the microscope, such close-up views of plants reveal the rapid pace at which botanical knowledge was being gathered, codified and disseminated.[26] They also attest to the growing culture of the material or visual fragment, a direct endorsement of the Baconian approach to studying nature with 'a fresh examination of particulars' that evinced the desire to reduce nature to its constitutive parts from which new bodies of knowledge could be created based on examining, comparing and contrasting those parts.[27]

But reduction, reconstitution and knowledge-building necessitated removing and dislocating plants and their parts. Might fragmentation then be read as a visual paradigm of dislocation and displacement so essential to the practices of plant collecting and botanizing? Can it be analyzed within the broader practice of plantation culture where plants, labouring bodies and planters were uprooted from their original habitats only to be transplanted in plantation landscapes? Such displacements hint at unruliness, signalling at the profound shifts that destabilized the very worlds from which plants and people were removed, and those in which they were relocated. Seen this way, the fragment can be understood as a metonymic reminder of the diasporas of plants and people bound up with the geographies of agriculture and botany, and indeed, more broadly with the mobilities and movements of people, objects, ideas, commodities and wealth across and within the British Empire. A word whose very etymology draws upon the Greek *dia* ('division' and 'dispersal') and *spiro* ('to sow the seeds'), the term 'diaspora' oscillates between 'the idea of dispersion' on the one hand, and the notion of 'stasis and stability' on

25. Turner, 'Roxburgh', pp. 22-23. Company artists were Indian artists employed by (mainly) high-ranking East India Company officials.
26. By 1918, a dissected view of *Indigofera Tinctoria, Linn.* would be included in K. R. Kirtikar and B. D. Basu's *Indian Medicinal Plants*. Influenced by Roxburgh, and also by John Forbes Royle's work on materia medica, Kirtikar and Basu attempted to weave together Ayurveda and Western botanical knowledge. See David Arnold, *Science, Technology and Medicine in Colonial India* (2004), p. 175.
27. Francis Bacon, as quoted in Dahlia Porter, *Science, Form, and the Problem of Induction in British Romanticism* (2018), p. 4.

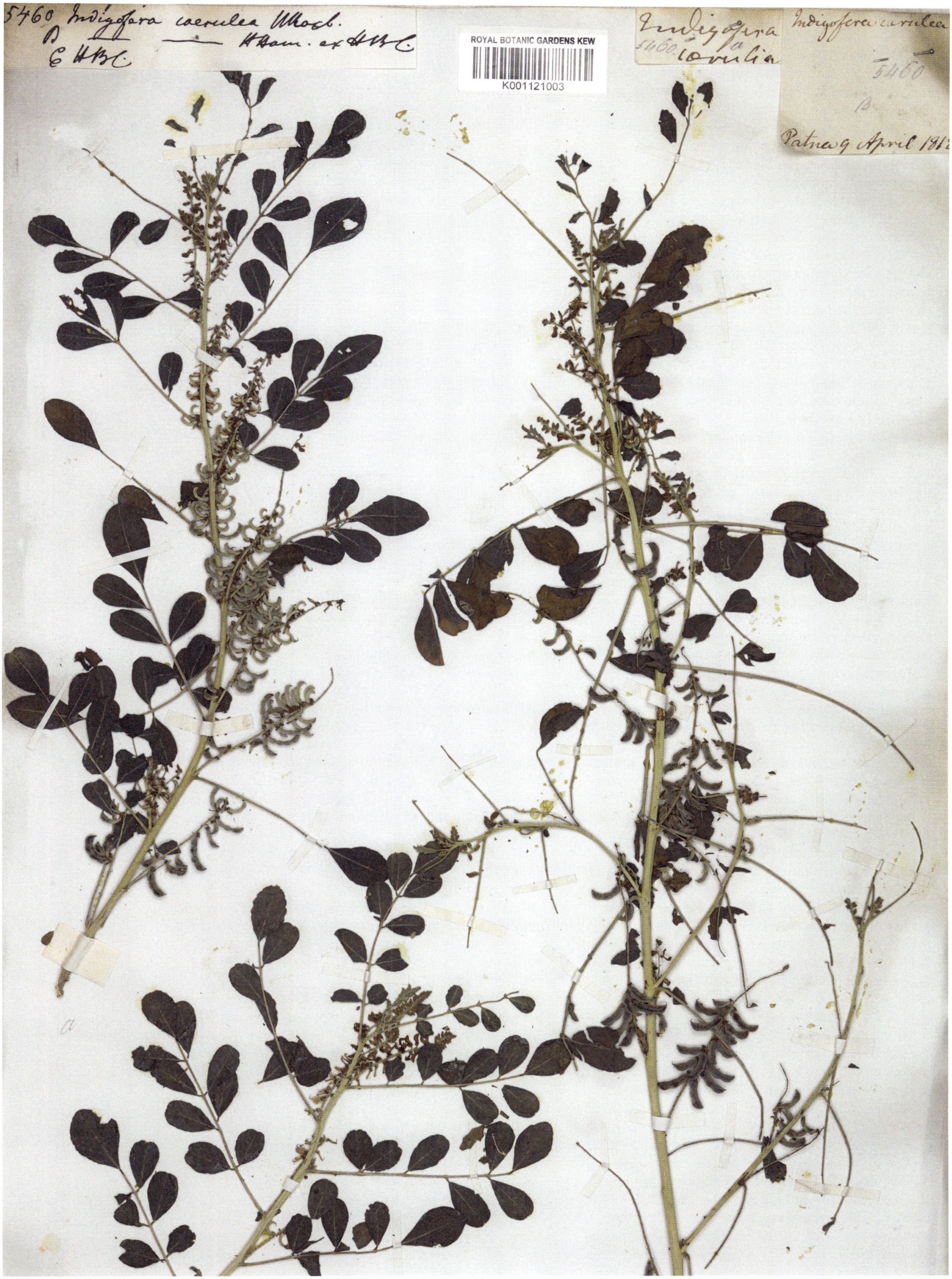


Indigofera caerulea Roxb, botanical specimen from the William Roxburgh collection, specimen no. K001121003. Collected in Patna, 9 April 1812. Indigo plant on paper, 26.7 × 42.6 cm.

the other, its origins rooted in the ontologies of dislocation, renewal and regeneration borne out by the movement and dispersal of seeds and plants, the very foundation of a plantation.[28]

Isolated from their natural settings, plants are palpable reminders of the ecosystems they once inhabited and the landscapes from which they were extracted. Quite simply, they remind us, in Anna Tsing's words, of the 'unruly edges and seams of imperial space, where we cannot ignore the inter-species interdependencies that give us life on earth'.[29] Pressed between herbarium sheets or sheets of drawings, those 'edges and seams' were transferred into the heart of scientific inquiry. With its place of origin blanked out literally and figuratively, the indigo plant was recalibrated as a botanical acquisition within a classification system that sought to 'erase the environmental and cultural contexts of plants'.[30] Yet cultural knowledge and, more specifically, indigenous knowledge was essential to growing the indigo plant and shaping a successful plantation economy. As Prakash Kumar notes, indigo cultivation in eighteenth century Bengal relied on Indian practices that existed well before the English, French and Dutch arrived in India, and on English, French and Spanish knowledge of indigo planting appropriated from indigenous cultures across the Caribbean and Central America.[31] The 'peasant-produced indigo' in the Spanish indigo empire, he points out, 'cornered major profits' for 'European traders'.[32]

The same can be said of plantations in Bengal that created vast fortunes for private merchants like Prinsep, who returned to England a rich and influential member of London society. But Prinsep's success was far from smooth sailing. His early attempts to apply the West Indian method of indigo planting had proven challenging in a foreign landscape. Several failures had ensued before the 'unruly seams and edges' of the colonial plantation in Bengal were tamed through trial and error, patience and perseverance; only then could the indigo plant flourish.[33] By 1828, Bengal indigo reportedly fulfilled 'four-fifths of the consumption of Europe, Asia, and America'.[34] Indigo blue's commercial success would continue to be forged through the close alliance between botany and commerce — one that would go on full display at a series of exhibitions in London and Calcutta, starting with the pioneering Great Exhibition of 1851 for which indigo plantations, or factories, supplied the indigo plant exhibits.[35]

## THE LABOR OF INDIGO

By the 1880s, Calcutta-based agency houses — trading firms that mediated between indigo factories and merchants — were also the primary suppliers of indigo to local and foreign markets, as well as the custodians of indigo specimens displayed at colonial exhibitions.[36] In sharp contrast to herbaria where plant specimens were stored in secluded cabinets, exhibitions drew the leafy fragments of the indigo plant into public sites of display. They also enabled the Indian government to openly promote 'natural indigo' to offset the growing popularity of synthetic indigo, whose market value now threatened the production of natural dye. Key to this strategy was exhibiting plant specimens near miniature dioramas or clay models of indigo factories that visualized the very processes through which indigo blue was coaxed from a plant.[37] Made by artisans from Krishnanagar, an indigo-growing area of Bengal, dioramas, along with plant specimens, presented convincing images of the plant's origins (indigo) and its places of cultivation (plantations) that together evoked an 'ideal industrial world' for exhibition visitors.[38] Even the detail of the reclining ryot glimpsed in the diorama displayed at the Calcutta International Exhibition of 1883–1884, while evocative of the prevailing stereotype of the idle native, can be linked more generally to Victorian aesthetics of leisure.[39]

Reduced to miniature scale in the diorama, the labour of indigo is turned into a delightful curiosity, yet the dollhouse-like charm of the clay model belies the harsh working conditions and (often) violent negotiations that permeated plantation life. As Michel Foucault observes, 'the body becomes a useful force only if it is both a productive body and a subjected body'.[40] Indeed, the visual imaging of indigo cultivation frequently drew attention to surveillance as an integral part of plantation life. Be it in dioramas, newspapers or photographs like Oscar Mallitte's image of European supervisors watching over ryots immersed up to their waists in vats filled with fermenting indigo, agrarian labour — and especially male labour — was shown as inseparable from the politics of discipline and control. Put another way, such picturizations asserted the role of plantations as both disciplined as well as disciplining environments where the unruly was kept at bay through routine inspections and punishment. Like the diorama and the newspaper illustration, Mallitte's photograph emphasizes discipline and industry, with plants, bodies and chemical residue entwined with one another in the production of indigo blue. Entrapped in the vat, labouring ryots are pressed into service like 'human machines' (borrowing from Michael Taussig), beating the soaked and fermented indigo plants with bamboo paddles to separate the dyestuff from plant matter. Liquid oxidizes, precipitating the indigo dye, foam, froth and the stench of chemical processes engulfing their half-naked bodies. Finally, the water is drained out and the remaining sludge is dried, 'cut into square cakes', and 'sent down to Calcutta' where it is sold as 'the indigo dye of commerce'.[41]

But beating was not simply confined to dye manufacture; it was also a means of keeping plantation labourers in line. 'Before, we felt sorrow in beating one man; now, we can beat ten persons with the *Ramkant* (leather strap), making them senseless,' declares Planter Rose in Dinabandhu Mitra's *Nil Darpan*, prompting Torap the rebellious ryot to give him a dose of his own medicine.[42] If the inescapable realities of violence underscored what historical geographer Caroline Cornish describes as 'economic botany in action', then the manually intensive processes of indigo production revealed the strict hierarchies of labour and violence upon which the smooth running of plantations relied.[43] Dioramas, newspapers, and photographs

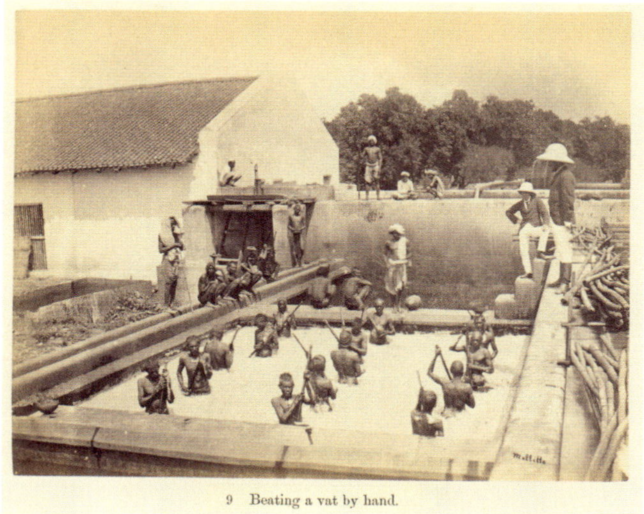

'Beating a Vat by hand', Oscar Mallitte, in The Planting & Manufacture of Indigo in India: 29 Photographic Views, Allahabad, India, 1877. 18.3 × 23.7 cm.

offered a more public realm of viewership in which these realities and hierarchies were laid bare. As such, they engendered a sort of voyeurism centred on bodies, liquids and plant worlds that constituted the secluded world of indigo plantations.

As if to demonstrate this, the hatted, suited and booted European planter in the photograph and the diorama looks down, literally and figuratively, upon the labouring ryot, his vantage point and uniformed figure instantly signalling his position of authority. Yet such positionings and modalities of viewing betray an underlying anxiety about losing control over the 'native' body in a space dominated by ryots. The threat of the unruly, rebellious subaltern could not be underestimated, especially in the wake of the Indigo Revolt triggered by the violence of plantation culture. Colour emerged as a means of taming the ryot.

In 1846, Thomas Machell, an assistant to the influential Bengal-based indigo planter James Forlong, observed that indigo blue began its journey in the skilled hands of the 'dark skinned' labourer:

> *Women and children flung sheafs of green indigo plants into the vats which were carefully and quickly stowed by the noisy coolies (...) but long before the last vat was filled ... there was a sound of wooden mallets hammering at huge wooden plugs and then a rush of orange coloured water pouring into the lower vats. It is from this fermented Indigo juice that the dye is made by the dark skinned sons of India — the dye which may colour the purple robes of royalty or the blue coat of the charity boy, the fair forms of our northern beauties or the dark uniforms of the British soldier. This is the dye for the sailors blue jacket and labourers Sunday coat — a tide golden to those who far from here know not and care not for the toil and groanings of the thousands whose lives are spent in one long struggle of want and toil for the benefit of those who know not even of their existence.*[44]

Colour mediates a complex network of bodies and plants, the dark complexion of the labourer invoking India's vast human resources that were mobilized, managed and exploited to meet the demands of British consumers. As working men, women and children were forced to contend with heat, sweat, fermentation, rotting smells and green and blue stains, skin emerged as the principal threshold where colour was registered and recalibrated within a highly racialized domain of indigo production. And it is this dualism between tactility and visuality, between the touch and stain of indigo blue, that the diorama made startlingly visible in its display of ryots and their supervisors staged in the midst of their collective performance of capitalist commodity production.

From the planter's perspective, an industrious ryot defined a well-run indigo factory where the very dynamics of labour were aligned with Victorian notions of work as a civilizing process and a morally edifying category. In reality, however, the factory was a site of strenuous and dangerous corporeal engagements. Here, like the

28. Eleni Sideri, 'The Diaspora of the term Diaspora' (2008), pp. 33-34.
29. Anna Tsing, 'Unruly Edges: Mushrooms as Companion Species' (2012), p. 141.
30. Beth Tobin, 'Imperial Designs' (1996), p. 269.
31. Kumar, 'Planters and Naturalists', pp. 720-734.
32. Ibid. pp. 725-726,
33. Ibid. pp. 731-735, 745-746. Prinsep became an alderman to the City of London and a Member of Parliament for Queensborough. Kumar observes that Prinsep probably consulted the Elias Monnereau's *The Complete Indigo Maker* (1769), based on growing indigo in Saint Domingue, the French colony in the Caribbean (first published in French in 1736). He also notes that little is known about Prinsep's experience of cultivating indigo in Bengal.
34. 'Free Trade and Colonisation in India' (1828), p. 405
35. George Watt, *Economic Products of India Exhibited at the Calcutta International Exhibition* (1883), p. 33; *Great Exhibition of the Works of Industry of All Nations* (1851), p. 880.
36. Thomas Wardle, *Colonial and Indian Exhibition* (1886), p. 147. Calcutta's agency houses oversaw the Company's advances made to indigo planters. The prominent agency house Thomas, Marten & Company, was established in 1851. Known today as J. Thomas, it is headquartered in Nilhat House, whose very name pays tribute to the indigo industry. See *The J. Thomas Story* (2012), p. 14.
37. A clay model of an indigo factory, now in the Indian Museum in Kolkata, was displayed at the Calcutta International Exhibition of 1883-1884. See *Official Report*, vol. 2 (1885), p. 535. Another clay diorama of an indigo factory made by Rakhal Chandra Pal was displayed in 1886 at the Colonial and Indian Exhibition in London. Pal's diorama is now in the economic botany collection at the Royal Botanic Gardens, Kew. See Caroline Cornish, 'Curating Global Knowledge' (2015), p. 140 and Frank Cundall ed, *Reminiscences of the Colonial and Indian Exhibition* (1886), p. 21.
38. Louise Purbrick, 'Introduction' (2001), p. 2. Sixty clay figures of Indian artisans at work made by Krishnanagar sculptors were displayed at the Great Exhibition. See Lara Kriegel, *Grand Designs: Labor, Empire, and the Museum in Victorian Culture* (2007), p. 117.
39. As seen, for instance, in James Tissot's rendering of a picnicker stretched out on the ground, teacup in hand, in *Holyday* (1876). Such visualizations were augmented by the valorisation of labour at the Great Exhibition, which set the tone for all subsequent exhibitions in Britain and colonial India to celebrate 'workers, of all types' who 'stand forth as the really great men.' See Nacy Rose Marshall et al, *James Tissot: Victorian Life/Modern Love* (1999), pp. 110-111 and Tim Barringer, *Men at Work: Art and Labour in Victorian Britain* (2005), p. 2.
40. Michel Foucault, *Discipline and Punish: The Birth of the Prison* (1995), p. 39.
41. For an analysis of indigo manufacture in colonial Bengal, see: Michael Taussig, 'Redeeming Indigo' (2008), pp. 5-8.
42. Mitra, *Nil Darpan*, p. 53.
43. Cornish, 'Curating', p. 136; Cornish, 'Collecting Photographs', p. 129.
44. Machell, as quoted in Balfour-Paul, 'Bengal to Blue Jeans', pp. 42-44.

'indigo plant of commerce', the ryot had to yield and comply. Consequently, plants and people were positioned as property, and the plantation was claimed as an unruly landscape to be disciplined by the planter.

## A PARTITIONED CITY

By 1831, there were nearly 400 indigo factories in Bengal with both Europeans and Bengalis at their helm.[45] As Bengal indigo dominated in global markets, the Governor-General Lord William Bentinck (1774–1839), along with wealthy Bengali plantation owners Ram Mohan Roy (1772–1833) and Dwarkanath Tagore (1794–1846), were convinced that indigo production was beneficial to the poor peasant farmer.[46] But by the 1850s, as public criticism of the exploitation of plantation workers erupted, Calcutta's elite could no longer ignore the plight of the ryot.

In 1859, poor weather conditions combined with extreme physical hardship culminated in the Indigo Revolt. Coming on the heels of the Indian Rebellion of 1857, the indigo riots and demonstrations were no less devastating, prompting Lord Canning, the Viceroy of India, to confess that they had 'caused [him] more anxiety' than the events in Delhi.[47]

Faced with a crisis, the government initiated a Commission of Inquiry in 1860 to determine what permanent changes could be put into place to protect the rights of both indigo planters and cultivators. That same year, hundreds of indigo farmers poured into Calcutta to present their petitions to the city's Lieutenant-Governor Sir John Peter Grant, prompting the protestant missionary James Long (1814–1887) to launch an acerbic attack on the credibility of the Indigo Commission in a letter to the editor of the *Bengal Hurkaru*. In May 1860, Long went on to address the indigo question at the all-Bengali Family Literary Club in Calcutta.[48] Just over a year later, he was jailed.

Long's imprisonment was spurred on by the English translation of Mitra's play *Nil Darpan*, whose critique of the brutal oppression of ryots unleashed a fresh wave of controversy about the indigo industry. Although the brilliant Bengali poet and dramatist Michael Madhusudan Dutt (1824–1873) had translated the play with Long's support, the prosecution representing the Landowners' and Commercial Association (to which the indigo planters belonged) targeted Long as the play's translator. The trial began on July 19, 1861, in the Supreme Court of Calcutta, where Sir Mordaunt Wells presided as the judge, and the fifteen-member jury, save for two individuals, was composed mainly of Britons.[49] Accused of libelling the indigo planters of Lower Bengal and the editor of the *Englishman*, Long was imprisoned in the Common Jail of Calcutta and fined the princely sum of 1,000 rupees, the latter paid promptly by the Bengali playwright Kaliprasanna Sinha (1840?–1870).[50]

Close economic and social ties with the British made it difficult for Calcutta's prominent Bengali citizens to agitate for 'radical reforms' or demand the 'overthrow' of 'British rule'.[51] But Long's indictment now eroded their steadfast loyalty to the British government and inspired them to find a

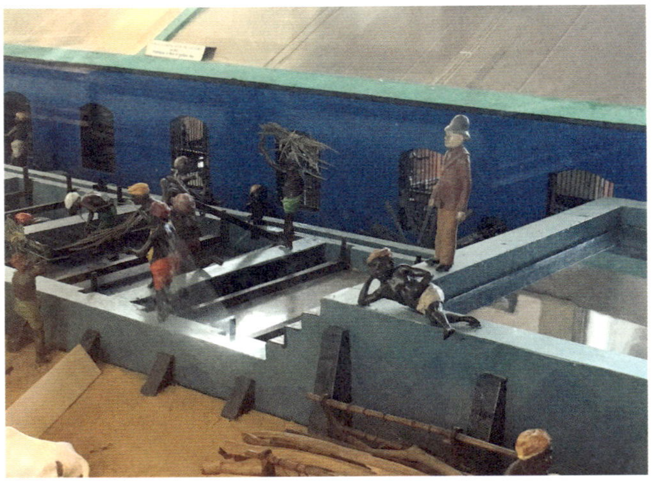

Krishnanagar artist, Model of an Indigo Factory, detail, 1883–1884. Clay, paint, glass, bamboo and other materials, 203.2 × 101.6 × 30.48 cm.

Models like these enabled the Indian government to visualize the production process of indigo blue and promote natural indigo as a profitable commodity, worthy of investment. They became a valuable prop in what became known as 'economic botany'.

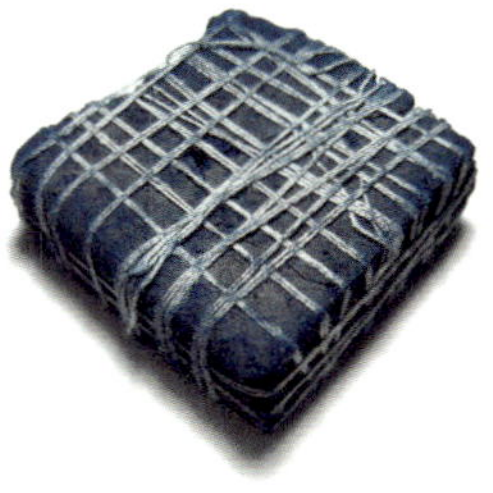

Piece of indigo dye from India.

45. U.R. Bansal et al, 'Industries in India during 18th and 19th Century' (1984), p. 219.
46. Ray, *Bengal Industries*, p. 232. See also: Blair B. Kling, *Partner in Empire: Dwarkanath Tagore and the Age of Enterprise* (1976), p. 87 and Subhas Bhattacharya, 'Indigo Planters, Ram Mohan Roy and the 1833 Charter Act' (1975), pp. 56-65.
47. Balfour-Paul, *Indigo*, p. 73.
48. Geoffrey A. Oddie, *Missionaries, Rebellion, and Proto-nationalism* (1999), pp. 111-112, 116.
49. Amiya Rao et al, *The Blue Devil: Indigo and Colonial Bengal* (1992), p. 123
50. Oddie, *Missionaries*, pp. 122-125.
51. Bhattacharya, 'Indigo Revolt of Bengal', p. 20
52. Rao, *Blue Devil*, p. 135. The performance took place at the Jorasanko residence of Madhusudan Sanyal. It was the first public Bengali theatrical event of its kind. See also: Sudipto Chatterjee, 'Performing (Domi-)nation', (1995) p. 3 and Claire Pamment, *Police of Pig and Sheep* (2009), pp. 234-236.
53. Rao, *Blue Devil*, pp. 136-37.
54. Appadurai, 'Introduction: Commodities and the Politics of Value' (1997), pp. 29-41.
55. Karl Marx, *Capital: A Critique of Political Economy* (1921), p. 516.
56. Kumar, *Indigo Plantations*, p. 154-155; Watt, Pamphlet, cover page. Levinstein would later take over the family firm of Levinstein Limited, one of the earliest and most important British dye-makers.
57. Kumar, *Indigo Plantations*, p. 294.

renewed sense of pride in their Bengali identity. Just over a decade later, a staged production of Mitra's *Nil Darpan* took place at the Calcutta National Theatrical Society in December 1872, pulling indigo back into the limelight.[52] Praised as 'an event of national importance' in Bengali newspapers, *Nil Darpan* was denounced as 'libel on the Europeans' in the *Englishman*, the chief mouthpiece for indigo planters who expressed surprise that the government had '[allowed] its representation in Calcutta'.[53] Indigo cultivation had exposed the cracks and fissures in colonial society, while simultaneously giving the ryot a new visibility in the partitioned city. Taking full advantage of a messy trail of government blunders and a sympathetic judge, irate planters went out of their way to punish their long-standing enemy, a Christian missionary who had dared to support the ryot. By collapsing the boundaries between plantation life and urban society, and between a plantation economy and urban commerce, they ensured that the politics of refusal and rebellion, once confined to unruly plantation landscapes, were now embedded in the city.

## CONCLUSION

Colonial plantations can be understood as microcosms of empire where transplanted people (labourers and planters) became entangled with transplanted plants (indigo). Haunted by the loss of identity and place, each determined the fate of the other. Nature ceased to be natural and landscapes turned into contested zones of imperial encounter. Plantation landscapes therefore urge us to consider how the indigo plant, once embedded in the flux and flow of human life, was reconstituted as an artifact that was meant to cater to, and indeed, to produce human 'desire and demand'.[54] Botanical specimens, fermented liquids and blue dyes track indigo's metamorphosis into a commodity that travelled from plantations to factories, settled into herbaria, and seeped into cloth. Dioramas and exhibitions extended these displacements into the public sphere where indigo was valorized as a product of Victorian industry, its plant form conceding to its blue dye in clay models depicting its laborious production. Prints, photographs, paintings and drawings, on the other hand, folded the plantation back into more intimate orbits of viewing, thus repositioning the complex dynamics of indigo production within the familiar contours of landscape painting and photography. But such picturizations glossed over the harsh realities of plantation life, sharpening instead British pride in a colonial industry that saw indigo labourers beaten and killed across rural Bengal. Might we then reframe indigo as a useful yet unruly plant whose material changes, chemical infusions and economic exigencies paved the way for violence and disorder on plantations, and thenceforth, in the city of Calcutta?

The systematic remaking of nature into specimens and dioramas underscores the web of plant-human interdependencies upon which nineteenth century modernity came to rely. As science and agriculture converged in plantations, the modern was lodged in the spectatorial. It was also rooted in the transformative potential of nature and in the productivity of landscapes that fuelled capitalist systems of wealth production. Modernity now insisted on merging 'the cheapness of the human sweat and the human blood, which were converted into commodities', in the words of Karl Marx (1818–1883), with the sensory pleasures of commodity culture and the optics of visual display.[55] Visitors to colonial exhibitions in Calcutta, London and Melbourne could marvel at miniature recreations of indigo factories or samples of indigo, while reading newspaper accounts about the brutalities of exploitation. Modernity was rife with such slippages in time and space. And emphasizing its precarity were plants like indigo that crystallized into sites of resistance, their leafy matter shoring up plantations as powerful nodes of culture and identity, and the trajectories of science as innovative yet fragile streams of knowledge.

By 1901, the British industrial chemist and dye-maker Herbert Levinstein (1878–1956) reminded every 'Yorkshire dyer and printer' to favour natural indigo, 'the product of our greatest dependency, India', over synthetic indigo invented by their German rivals. That same year, fellow chemist Raphael Meldola (1849–1915) observed that Germany's display of coal tar products at the 1900 Paris Exposition was a troubling sign of Britain's decline as an industrial power. Indigo planters, he surmised, had failed to take seriously Germany's advances on synthetic indigo production.[56] If these scientists sensed that natural dye was on its way out, they were not wrong. By World War I, 'factory-produced synthetic indigo' had replaced the agricultural dye, rendering a plantation industry obsolete.[57] Even so, the traces and shadows of indigo continued to linger on in Calcutta where, to this day, vestiges of Bengal's indigo culture can still be found at the palatial Tagore Villa, once an indigo planter's estate (now quarters for officers of the Border Security Force), Nilhat House, headquarters of the erstwhile indigo brokers Thomas, Marten and Company (J. Thomas), and the Tollygunge Club built on a former indigo plantation.

MOUNIRA AL SOLH is a visual artist born in Lebanon, raised between Lebanon and Syria, and currently based between the Netherlands and Lebanon. She studied painting at the Lebanese University in Beirut, Fine Arts at the Gerrit Rietveld Academy in Amsterdam and was a resident at the Rijksakademie Amsterdam between 2007–2008. Mounira Al Solh's art practice embraces inter alia drawing, painting, embroidery, performative gestures, video and video installations. Irony and self-reflectivity are central strategies for her work, which explores feminist issues, tracks patterns of micro history, is socially engaged, and can be political and escapist all at once.
Her work was presented at Documenta 14, Athens and Kassel (2017) and the Venice Biennale, both in the exhibition curated by Okwui Enwezor (2015) and in the Lebanese Pavilion (2007 and 2024). In 2017 the Art Institute of Chicago organized her first US solo exhibition, *I Strongly Believe in Our Right to Be Frivolous*. Other recent solo exhibitions include *A land as big as her skin*, Bonnefanten Museum, Maastricht (2025/2026); *Stray Salt*, Sfeir-Semler Gallery, Beirut (2025) and *A day is as long as a year*, BALTIC Centre for Contemporary Art, Gateshead (2022). Recent group exhibitions include *BEDROCK, Liverpool Biennal, Liverpool (2025); Unravel: The Power and Politics of Textiles in Art,* Barbican Art Gallery, London and Stedelijk Museum Amsterdam (2024) and *Artes Mundi 10*, National Museum Cardiff (2023).

RACHEL DEDMAN is a curator, writer and art historian who lives in London. She studied history of art at the universities of Oxford and Harvard. Her work examines the material and political lives of things, and challenges established narratives around cultural production in the Global South. Dedman is the Jameel Curator of Contemporary Art from the Middle East at the V&A, London, where she curates the triennial Jameel Prize exhibition and the Jameel Fellowship artist residency programme.
Recent projects on *tatreez* have taken place in Kettle's Yard, Cambridge; The Whitworth, Manchester (both 2023 and 2024); V&A South Kensington, London; V&A Dundee and Hayy Jameel Jeddah (all 2025). These exhibitions grew out of years of research and curatorial work for the Palestinian Museum, West Bank, where Dedman was curator between 2014 and 2019. Additionally, Dedman maintains an independent curatorial practice, her research and writing are widely published, and she is the author of three books on Palestinian embroidery and dress.

ANTONIO JOSE GUZMAN lives and works between Amsterdam, Gujarat and Panama City. He studied fine arts at the Gerrit Rietveld Academie and was artist resident at the Rijksakademie van Beeldende Kunsten (both Amsterdam). His practice engages with social justice, pattern research and the colonial history of textiles, foregrounding the positive role of migration, social transformation and community engagement. Working across installation, textiles, collage, video, photography, music, performance and painting, Guzman creates multidisciplinary works inspired by diasporic identities, storytelling and cultural analysis. He currently collaborates with visual artist Iva Jankovic on the project 'Electric Dub Station'. Their joint works have been exhibited internationally in venues and events including the Liverpool Biennial and Museo de Arte Contemporánea de Panamá, Panama City (both 2025); 60th Venice Biennale (2024); Haus der Kulturen der Welt, Berlin (2023); Barbican Art Gallery, London & Stedelijk Museum Amsterdam (2024), as well as Sonsbeek 20→24, Arnhem (2021) and OSCAM – Open Space Contemporary Art Museum, Amsterdam (2020). Jankovic and Guzman are also founders of *'Messengers of the Sun'*, a performance art initiative recently presented at the 60th Venice Biennale. As solo artist, Guzman exhibited amongst others at the Havana Biennial (2019); Museum of Contemporary Art, Panama (2018) and Nieuw Dakota, Amsterdam (2017).

IVA JANKOVIC is an artist and designer who lives in Amsterdam and works in the Netherlands, Gujarat and Serbia. She studied philosophy at the University of Belgrade and fine arts at HKU University of the Arts, Utrecht.
In 2012 Jankovic founded a sustainable clothing brand which serves as a platform for her artistic research into the use of patterns and symbols across the world. Merging her traditional fine arts education with crafts, she transforms her ideas into performances, installations and unique fashion garments. Her fascination for communal memories is furthering a theory of homogeneity in human thinking. Since 2017 she has been working with visual artist Antonio Jose Guzman on the project 'Electric Dub Station'. Their joint works have been exhibited internationally in venues and events including the Liverpool Biennial and Museo de Arte Contemporánea de Panamá, Panama City (both 2025); 60th Venice Biennale (2024); Haus der Kulturen der Welt, Berlin (2023); Barbican Art Gallery, London & Stedelijk Museum Amsterdam (2024), as well as Sonsbeek 20→24, Arnhem (2021) and OSCAM – Open Space Contemporary Art Museum, Amsterdam (2020). Jankovic and Guzman are also founders of *'Messengers of the Sun'*, a performance art initiative recently presented at the 60th Venice Biennale. Her other creative work includes collaboration with Stichting de Vrolijkheid, developing art projects in Dutch asylum-seeker centres.

NICO DE JONGE is an expert on Indonesian art and culture. A graduate of the Free University Amsterdam and the Royal Tropical Institute, in Amsterdam, he conducted anthropological fieldwork in the Moluccas (eastern Indonesia) between 1981 and 1983, and again in 1987, specializing in traditional religion and material culture. He was a lecturer at Leiden University before leaving academia in 1997 to join the National Museum of Ethnology, in Leiden, where his co-curated projects included the permanent exhibition of the Insular Southeast Asian collections and *Indië Ontdekt*, marking the 150th anniversary of the Royal Institute for Linguistics and Anthropology in (2001). From 2002 until his retirement in 2020, he served as Vice-Director of the University Museum at the University of Groningen. During this time, he contributed to several major international exhibitions, including at the National Museum of Indonesia, Jakarta (2005); the Nieuwe Kerk, Amsterdam (2006); the Dallas Museum of Art (2013) and the Europalia Indonesia exhibition, Brussels (2017). De Jonge has published extensively on the arts and cultures of Indonesian ethnic groups. He has edited and contributed to award-winning publications, some of which remain key references on the region.

ELISA VAN JOOLEN is an artist who lives and works in Amsterdam. She studied at Gerrit Rietveld Academie in Amsterdam, and Parsons School of Design, New York City. Van Joolen has been artist in residence at IASPIS in Stockholm and at the Jan van Eyck Academie, Maastricht. In her work she exposes the relational aspects of clothing and subverts processes of value production. Her projects often reflect specific social contexts and emphazise collaboration and participation. Her work has been exhibited at events and venues including Stedelijk Museum Amsterdam (2022); Het Nieuwe Instituut, Rotterdam (2021); Museum Boijmans Van Beuningen, Rotterdam (2017); New York Fashion Week (2017); Brazilian Design Biennial, Florianópolis (2015); Museum für Kunst und Gewerbe, Hamburg (2015); OCAT Art Terminal, Shenzhen (2014) and Arnhem Fashion Biennial (2011). She is head of the fashion department at the Gerrit Rietveld Academie and co-founder of Warehouse | A Place for Clothes in Context, in Amsterdam.

ANANYA JAHANARA KABIR is professor of English literature at King's College London. Her research spans creolization across the Atlantic and Indian Ocean worlds, critical philology, and the relationship between literary texts, embodied and material culture and memory. Between 2013 and 2018, she directed the ERC Advanced Grant-funded project 'Modern Moves' (on the global popularity of African-heritage dance). Currently, she is completing a monograph on Africanity, dance and reparation, and developing a new project on the Dutch, the Portuguese and transoceanic creolization. Kabir has been awarded India's Infosys Prize and Germany's Humboldt Research Prize and is elected Fellow of the British Academy. Recent publications include 'Archipelagic Memory', co-edited with Luca Raimondi (2024); 'Archive-Repertoires of Memory: Knowing Migration through Shailesh Bahoran's Dance' (2023); 'Creolising Universality', (2023) and 'Crypt, Cornucopia, and the Surface of Pattern: Vlisco's Designs' which appeared in *Third Text* (2023).

PATRICIA KAERSENHOUT is an Afro-Dutch artist of Surinamese descent. They studied Social Sciences at the Sociale Academie 'De Aemstelhorn' and fine arts at the Gerrit Rietveld Academie, both in Amsterdam. Their practice expands across multiple mediums including textile, collage, sculpture, performance, video and film, and encompasses an artistic journey in which they investigate their Surinamese background in relation to their upbringing in a West-European culture. The political thread in their work raises questions about the African Diaspora's movements and its relation to feminism, sexuality, racism and the history of slavery.
Their work is widely exhibited in the Netherlands and abroad. Recent solo exhibitions include *Into the deep loving darkness*, Künstverein Braunschweig (2024); *Visions of Possibilities*, Bonnefantenmuseum, Maastricht (2023) and *Of Palimpsests & Erasure* Blackwood gallery Toronto (2024). Recent group shows include *Avant Garde and Liberation MUMOK Vienna* (2024). kaersenhout regular speaks about her work in public addressing the ongoing legacies of slavery. Their films and videos are screened worldwide.

KATHY M'CLOSKEY is Adjunct Associate Professor of Anthropology in the Department of Sociology and Criminology at the University of Windsor, Canada. Her research focuses on globalization, gendered injustice, intellectual and cultural property rights, and the political economy of 'collectibles', with a focus on historic and contemporary Native American production in the southwestern United States. She is Research Affiliate at the Southwest Centre, University of Arizona, and served as Research Director for the award-winning documentary *Weaving Worlds* (2009, Native American Public Telecommunications, Inc.). She has received funding from the Social Sciences and Humanities Research Council of Canada and two social justice awards from the University of Windsor and Diné (Navajo) Studies (2018) respectively, in recognition of her activism which includes serving as a consultant for the Indian Arts and Crafts Board, Washington, DC, and as a member of the Association on Indian Affairs. Between 1988 and 2004, Kathy curated five exhibitions of women's fiber work.

ROMITA RAY is associate professor of art history at Syracuse University. She is the author of *Under the Banyan Tree: Relocating the Picturesque in British India* (2013) and *The Eternal Masquerade: Prints and Paintings by Gerald Leslie Brockhurst (1890-1978) from the Jacob Burns Foundation* (2006). Ray has published widely on the art and architecture of the British empire in India and has curated exhibitions at the Georgia Museum of Art (University of Georgia), the Syracuse University Art Museum, and the National Portrait Gallery (London). She has initiated and overseen two Digital Humanities projects: *Landscape Studies at Syracuse University* and *Reflections on Take Me to the Palace of Love*. Ray is currently working on a book manuscript on the visual cultures of tea in colonial and modern India tentatively titled, *Leafy Wonders: Art, Science, and the Aesthetics of Tea in India*. Her research has been supported by the National Endowment for the Humanities, the National Endowment for the Arts, Royal Museums Greenwich (London), Huntington Library, Houghton Library, the Lewis Walpole Library and the Yale Center for British Art. Ray serves on the Advisory Board of the Paul Mellon Centre for Studies in British Art (Yale University, London) and on the Advisory Committee for the Plant Humanities Initiative at Dumbarton Oaks (Harvard University).

JENNIFER TEE was born in Arnhem, and lives and works in Amsterdam. She studied at the Gerrit Rietveld Academy and the Sandberg Institute (MFA), both in Amsterdam. She was a resident artist at the Rijksakademie, Amsterdam and ISCP, New York. Tee embraces a wide range of artistic mediums, including sculpture, textiles, installation, performance and collage made with dried tulip petals. Her artwork can be seen as material representations of the journey of the soul, questioning the relationship between spirit and matter. The work responds to experiences of cultural diasporic narratives and heritage, identity and language, migration and trade routes between people, commodities and objects from nature.
Tee has exhibited widely, both in the Netherlands and abroad. Recent solo exhibitions include: *Still Shifting, Mother Field*, co-produced by Secession, Vienna and MELLY, Rotterdam (2022/2023); *DRIFT*, Stedelijk Museum Amsterdam (2020); *Let it Come Down*, Camden Arts Centre, London (2017); *Tulip Palepai, Navigating the River of the World*, Rijksmuseum, Amsterdam (2017); *The Soul in Limbo*, Cobra Museum, Amstelveen (2016); *Practical Magic*, Project Art Centre Gallery, Dublin (2013) and *Local Myths*, Eastside Projects, Birmingham (2010). She was awarded among others the Amsterdam Prize for the Arts (2020) and the Dutch 'Prix de Rome' (1999).

CHRISTEL VESTERS is a curator, writer and lecturer based in Amsterdam. She studied art history and curating in Amsterdam, New York and London. Her practice is research-based and that links contemporary art with other fields of knowledge, including art history, critical theory, textile history and material culture. She is the initiator of two independent curatorial research platforms: *Unfinished Systems of Non-Knowledge*, which explores art's agency as another form of knowing, and *Touch/Trace: Researching Histories through Textile*, which investigates the intricate connections between contemporary art, textiles, history and society.
Over the past two decades, she has curated numerous exhibitions and public programmes, including the group exhibition *Interwoven Histories: Researching Histories through Textiles*, which, together with its accompanying catalogue, forms the prelude to this book. Vesters regularly writes on contemporary art, design and cultural history for national and international publications. Recent essays on textile in art include 'Hella Jongerius: Loom Room' (2023); 'Kristina Benjocki' (2022); 'Kente Cloth Unravelled' and 'Activist Threads' (both 2021); 'Verknoopte Verhalen' (2019); 'Textiles as Storage of Cultural Heritage and Collective Memory' and 'Some Notes on Women, Labour and Textile Crafts' (both 2018)

VINCENT VULSMA is an artist and educator based in the Netherlands. In his work he explores the tension between autonomous art and the socio-political relations on which its production is based. The history and economy of global trade, as well as questions of cultural appropriation, are important points of departure in his practice. His work has been included in international group exhibitions at venues including Musée d'Art Moderne, Paris (2017); Fondazione Sandretto Re Rebaudengo, Turin (2015); Museum Abteiberg, Mönchengladbach (2014); Kunstverein für die Rheinlande und Westfalen, Düsseldorf (2013); Centraal Museum, Utrecht (2010) and Stedelijk Museum Amsterdam (2008).
Vulsma received the Villa Romana Prize fellowship and the Prix de Rome in 2011, and has undertaken residencies at WIELS Contemporary Art Centre, Brussels (2012); Arts Initiative Tokyo (AIT, 2007) and De Ateliers, Amsterdam (2004–2006). Since 2013, he has been Tutor of Fine Art at Base for Experiment, Art and Research (BEAR), Arnhem.

LIST OF WORKS CITED
(per chapter)

INTRODUCTION
p. 7-11

Ingold, T, *Being Alive: Essays on Movement, Knowledge and Description* (London: Routledge, 2011).
Vesters, C, 'Kente Cloth Unravelled', essay for *The Palace of Typographic Masonry* (May 2021).
Vesters, C, *Interwoven Histories: Researching History through Textiles*, exhibition catalogue, *Touch/Trace*, ROZENSTRAAT (Amsterdam: Stichting Par&H, 2021).
Vesters, C, 'Activist Threads', in *Active Threads*, exhibition catalogue (Düsseldorf: KAI10 – Arthena Foundation, 2021).
Vesters, C, 'Travelling Carpets' in *MacGuffin Magazine*, no. 9 (Winter 2020/Spring 2021), pp. 135-146.
Vesters, C, 'Jacquard's Machine', in G Houzé, F Quintin eds, *Hella Jongerius: Interlace, Woven Research*, exhibition catalogue (Cologne: Koenig Books, 2019).
Vesters, C, 'Verknoopte Verhalen', *De Groene Amsterdammer*, no. 6 (2019).
Vesters, C, 'Textiles as Storage of Cultural Heritage and Collective Memory', in *Cultural Threads*, exhibition catalogue (Tilburg: TextielMuseum, 2018).
Vesters, C, 'Some Notes on Women, Labour and Textile Crafts', in N Folkersma ed, *The Female Perspective* (2018).
Warner, M, *Stepping beyond Words: Narratives on the Move in Cultural Conflicts*, lecture presented at the Warburg Institute, London, 2018, at the symposium *Aby Warburg 150: Work, Legacy, Promise*.

SETH SIEGELAUB
pp. 13-15

Benjamin, W, 'Unpacking My Library: A Talk about Collecting', in *Selected Writings: Volume 4, 1938-1940* (Cambridge, MA: Belknap Press of Harvard University Press, 2006 [July 1931]), pp. 486-493.
Center for Social Research on Old Textiles and Siegelaub, S eds, *Bibliographica Textilia Historiae: Towards a General Bibliography on the History of Textiles Based on the Library and Archives of the Center for Social Research on Old Textiles* (New York: International General, 1997) [CSROT 5100]
Coelewij, L and Martinetti, S eds, *Seth Siegelaub: Beyond Conceptual Art* (Cologne: Verlag der Buchhandlung Walther König, 2016).
Motard, A and Sainsbury, A, 'Nothing Personal... An Interview with Seth Siegelaub', in S Martinetti, A Motard and A Sainsbury eds, *The Stuff That Matters: Textiles Collected by Seth Siegelaub for the Centre for Social Research on Old Textiles* (London: Raven Row, 2012).
'Seth Siegelaub in Conversation with Rike Frank and Grant Watson', in R Frank et al, *Textiles – Open Letters* (Berlin: Verlag der Buchhandlung Walther König, 2012), pp. 224-231.
Vesters, C, 'Weefsels en patronen: Seth Siegelaub—portret van een tegendraadse doener en denker', *De Groene Amsterdammer*, no. 7 (17 February 2016).

KUMKAPI
pp. 16-20

Appadurai, A ed, *The Social Life of Things: Commodities in Cultural Perspectives* (Cambridge: Cambridge University Press, 1986).
Balpinar, B, 'A Discussion on Central Asian Türkmen Influence on Anatolian Kilims', in *Oriental Carpets and Textile Studies VI* (2001), pp. 7-16.
Bensoussan, P, 'The Master Weavers of Istanbul', *Hali* 26 (1985): pp. 34-41
Bode, W and Kühnel, E, *Antique Rugs from the Near East*, 4th edition (Braunschweig/Berlin, 1958 [originally published in German, 1902]).
*Carpets of the East in Paintings from the West*. New York, Metropolitan Museum of Art, March 11-June 29, 2014, exhibition page, https://www.metmuseum.org/exhibitions/listings/2014/carpets-of-the-east (accessed 6 November 2022).
Cengiz, K, *The Tale of Industrialization in a Small Town in Turkey: Hacılar - Kayseri*, PhD diss, Middle East Technical University, 2012.
Day, S 'Between a Tribal and a Court Art: The Turkish Carpet', in S Day ed, *Great Carpets of the World* (New York: Vendome Press/Thames & Hudson, 1996), pp. 50-161.
Farrow, G F with Harrow, L, *Hagop Kapoudjian: The First and Greatest Master of the Kum Kapi School: From Examples in the George Farrow Collection of Silk Rugs and Carpets* (London: Scorpion Publishing, 1993), pp. 96.
Kouymijan, D, 'The Berlin Dragon-Phoenix Carpet and Its Probable Armenian Origin', in *Armenian Rugs and Textiles. An Overview of Examples from Four Centuries*, exhibition catalogue (Vienna: Armenian Rugs Society, 2014), pp. 5-8.
'Kum Kapı Rugs from the Arkas Collection', Turkish and Islamic Arts Museum (Istanbul), 5 October-20 November 2017, exhibition catalogue / announcement page, 'Kum Kapı Rugs from the Arkas Collection', HALI, https://hali.com/news/kumkapi-rugs-arkas-collection-tiem-istanbul/ (accessed 12 December 2023).

THE POLITICS OF DISCLOSURE
pp. 39-46

Abeita, A, 'Pressing Concerns for the Future of Native American Arts and Crafts', *Navajo Studies Conference* (Albuquerque, University of New Mexico, November 2, 2006).
'Is It All Loot? Tackling the Antiquities Problem', *The New York Times* (March 29, 2006), http://www.nytimes.com/2006/03/29/arts/artsspecial/29panel/html (Accessed 10 November 2024).
'Fake Navajo Rug Alert', *ATADA*, 2005, http://www.atada.org/news.html (downloaded 23 September 2005, link no longer available).
Bahr, H M, *Diné Bibliography to the 1990s* (Lanham: Scarecrow Press, 1999).
Berlant, T and Kahlenberg, H M, *Walk in Beauty* (New York: Little Brown, 1977).
Bernstein, B, 'Remarks', Indian Arts and Crafts Association. The Business of Art Seminar. Albuquerque Convention Center, April 21, 2010.
Bigelow-Sanford Carpet Company Records, Baker Library Historical Collections, Harvard Business School. Cambridge, MA.
Brugge, D, *Hubbell Trading Post, National Historic Site* (Tucson: Southwest Parks and Monuments Association, 1993).
National Association of Wool Manufacturers, *Bulletins of the National Association of Wool Manufacturers 1866-1925* (Chicago, Newberry Library).
National Association of Wool Manufacturers, *Bulletins of the National Association of Wool Manufacturers 1926-1943* (Cambridge, Harvard University Baker Business Library).
Denetdale, J, *The Long Walk: The Forced Navajo Exile* (New York: Chelsea House, 2008).
Denetdale, J N, *Reclaiming Diné History. The Legacies of Navajo Chief Manuelito and Juanita* (Tucson: University of Arizona Press, 2007a), cited in Lee, L L, 'Navajo Transformative Scholarship in the Twenty-First Century', *Wicazo Sa Review* 25 (2010): pp. 33-45.
Denetdale, J N and Coulter, Lane, ed, 'Navajo Saddle Blankets: Textiles to Ride in the American West', *New Mexico Historical Review* 78, no. 4 (2003).
Goldfarb, B, 'In His Element', *Architectural Digest*, September 2013, (NYC: Condé Nast), pp. 148-161.
Edmund Pike Graves Papers, 1865-1919. (Mss 761 G 776) Baker Library Historical Collections, Harvard Business School, Cambridge, MA.
Haraway, D, *Staying with the Troubles: Making Kin in the Chthulucene* (Durham, NC: Duke University Press, 2016).
Hedlund, A L, *Navajo Weavings from the Andy Williams Collection* (St. Louis: St. Louis Art Museum, 1997).
Henson, D and Henson, B, *Rugs to Riches: The Amazing Story of the El Paso Saddle Blanket Company* (El Paso: Trego-Hill Publication, 2001).
The Hubbell Trading Post Papers 1882-1968 (AZ 375). Special Collections Library, University of Arizona, Tucson.
Hudson, K, 'How Misleading Does an Ethnographical Museum Have to Be?', in I Karp and S Lavine, eds, *Exhibiting Cultures: The Poetics and Politics of Museum Display* (Washington, D.C.: Smithsonian Institution Press, 1991), pp. 457-64.
Kent, K P, 'Pueblo and Navajo Weaving Traditions and the Western World', in N H Graburn, ed, *Ethnic and Tourist Arts* (Berkeley: University of California Press, 1976), pp. 85-101.
Leuthold, S, *Indigenous Aesthetics: Native Art, Media and Identity* (Austin: University of Texas Press, 1998).
Lonetree, A, *Decolonizing Museums. Representing Native America in National and Tribal Museums* (Chapel Hill, NC: University of North Carolina Press, 2012).
Mattei, U and Nader, L, *When the Rule of Law is Illegal* (Oxford: Blackwell, 2008).
M'Closkey, K, *Why the Navajo Blanket Became a Rug: Excavating the Legacy of Modernization and Development* (Albuquerque: University of New Mexico Press, forthcoming).
M'Closkey, K, 'Diasporas of and by Design: Exploring the Unholy Alliance between Museums and the Diffusion of Navajo Textile Designs', in R Darnell and F W Gleach, eds, *Disruptive Voices and the Singularity of Histories, Histories of Anthropology Annual* 13 (2019): pp. 111-149.
M'Closkey, K, 'Up for Grabs: Assessing the Consequences of Sustained Appropriations of Navajo Weavers' Patterns', in T Berman, ed, *No Deal! Indigenous Arts and the Politics of Possession* (Santa Fe, NM: SAR Press, 2012a), pp. 128-154.
M'Closkey, K, 'The Politics of Pastoralism: Navajos, Churras and the Challenges of Sustainability in a Globalizing World', in *Textile Society of America Symposium Proceedings,* p. 715 (2012b).
M'Closkey, K, 'Unravelling the Narratives of Nostalgia: Navajo Weavers and Globalization', in C Williams, ed, *Indigenous Women and Work. From Labor to Activism* (Urbana: University of Illinois Press, 2010a), pp. 120-135.
M'Closkey, K, 'Novica, Navajo Knock-offs and the 'Net: A Critique of Fair Trade Marketing Practices', in S Lyon and M Moberg, eds, *Fair Trade and Social Justice: Global Ethnographies* (New York: New York University Press, 2010b), pp. 258-282.
M'Closkey, K, 'Towards an Understanding of Navajo Aesthetics', *SEE: Semiotics, Evolution, Energy* 4, no. 1 (2004a), pp. 191-117.
M'Closkey, K, 'The Devil's in the Details: Tracing the Fingerprints of Free Trade and its Effects on Navajo Weavers' in B Hosmer and C O'Neill, eds, *Native Pathways: Economic Development and American Indian Culture in the Twentieth Century* (Boulder: University of Colorado Press, 2004b).
M'Closkey, K, *Swept Under the Rug: A Hidden History of Navajo Weaving* (Albuquerque: University of New Mexico Press, [2002] 2008).
Meyer, K, *The Plundered Past* (New York: Atheneum, 1973).
Montano, R and Yohe, J A, 'Blanketing the Plains. *Hanoolchaadi* in Indian Country' *First American Art Magazine* 14 (2017): pp. 20-25.
O'Neill, C, *Working the Navajo Way. Labor and Culture in the Twentieth Century* (Lawrence: University Press of Kansas, 2005).
Parezo, N, 'The Challenge of Native American Art and Material Culture', *Museum Anthropology* 14, no. 4 (1990): pp. 12-29.

Pete, L T and Teller, B O, *Spider Woman's Children: Navajo Weaving Today* (Loveland, CO: Thrums Books, 2018).
Pete, L T and Teller, B O, *How to Weave a Navajo Rug, and Other Lessons from Spider Woman* (Loveland, CO: Thrums Books, 2020).
Reichard, G, *Navajo Shepherd and Weaver* (New York: J J Augustin, 1936); repr. as *Weaving a Navajo Blanket* (Mineola: Dover Publications, 1974).
Rodee, M, *Old Navajo Rugs: Their Development from 1900 to 1940* (Albuquerque: University of New Mexico Press, 1981).
Stephen, L, 'Weaving in the Fast Lane: Class, Ethnicity and Gender in Zapotec Craft Commercialization', in J Nash, ed, *Crafts in the World Market* (New York: State University of New York Press, 1993), pp. 25-57.
Stephen, L, 'Export Markets and Their Effects on Indigenous Craft Production: The Case of the Weavers of Teotitlán del Valle, Mexico', in M B Schevill, J Berlo and E Dwyer, eds, *Textile Traditions in Mesoamerica and the Andes* (New York: Garland, 1991a), pp. 381-399.
Stephen, L, 'Culture as a Resource: Four Cases of Self-Managed Indigenous Craft Producers in Latin America', *Economic Development and Culture Change* 40, no. 1 (1991b): pp. 101-103.
United Nations, *United Nations Declaration on the Rights of Indigenous Peoples (UNDRIP)*, Division for Social Policy and Development, Indigenous Peoples, 2007 https://www.un.org/development/desa/indigenouspeoples/declaration-on-the-rights-of-indigenous-peoples.html
Weiss, L, 'The Development of Capitalism in the Navajo Nation: A Political Economy History', in *Studies in Marxism* 15 (1984).
Wheat, J B, and Hedlund, A L, ed, *Blanket Weaving in the Southwest* (Tucson: University of Arizona Press, 2003).
Wheat, J B, *"Navajo Blankets" from the Collection of Anthony Berlant* (Tucson: University of Arizona Museum of Art, 1974).
Whitaker, K, *Southwest Textiles: Weavings of the Pueblo and Navajo* (Seattle: University of Washington Press, 2002).
Wikicollecting http://en.wikicollecting.org/andy-williams-navajo-blankets-auctioned-at-sothebys (Downloaded 30 August, 2013, page no longer available).
Willink, R and Zolbrod, P, *Weaving a World: Textiles and the Navajo Way of Seeing* (Santa Fe, NM: Museum of New Mexico Press, 1996).
Witherspoon, G, 'Navajo Weaving: Art in its Cultural Context', *MNA Research Paper*, no. 36 (Flagstaff: Museum of Northern Arizona, 1987).
Yazzie, B B, 'Spider Woman, Our Grandmother's Teachings Woven into Our Diné (Navajo) Lifeways', personal files, n.d.

LAMPUNG SHIP CLOTHS
pp. 65-72

Aeckerlin, J A, 'De pangkat papadon in de Lampongsche Districten', *De Indische Gids* 16 (1894): pp. 1532-1542.
du Bois, J A, 'De Lampongsche Districten op het eiland Sumatra', *Tijdschrift voor Nederlandsch-Indië* 14, no. 4 (1852): 245-275; no. 5 (1852): 309-333.
Broersma, R, *De Lampongsche Districten* (Batavia, Rijswijk: Javasche Boekhandel & Drukkerij, 1916).
van Dijk, T and de Jonge, N, *Shipcloths of the Lampung, South Sumatra* (Amsterdam, Galerie Mabuhay, 1980).
Degroot, V, Chutiwongs, N and Hardiati, E S eds, 'Early History and Archaeology of Sumatra: An Overview', in F Brinkgreve and R Sulistianingsih, eds, *Sumatra: Crossroads of Cultures* (Leiden: KITLV Press, 2009) pp. 41-50.
Forbes, H O, *A Naturalist's Wanderings in the Eastern Archipelago* (London: Sampson Low, Marston, Searle and Rivington, 1885).
Funke, F W, *Orang Abung: Volkstum Süd-Sumatras im Wandel. Band I –Kulturgeschichte der Abung-Stämme von der megalithischen Zeit bis zur Gegenwart* (Leiden: E. J. Brill, 1958).
Funke, F W, *Orang Abung. Volkstum Süd-Sumatras im Wandel. Band II – Das Leben in der Gegenwart* (Leiden: E. J. Brill, 1961).
Gittinger, M, 'A Study of the Ship Cloths of South Sumatra: Their Design and Usage', PhD diss, Columbia University, 1972.
Gittinger, M, 'A Reassessment of the Tampan of South Sumatra', in M Gittinger, ed, *To Speak with Cloth: Studies in Indonesian Textiles* (Los Angeles: UCLA Museum of Cultural History, 1989a), pp. 225-39.
Helfrich, O L, 'Bijdragen tot de geographische, geologische en ethnographische kennis der afdeeling Kroé', *Bijdragen tot de Taal-, Land- en Volkenkunde van Nederlandsch-Indië* 5, vol. 4 (1889): pp. 517-629.
Hissink, J H, 'Het pepadonwezen en zijne attributen in verband met de oude staatkundige indeeling in marga's en het huwelijks- en erfrecht in de afdeeling Toelang Bawang der Lampongsche Districten', *Tijdschrift van het Bataviaasch Genootschap* 47 (1904): pp. 69-167
Holmgren, R and Spertus, A, *Early Indonesian Textiles from Three Cultures: Sumba Toraja Lampung* (New York: The Metropolitan Museum of Art, 1989).
van der Hoop, A N J Thomassen a Tuessink, 'De Megalitische hoofdenzetel oorsprong van den Lampongschen Pepadon?', *Tijdschrift voor Indische Taal-, Land- en Volkenkunde* 80 (1940): pp. 60-77.
Horridge, A, *Outrigger Canoes of Bali and Madura, Indonesia* (Honululu: Bishop Museum Press, 1987).
Horridge, A, 'A Summary of Indonesian Canoe and Prahu Ceremonies', *Indonesia Circle* 39 (1986): pp. 3-17.
de Jonge, N and van Dijk, T, *Forgotten Islands of Indonesia: The Art and Culture of the Southeast Moluccas* (Singapore: Periplus Editions, 1995a).
de Jonge, N, *The Religious Art of the Southeast Moluccas* (digital publication RMV-Leiden, 2002).
op 't Land, C, 'Een merkwaardige "Tampan pengantar" van Zuid-Sumatra', *Kultuurpatronen* 10, 11 (1968-69): pp. 100-117.
van der Lith, P A, Fokkens, F and Spaan, A J, *Encyclopaedie van Nederlandsch-Indië* (The Hague: Martinus Nijhoff; Leiden: E. J. Brill, 1896-1905).
Maxwell, R, *Textiles of Southeast Asia. Tradition, Trade and Transformation* (Singapore, Periplus Editions, 2003), footnote 19 (1990).
Palm, C H M, 'De Cultuur en Kunst van de Lampung, Sumatra', *Kultuurpatronen*, part 7 (1965): pp. 40-80.
Schefold, R, Dekker, V and de Jonge, N eds, *Indonesia in Focus: Ancient Traditions—Modem Times* (Meppel, Netherlands: Edu'Actief Publishing Company, 1988).
Schefold, R and Alpert, S G eds, *Eyes of the Ancestors: The Arts of Island Southeast Asia at the Dallas Museum of Art* (Dallas, TX: Dallas Museum of Art and Yale University Press, 2013).
Snelleman, J F 'Nog een merkwaardig weefsel uit de Lampongs', *De Aarde en haar Volken* 46, no. 18 (1910): pp. 75-76.
Steinmann, A. 'Enkele opmerkingen aangaande de z.g. Scheepjesdoeken van Zuid-Sumatra', *Cultureel Indië* 1 (1939): pp. 252-256.
*Steinmann, A, 'Das Seelenschiff in der Textillkunst Indonesiens', *Kultuurpatronen*, part 7 (1965): pp. 23-39.
Sundari, E, 'Trade Ceramics from Sumatra in the Collection of the National Museum (Jakarta)', in F Brinkgreve and R Sulistianingsih, eds, *Sumatra: Crossroads of Cultures* (Leiden, KITLV Press, 2009), pp. 97-106.
Taylor, P M and Aragon, L V, with assistance from Rice, A L, *Beyond the Java Sea: Art of Indonesia's Outer Islands* (Washington, D.C.: The National Museum of Natural History, Smithsonian Institution, in association with Harry N. Abrams, 1991).
Schefold, R and Alpert, S G eds, *Eyes of the Ancestors: The Arts of Island Southeast Asia at the Dallas Museum of Art* (2013).
Gittinger, M, 'The Ship Textiles of South Sumatra: Functions and Design System', *Bijdragen tot de Taal-, Land- en Volkenkunde* 132, no. 2-3 (1976): pp. 207-227.
Schnitger, F M, *Forgotten kingdoms in Sumatra* (Leiden, E.J. Brill, 1939).

MIGRATION'S MATERIAL TRACES
pp. 91-98

de Cesari, C, 'Heritage, ethnography and the making of nationalist agents', in R Dedman and S Harb, eds, *Labour of Love: New Approaches to Palestinian Embroidery* (Ramallah: Palestinian Museum, 2018).
Davis, R, 'Mapping the Past, Re-creating the Homeland', in A H Sa'di and L Abu-Lughod, eds, *Nakba: Palestine, 1948 and Claims of Memory* (New York: Columbia University Press, 2007).
Dedman, R, *At the Seams: A Political History of Palestinian Embroidery* (Beirut: Palestinian Museum, 2016).
Dedman, R, 'Labour of Love: New Approaches to Palestinian Embroidery', in R Dedman and S Harb, eds, *Labour of Love: New Approaches to Palestinian Embroidery* (Ramallah: Palestinian Museum, 2018).
Frank, G, 'Crafts production and resistance to domination in the late 20th century', *Journal of Occupational Science* 3, no. 2 (1996).
Halaby, S, *Liberation Art from Palestine* (New York: H.T.T.B. Publications, 2001).
Kawar, W, *Threads of Identity* (Cyprus: Rimal Books, 2011).
Mansour, S and Tamari, V, 'Art Under Occupation', in *Natura Cultura* (Salerno, 1990).
Sayigh, R and Peteet, J, 'Between Two Fires: Palestinian Women in Lebanon', in R Ridd and H Callaway, eds, *Women and Political Conflict: Portraits of Struggle in Times of Crisis* (New York: New York University Press, 1987).
Sayigh, R, 'Gender, Conflict and Displacement in Palestine', from *Displacement: A Palestinian Women's Voice Archive,* last modified 24 June 2004 (accessed 16 July 2020, link no longer available).
Scholch, A, 'European penetration and the economic development of Palestine, 1856–82', in R Owen, ed, *Studies in the economic and social history of Palestine in the nineteenth and twentieth centuries* (Illinois: Palgrave Macmillan, 1982).
Sherwell, T M, 'Imaging Palestine as the Motherland', in T B Zvi and Y Lerer, eds, *Self-Portrait: Palestinian Women's Art* (exhibition catalogue) (Tel Aviv: Andalus Publishing, 2001).
Weir, S, *Palestinian Costume* (London: The British Museum Press, 2004).

VLISCO'S ANGELINA
pp. 117-121

Aronowsky Cronberg, A, 'The Story of Vlisco and Real Dutch Wax: From Helmond to Accra to Paris and Back Again', in R Gerards and S M Sho, eds, *Vlisco Fabrics,* (Arnhem: ArtEz Press, 2012).
Apter, A, and Derby, L, eds, *Activating the Past: History and Memory in the Black Atlantic World* (Cambridge: Cambridge Scholars Publishing, 2009).
Bijlsma, G W, and Rodenburg, G H, *Van Vlissingen and Co's Gedenksboek, 1846–1946 Honderd Jaren van Vlissingen and co: Over de Kunst van het Drukken* (Helmond: Vlisco, 1948).
Chakrabarty, D, *Provincialising Europe: Postcolonial Thought and Historical Difference* (Chicago: University of Chicago Press, 2000).
Ford, T, 'The "Afro Look" and Global Black Consciousness', *Journal of Contemporary African Art*, 37 (2015): pp. 28-37.
Greenblatt, S, *Renaissance Self-Fashioning: from More to Shakespeare* (Chicago: University of Chicago Press, 2012).
GTP Fashion, *Our Story*, https://shop.gtpfashion.com/our-story (accessed 7 November 2024).

Mitchual, G, 'The Amazing History And Evolution Of The Dashiki', *Unorthodox Reviews*, https://unorthodoxreviews.com/dashiki-history-evolution (accessed 7 November 2024).

Kabir, A J, '*Rapsodia Ibero-Indiana:* Transoceanic Creolization and the Mando of Goa', *Modern Asian Studies* 55, no. 5 (2021): pp. 1581-1636.

Kabir, A J, 'Crypt, Cornucopia and the Surface of Pattern: Vlisco's Designs', *Third Text* 37, no. 2 (2023): pp. 193-206.

Kent, R, 'Time and Transformation in the Art of Yinka Shonibare MBE', in R Kent, R Hobbs, and A Downey, *Yinka Shonibare MBE* (New York and London: Prestel, 2008), pp. 12-23.

Khar, S S and Ayachit, S, 'Looking Backwards to Go Forward: Use of Traditional Indian Pattern Making to Develop Contemporary Methods for Global Fashion', *International Journal of Fashion Design, Technology and Education* 6, no.3 (2013): pp. 181-189.

Nielsen, R, 'The History and Development of Wax-Printed Textiles Intended for West Africa and Zaire', in J Cordwell and R Schwartz, *The Fabrics of Culture: The Anthropology of Clothing and Adornment* (The Hague: Mouton Press, 1979), pp. 467-69.

Pankhurst, R, 'Indian Trade with Ethiopia, the Gulf of Aden and the Horn of Africa in the Nineteenth and Early Twentieth Centuries (Le commerce indien avec l'Éthiopie, le golfe d'Aden et la Corne de l'Afrique au XIXe siècle et au début du XXe)', *Cahiers d'Études Africaines* 14, no.55 (1974): pp. 453-497.

Picton, J, *African Textiles* (New York and London: Routledge, 2021).

Picton, J, 'Laughing at Ourselves', in Y. Shonibare, *Double Dutch* (Rotterdam: Nai Publishers, 2004), pp. 45-63.

Picton, J, 'Yinka Shonibare: Undressing Ethnicity', *African Arts* 34, no.3 (2001): pp. 66-95.

Prakash, O, 'The Dutch and the Indian Ocean Textile Trade', in G Riello and P Parthasarathi, eds, *The Spinning World: A Global History of Cotton Textiles, 1200-1850* (Oxford: Oxford University Press, 2011), pp. 145-160.

Sylvanus, N, 'Archival Prints: Alternative Histories of Taste and Circulation', in N Sylvanus, *Patterns in Circulation: Cloth, Gender, and Materiality in West Africa* (Chicago: University of Chicago Press, 2016), pp. 49-77.

Vaughan, M, 'Africa and the Birth of the Modern World', *Transactions of the Royal Historical Society* 16 (2006): p. 150.

Young, P, 'Ghanaian Women and Dutch Wax Prints: The Counter-appropriation of the Foreign and the Local Creating a New Visual Voice of Creative Expression', *Journal of Asian and African Studies* 51, no.3 (2016): pp. 305-327.


KENTE CLOTH
pp. 122-124


Adler, P and Barnard, N, *African Majesty: The Textile Art of the Ashanti and Ewe* (London: Thames & Hudson, 1992).

Ofori-Ansa, K, *Kente Is More Than a Cloth: History and Significance of Ghana's Kente Cloth* (poster, Sankofa Publications, Ghana, 1993).

Félix, D St., 'Embarrassment of Democrats Wearing Kente-Cloth Stoles', 9 June 2020, www.newyorker.com (accessed 21 August 2024).

Rattray, R S, *Ashanti Proverbs: The Primitive Ethics of a Savage People* (Oxford: Clarendon Press, 1916).

Rattray, R S, *Religion and Art in Ashanti* (Oxford: Clarendon Press, 1927).

Rattray, R S, *Ashanti Law and Constitution* (Oxford: Clarendon Press, 1929).

Ross, D H, *Wrapped in Pride: Ghanaian Kente and African American Identity* (Los Angeles: University of California, 1998).


UNRULY INDIGO?
pp. 143-153


Appadurai, A, 'Introduction: Commodities and the Politics of Value', in A Appadurai, ed, *The Social Life of Things: Commodities in Cultural Perspective* (Cambridge: Cambridge University Press, 1997), pp. 3-63.

Arnold, D, *Science, Technology and Medicine in Colonial India* (Cambridge: Cambridge University Press, 2004).

Balaram, P T, 'Indian Indigo', in M Feeser, D Goggin, and B Fowkes Tobin, eds., *The Materiality of Color: The Production, Circulation, and Application of Dyes and Pigments, 1400–1800* (Farnham, UK: Ashgate, 2012), pp. 139-54.

Balfour-Paul, J, *Indigo: Egyptian Mummies to Blue Jeans* (London: Firefly Books, 2011).

Balfour-Paul, J, 'Indigo: From Bengal to Blue Jeans', *Marg* 65, no. 2 (2013): pp. 38-49.

Bansal, U R, and Bansal, B B, 'Industries in India during 18th and 19th Century', *Indian Journal of History of Science* 19, no. 3 (1984): pp. 215-23.

Barringer, T, *Men at Work: Art and Labour in Victorian Britain*, (London: The Paul Mellon Centre for Studies in British Art, Yale University Press, 2005).

Bhattacharya, S, 'Indigo Planters, Ram Mohan Roy and the 1833 Charter Act', *Social Scientist* 4, no. 3 (October 1975): pp. 56-65.

Bhattacharya, S, 'The Indigo Revolt of Bengal', *Social Scientist* 5, no. 12 (July 1977): pp. 13-23.

Brockway, L H, *Science and Colonial Expansion: The Role of the British Royal Botanic Gardens* (New York: Academic Press, 1979).

Chatterjee, S, 'Performing (Domi-) nation: Aspects of Nationalism in Nineteenth Century Bengali Theatre', Unpublished paper, Thirtieth Anniversary Bengal Studies Conference, University of Chicago, April 28, 1995. pp. 3-6, http:// www.lib.uchicago.edu/e/su/southasia/TESTold/Sudipto.html (accessed March 13, 2021).

Cornish, C, 'Collecting Photographs, Constructing Disciplines: The Rationality and Rhetoric of Photography at the Museum of Economic Botany', in E Edwards and C Morton, eds, *Photographs, Museums, Collections: Between Art and Information* (London: Bloomsbury, 2015), pp. 119-38.

Cornish, C, 'Curating Global Knowledge: The Museum of Economic Botany at Kew Gardens', in D A Finnegan and J J Wright, eds, *Spaces of Global Knowledge: Exhibition, Encounter and Exchange in an Age of Empire* (Farnham, UK: Ashgate, 2015), pp. 119-42.

Cundall, F, ed, *Reminiscences of the Colonial and Indian Exhibition* (London: William Clowes & Sons, 1886).

Das Gupta, R, 'Plantation Labour in Colonial India', *The Journal of Peasant Studies* 19, nos. 3-4 (1992): pp. 173–98.

Edelson, S M, *Plantation Enterprise in Colonial South Carolina* (Cambridge, MA: Harvard University Press, 2006).

Foucault, M, *Discipline and Punish: The Birth of the Prison*, Alan Sheridan, transl. (New York: Vintage Books, 1995).

'Free Trade and Colonisation in India', *The Oriental Herald* 17, no. 54 (June 1828): pp. 399-429.

*Great Exhibition of the Works of Industry of All Nations, 1851: Official Descriptive and Illustrated Catalogue* (London: Spicer Brothers, Wholesale Stationers; W. Clowes and Sons, Printers, 1851).

Guha, R, 'Neel-darpan: The Image of a Peasant Revolt in a Liberal Mirror', *The Journal of Peasant Studies* 2, no. 1 (1974): pp. 1-46.

Gupta, J, 'The Travels and Travails of Indigo in Bengal: Anglo-French Rivalry in the Early Nineteenth Century', in N Goswami, ed, *Desiring India: Representations through British and French Eyes 1584–1857* (Kolkata: Jadavpur University Press, 2020), pp. 175-88.

'Indigo Culture in Bengal', *Illustrated London News*, Saturday, October 16, 1869.

*The J. Thomas Story: One Hundred and Fifty Years of Excellence in Tea* (Kolkata: J. Thomas and Company Private Limited, 2012).

Jasanoff, M, 'A Passage through India: Zoffany in Calcutta & Lucknow', in M Postle, ed, *Johan Zoffany RA Society Observed* (New Haven, CT: Yale Center for British Art; London: Royal Academy of Art; New Haven, C T: in association with Yale University Press, 2011), pp. 124-39.

Jones, Sir W, 'A Catalogue of Indian Plants, Comprehending Their Sanscrit, and as Many of Their Linnæan Generic Names as Could with Any Degree of Precision be Ascertained', *Asiatick Researches: Or, Transactions of the Society Instituted in Bengal, For Inquiring into the History and Antiquities, The Arts, Sciences, and Literature, of Asia* 4 (1795): pp. 229-36.

Kling, B B, *Partner in Empire: Dwarkanath Tagore and the Age of Enterprise in Eastern India* (Berkeley and Los Angeles: University of California Press, 1976).

Kriegel, L, *Grand Designs: Labor, Empire, and the Museum in Victorian Culture* (Durham, NC: Duke University Press, 2007).

Kumar, P, *Indigo Plantations and Science in Colonial India* (New York: Cambridge University Press, 2012).

Kumar, P, "Planters and Naturalists: Transnational Knowledge on Colonial Indigo Plantations in South Asia." *Modern Asian Studies* 48, no. 3 (May 2014): pp. 720-53.

Kyd, R, 'Letters to Government from Colonel Robert Kyd reporting on various botanical subjects', Bengal Public Proceedings, Fort William 2nd July 1790, pp. 350-72. British Library, IOR/P/3/53.

Llewellyn-Jones, R, ed, *A Man of the Enlightenment in Eighteenth-Century India: The Letters of Claude Martin 1766–1800* (Delhi: Permanent Black, 2003).

Macpherson, Governor-General J, 'Extract from a Public General Letter from the Governor-General and Council, Calcutta, to the Hon'ble the Court of Directors—dated the 21st of August 1786, paragraphs 50 to 53', in George King viii, ed, *Annals of the Royal Botanic Garden, Calcutta*. Vol. 4, *The Anonaceæ of British India* (Calcutta: Bengal Secretariat Press, 1893).

Marshall, N R and Warner, M, *James Tissot: Victorian Life/Modern Love* (New Haven, CT: Yale University Press, 1999).

Marx, K, *Capital: A Critique of Political Economy*, vol. 1, F Engels, ed (Chicago: Charles H. Kerr & Company, 1921).

McCracken, D P, *Gardens of Empire: Botanical Institutions of the Victorian British Empire* (London and Washington: Leicester University Press, 1997).

Mitra, D, *Nil Darpan; or The Indigo Planting Mirror, A Drama. Translated from the Bengali by a Native*, M M Dutt, transl. (Calcutta: C. H. Manuel, Calcutta Printing and Publishing Press, 1861).

Nandi, P S, 'One Mirror, Myriad Reflections: The Politics of Indigo Cultivation and Its "Representation" in D Mitra's *Nil Darpan, or The Indigo Planting Mirror*', *Colloquium: A Journal of the Arts Department* 3 (2016): pp. 48-55.

Oddie, G A, *Missionaries, Rebellion, and Proto-nationalism* (Richmond, Surrey: Curzon Press, 1999).

*Official Report of the Calcutta International Exhibition, 1883–1884: Compiled Under the Orders of the Executive Committee*, vol. 2. (Calcutta: Bengal Secretariat Press, 1885).

Palchoudhuri, R, 'Neel in Bengali Culture', in K Vatsyayan, ed, *Culture of Indigo in Asia: Plant, Product, Power* (New Delhi: Niyogi Books, 2014), pp. 163-70.

Pamment, C, '*Police of Pig and Sheep*: Representations of the White *Sahib* and the Construction of Theatre Censorship in Colonial India', *South Asian Popular Culture* 7, no. 3 (2009): pp. 233-45.

Philip, K, *Civilizing Natures: Race, Resources, and Modernity in Colonial South India* (New Brunswick, NJ: Rutgers University Press, 2004).

Porter, D, *Science, Form, and the Problem of Induction in British Romanticism* (Cambridge: Cambridge University Press, 2018).

Purbrick, L, 'Introduction', in L Purbrick, ed, *The Great Exhibition of 1851: New Interdisciplinary Essays* (Manchester: Manchester University Press, 2001), pp. 2-25.

Rao, A, and Rao, B G, *The Blue Devil: Indigo and Colonial Bengal with an English Translation of Neel Darpan by Dinabandhu Mitra* (New Delhi: Oxford University Press, 1992).

Ray, I, *Bengal Industries and the British Industrial Revolution (1757–1857)* (New York: Routledge, 2011).

Ray, I, 'The Indigo Dye Industry in Colonial Bengal: A Re-examination', *The Indian Economic and Social History Review* 41, no. 2 (2004): pp. 199-224.

Roxburgh, W, 'Account of a New Species of *Nerium*, the Leaves of which Yield Indigo, with an Engraving of the Plant, and Descriptions and Engravings of the Necessary Apparatus for Manufacturing the Indigo. To Which is Added, a Brief Account of the Result of Various Experiments Made with a View to Throw Some Additional Light on the Theory of that Artificial Production. Also Descriptions of Two Other Plants Which Yield Indigo, and One from Pegu, Said to Yield a Green Dye', *Transactions of the Society, Instituted at London, for the Encouragement of Arts, Manufactures, and Commerce; With the Premiums Offered in the Year 1810* 28 (1811): pp. 251-307.

Sideri, E, 'The Diaspora of the Term Diaspora: A Working-Paper of a Definition', *Transtext(e)s Transcultures: Journal of Global Cultural Studies* 4 (December 2008): pp. 32-47.

Smith, C H F, and Stevenson, M, 'Modeling Cultures: 19th Century Indian Clay Figures', *Museum Anthropology* 33, no. 1 (2010): pp. 37-48.

Taussig, M, 'Redeeming Indigo', *Theory, Culture & Society* 25, no. 3 (2008): pp. 1-15.

Thomas, A P, 'The Establishment of Calcutta Botanic Garden: Plant Transfer, Science, and the East India Company, 1786–1806', *Journal of the Royal Asiatic Society* 16, no. 2 (2006): pp. 165-77.

Tobin, B, 'Imperial Designs: Botanical Illustration and the British Botanic Empire', *Studies in Eighteenth-Century Culture* 25 (1996): pp. 265-92.

Tsing, A, 'Unruly Edges: Mushrooms as Companion Species', *Environmental Humanities* 1 (2012): pp. 141-54.

Turner, I M, 'William Roxburgh and the Names of Some Indian Indigos', *Willdenowia* 44, no. 1 (March 2014): pp. 21-25. Varadarajan, L, 'Indigo: The Indian Tradition', in Kapila Vatsyayan, ed, *Culture of Indigo in Asia: Plant, Product, Power* (New Delhi: Niyogi Books, 2014), pp. 78-88.

Wardle, Sir T, *Colonial and Indian Exhibition, 1886: Empire of India: Special Catalogue of Exhibits by the Government of India and Private Exhibitors* (London: William Clowes and Sons, 1886).

Watt, G, *Economic Products of India Exhibited at the Calcutta International Exhibition, 1883–1884. Part II, Dyes, Tans, and Mordants* (Calcutta: Printed by the Superintendent of Government Printing, India, 1883).

Wheeler, M, Burgio, L and Shulman, M, 'Materials and Techniques of Kalighat Paintings: Pigment Analysis of Nine Paintings from the Collections of the Victoria and Albert Museum', *Journal of the Institute of Conservation* 34, no. 2 (September 2011): pp. 173-85.

Williams, R, *Culture and Materialism: Select Essays* (London: Verso, 2005 [first published 1980]).

INTERWOVEN HISTORIES
p. 8 © Ashmolean Museum, University of Oxford.
p. 11 FRAC Collection Burgundy, France, © Alighiero Boetti, Territori occupati, 1969, c/o Pictoright Amsterdam 2024

A TAPESTRY OF THOUGHTS
p. 13 [+ cover] Courtesy of the artist. Photo Gert Jan van Rooij.
p. 14 [top left + right] Courtesy Stichting Egress Foundation. Photo Marja Bloem; [bottom] Courtesy Stichting Egress Foundation.

KUMKAPI
p. 16 [top left + bottom left + bottom right] Calouste Gulbenkian Foundation, Lisbon – Calouste Gulbenkian Museum. Photo Carlos Azevedo; [top right] Corporate collection of Arkas Holding - Arkas Collection, Istanbul.
p. 17 Sevan and Loris Tchokazian, Armenian Rugs Society.
p. 18 [a + b] CC BY-SA 2.5; [c] Illustration by Seppie Groot.
p.19 [top] Haarlem, Frans Hals Museum, Inv. os i-32. Photo Tom Haartsen; [bottom + cover] CC BY 3.0.

THE MIGRATION OF A PATTERN
p. 21-22, 24, 25 [+ cover] Courtesy ifa (Institut für Auslandsbeziehungen). Photo Stefanos Tsakiris.
p. 26-27 Courtesy ifa (Institut für Auslandsbeziehungen). Photo Uwe Walter.
p. 28 [top right + bottom] Courtey of the artists. Photo Isabelle Arthuis.
p. 28 [top left], 29 Courtesy ifa (Institut für Auslandsbeziehungen). Photo Stefanos Tsakiris.
p. 30 [1] Southern Navajo Agency, 1933. NARA – 298601; [3] Photo used with permission from The Woolery; [4] Photo Nikyle Wes Begay; [5] Gift of John and Margot Ernst, in celebration of the Museum's 150th Anniversary, 2019. The Metropolitan Museum of Art (CC0); [6] Public domain; [7 + 8] Arizona State Museum, University of Arizona; [10] Courtesy of the artist and Garth Greenan Gallery, New York; [11] Courtesy National Park Service, Museum Management Program and Hubbell Trading Post NHS, HUTR 3444; [12] Denver Public Library Special Collections; [13] Photo Jerrye & Roy Klotz; [14 + cover] Garland's Sedona, Arizona. shopgarlands.com.
p. 32 [left] Courtesy ifa (Institut für Auslandsbeziehungen). Photo Stefanos Tsakiris; [right] Courtey of the artists. Photo Isabelle Arthuis.
p. 33 [15 + 16] Public domain; [17 + 18] Jacksonville Area Museum; [19 + 20] Special Collections & University Archives, University of Oregon Libraries. Photo Lee Moorhouse; [21] Photo Timothy Dahl.
p. 34 Courtesy ifa (Institut für Auslandsbeziehungen). Photo Stefanos Tsakiris.
p. 35 [22 + cover] Photo Stedelijk Museum Amsterdam; [23] Used with the permission of Inter IKEA Systems B.V; [24] Photo Ruth Harriet Louise; [25] Bernhard Willhelm. Photo firstVIEW; [26] Eighth Generation, owned by the Snoqualmie Tribe; [27] Photo Angel Wynn/ Nativestock.com; [28] Courtesy UNC Greensboro. Photo Martin W. Kane.
p. 36 Courtesy of the artist and Stichting PAR &H. Photo Floris Leeuwenberg.
p. 38 Courtesy ifa (Institut für Auslandsbeziehungen). Photo Stefanos Tsakiris.

THE POLITICS OF DISCLOSURE
p. 40 Pennington & Rowland, Navajo Weavers. Photo retrieved from the Library of Congress.
p. 41 Courtesy Herb and Dorothy McLaughlin. Photo Greater Arizona Collection, Arizona State University Library.
p. 42 [top] Photo Stedelijk Museum Amsterdam; [bottom] Lord Decor.
p. 44 [top] Diagram by Karen M'Closkey; [bottom] Photo by the author.
p. 45 Diagram by Karen M'Closkey.

RITE OF PASSAGE
p. 47-48, 50-54 [+ cover] TextielMuseum. Photo Josefine Eikenaar.
p. 56 [1] Photographed by G.F.M. Liebert, first published in the magazine Eigen Haard, 1900, no 44; [2] Photo taken by C.B. Nieuwenhuis and published in the magazine Eigen Haard; [3] The Met Collection API. Gift of Anita E. Spertus and Robert J. Holmgren, in honor of Douglas Newton, 1990; [4] CC-BY-SA 4.0. Collection Wereldmuseum [TM-1969-1]; [5] CC-BY-SA 4.0. Collection Wereldmuseum [TM-1772-1521]; [6] Collection Wereldmuseum [7082-S-493-1]; [7] CC-BY-SA 4.0. Collection Wereldmuseum [TM-1969-4]; [8] Photo taken by C.B. Nieuwenhuis and published in the magazine Eigen Haard; [9] KB, national library of the Netherlands.
p. 59 [10 + cover] Bequest of Edwin De T. Bechtel, 1957. The Metropolitan Museum of Art (CC0); [11 + cover] CC BY-SA 3.0. Jean-Pol GRANDMONT; [12] National Gallery of Australia; [13] Collection Fries Museum, Leeuwarden; [14] Copyright © 2009 by the Foundation of the Works of C. G. Jung Translation copyright (c) 2009 by Mark Kyburz, John Peck, and Sonu Shamdasani. Used by permission of W. W. Norton & Company, Inc; [15 + cover] Steve Munsell Collection. Photo courtesy of the Moab Museum; [16] CC BY 2.0. Illustration from a book by Magnusen, Finn, 1859, published by Bohn, Henry G; [17] Image courtesy of Nelson-Atkins Digital Production & Preservation, Jamison Miller.
p. 60 [top + bottom] Courtesy of the artist and Galerie Fons Welters, Amsterdam.
p. 61 [18] CC-BY-SA 4.0. Gupuinsas1993; [19] Private Collection; [20] CC-BY-SA 4.0. Tigerente; [22] Photo Jukurae/ Shutterstock; [23] Orange Wayfarer; [24] Photo imageBROKER/Muthuraman V; [25] Photo SOPA Images; [26] Public domain. Made by unk Indian weavers.
p. 62 [top + bottom] Courtesy of the artist and Galerie Fons Welters, Amsterdam.
p. 64 TextielMuseum. Photo Josefine Eikenaar.

LAMPUNG SHIP CLOTHS
p. 65 CC-BY-SA 4.0. Collection Wereldmuseum [RV-A78-41]. Courtesy of KITLV/Royal Netherlands Institute of Southeast Asian and Caribbean Studies 3897.
p. 69 [top] Collection Museum National Indonesia, Jakarta (inv nr 577); [bottom] Photo Historisches Archiv mit Rheinischem Bildarchiv, Wolfgang F. Meier, rba_d005896.
p. 70 [top] Dallas Museum of Art, the Steven G. Alpert Collection of Indonesian Textiles, gift of The Eugene McDermott Foundation; [middle + cover] Photo by missionary Petrus Drabbe; [bottom] Public domain. Leiden University Libraries.

MOVING STORIES
p. 73-74, 99 Courtesy the artist and The Art Institute of Chicago/Art Resource, NY/ Scala, Florence.
p. 76-77 Courtesy the artist and Sfeir-Semler Gallery. Photo Yiannis Hadjiaslanis.
p. 78-79 [+ cover] Image courtesy of Mathaf: Arab Museum of Modern Art, Doha.
p. 80 [top] Courtesy the artist and Sfeir-Semler Gallery. Photo Yiannis Hadjiaslanis; [bottom] Courtesy the artist and The Art Institute of Chicago/Art Resource, NY/Scala, Florence.
p. 82 [1 + 2] © 2024 by Benaki Museum Athens; [3] Piri Reis. Acquired by Henry Walters; [4] Public domain. Félix Bonfils; [5] Public Domain.
p. 83 [6 + cover] The Cleveland Museum of Art. Purchase from the J. H. Wade Fund. 2014.388; [7] From the British Library archive; [8] CC BY 3.0. David Shankbone; [9] Emily Jacir; [10] © Tracey Emin. All rights reserved, DACS 2024. Photo © Stephen White Courtesy White Cube; [11] CC BY 2.0. Christopher Paquette; [12] CC BY-SA 3.0. Yves6; [13] Copyright 2012 AP. All rights reserved. Photo Bilal Hussein.
p. 84 [top + bottom] Courtesy the artist and Sfeir-Semler Gallery, Beirut/Hamburg; [middle] Courtesy the artist and The Art Institute of Chicago/Art Resource, NY/ Scala, Florence.
p. 85 [14] Public domain; [15] Folklore Museum of Archangelos, Rhodes; [16] Courtesy The Textile Museum Collection, George Washington University. Acquired by George Hewitt Myers before or in 1925; [17 + 18] © 2024 by Benaki Museum Athens; [19] The Textile Museum Collection 81.29. Acquired by George Hewitt Myers prior to March 1940; [20] © Victoria and Albert Museum, London.
p. 86 Courtesy of the artist and Stichting PAR &H. Photo Floris Leeuwenberg.
p. 87 [21] Collection Dutch Resistance Museum; [22] Common Threads Project; [23] Fondo Isabel Morel Gumucio. Colección Museo de la Memoria y los Derechos Humanos; [24] A.T. Casdagli; [25] Palestine History Tapestry. Photo Theo Chalmers Oxford UK; [26] TRC Leiden; [27] Textile Research Centre, Leiden, TRC 2014.0142h; [28] Public Domain. Xia Xiong 5200 (refugee camp registration number) History Trust of South Australia (HT 2003.0159).
p. 88 [top] © BALTIC. Photo Rob Harris; [bottom] Courtesy of the artist and Stichting PAR &H. Photo Floris Leeuwenberg.
p. 99 Courtesy the artist and The Art Institute of Chicago/Art Resource, NY/ Scala, Florence.

MIGRATION'S MATERIAL TRACES
p. 92 [top left] From the collection of Dar Al-Tifel Al-Arabi Musuem for Palestinian Heritage. Photo Kayané Antreassian for the Palestinian Museum; [top right] From the collection of Widad Kawar. Photo Tanya Traboulsi for the Palestinian Museum; [bottom left] From the collection of Maha Abu Shosheh. Photo Kayané Antreassian for the Palestinian Museum; [bottom right] Courtesy of Raja El-Zeer. Photo Kayané Antreassian for the Palestinian Museum.
p. 93 [top] Philip J. Baldensperger, published in The Immovable East; [bottom] Courtesy of the Palestine Costume Archive's collection.
p. 94 [top] Palestinian Poster Project; [bottom] Photo Abdallah Aljamal, Palestine Chronicle.
p. 96 From the collection of Widad Kawar. Photo Tanya Traboulsi for the Palestinian Museum.
p. 98 [bottom] Copyright 2018 The Associated Press. All rights reserved. Photo Carolyn Kaster.

THE THREADS THAT BIND US
p. 99-106 [+ cover] Courtesy the artist and Stichting PAR &H. Photo Hannah Jung.
p. 108 [1 + cover] Collection Foundation Nationaal Museum van Wereldculturen; [2] 116863: Coll.RHCe/Municipality Helmond. Photo Tonnie van Deursen; [3] G.P.J. Verbong: Katoendrukken in NederLand vanaf 1800, in Brommer, B. (ed.); Katoendruk in Nederland, Helmond/ Tilburg, 1989; [4] 116846: Coll.RHCe/ Municipality Helmond. Photo Tonnie van Deursen; [5] Photo Maria van der Heyden i.o.v. TextielMuseum. Photo Maria van der Heyden for TextielMuseum.
p. 109 [6-11] Vlisco Archive, © Vlisco B.V.
p. 110 [left] Courtesy The Black Archives, Amsterdam; [right] Courtesy the artist. Photo Aatjan Renders.
p. 111 [12] CC-BY-SA 4.0. Collection Wereldmuseum [TM-5491-17]; [13] CC-BY-SA 4.0. Collection Wereldmuseum [TM-3325-211]; [14 + cover] Collection Wereldmuseum Rotterdam [TM-6384-35]. Collection ing. S.A. Bruijning; [15] CC-BY-SA 4.0. Collection Wereldmuseum [TM-3325-216]/Collection Wereldmuseum [TM-5491-13]/CC-BY-SA 4.0. Collection Wereldmuseum [TM-3325-188]; [16] Fotocollectie Elsevier Binnenland © ANP; [17 + cover] Photo Jaasir Linger; [18] Collection Wereldmuseum [TM-60008917]. Photo J.E. Julius Eduard Muller.
p. 112 TextielMuseum. Photo Josephine Eikenaar.
p. 113 [19 + 20] Collection of the Smithsonian National Museum of African American History and Culture; [21] Courtesy People's History Museum Manchester; [22] Library of Congress Prints and Photographs LC-USZ62-106646; [23] LSE Library, World's Graphic Press Limited, 36-38 Whitefriars Street, Fleet Street, London; [24 + cover] Thalia and Ian Campbell. Campbell Archives; [25] Thalia Campbell & Lucy Campbell. Campbell Archives. Courtesy of The Peace Museum; [26] Val Dunne Photography/ Shutterstock; [27] © David Hammons. Photo Aurélien Mole.
p. 114 [left] Courtesy the artist, Commissioned by Art Labour Archives; [right] courtesy the artist and PAR &H Foundation. Photo Hannah Jung.
p. 116 Courtesy the artist and PAR &H Foundation. Photo Hannah Jung.
p. 117-118 Vlisco Archive, © Vlisco B.V.
p. 119 [top] © Victoria and Albert Museum, London; [bottom] Katya Golovchyn.
p. 120 [top + middle] Vlisco Archive, © Vlisco B.V.

KENTE CLOTH
p. 122 © The Trustees of the British Museum.
p. 123 The National Archives UK. Open Gouvernment Licence.
p. 124 Copyright 2020 The Associated Press. All rights reserved. Photo Manuel Balce Ceneta.

THE DEEP OF INDIGO
p. 125-126, 128 Courtesy of the artists and Stichting PAR &H.
p. 129 Photo Stedelijk Museum/Gert Jan van Rooij.
p. 132 Courtesy of the artists and Stichting PAR &H. Photo Virginie Gauthier.
p. 134 [1] CC-BY-SA 4.0. Wellcome Collection; [2] KITLV 37A36//kitlv.nl; [3] Digital image courtesy of Getty's Open Content Program; [4] Economic Botany Collection, Royal Botanic Gardens, Kew (EBC 79733). Photo Paul Little; [5] Photo Kremer Pigments, 2020; [6] © The National Gallery, London; [7] Bijzondere Collecties Universiteit van Amsterdam.
p. 136 [left] Public Domain; [right] Courtesy of the artists. Photo Petra Katanic.
p. 137 [9] 2006/136/2 Powerhouse Collection. Gift of Clare Maguire, 2006. Photo Marinco Kojdanovski; [10] Arnold and Deanne Kaplan Collection of Early American Judaica (University of Pennsylvania); [11] Collection Dutch Open Air Museum; [12 + cover] Collection Vereniging Vrienden van het Zuiderzee-museum. Photo Wim Zandbergen/ Freelensmedia; [13] 98/126/116 Powerhouse collection. Purchased 1998. Photo: Geordie McRae; [14] ©Kerry Taylor Auctions.
p. 138 [top + bottom] Courtesy of the artists.
p. 139 [15] Museum Rotterdam; [16] Photo Jaasir Linger; [18] Javier Martinez, Virgin de Regla; [19] Giovan Battista Salvi detto il Sassoferrato, Vergine Annunziata, Pinacoteca Comunale di Cesena; [20] InnerPeaceSeeker/Alamy Stock Photo; [21] © Taiwo Adejoke Bamidele; [22] CC-BY-SA 4.0. Collection Stichting Nationaal Museum van Wereldculturen [TM-20017656].
p. 140 Courtesy of the artists.
p. 142 Courtesy of the artists and Stichting PAR &H.

UNRULY INDIGO?
p. 145 © Holburne Museum, Bath.
p. 146 + 149 © The Board of Trustees of the Royal Botanic Gardens, Kew.
p. 151 Digital image courtesy of Getty's Open Content Program.
p. 152 [top] Botanical Survey of India, Kolkata; [bottom] CC BY-SA 2.5. Photo Evan Izer (Palladian).

[COVER] Spinning wheel made by Wim Vogel based on plans by the Norske Husflidsforening. Photo: Susanne Visch, La Visch Designs - www.lavisch.com; Courtesy Antonio Jose Guzman. Photo Marlies Steenman; Courtesy Stichting Egress Foundation; Public domain.

INTERWOVEN HISTORIES
Contemporary Art, Migratory Narratives and Textiles

WRITER & EDITOR:
Christel Vesters

CONTRIBUTORS:
Rachel Dedman, Nico de Jonge, Ananya Jahanara Kabir, Kathy M'Closkey, Romita Ray, Christel Vesters

COPY EDITING:
Billy Nolan, Christel Vesters, Mariëtte Wijne

DESIGN:
Virginie Gauthier, after a proposal by Sandra Kassenaar

TYPESET IN:
Catalogue, Akkurat mono (Lineto)

PRINTING & LITHOGRAPHY:
die Keure printing (part of INNI group), Kortrijk, Belgium

EXTRA LITHOGRAPHY:
PRDigitaal (Pieter Reinink)

PAPER:
Etibulk 115 gr/m, Emotion 120 gr/m, Invercote 240 gr/m, Wibalin Finelinen

PRODUCTION:
Christel Vesters, PAR &H Foundation; Sara Duisters, nai010 publishers, Rotterdam

PUBLISHER:
Eelco van Welie, nai010 publishers, Rotterdam

THANK YOU:
It took many hands and minds to bring this publication to life. My gratitude goes to the artists for their trust and generosity in sharing their work, and the authors for their insightful contributions. Warmest thanks to Mariëtte for her generous support throughout the writing process, and to Billy for teaching me about the Oxford comma. Heartfelt thanks to Virginie for her dedication and tireless work—all the way to the end—and to Eelco and Sara at nai010 publishers, without whom this publication would not have come into the world. And to my family, S & S, this book is for you.

This publication was made possible by financial support from the Amsterdam Fund of the Arts, Creative Industries Fund NL, Mondriaan Fund, Jaap Harten Fonds and PPO.



nai010 publishers is an internationally orientated publisher specialized in developing, producing and distributing books in the fields of architecture, urbanism, art and design. www.nai010.com

nai010 books are available internationally at selected bookstores and from the following distribution partners:

North, Central and South America — Artbook | D.A.P., New York, USA, dap@dapinc.com

Rest of the world — Idea Books, Amsterdam, the Netherlands, idea@ideabooks.nl

For general questions, please contact nai010 publishers directly at sales@nai010.com or visit our website www.nai010.com for further information.

Printed and bound in Belgium.

ISBN 978-94-6208-730-9
NUR 655, 651
BISAC ART000000, DES013000
THEMA AFW

The inside cover of this book features a selection of textile fragments from the Seth Siegelaub Textile Collection (SST). Siegelaub catalogued each fragment diligently, leaving question marks where further research was needed to confirm information, though this research remained incomplete. He conceived SST as a research collection that, once digitized, would be open to everybody. People could fill the gaps or add new information, keeping the archive alive. All items can be studied in an online database, which can be accessed via the website of the Egress Foundation: http://egressfoundation.net.

01. [SST 209]
Five silk fragments in yellow, white and red on dark green ground, sewn together. France, 18th century. Silk, lampas weaving, 34.5 × 21.5 cm.

02. [SST 043]
Silk cannellé panel with small flowers on striped green ground, one selvedge. France, mid-late 18th century. Silk, metal thread, brocade weaving, 66 × 63 cm.

03. [SST 110]
Silk panel with embroidered floral motifs in silver and gold on red ground. Heavy corded edge, lined and interlined. Turkey, 19th century. Silk satin, metal thread, linen and metal thread cord, embroidery and sewing, 70 × 48 cm.

04. [SST 238]
Fragment of textile woven of dark and light brown wool with bird motifs and two borders. Peru, Chancay period, c. 14th century. Wool, double weaving, 41 × 23 cm.

05. [SST 288]
Fragment of embroidered panel consisting of four parts sewn together with red motifs on natural ground; probably pieces of a border; selvedges in different directions; pattern rotated in middle section. Italy, 17th century. Linen and silk, ajour embroidery, one knotted edge, 26 × 66 cm.

06. [SST 131]
Reverse side of three pieces of velvet with large floral motifs, red on golden ground, sewn together, pieces of selvedge. Italy (Genoa?), 17th century. Silk, metal thread, weaving (voided ciselé velvet), 101 × 33 cm.

07. [SST 271]
Multi-coloured and gold textile with a woven pattern of 5 rows of seated Buddhas on lotuses; in two parts, one with a selvedge (fragment). China-Tibet, 10th century (Liao period?). Silk, metal thread (gold leaf on a membrane), weaving, 33 × 26 cm.

08. [SST 291]
Silk velvet panel with dark blue floral motifs on golden ground; two pieces sewn together (fragment). Italy, 17th century. Silk, metal thread, weaving (cut velvet), 82 × 41 cm.